Reflexion

Reflexion

Lynette Fromme

First Printing

The Peasenhall Press — 2018

First printing 2018

ISBN   978-0-9913725-1-5

Library of Congress Catalog Number   2018947665

Cover design by Lynette Fromme and Red Wolf

The persons and events described in this book are real and true. In some instances pseudonyms have been used to protect the privacy of individuals. In such cases the altered names are indicated by an asterisk (*) the first time they appear.

Printed on recycled paper

You likely heard of the murders. This book is what happened before and after them along California's beaches and bluffs, San Francisco's Haight-Ashbury, the redwoods, Topanga Canyon, Beverly Hills, the Santa Susana Mountains, and the outback of the Mojave Desert. It's about the Charles Manson I perceived and a gathering of people like me preparing to survive either a revolution or the static institutions that were systematically trading all of our vital necessities for money.

— L. F., 2018

1963 - 1967

In 1963, when President Kennedy was murdered, I was in an eighth grade English class waiting for lunch break. A wall speaker delivered the news, and, as the class stared dumbly, our mature and stable teacher turned her back to us, sobbing *"Now the Russians will come for us!"*

I didn't know which was more shocking, the tragedy in Dallas, or our teacher's emotional breakdown. Scanning my brain for anything "Russian," I landed upon a vintage foreign film dubbed into English and shown on Saturday afternoon TV: An underage Russian soldier, traveling by train on a pass to see his sick mother, shares a fleeting romance with a beautiful peasant girl. Such appealing young soldiers on our doorsteps didn't seem like such a bad deal. I felt that our teacher's response was overblown. Anti-Soviet hype aside, wasn't our country stronger than just one man?

Outside the classroom, my best friend and I bumped through gloms of other slightly hysterical teens until officials closed the school and sent us home. She probably knew as little as I did about Russians, though her father was on the verge of promotion to Army General and a prestigious post at the San Francisco Presidio. Her house was farther, so we ended up on the piano bench at my house pounding out anxious duets and excess adrenaline, until my father rushed in from the back of the house roaring about our lack of respect. I didn't know that he cared about President Kennedy or that he was even at home. He ordered my friend out of our house and returned to his den. It was a sad and discombobulated time.

Charlie, as I knew him, was born out of Terminal Island Federal Prison near the shipyards of San Pedro, California, in March of 1967. He was thirty-two. He wore a 1950s-era prison-issue suit, and a Buddy Holly haircut to go with it. I was beginning my first semester of community college ten miles away in suburban Torrance. I was eighteen years old, restless to flippant, in a two-story condo belonging to my parents. I had red hair to my shoulder blades and an old-fashioned skate key on a chain around my neck; I didn't want a diamond ring.

Charlie took a bus to San Francisco where his parole officer was expecting him. Without money for food or hotel, he tapped the parole officer for ten, and was escorted by a young stranger to the crossroads of Haight and Ashbury streets where he was a clean-cut anomaly amid streams of bearded, longhaired hippies.

I didn't know anyone in Torrance, as my family had just moved inland from Redondo Beach, and by May of that year I was disillusioned. College in Torrance was not the mind-expanding exchange of ideas and information that I had imagined. One night my father and I clashed over something silly — a word or a definition. Suddenly enraged, he pointed to the door and yelled, "You get out of this house and never come back!" I cried, stuffing a big purse full of books and make-up and miscellaneous junk. I called my college boyfriend to pick me up, but he said he was too drunk to drive and suggested I hitchhike. It was nearly 9 p.m. when I trudged to the nearest freeway on-ramp and stuck out my thumb — but I wasn't going to see my boyfriend.

When we were sixteen, two friends and I, on weekend explorations, had discovered the boarded up, apparently deserted town of Venice, one of a handful of L.A. beach towns that periodically boom and bust. We'd wondered what bomb had left this devastation — the cracked cement and shattered glass, an empty theater with a few red plastic pieces still dangling from its marquee. What monster had devoured the population of this bright, stucco suburb to leave it so eerily empty?

After kicking around the rubble of a block of vacant shops, we had followed our curiosity through silent neighborhoods where only a curtain moved, or a thick-shoed old woman plotted her daily constitutional with a cane. Tidy pre-WWII duplexes were still clean, their lawns edged. The few people in evidence were old, and dressed in the style of the Churchills and Roosevelts. The Second World War, that had sloughed off the heels of the first "war to end all wars," had just moved on, a part of it now in Vietnam. But for us, on street after sunny street, the whole world might've been peacefully snoozing until, on turning a blind corner, we were struck and mugged dumb by the vast Pacific and a beach that was startlingly populated.

On the sand, on the strand, and beneath the gazebos, beside a rusty snack wagon and the mute jukebox of an abandoned patio café, people ranging spectrums of age, race, and culture leaned and lay dozing, skated and strolled — women with loose long hair and men with *beards.* There were painters at sidewalk easels, bookworms stretched out on the sand, bikers, Beatniks — odd-and-end people so cool and comfortable compared to the stiff, cinched-in "straight people" of the early '60s — rough travelers and homeless squatters in a parallel universe with housewives, bare-limbed preschoolers, and the tanned, elderly residents of the low-rent community.

We'd read about Beatniks but had never seen one. Passing small groups, we heard conversations, and the ideas we had read about: existentialism, transcendentalism, disestablishmentarianism. There was talk of Alan Watts, Tim Leary, and Ken Keasy, discussions about Buddhism, reincarnation, timelessness, and universality. Older black men in berets gathered at a bookstore where the only books on display were by W. E. B. Dubois. And signs everywhere read "MAKE LOVE NOT WAR."

Some of the Beatniks didn't speak, and some spoke in similes — "like" this and "like" that — about New York City and "Frisco," freight trains, saxophone players, "rounders," "reefer," "spare change," and "goin' through changes." To us, they were gems of true character, unlike the frightened shadows who cheerlessly admitted to being our parents. These were the REAL people, and if we were respectful, and hung around long enough during that year of getaway weekends, they would tell us their stories. They are blended in my memory with the scents of seaweed and yellow mustard and hot grease, with tin-toned transistor radios, distant bongo drums, waves with children's voices in them, and, from the toothpick-looking roller coaster tracks high over Pacific Ocean Park, the rhythmically recurring choral crescendos.

10

Only two years later, Venice Beach was dark, damp, and utterly deserted, all familiar landmarks gone. A light far down the strand turned out to be from a new bookstore/gallery whose proprietor and customers seemed too cool to notice me searching for a face I could trust. The man behind the counter began to close out the cash register, but I could not bring myself to speak.

Outside, I moved for cover beneath a gazebo, facing a gloomy sea. The store's light behind me was doused from the sidewalk, its glass doors locked, and as footsteps and car engines faded, I was left in the dark, completely alone, and at a standstill.

My dilemma was broken by a blur — a man in a smuggler's cap, flight jacket, and jeans hopped the half-wall in front of me and leaned against it. Animated, smiling, he was old — or young — I couldn't tell. He had a two-day beard and reminded me of a fancy bum, elegant — but my fear was up.

"Name's Charlie," he said, looking directly in my eyes. "In San Francisco they call me 'The Gardener.'" Sensing my alarm, he said simply, "It's alright," and I felt, within the tone of his voice, that it was. He moved with smooth confidence. He appeared both big and small. I was enchanted, yet flustered and mentally hiding — and then he wasn't there at all — until I sought him back in earnest, and he was seated on the wall. I gathered in the pieces of my mind.

"So, your father kicked you out," he said with certainty, and once again my mind went with the wind. But before I could ask how he knew, I began to tell him about a life I imagined living, and the so-called reality in which I felt trapped. He said, "The way out of that room is not through the door." I puzzled and considered trying windows.

"Don't want out," he said, "and you're free. The want ties you up. Be where you are. You got to start some place." He had a cleft chin and a Southern country accent I would later recognize as typically West Virginian, more a strum than a twang. He said that what I wanted OUT of was "thought" rather than "place." Instead of sounding cockeyed, this reminded me of a poem I'd written one sleepless night in a dead-end depression after staring at my grey-and-red-checkered pajamas. Just as children imagine being small enough to walk around the designs in curtains and blankets, I'd found myself on the grey and red checkerboard, trapped in one grey square; I could not cross its borders. Around and round its edges I'd paced like a caged animal, collapsing in one corner "to gnaw the bare bones of despair." But when I'd looked up, within this fantasy, my square had become a diamond; changing my perspective had changed my world. Within Charlie's laugh, I felt understood. It seemed ironic that it would take a stranger for me to know this comfort.

I was most arrested by his eyes. They knew me. He was a present and active intelligence. I didn't understand it. I didn't know what made his face a comfortable place to rest my eyes. He was an older man, I was sure now, with loose brown curls showing beneath his cap, and a jaw line that could've been used in shaving commercials. He, in fact, had recently shaved, leaving only the stubble of a full mustache to run down the sides of his mouth and connect with the shadow of a goatee. It was not attractive to me, this sandpapery facial hair. It was too bum-like, too much like neglect, but beneath it were decent features; he was neat, and appeared clean. He knew something about being trapped, he said, because he'd only recently been released after seven and a half years in prison. Then he revealed to me a glimpse of a life spent in and out of confinement, of the hurt, the anger, and the peace he said finally came with knowing and accepting himself. He was going north to see his mother, he told me, and I could come with him if I wished. I thought about my boyfriend, far from that moment, but this man was a complete stranger.

He glanced down the walk; apparently, someone was waiting for him. I struggled with the decision. Finally, he said, "I can't make up your mind for you." He smiled sympathetically and was on his way. I watched him go half a block before grabbing up my bag of books and running to catch up with him.

A bulge of male bodies and one teenage girl were waiting in a beat-up car. Charlie encouraged me to squeeze into the dark between these dim figures who only grunted acknowledgment. Darlene, a bandanna-ed brunette, looked hard, and didn't speak, even when introduced. Half an hour later when we stopped at a house in the suburbs, I felt relieved. More men were inside, but also Ginger, a stylish, sensible-looking blonde who owned the place. The group in the car had begun to look to me like they might be on an interstate crime spree.

Ginger had a "square job" and only minor friction with "the law" but through some contact of her past, and in common with Charlie, she knew ex-convicts and had a habit of helping them out. That's what she told me while we looked through her closets to find me some clothes.

I don't recall what I was wearing. My parents wore gray and beige. During high school, I'd ditched the blands for paisley dresses, and a raw walnut as a pendant, but after graduation, I was back to loafers, slacks, and knit pullovers — ordinary middle-American moderation, skate-key aside. Ginger wasn't that different, but at my height, five-three, she weighed less than 125 pounds. Still, she found me some nice fitting jeans, cotton blouses, and a lightweight jacket. Then she invited me into the kitchen.

The mean Darlene, who was obviously another of Ginger's beneficiaries, was actually pretty in the light. She had claimed a section of the living room where she sat bent over poster paper, drawing. Ginger considered her a true artist. Darlene, it turned out, was a seventeen-year-old runaway. Arriving in San Francisco two months before, she had been hustled by a street pimp who was handling her luggage when Charlie had recognized and embraced her. Thanking the pimp, he'd taken her bags, and headed her in another direction. She had never met Charlie before then.

The men at the house were cordial with one another but not friendly. Referring to each other by last names, Charlie was "Manson" to them. The other names I've long since forgotten, as we would not see Ginger nor any but one of the men again. All I knew, when four of us got back into the car around midnight, was that I would be continuing my travels with several more sets of clothes, a stomach full of strawberry shortcake, and three companions that Ginger had known for more than an hour.

Darlene fell asleep on the lumpy guy in the back seat while Charlie drove and talked, and I listened. His cap was gone now, revealing well-cut, wavy hair, the leather jacket replaced by a black Mac or trench

14

coat. All night long, as geometric shapes of shadow and light flickered across his face, he told me about their travels. He had zest, and a knack for storytelling; but how he and Darlene had gone all over the state without being questioned — he being nearly twice her age and an ex-convict — and why, if she was his girlfriend, she was sleeping all over the man in the back seat, I did not know. Whether in answer to my thoughts or his own, he addressed these questions with candor beyond my comfort. He said, "Darlene is bright. Darlene is talented. Darlene is a beautiful girl — but Darlene clings to gloom. I can't seem to talk her out of it."

I wondered if Darlene was awake.

"She's had a hard life," he said, "...raped when she was eleven, had a baby at twelve..."

I could not imagine.

"She was self-conscious about her stretch marks when I met her. She wanted to make love in the dark."

How gauche. He was telling me the secrets of this girl's anatomy.

"I told her, 'Those stretch marks are beautiful; those stretch marks are like a badge; they're part of what you went through to be you. Don't think those marks are ugly. That's somebody else's thinking.'"

I thought to raise another subject.

"But Darlene is headstrong," he went on, "...started running away when she was just a kid. And angry all the time — fight you in a minute."

I'd figured that.

"She's taught me," he counterbalanced. "Like most men I thought I knew what I was doing; I thought I was doing all I needed to to make her happy. We had a room in San Francisco, and I was out with some people. This was a few weeks after I met her. She didn't want to go. So I come back to the pad that night, and just as I start to open the door..."

He acted this out.

"...I hear her in there and she's going 'oohhhh' and 'aahhh' — and I know what she's doing but I can't believe it. She's got some guy in there. Not only that, but she's NEVER SOUNDED LIKE THAT WITH ME!"

Charlie looked shocked. I laughed, and he smiled.

"It was an ego death," he said blithely (a comic at the funeral). "I mean, I wanted to go in but I felt like a fool. I couldn't very well — she was obviously enjoying herself! I was so mad I walked the streets half the night on fire. I realized I wasn't giving her what she wanted, and I didn't know I felt that inadequate to be that jealous. You know, a man wants to think he's all a woman could want or need. He's the man. Little girl comes along and sets him straight."

This combination of braggadocio and self-realization sounded true to me, and I felt somehow rewarded by his comeuppance. I was just beginning to gloat when he countered, "But then it's her turn. And she don't want to give up her ego. She wants to be on top. But she wants a He-Man to look up to. She wants a lord, but she wants to dictate what he thinks. She thinks she wants to be happy, but she's not happy unless she's miserable!" He was grinning. I was taken by his honesty and humor, but the subject matter was embarrassingly personal, his language from the streets or below. How could I assent to this? I felt like I was stepping down.

As the sun rose, huge and golden, I was weary and suddenly struck by memories of everyone I was leaving behind. He smiled at my tears and sang, the tenderness in his voice both a catalyst and a comfort to my sadness. When we stopped for gas and to stretch our legs, Darlene and I went into the restroom together. I felt much better. I splashed cold water over my red face and said something simple, but she didn't speak to me.

In Berkeley, three of us got out on a street corner, and the big man drove away. Then we walked up a flight of stairs to see Mary in her second floor apartment. Tall and sweet-faced, a natural blonde, Mary had recently quit her job as librarian for the university down the block. She had straight birch-blonde hair to her shoulders, round blue eyes, a straight nose, and a well-defined jaw. Poised and articulate, she easily made cornmeal muffins while she and Charlie talked. By the sound of it, we were all going to the woods. I liked the idea, just for a trip. I pulled a pen and tablet from my purse to write a letter to my boyfriend, but it didn't go beyond three lines. I was listening.

Darlene was pacing the living room when Charlie finally joined her. Their voices were too low for me to understand, but she was obviously angry. His tone was conciliatory but she was un-reconciled. The talk rose and fell. She was absolutely refusing something. He said something as if giving her permission or telling her he wasn't going to object. Then he walked out of the room.

In less than half an hour, Darlene had gathered her belongings and called the big guy to come and take her away. It was so fast and final that I thought I ought to feel something, but I didn't.

While Mary took a shower, Charlie spoke highly of her. He and Darlene had been homeless until they'd knocked on Mary's door and she'd taken them in. He told of how funny it was when Mary had discovered him using her toothbrush. I was disgusted. He wouldn't be using my toothbrush either. At the same time, I had already imagined him kissing me. The attraction was disconcerting. Something about his moves and casual postures made him interesting to watch.

In the evening, after the cornbread and a thick soup that Mary had cooked up, she did the dishes while Charlie sat at the kitchen counter, and I sat in a stuffed chair in the living room. I ceded the chore to her because it was her apartment, her meal, and because, although she was soft-spoken, everything she did was in a deliberate, almost commanding way. She was four or five years older than me, and possibly as many inches taller, the height emphasized by her thinness and posture. Her clothes were the well-made, expensive college-edition Bass, Bauer, and Bean, but they were not new, and she appeared to dress practically rather than to affect an image. After drying and putting the dishes back into the cupboards, she told us that her taffy-colored dog, a retriever mix, needed to take a walk.

"*She can't wait to get out of the city,*" Mary sang as they went out the door.

Mary and Charlie's relationship seemed both nonchalant and formal. I couldn't tell if it was more than a friendship. He was so enthusiastic about my getting to know her that it sounded like boasting. He said, "Mary come all the way out here from Wisconsin by herself. She's been living alone, just the dog to talk to, working — going to school — working — eighteen hours a day. No dates. No movies. No music. She can play the flute as well as any member of a symphony orchestra but she's got it hidden in the closet. She's already got two college degrees..." I wasn't sure if he was telling me how smart she was, or wondering

18

aloud how much education a person needs; earlier I'd heard him tell someone that his own schooling had been cut short in the third grade.

When she returned, Mary went to the kitchen and filled the dog's bowl with water. Then she joined us in the living room where Charlie was tuning a guitar. He asked her if she intended to play the flute with him, and she just smiled.

"Not now," she begged off. So he played for us. He sang popular love songs and ballads, a cowboy tune, and a few he said he'd written in prison. He strummed jazz and fingered Spanish classical, but it was his voice I thought most worthy of attention. It sounded like one of the crooners I grew up hearing on radio, a Crosby or Sinatra — its quality was that good. And he was unselfconscious about it, a natural. At times, I saw him as robustly handsome, not just for the shape and features of his face, but for its expressive content.

Later that night I watched cards, coins, and cigarettes disappear and reappear, slipping through his fingers. Not only did the tricks capture my awe, but his showmanship and spirit did too. I had to remind myself that this person could barely read, and that I looked down on him — for in a world of novels, he was just one fascinating character.

In a dark bedroom, I sat fully dressed, thinking of the old life, and here, the new. I wanted to hold on to both. As I expected, he came in, put his arms around me, and I, in my actions, said yes-no-yes-no with a history of old movies in mind and no intention of giving in at all. He gently pushed me away from him; I pushed him back. He laughed, but said, "Who do you think you're fooling?" and walked out of the room. I was glad it was dark.

In the misty morning, I ignored a wish to sleep, got up, straightened my clothes, and made the bed. Mary came in, stripped the bed, and began gathering things we might need for the trip. After toast and coffee, we loaded the trunk of her elderly sedan with plenty of her clothes Charlie said we wouldn't need, all the food from her cupboards, her stereo and speakers, and a stack of her record albums — The Beatles, Ravi Shankar, Country Joe and the Fish — her dog, Muffet, and her last paycheck. I had no money at all. But since I'd regularly tanked up the family car, I happened to have my dad's Standard Oil credit card.

Charlie began the drive north, asking Mary to take over so that he could look at the scenery. He didn't call it "scenery." That's the word I would've used, as in "backdrop" for the all-important actors. I cannot tell you which route we took or whether those were Douglas firs or Loblolly pines we were passing. I was just a tired hitchhiker on their vacation. I thought we would arrive at his mother's house, but they began looking for cabins to rent near Mendocino, a speck of a coastal town two hours north of San Francisco. Whether they found one in a newspaper or by conversation, Mary paid rent to a bent and barnacled landlady who lived far from the property.

The dark wood cabin denned at the end of a retired resort road, had only three rooms — a bathroom, a large kitchen, and a combination living room/bedroom with one double bed. The landlady had offered to rent us an extra bed, but Mary and Charlie had declined, and I'd felt embarrassed at what she must think. By the time we got to the cabin, we had all taken showers, and Mary had made the bed, I was exhausted, but uneasy when they began to undress. Charlie didn't wear anything to bed; Mary stripped down to her un-

20

derwear and a cotton camisole. When they got into bed and turned out the light, I got in beside her. I kept my clothes on.

Charlie slept soundly, and rose early. Mary and I woke and tried to go back to sleep. We heard him talking to the dog, and they went out together. Soon Mary rolled out of bed, making motorboat sounds with her mouth. Turning her long, thin back to me, she dressed in jeans, a flannel shirt, and thick cotton socks. She handed me a pair with a shy smile and encouraging blue eyes. She was unquestionably Scandinavian, raised in the northern Midwest where they speak in short, chopped sentences, like in the cold. I perceived something else in her large, direct eyes. It was fear. Neither of us was accustomed to sharing a bed with two people we barely knew.

While Mary was in the bathroom, I lingered in bed, trying to decide what to do that day. I thought about my boyfriend. He was tall, tan, and mentally keen, an experienced surfer, and as good-looking as any male model. He was also moody, could be mean, and even when we were together, neither of us felt complete. I was too inexperienced for him. Maybe when I went back, things would be better between us.

Outside our cabin, the sun-dappled foliage reminded me of summer camp, the air cool, crisp, and silent. Muffet appeared between the trees with Charlie behind her, his face radiant. Bending to run his hands through her fur, he said that they had seen this and they had done that, as if he and the dog were in the same mindscape. Mary started breakfast, and they talked about going to the beach. I grabbed the moment to read.

I had planned to get a number of books read that summer — mainly so that I could return to school and say I'd read them. I wanted erudition, but I also wanted credits in my educational account. I was reading *Steppenwolf* by Herman Hesse when Charlie said something remarkably similar to what I'd just read. This first thrilled, then made me suspicious. He'd said he didn't read. He read road signs — he *could* read — but he didn't read books. How could he know *anything*?

California Highway 1, the narrow, two-lane Pacific Coast Highway, winds high above giant sea-sloshed rocks and little alcove beaches. An East Coast hippie couple renting a red farmhouse across the road showed us the anchored rope that locals used to get down the cliffs. The prospect of trusting this rope for the steep descent halted me cold, but seeing the big mustachioed man take hold of it and lean back from the cliff with all his weight spurred me to flip off fear and step forward. Charlie quipped, *"No! Let me be the hero!"* as he reached for the rope. His impish smile and a glint in his eye contacted a deeper part of my consciousness and I felt simultaneously thrilled and embarrassed to be busted displaying bravado. I was an undercover tomboy; I believed I could do almost anything the guys could do, but I would never have made such a claim.

On the beach we stripped off our shoes and socks, and rolled up sleeves and pant legs. We spent the afternoon by ourselves, searching for natural treasures, soaking up the faint warmth, and watching the sun sink into its own red lake. I lost most of the experience in a blinding preoccupation with my skin: my legs were ugly, so pale you could see the red and blue vessels. On the southern California beaches where surfers ruled and all respectable people were tan, a teenage friend had once hollered, "Lyn! Where are

you? You blend in with the sand! Ha ha!" I took it seriously. It was a matter of status to be dark, a matter
of popularity. I had blistered and lobstered myself in
the attempt. The only melanin I seemed to have was
in spots.

As a new teen, I'd been embarrassed to learn
through a magazine ad of a skin cream that would
"Remove ugly blotches, freckles and flaws!" Another
page advertised the glossy, bronzed bodies of people
using "quick tanning" cream. The results on me were
freakish. The dye turned me iodine orange, and I
spent about a month looking like the victim of a violent car crash.

Charlie suddenly told Mary to look at my legs. I
shunned him. He told her, "Look at all the colors." I
covered my legs and wanted to hide. I was angry. He
adopted it.

"Haven't those legs served you? Haven't they carried you everywhere you wanted to go since you got
up on them?" I reluctantly considered this. It was
true that I took them for granted; they were function-
ally more than adequate; I'd been a dancer. He said,
"Neither of you know how perfect you are." I wanted
to believe him but hid the thought quickly so as not
to be taken for a fool. Nobody else had ever said that
to me before.

Mary didn't seem suspicious of Charlie,
not that we talked about it. Charlie did most of the
talking by our preference. He made observations and
sometimes told us stories about the prison on McNeil
Island in Washington State where he had spent the
majority of his last federal sentence. He was twenty-
four when a judge in Los Angeles sentenced him to
ten years for trying to cash a check he won in a poker
game. He sounded blasé about it, a little surprised

that this "rinky-dink thirty-seven dollar fifty-cent check" had gotten him so much time.

That first week we drove to the peninsular town of Mendocino for groceries and so Mary could rent a post office box; her parents and Charlie's parole officer had to have a point of contact. Architecturally, Mendocino, like San Francisco, was a New England transplant, a replica of its early inhabitants' origins, with both fine Victorian homes and patched wood shacks. By remnant and recent renewal, it had the look of a sepia photograph of many nineteenth century western towns, with a cracker barrel grocery, a leatherworks shop, the original timbered hotel, and a garage, once a livery stable and blacksmith's. Some of the streets were still lined with boardwalks, no doubt because, before asphalt, they became muddy and puddled. I could see the women's long skirts dragging in the dirt — right then. In 1967 pioneer skirts were back in fashion, along with fringed buckskins, boots, high-necked lace blouses, and other antique garments that had been stored for years in attics and trunks and were showing up in second hand stores.

I waited outside while Mary and Charlie went into the grocery. Nothing had been built along one side of the street to ruin the view of the grassy promontory to its cliffs and the sea. Two wind-wild horses frisked there, up to their fetlocks in spring grass. Their flying manes before the ocean looked like the illustrations in horse books I'd checked out of the public library while I was in elementary school.

Most of my classmates' parents, like mine, had come to Los Angeles in the 1940s from other parts of the country or world for the job opportunities. NASA and the aircraft companies drew them, the military got a big batch, and all of the human service profes-

24

sions needed people. One of my classmate's parents was a gardener, another a homicide detective, a third an astronaut. My dad worked for Northrup Aircraft as an aeronautical engineer designing planes for the military. My mother looked after him, me, my younger brother, and later a sister. She was good at it; she'd been obliged to quit high school at the age of fourteen to help with farm work and the raising of younger siblings. She had never gone back for the requisite papers to qualify for professional employment, but she was proud of my father's position and education. He earned all of the household money and he controlled it. She wouldn't have thought to have it any other way.

But my father's job was not secure when there was no need for the product. During the '50s after the Korean War, his company periodically announced pending layoffs, and he, being one of the younger engineers, bore the news home with cynical jokes about our future in "the poorhouse." He was smiling, but real fear was in his eyes, and although he never lost his job, he desperately strove to secure it by taking advanced math, physics, business, and language courses. He would just get home from work and sit down to eat with us when it was time for him to be hurrying back to the car for the hour-long drive to the university. On nights when he stayed at home, he isolated himself so that he could study. He was very serious and wanted no interruptions.

Charlie was talking with a stranger on his way out of the store. When we walked down the streets to view the town, he spoke with half the people who looked in his direction. Many replied as if resuming conversation with a friend. A couple of times when he spoke with young women, I felt illogically jealous, both of his directing his attentions elsewhere, and of their apparent ease in the exchange. I didn't even *look* at most people for fear of invading their privacy. Privacy was a major concern of my parents who were easily embarrassed. From the beginning, I was the odd "show off" in the family. My father had pointed this out to me in a manner of scolding even before I had started kindergarten. Actually, he was right: I didn't know how to ride a horse at the age of five, no matter how many times I'd seen it on TV. He was probably protecting me, but his reprimands made me tuck myself in like a hedgehog.

On the roads through the woods to and from our cabin, Charlie explored. He was a safe driver, but whimsical, backing up or turning onto side roads to suit his curiosity, all while conversing, singing, or being silent, giving no hint of his purposes. Sometimes he "read" houses, speculating on their owners.

"These people have a lot of love, probably got grandchildren that come up in the summer." "These people are afraid — look at all those locks." On a whim, he would jaunt up to the doors. At first, I couldn't believe he could be so sanguine. You could have dropped him anywhere on earth and he'd have had an extraordinary experience. He said that in prison he'd realized he could be free wherever he was. He told a story about being in "the hole" in Terminal Island. A warden had stopped to ask him why he never asked to get out. "You know," he quoted the warden, "If you *acted* right and asked me, you might get out of here early."

"Get out of where?" Charlie asked him.

"Out of this penitentiary!" The warden barked.

"What penitentiary?" Charlie asked. "Are you in a penitentiary? I'm not."

I enjoyed watching and listening to Charlie but balked when he tried to coax me into his enjoyment. I didn't know *what* I wanted. I couldn't go home. It hadn't been my real home for years. I wondered about my mother, brother, and sister, but we had been apart many times before.

Mary made small dinners in the cabin while Charlie talked with the dog, and then with his guitar — private conversations, venturing out on chords, repeating sequences, and fingering single strings — his body bowed over it, his face blank, as if listening to its confidences. Some of Charlie's original music was catchy, and some of it complex, with pivotal chord and key changes. The words were simple:

> "Your home is where you're happy. It's not where
> you're not free.
> Your home is where you can be what you are 'cause
> you were just born to be…"

The notion that we might be born simply to experience existence was not mainstream thinking at the time.

> "Anywhere you might wander, you could make that
> your home.
> And as long as you've got love in your heart, you'll
> never be alone."

Hardly new, a little sappy, yet hopeful and timely and I liked it a lot. But some of his phrases were embarrassingly vacuous.

> "They'll show you their castles, and diamonds for all
> to see…"

Redundant — and ridiculous; nobody lives in castles.

"But they'll never show you their peace of mind,
'cause they don't know how to be
free."

True or not, those lyrics sounded faux folk-and-freedom to me. My English Lit teacher would've snarled at them. One morning, for some reason, we left the car and took a ride to a wide lake or bay where one of Charlie's new acquaintances had a wooden rowboat that we pushed off the pebbled shore and paddled to the center of some spectacular coniferous scenery. As the sun lifted mist off the water, an otter floated by on its back, gnawing a gristly mollusk clutched between its paws. The day became hot and stunningly blue, cool water slapping the sides of the boat as it rocked us. But I got sunburned and lost my book. It left in the car of the stranger who brought us. I was sorely disappointed and blamed Charlie because he clearly didn't sympathize. I didn't say anything; I just thought he was careless, arrogant, and obviously illiterate. A few days later, he surprised me with another copy of the same book. He'd seen it in someone's cabin and had simply asked for it.

Mary was generous, providing me with shampoo and all of the necessities without making me feel in the least indebted to her. Charlie was considerate, deferential, almost solicitous. I was flattered but I didn't like it. I wasn't used to it. I liked him better when he was aloof.

"Your Ego Is a Too-Much Thing" was one of
Charlie's prison compositions, with minor chords and
an insinuating, snaky sound. He sang it to neighbors in the red farmhouse, but I knew it was really to
me. I felt pulled to attention, personally attacked, and
disdainful of the peculiar lyrics. The expression "too
much" dated it. Four or five years earlier, "too much"
was common teen slang for amazement, delight, and
even disgust. Everything was too much.

"Your ego is a too much thing. Your ego is a too
much thing.
It'll make you fool yourself, you'll think you're some-
body else —
Look out for the trouble it brings ...
You get afraid you're gonna act like a clown
And you get mad when somebody puts you down
Your heart's a pumpin' and your paranoia's jumpin'
Your ego is a too much thing.
When everything seems going so fine/ old ego puts
itself on in a bind
Your certainty turns to doubt/ then you start flippin'
out
And you ease on out of your mind."

While singing, Charlie grazed me with the ego-eye.
This was a tête à tête. Something was definitely going
on here.
The East Coast couple had given us an open invitation to visit their farmhouse. Their hospitality and
fascination with Charlie kept us coming back. The
man and Charlie discussed music and most things
mechanical, while the woman offered coffee, and

whatever she had baked or cooked. Other neighbors sometimes filled the house.

One day Charlie was telling a group of us about a forty-day stint in solitary confinement. He said, "When I got there, the guy in the next cell was whistling and banging a tin cup on the cement wall." Charlie demonstrated, whistling the United States Marine Corps anthem while tapping a spoon against a ceramic cup. "Over and over, night and day, the same tune, and that cup — and I thought I'd go crazy. The first three, four days I yelled — I cursed — I did everything I could think to shut that guy up. And one day — he stopped." Charlie straightened, as if listening. A comically hopeful expression crossed his face. "And then," he said, "I heard..." In monotone, he resumed the anthem. "I tried to cover my head," he bleated. "I stuffed my ears. It was *killing* me!"

Charlie looked farcically pathetic. I broke up laughing. He was a raconteur but also a mime. His face contained more comedy than his words.

"Did he *ever* stop?" someone finally asked.

"Hey, I don't know," Charlie replied, grinning. "After about ten days, I was humming and tapping my foot." With that, he stroked the strings of the guitar and began to play it.

Later he told us that the fellow with the tin cup was a "Section Eight" military psychiatric discharge. As a prisoner in the 1950s, Charlie had helped to convert the Navy prison on Terminal Island to a standard U.S. prison. He had met "Crazy Eights" from World War II and every military conflict since.

Federal prisoners are those convicted of crimes on or against federal employees or properties. Crossing state lines in the commission of a crime is federal, as are crimes committed on military bases and Indian reservations, and crimes under the jurisdiction of the

Department of Alcohol, Tobacco and Firearms, the Drug Enforcement Agency, the Treasury Department, the U.S. Postal Service and so on. They were bank robbers, embezzlers, counterfeiters, racketeers, drug traffickers, gunrunners — even moonshiners.

Charlie remembered a Kentucky moonshiner who claimed that the only reason he got caught was that the Feds had double-crossed him. Early one morning, they had raided one of his stills and chased him up a mountain, managing to keep within yelling distance. They had begged him to stop just long enough to give them a breather. He had agreed, and kept his word. They hadn't. Charlie said that this "country boy" was just more honest than other people. He said, "Everybody laughed and thought he was a dumb rumpkin who got out-run by the Feds until he went out to the track, took off his shoes, and showed them he could outrun just about anybody."

I didn't know the affinity Charlie had with such men, or that he had relatives in Ohio, West Virginia, and Kentucky — some of them genuine hill people.

Our cabin smelled like weathered wood, sun-bleached canvas, patched cotton quilts, a little must, rust, stick matches, kerosene, and candle wax. It also smelled of evergreen air that we welcomed inside whenever it wasn't cold. The cumulative scents both indoors and out crept into my sense of self and made me feel like something more than lonely. There were possibilities in those scents.

The kitchen had a short, pudgy grandmother refrigerator, a white enameled stove with black iron burners, and lots of counter and cupboard space containing only a dented sieve and a midnight blue turkey pan. Mary had brought a twenty-five pound sack of soybeans — "superfood" the guy at the store had told her. We filled the turkey pan with water to soak the soybeans for later cooking.

Traveling through redwood country would prove educational. Two types of redwoods live in California, the Giant Sequoia, growing inland and generally of greater girth, and the Coastal Redwood, considered *the world's tallest tree.* Some of both have bases bigger than the average garage, and make humans appear the size of chipmunks.

The Coastal Redwood is California's State Tree. It is not — but should be — on the State Flag beside *ursos arctos horribilus,* the grizzly bear that has long been gone from California. When the first Americans unofficially moved in to take possession of Mexican California, they called themselves (in their adversary's tongue) Los Osos, after those very present, much feared, and respected beasts. Several skirmishes and a rowdy battle later, the men raised their "Bear Flag" of victory — according to one diarist, a torn piece of petticoat on which was hurriedly drawn a bear that looked more like a Berkshire hog. The grizzly on California's state flag is symbolic of *that* bear.

I had seen redwoods when I was young. My dad took us in our station wagon to see the tallest of these trees, some of which were carved at their bases so that, for a small fee, tourists could drive through them while the trees continued to grow. A couple of miles up the coast from our cabin was a point of land and an empty lighthouse, both named for the explorer whose expedition unwittingly gave California its name.

"Point Cabrillo," Mary read from a limp map. "Named for Juan Rodríguez Cabrillo."

"Friend of yours?" Charlie queried.

"An explorer," she said, smiling. "Some say he discovered California and some say he named it."

I've heard Charlie say only a few things regarding such discoveries and one was this: "Discovered right out from under the people who were already living there." (Which is true; Europeans found an uncounted number of native tribes in California, and anthropologists at the turn of the twentieth century ran to catch a glimpse of the last of them.) Charlie also said, "Someone said that someone said that someone told them that someone said..." He seemed to think that a large part of history was hearsay.

"It's people who know what they're talking about," I wanted to argue. "It's years of research."

"I don't have anything against it," he said. "I just look at it for what it is." He was too calm to argue with, so I argued silently and later looked it up. As if to prove his point:

History tells that Juan Rodriguez Cabrillo left his Portuguese home in the early 1500s, joined the Spanish army in Cuba, and, serving under Hernan Cortes in 1521, helped to take Tenochitlan (now Mexico) from Montezuma and the Aztecs, and rename it New Spain. It says that twenty years later, New Spain's viceroy commissioned Cabrillo to take two ships north, charting the unmapped Pacific coast, and searching for the fabled "El Dorado" or "Seven Cities of Gold." Here, legend and fable join hearsay and fantasy.

It is recorded that Cabrillo explored the entire western coast to what is now the state of Oregon. It is also recorded that Cabrillo sailed only as far north as present day San Francisco, where a violent storm repelled him to the south and he died on one of the islands off Santa Barbara. Further encyclopedic research explains that Cabrillo's northward expedition never got farther north than the current San Diego Bay, and it was there that he drew his last breath.

One version states that on Sunday, July 2, 1542 Cabrillo's party "sighted California." California? Allegedly, no historical reference to the name was known until the re-discovery of a Spanish novel *The Exploits of Esplandian*, a fantasy-adventure published in Madrid in 1510 by Ordonez de Montalvo (or in 1500 by Garci Rodriguez de Montalvo). The book told of Christians in Constantinople fighting an army of black Amazons led by Queen Califa (or Califia) from the island of "California." (In the novel, the gold-rich island is guarded by flying beasts that can carry men into the air and drop them from un-survivable heights.) "California" could have been sixteenth century slang for "the boondocks" but some historians found it plausible that Cabrillo and crew had at least heard about the novel and made use of the name.

Whether or not Cabrillo ever saw "Cape Mendocino" which is 110 miles north of the town, he is credited with having named that westernmost point of California in honor of his patron, Don Antonio de Mendoza, Viceroy of New Spain, and thus with naming the county and town of Mendocino. Another Mendoza, a later Viceroy, muddles certainty about this point, and what is absolutely clear to me is why they *didn't* teach this in school.

Critical comment on schools and books often surfaced in Charlie's conversations. While traveling one day, he sang this:

"If a pound of prunes costs thirteen cents at half past one today,

And the grocer is so bald he wears a dollar-five
toupee,
If with every pound of tea, he gives out two cut-
glass plates,
How long before Willy falls on his roller skates?

Oh, put down six and carry two, gee but this is hard
to do
You can think and think until your brains are
numb
I don't care WHAT Teacher says — I can't find that
sum."

I was amused, but wondering how to contest these
subversive lyrics, when he leaned in my direction.
"Victor Herbert," he informed me helpfully. Herbert
was an Irish-American composer known for comic op-
erettas. I'd never heard of him.

On a whim and a tip about an art show, we
drove up the coast beyond Point Cabrillo and found
that the whole town of Caspar was for sale. All I could
see of it were three dilapidated buildings that appeared
never to have left the 1930s. A faded FOR SALE sign
stood post in front of a former lodge or cocktail lounge,
and in the dust around it, brittle weed clumps waited
like winos for another drop. Locals told us that the
legendary racehorse Seabiscuit had lived out his final
days nearby, and I pictured fedoras passing through
Caspar.
    The "art show" consisted of a few bland landscapes,
the others allegedly having been sold, but here of all
places, on a warped boardwalk in a desolate shanty-
town, we ran into another ex-convict who knew Charlie (what are the odds?) and *didn't* like him, I could

tell. What an awkward coincidence. He looked like Jack Knife of the Yukon with his beautiful Wolf-Girl, and we looked — just *odd*. My hair was haywire, I had on Mary's clothes and no makeup. The girl was magazine perfect in expensive leather from her knee boots to the Russian fur hat pulled over curtains of satiny hair. I felt like a hillbilly next to her — or worse, middle-class.

There was an animal thing between Jack and Charlie — a sense of hair-raising and laying back of ears — flashes of teeth played out as smiles. They circled each other. What was Charlie doing with two women? What did Charlie think of Jack's? Was Jack laughing at Charlie? Was Charlie gloating? How primitive! How embarrassing! They were competing.

Jack threw back his head, teeth to the sky. He was a cold dog, all right, and not a bit handsome, crooked and bony at both ends, but there was something sharp and superior about him, the cruel curl of his lip, or that sniffing smugness. It made me think something was definitely wrong — with Charlie; I already knew something was wrong with me. They exchanged a few growling attaboys and we parted, but I was so embarrassed at possibly having been perceived as a ménage a trois that I couldn't see straight. As for Charlie, he was a shameless showoff; he was too confident. And he was SHORT. He should've been taller but he didn't stand up to his full height. I had seen that stance before. It wasn't a slouch or a slump but the slightly rounded shoulders and ducked head of a boxer.

Kathleen Maddox, Charlie's mother, was certified born in Morehead, Kentucky on the first Armistice Day signaling the end of World War I, November 11, 1918. Her parents were a railroad conductor

and his strict Nazarene Christian wife. Nineteen-eighteen, at its outset, could have announced the Apocalypse. The number of war dead continued to rise as a lethal flu swept the globe, killing *millions*. But from the day Kathleen was born, war energy was redirected and America began rebuilding. Women voted in national elections for the first time, and home commodities — radios and automobiles among them — became affordable and plentiful. For eleven years, American expectation and the be-all end-all economy were on the up and up — until 1929 when the stock market abruptly avalanched, taking a shocked country into a cold depression.

Kathleen Maddox turned eleven in 1929, and only a few years later, she ran away from home. She told family that she'd hooked up with an older man named "Colonel Scott," but by November of 1934 when Charlie was born at Cincinnati General Hospital in Ohio, it was "William Manson," a twenty-four-year-old day laborer for a dry-cleaning service, whose name appeared on the birth certificate. The baby's name was recorded only as "Manson." Barely sixteen, Kathleen had given her age as eighteen and claimed an address on a Cincinnati street that — if city records are reliable — never existed. Shortly thereafter, for reasons unknown to me, Kathleen Maddox and her brother, Luther, were arrested and convicted of strong-arm robbery. William Manson was out of the picture.

In West Virginia the baby "Manson" was renamed Charles Milles Maddox after his late grandfather, and raised for six years by his maternal grandmother and a succession of relatives. He visited his mother at the West Virginia State Penitentiary in Moundsville.

In a dim tackle shack in Caspar, California, Charlie inquired of a prickly old man about the prospective sale of the town. He bought dime candy bars, and emerged in the sunlight, handing one to each of us. "We can't afford the two million," he said, "...so I got these." He liked Paydays, a sweet caramel roll thickly studded with salted peanuts.

At night in the cabin, Mary lit a candle, some incense, and a single marijuana cigarette that we passed between us in the age-old ceremonial style. I had occasionally smoked the dried leaves of this plant with friends for at least three years, and invariably received from it both heightened awareness and hallucinatory paranoia. The fixed notion that people were laughing at my stupidity blocked perception of the world around me. An acquaintance had told me that marijuana seeds could be popped in an oiled skillet like popcorn. He'd persuaded me to go into the kitchen to make up a batch. It was a light-hearted joke — I didn't feel that he was being malicious — but I couldn't get over the idea that I really was stupid, because while he and other friends could sit in the living room having a good time, I was in a partial stupor, trapped in thoughts about myself.

Charlie and Mary's relationship is more developed than mine is with either of them. It's as though I'm watching from behind soundproof glass, unable to communicate or to understand what they're saying. I go in and out of consciousness of the scene. They are standing near a candle talking, their inflated shadows enhancing them. Her posture is of open interest, her shoulders relaxed and neck long. He makes her laugh and her eyes become more hugely blue and shining. I think she may be in love with him. They disappear and reappear. I try to be invisible, until I can hide in sleep.

If he had wanted to be alone with her, if they had wanted to be more intimate, they didn't embarrass me by showing it. I still slept in my clothes. Charlie raised an eyebrow, grinning as he looked past Mary at me one night, but he settled into his comfort and fell asleep. Apparently, he was not out to conquer. I think I wanted him to, because I was struggling; I think I was waiting for someone to jump into my mind and pull me out. On a walk the following day, I fell into the same quandary. In the patches of woods, never mind the forest, I could not see the trees.

Here, in the open, where a mind can expand, my view is narrowing. I'm struggling to keep a normal face, but under it, I believe I might embody all the badness, wrongness, and stupidity of the world and I don't know how to carry it. Just guarding the secret is exhausting.

In this obsessive self-consciousness, I nearly ran into Mary and Charlie, but rather than demonstrating scorn, they showed me the den of an unidentified animal. Charlie said that with Muffet along, we were unlikely to catch a glimpse of it, and we walked on. They didn't seem to have noticed my conflict.

Charlie talked to Muffet as though she understood him. She was a lustrous, intelligent animal with the sort of dog ears that teachers told us not to put at the corners of pages in our books. They expressed her character but to him they were beacons. He said that she sensed more, and that he was learning from her. I wondered if Mary was ever jealous of her dog's devotion to Charlie. Mary wasn't selfish but she was private, like I was, with personal sensitivities that were sometimes mysterious. She surprised us one night, kneeling beside the bed, unlatching her flute case and assembling the silver pieces with conflicting emotions on her face. The instrument was clearly a treasured and difficult friend.

My father had displayed such emotions when I was six and saw him put together a clarinet that, to my excitement, he had brought from the attic. He was a fair piano player, reading from classical and popular sheet music, sometimes even singing, and I sang along. I idolized this aspect of him, but, when his audience was impressed, a smirk quickly replaced his sincerity, as if to protect himself from ridicule by pretending to be joking, and he never allowed himself to be taken by the music. This was true on the day that he played the clarinet. His face reddened and I felt in him a scorching humiliation. Without completing the piece, and despite our entreaties, he silently, almost angrily, put the clarinet away, and I never saw it again.

Kneeling, straight backed, the candle flame sparking off her flute, Mary pressed a deep breath through taut lips into the instrument. She played haltingly at first but with courage. Then, catching a muse and releasing herself, she exhaled enchanting music, lifting my mood, my spine, and my admiration of her.

Mary was twenty-three and had attended two colleges — Wisconsin State and the University of Wisconsin — earning two degrees before I got out of high school. An efficiency expert, in a hurry she might put on the first two shoes she could find, even if they didn't match. Charlie loved it. The downside of her efficiency was impatience. She could be frustrated by delay, and her irritation showed, but she didn't often speak it. She might have been called taciturn, tough — at worst, abrupt, stub-jawed, button-lipped, and close-minded — but never for long. She was bright and attractive, her will was good, and she didn't bother with grudges. Charlie leaned on her for any necessary business and often said she had a lot of love.

Mary and I were soon joining him on his morning expeditions, exploring the forest of redwoods, oak, bay laurel, rhododendron, poison oak, and who knew what else. Seeming random swatches of land had been cut bare while others were overgrown with brush. We stayed, for the most part, on denuded paths where we could walk with ease. When Charlie ventured into the thickets, I found myself feeling edgy about getting spiders in my hair.

I thought I loved the woods, but not like he did. He seemed to think they called to him. We followed him one day on an exhaustive journey he felt compelled to make in response to something he could not specify. At last he declared it to be a circle of three tall redwoods he seemed to consider personages. Despite my ordinary lack of concentration, I lay on my back in the center of this circle with Mary and him for most of the afternoon.

Young sequoias look like Christmas trees, with needled branches from bottom to top, but mature trees often are bare on their lower halves. From this perspective, the three trees appeared to get closer at the top, as if confiding in one another. I think of Charlie's trees as "The Three Graces" of classical myth and art. Whatever they communicated to him, he kept to himself. He certainly had more stamina and patience than I did. I got cold sooner; I itched; I was unused to being still for half an hour, much less three. He liked to explore until his stomach growled; then he looked to us for food.

The soybeans we'd set out to soak had sprouted. Aside from nibbling their bitter roots, we didn't know what to do with them. When food ran lowest, we got into the car and drove ten miles to Fort Bragg, a commercial fishing town — all nets, creaking docks, and clanking metal — for cheap hamburgers from a take-out window.

Charlie ate in the way he did everything, not primly but with finesse. He appreciated any offer of food or drink whether he accepted it or not. If he liked it, he ate without saying much; if he didn't like it, he just didn't eat much. His tastes were Depression era or prison issue. Mary and I were amused to learn that he keenly liked canned "fruit cocktail," and that, given a choice of any cheese in the world, he'd ask for Velveeta. We had no notion of how differently he'd been raised, first by many individuals and never in one place for long. He didn't know his father. His original birth certificate marked him not legitimate, and in the 1930s the word "bastard" was still in use as a scarlet degradation. His mother had filed a paternity suit against "Colonel Walker Scott" in 1935 but Charlie didn't speak of it.

From immediate and extended family, he went to foster homes, boys schools, juvenile halls, jails, and prisons. He didn't — then wouldn't — go to school. Tests later assessed his I.Q. at far above average, but he refused a normal education. His English was colorful but limited, his grammar un-ruled. He said "ain't" and used double negatives and common, unnecessary indecencies. Paradoxically, he was a grade-A communicator. He compensated, using his face, body, and, mainly, his brain. He likened the brain to a computer, and the mind to its operator. (Back then, computers were the size of rooms, and his concept was uncommon). His own computer files were extensive. He'd been exposed to the behaviors, ideologies, and experiences of hundreds of mostly men by the time he was twenty.

But we didn't learn about Charlie's early life until later. Instead, he entertained us with anecdotes about his more recent past in each of the two federal prisons off the West Coast. He mimicked the sometimes pathetic or unsavory characters with a fondness and honesty that broke us in half laughing. One memory was of a couple of old glue sniffers on a recreation yard, one standing rigid, looking skyward, sniffing a rag doused in factory glue, the other one approaching, and asking, *"What're you doin'?"*

"They're comin' for me," the first one answered. "This is the spot."

"Who? Who's comin'?"

"They're comin' for me. They're gonna send down a beam."

"Who's comin'? *I wanna go."*

"You can't go."

"Why? I WANNA GO!"

"YOU CAN'T GO! THERE'S ONLY ROOM FOR ONE!"

They began wrestling for a place on the imaginary spot, the first one hollering, "NO, MAN, YOU'RE GONNA RANK IT! "

Mary and I were getting glimpses into one of the world's remaining inner sanctums and we were intrigued. What I believed about prisoners came from the usual media sources and seemed to be a mixed message: there were true bad people who had to be kept away from the rest of us, and there were people who just ended up in the wrong places at the wrong times. I focused on the latter, because, since people were fundamentally good, some people were in prison because mistakes had been made, sometimes by police and prosecutors. One look at police brutality against civil rights marchers told that story. Throughout time and great literature, soldiers, scientists, artists, clerics, philosophers, kings and queens had all been imprisoned. If I had any objection to the convicted class, it had more to do with morality than illegality.

Charlie told a few stories about shirking the requisite prison jobs. In one, he had taken a job in the Music Room, furnishing, equipping and maintaining it, while listening to and playing music all day. It was the perfect job for him until a guard found out that there was no Music Room before Charlie had opened one. He'd had jobs in the kitchen, on a paint crew, and as an orderly; all were short-lived. Sent to work in the prison factory, he did an investigation and started making speeches.

"Fred," he'd say, "I thought you were against war. What're you doing making parts for the military?" "Joe, how long you been workin' here? You say you didn't get parole? Don't be surprised. They need you, man. You're *buildin'* their penitentiaries." He said that he even got kicked out of group therapy because the psychologist said that he confused people. Delighted at having successfully failed so many positions, called "Crazy Charlie" by some of the staff, he was free to pursue his music.

I laughed at these stories but questioned the morality of avoiding one's share of work. Where I was from, peoples' pride was neither in inherited wealth nor in the ability to beg, swindle, and steal it, but in punctuality, reliability, and steady hard work. Shyness aside, we were a prideful people who didn't call in sick unless we couldn't stand up, and stayed well just to keep our noses in the air.

Charlie, Mary, and I were partly supported by money that Mary had saved. It didn't seem offensive or irresponsible, but as though we were furthered by providence. And contrary to being a malingerer, Charlie was perpetually engaged. In Mendocino his explorations led him to facilitate exchanges between strangers — a man looking to unload an old Mercury with the father of a teen who wanted a fix-up car, a woman seeking a cheap propane stove with somebody clear across town who never used his and gave it up for free. Charlie had a knack for this, and he didn't make a thing for it but new acquaintances and invitations to dinner. His alertness and ability to entertain people were sometimes the only resources supporting us.

My memory of the people we visited is a vague amalgam of artistic, do-it-yourself couples in well-constructed rented cabins living the good life, unmolested. Besides no fast food franchises, no supermarkets, and no neon at all, Mendocino had no visible police force. Laissez faire was law and seemed to promote respect; far from being based in passive weakness, it assumed right behavior and would deal forthrightly with transgression. (Northern woods hippies were no more likely to be bullied than any self-reliant people.)

The cabins were comfortably furnished with antiques or cleverly salvaged scraps of natural, nearly edible materials, instruments of art and music, colorful quilts, weavings and embroideries, dried flowers, clay vessels, incense, candles, and books galore. This life was my ideal — fresh air, privacy, the forest, the sea — what more could an artist, writer, or naturalist want? However, Mendocino offered no jobs with which to support this lifestyle. Jobs engendered by entrepreneurs were worked by their families and friends. In fact, after the lumber mills were shut down, Mendocino had almost no economy until the late 1950s when a group of local artists formed what was already loosely an "art colony." This, and the tide pools, brought in more tourists and retreaters for the cabins and exclusive inns. There was talk amongst travelers of "a spiritual presence."

Charlie remembered waking one night as he felt something leaning on his feet at the end of the bed. Muffet sat tensely watching beside him. They'd both stared into the dark for some time before Muffet had lain down again, and he had drifted to sleep. He wondered if we'd been awake.

I didn't believe in ghosts. Mendocino had its legendary phantoms — a Victorian lady staring out to sea from a window of one of the finer old houses, a veteran soldier said to have been murdered at Big River's sawmill, and spirits cut adrift by shipwrecks — but these were clearly insubstantial. The East Coast couple, who seemed practical in other respects, said that they had a "baby ghost" they sometimes heard laughing or crying in a bedroom upstairs. I figured this had to do with their wanting a baby and being unable to conceive. But while crossing the bridge over Big River one night, Charlie, Mary, and I all saw something. It could've been a bum; it was dark. Charlie braked the car, and backed it up on the bridge. My pulse bumped into my nerves. No one or thing was visible, but you could never know when a semi might come barreling at can't-stop miles an hour while you're in the middle of a dark highway *looking for ghosts*. We said and saw nothing but a light far out at sea, and we drove on.

A surprising sense of the supernatural came to me the first time I saw Charlie dance. We were in a cabin listening to record albums. Mary had gone to town with our hosts. I don't remember the music, but that it moved him. His countenance lifted, and his body appeared weightless, each finger and limb moving without effort and in perfect rhythm. I was *not* hallucinating, yet his face kept changing as he dipped and dodged, crept and leapt a footstool, winking at me. He moved through the dances of different eras and cultures, nimbly, and in a progression so quick that I could just recognize each before it fell into another. Then he switched to enacting everyday motions in sync with the music — showering, dressing, brushing his teeth. I'd been trained in dance since childhood, but *I had never seen anyone dance like that.* This shocking surge of talent and creativity frightened me, and I ran out of the cabin. He found me sitting beside it with my knees drawn up to my chest. Chuckling tenderly, he said that he was just as surprised as I was. He had never danced like that, he explained, because in prison "tough guys don't dance."

He had, however, learned to box. At one of the boys' schools the Catholic monks taught their charges using gloves and rules of fairness. Charlie remembered being called a "duke" and earning a gold and green jacket. He had an edgy but abiding respect for the monks who taught him "handball, basketball, and things that would later save my life."

Under the bridge at Big River, Mary spread a woven blanket on the sand and unpacked sandwiches she had made at the cabin. She had taken to wearing shorts, her long legs tanning nicely now despite days dimmed by a vague fog. I wore one of her thin skirts that were too long on me, but I could drape it above my knees when seated, and consider myself bohemian. I had quit wearing makeup — Mary didn't wear any — and hadn't shaved my legs or underarms since leaving L.A. This was becoming the fashion anyway. My high school friends had read that European women didn't shave and were considered very sexy.

Last to come from Mary's satchel was lemonade. Wine would have suited my picture better, but Charlie didn't drink it. He said he'd quit drinking alcohol when he'd admitted to himself that he didn't like the taste. I was surprised to hear him say it. Where I was from, people *learned* to like the taste. Liquor ads showing sophisticated bons vivants with relaxed bodies and fluid wit were encouragement enough for me to keep trying, even when I didn't like it.

But sweet-tart lemonade goes well with salty ham and sea air. And a mix of warm sand with the distant shush of white water makes a potent sedative.

Big River flows beside the Mendocino peninsula from the forest to the sea. Historical archives recount a boat wreck near Big River survived by German immigrant William Kasten in 1850. They say that Kasten saw wealth in the redwoods, built himself a crude cabin, and stayed. Maybe, maybe not. It wasn't Kasten who set up the sawmill.

On record for the same year that Kasten came to land, the trade cargo ship, *Frolic*, a double-masted square-rigger sailing from China to gold-booming San Francisco, ran aground on a reef less than a mile from the beach at Point Cabrillo. Long after passengers had clambered onto land and left the area, the wreckage of *Frolic* drew scavengers and treasure hunters, among them a lumberman named Jerome Ford, traveling from San Francisco. In his archived diary, Ford describes the largely unmapped area with no roads, only narrow trails, and numerous swollen rivers to cross, one of which carried off two mules and most of his crew's food and blankets. But Ford recognized that he was surrounded by a fortune in timber.

Back in San Francisco, he consulted a wealthy city council member and developer named Henry Meiggs. Meiggs, who had orchestrated the creation of Fisherman's Wharf and other city venues renowned to this day, sent Ford on a second trip north to secure land for a sawmill. In his diary, Ford reports finding only six men living near Big River, one of them William Kasten who had taken out a land claim. Ford arranged to pay Kasten one hundred dollars, plus first timber, for land on which the Big River mill would be erected.

According to record, the mill was constructed on the east coast of the U.S. and shipped whole — in a schooner that Henry Meiggs had purchased — around South America and up the west coast to San Francisco, and then, with a full crew of managers and laborers, north to Big River.

In the late 1800s a visiting journalist explained Northern California's lumber business to readers of *Harper's Magazine* as follows:

> "...the coastline is broken at frequent intervals by the mouths of small streams... sawmills are placed... wherever a river-mouth offers the slightest shelter to vessels loading ...There are even mills which offer no lee... and here the adventurous schooner watches her opportunity, hauls under a perpendicular cliff, receives her lading in the shortest possible time, and her crew think themselves fortunate if they get safely off ... "Big River" is one of the best of the lumber ports; but even here, vessels are lost every winter. One of the old residents told me he had seen more than one hun-

dred seamen perish in the twenty years he had lived here..." (I also was shown) "...the strange and terrible cave into which a schooner was sucked in a sudden gale... Her masts were snapped off like pipe-stems, and the hull was jammed into the great hole in the rock, where it began to thump with the swell so that two of the frightened crew were at once crushed on the deck by the overhanging ceiling of the cave. Five others... hung on until ropes were lowered to them... a more terrifying situation... can hardly be imagined outside of a hasheesh [sic] dream."

Thus began the export of Mendocino's forests, the sawn redwoods taken by boatload not only to San Francisco, but across the world. One of the first mill operators later lamented his part in "what now looks like a desecration." But the town of Mendocino grew, passing through several names including Big River Township and Meiggsville. Fine homes were built, a church, a hotel, families were brought in, and along the riverbanks and the outskirts in places colloquially known as Portagee Flat and Fury Town, sawyers, mill workers, and cooks lived in digs to which they were accustomed. They were immigrants from the Azores, China, Denmark, Finland, Germany, Italy, and Sweden.

Within three years of selling property for the Big River mill, William Kasten told people that the area had become too populated for him. From the six men in 1851, it now counted more than 600. So Kasten sold his remaining land to a William Kelley, whose name remains prominent in Mendocino to this day. Developer Henry Meiggs' name, however, does not.

After finding himself in deep debt, Meiggs, still a well regarded San Francisco Alderman, stole blank city warrants from the San Francisco Treasurer's office and made them out to himself, increasing his account by $800,000. In October of 1854, knowing that discovery of his theft was imminent, he absconded "during the hours of darkness," taking his entire family out of the country and leaving "a financial shock wave that rocked the city from one end to the other." Though Meiggs was unknown to have ever actually been in Mendocino, and despite his outlaw status, he would manage to have much of Mendocino shipped to him.

Charlie pulled Mary's car to the roadside nesome salt-corroded resort trailers and a scallop of sheltered shore. In the distance, gulls and pipers glided above the water and tiptoed along its edges. It looked like another good place to spend an afternoon. Kicked back on the heels of our hands, Mary and I fiddled driftwood bits between our toes, and let the waves lull us while listening to Charlie fine-tune his hobby.

He had made his first guitar from a cigar box strung with rubber bands, and later constructed one in a prison woodshop. He said that he had played in state institutions during the '40s and '50s, but that Alcatraz had the only "music program" in the federal system, and it took him four years to get a guitar into another federal prison. Other prisoners had given him pointers. Among them was former gangster, Alvin Karpis, doing the end of a long federal term for crimes committed in the 1930s with the press-labeled "Ma Barker Gang." Charlie didn't give us details. I read about it in the newspaper a few years later. Interviewed from his home in Canada, Karpis was quoted as saying that he'd taught Charlie to play the steel guitar back when Charlie gambled and was known as "Tips." Incrementally, I learned that Charlie had been in custody in Kentucky, Ohio, West Virginia, Illinois, Indiana, Virginia, New York, Florida, California, and some states in-between.

Squinting through the splintered sun, thoughts came to me unbidden and passed unanalyzed until three barelegged children stood over us — none older than seven — staring at Charlie and at the guitar. He engaged them in conversation and they proceeded to tell him that they were living in one of the trailers by the road, and that their mother allowed them the run of the beach as long as they stayed away from the water. I was impressed by their directness, and by their independence; I thought they were cute, but I listened to little of what they said. Charlie, on the other hand, asked them philosophical questions I considered beyond their understanding, and gave their answers more import than I thought they warranted. He demonstrated guitar chords, and entertained them for much of the afternoon with lively songs that seemed to excite them, until their fidgeting quieted and they stood lit with sunset watercolors and wondrous expressions.

The faint voice of a woman turned them toward the highway, and back to Charlie. Mary and I waved to a distant figure leaning from one of the trailers. Dancing foot to foot, they waited until she had called again, and Charlie looked up, nodding to them. Then they excitedly said goodbye and ran to her.

I was a little stunned by this exchange, and none of us spoke. We watched the sun through a thickening mist that threatened to run ashore. (I cringed. Fog, to me, was like dawn to a vampire; the halo of fuzzy curls it fashioned hadn't been stylish since the 1800s.) As we got up to leave, Charlie asked, "How're you gonna learn from what you look down at?" I knew he was talking to me about those kids. How're you gonna learn from what you look down at? I wanted to deny it and defend myself, but he was right; I did look down on children for being uneducated and untrained. I thought everybody did. I liked to think myself a humble egalitarian, but in fact I looked down on about half of all adults for being too trained, on rigid religious types, on most "rich people," *all* of the white people of the Southern United States, and a long list of other people I'd never met, not to get into the animal and plant kingdoms. I felt a slow seep of shame hemorrhaging across my face. And just as I felt shame, we were stopped short when a white-haired, spook-eyed fisherman scuttled across our path muttering something dreadful about fog, as though it could overtake and drown him. I felt clammy and queasy. A swollen roller walloped the rocks and we left that beach.

Discomfort plagued me during those tepid days, the woods splintered and sticky, the rough coastal bluffs damp and dangerous. Even the cabin was unwelcoming. I couldn't find a place to rest. Aloof by appearances, I hoped Charlie would approach me. When he did, I snubbed him. One day, Mary purposely left me alone with him in a neighbor's cabin. Something important was happening and I wanted to follow it through. I had read and believed that LSD could be used for psychological cleansing. I had taken it several times before, but this time was different.

Slowly becoming conscious, I see the games I've been playing with him. He isn't playing. He walks outside of the cabin. I survey its interior, pretending intention, but I wonder what he's doing. From the porch, I can see him looking into a flowering bush. I have to be closer to see — bees; he's watching honeybees. *What century is this?*

I am in and out of consciousness. The car is against my back, I see him walking toward it, getting in and starting the engine. Climbing in, I'm comfortably terrified. Am I always terrified?

On the rubbery black asphalt down to the sea, I feel him beside me, and, strangely, within me. He's not what I have thought — not the back alley boot-scuff or social bottom brick, not a lost child, a sex-starved ex-con, a huckster or trickster, though surely all of those. Transforming before me, he is grand and humble, godly and infernal, in metamorphosis, a startling substantial phantom. Is it the drug or my mind creating these changes in him? And if so, why do other people not appear in so many forms?

The sky shades and rains tenderly. I've badly short-changed him. I swallow a queasy mouthful of panic, and the narrow tar road becomes a sprawling tongue that is swallowing us whole — but he is no comfort, for now he has no face. No features. He is nothing but a chilling emptiness that drops the bottom out of my illusions, leaving me horribly alone. He might be Charon hauling me to Hell.

At the bottom of the hill, he restrains the panting beast and looks to me for direction. The crossroad offers no hope of escape, and across it, spread before us stands a gothic family cemetery, encrusted tombstones and crosses bulging unevenly from rocky ground. I'm stunned. His disembodied voice sounds sinister: "Oh, that's where you want to go," and we roll across the dark divide to a packed dirt drive that passes between the tombstones. Sharp rocks crack and flick from beneath the tires, stirring the startled cry of a dove, and *the sudden flapping of its wings. I think I may have made my final decision. Does Death walk alongside Life, or are they opponents, or both, and why? Why is it necessary? Could I kill myself to avoid this painful end, or am I dying in fear of it?*

Fear, born of doubt, brings violent visions rolling down on me like the salty undertow grabs and plunges the panicky swimmer until up and down are indistinguishable. Experience comes without the buffer of words, in sensations and symbols, the brain code of dreams: I am standing on ridge rocks in the sun, windwhipped, and mesmerized by a gorge of roiling water below; dank breath rises from the troubled gut. I am padding along the barren shoreline examining curious rock arches and sea sculptures, when the cold chisel bites my feet. I am staring horizon-ward at dusk, seeing restless, white-capped ghosts in the turbulence.

My experience is little. I have paddled southern California waters for most of my life with barely a tug from the undertow or a salty tumble, but this pacific sea can be bitterly cold and hard-handed as it slaps the northern shores. I've seen its elegance sliding like liquid glass, its playful gushes in frilly lace to flirt and fuss about the necks of the craggy old rocks. But I am blind. That shock-headed old fisherman may be crazy, but he knows that this gentle, yielding liquid can kiss and nibble until pits become caverns, that it can bash and batter the life out of him.

Hell aches and groans inside me, sharp and hot, frozen and stinging, the hollowness of unwholesome hunger, the slow leak of bleeding dry. It is choking, smothering, swallowing the tongue and swallowing the sea, pressure without relief, the cramp of the womb before it expels us, the awful openness into which we are thrust. It's abandonment in a wet blanket, a howling wind through broken windows, and running in search of something I can't name. I'm hiding so hard that I cannot see, and, inside, faced with eternity.

When I opened my eyes, Charlie was at the wheel where I left him, watching the sun go down. He did not assault me, even by looking. At dusk, he started the engine and we moved on to Mary in the musical house of friends, and that night, as we sat listening to records, Charlie asked me for my skate key. Slipping the chain around his neck, he said something ironic and partly to himself, something about how he couldn't get over it, "people outside are more locked up than the ones who are in prison."

I grew up in a Los Angeles suburb on a block with eleven boys, no girls. I had a western six-shooter, an army automatic, and a replica of a pirate pistol that my dad had brought me from a business trip to New Orleans — all cap guns. Our neighborhood was partially un-landscaped, leaving piles of dirt and gravel for trenches and hideouts. Every day we couldn't wait to get outside to play "Cowboys" or "War." The boys let me play, even as they sometimes complained that my hair gave away the hiding places. One year, while we were dodging Germans, a tall soldier took me to a chimney corner, kissed me on the forehead and whispered, "You stay here. When all this is over, I'll be back to get you." He was in a different movie. Despite ridicule from the ranks, I became his personal nurse, until, in a moment of wellness, he left me for some girl in his grade at school. That little romance changed my channels. My mother had the wisdom to channel me into dance classes.

The Westchester Lariats were a community group of over sixty young people aged, roughly, seven to twenty-seven, and the ardent personal project of a University of Southern California professor of folk dance and physical education. Dr. Tillman Hall had taken the reins of a small square dance group, expanding its repertoire to include folk, popular, and modern dances as his knowledge and personal contacts grew. Besides traditional and acrobatic square dances, we learned to polka, schottische, rumba, samba, and Cha-cha-cha. We did a showy Viennese waltz, a snappy fox trot, the Can-Can, the Highland Fling, the Tarantella, the Hula, the Charleston of the '20s, Jitterbug of the '40s and the '60s Twist. We learned new dances, practiced for hours each week, and returned home damp with sweat.

I was ten when I took the first of four cross-country tours with the troupe in a chartered bus and without my parents. Nearly every night in a different city, we performed a two-hour song and dance show in theaters and auditoriums, military bases, and outdoor arenas. For six to eight weeks of each summer we slept in campgrounds, barracks, and often as guests in private homes from farmhouses to mansions. I saw more lifestyles than I then realized, and nearly every state in the Union. My mother helped to sew a large collection of ethnic costumes. My father financed my trips.

His parents lived in Brooklyn, New York, and I was allowed to spend several days with them that first summer when our troupe passed through the city. My old grandpa in his dapper hat, suit, and vest, took me by the hand to see all his proprietor friends downtown, and everywhere we went, he introduced me as "my little granddaughter from Hollywood," "a dancer from Hollywood." Grandpa seemed to think that all of Los Angeles was Hollywood.

After the public fanfare and handshaking, Grandpa treated me to a big meal at Schraft's, and when I couldn't eat it all, he scolded me severely for ordering it. He was embarrassed by even the suggestion that we take the food home.

Grandma served her meals on china plates with fancy white linen. Dinner was a solemn affair during which she criticized my use of the salad fork on my meat. Grandma carried herself like Queen Victoria and looked a little like her too. In reality, she was the wife of a retired tool-and-die factory foreman, and the comfortable 76th Street row house she and Grandpa had occupied for years was owned by one of her two sisters who occasionally lived with them. I don't know where these great aunts were during my visit, or who the old woman was in a bedroom at the top of the stairs, but I found her sitting in a rocking chair by a lace-curtained window. She apparently thought I was my father's sister. I was fascinated by the things she was saying, but suddenly my grandfather found me, Grandma right behind him. They were embarrassed and angry. The old woman asked them a question that Grandpa answered tersely. When she asked again, he snapped at her. They pulled me out of the room and scolded me for entering without their permission. It hurt. I liked her.

The dance troupe occupied my time, and gave me a sense of camaraderie. I looked forward to each summer trip and was always a little sad to come home. We traveled to the new state of Alaska when the Al-Can Highway was still partly gravel, performed on TV variety shows, and in big theater productions at the Hollywood Bowl, marched in the parade at Disneyland each year, met Lassie and Timmy, Walt Disney, and other Hollywood personalities.

I turned eleven ready to find a real job. It was in the local newspaper: Lt hs cleaning 3 dys wk/2 hrs pr dy at a residence only two blocks from my elementary school. I was thrilled that first day after school, walking to work; I was exhausted walking home. My new boss, a humorless middle-aged woman, was demanding. She and her family lived in a giant laundry pile that they never completely picked up. It was disconcerting to see that her girls were about my age. Though apparently studious, they traipsed in, dropping their sweaters, while I washed stacks of crusted dishes in various saucepans of cold water, keeping separate the dishes that had served meat from those that had held cheese. The religious custom was never explained to me. At eighty cents an hour, it wasn't the job of my dreams, but I wanted to work.

On Saturdays and Sundays, I was educated in the Catholic faith for my mother; my dad was relatively Lutheran but he didn't go to church. I enjoyed the company of my younger brother and baby sister, and, alternately, tussled with them. I could do flips on the trampoline and off the diving board at the "Y," nailed a plank to my skates for a skateboard, and later learned to ride a surfboard. I liked being a kid and resisted the obligatory bras, garter belts, razors, and stockings pushed by excited young mothers, along with "Charm School" and ideals that made me feel less than adequate. Walking to the store, I was cruised by a carload of older boys.

"Hey, honey, you wanna come for a ride?" Flattered, excited, I pretended to ignore them. They cussed, laughed, and yelled, "Uggllee!" burning rubber as they peeled away. I never even got a look at them, but for years, in times of doubt, I could hear them yelling "Uggllee!" and going away.

It was a common lack of confidence. I felt nakedly *un*exposed and stupid, but also intensely curious about all natural phenomena, firstly birth and death. I wanted to witness birth, observe surgery, and sit in on an autopsy. At the time, not even expectant fathers were allowed in hospital rooms. I was told so by nurses who invariably advised me to go to school for the experience.

School was a blur. My dad bared his teeth when he tried to teach me algebra. He had large, even teeth that clamped fiercely in anger. The suggested "few home lessons" turned out to be a mistake — one after another. I blocked. His anger happened quickly. The angrier he got, the more I blocked. He ended up telling me I was "dumber than the cat," and I had to learn algebra in summer school.

As I turned twelve, my father was in mid-life; he bought himself a sports car and a twenty-six-foot Chris Craft that he rarely took out of the harbor after the six months of its novelty. None of his acquisitions seemed to satisfy him. Before smog obscured the view, I climbed to the slanted roof of our garage and lay staring into the sparkling darkness. I talked to God there, and infinity embraced me, but upon my descent, the flickering magic vanished and reality labored on.

About that time I read a fascinating book about the experimental use of the new drug, lysergic acid diethylamide, in psychoanalysis. Not long after, I saw a Harvard professor on television discussing that same little-known substance. Contrary to adult drones, the world was still a wonderfully mysterious place.

A strong desire for harmony and justice gave me angry indignation over news reports of stubborn, often thuggish *injustices* dispensed by common white people in the South. I had been through the southern states, had seen the literal signs of segregation and contempt. What was wrong with these adults? I had no real knowledge of my civil rights, of what it took to get them, or what it would be like without them, but the realization that a whole group of people had to go out into the streets and be clubbed in the head to obtain what I already had was shocking and shameful to me. Why weren't the American people correcting this injustice with the same vigor that sent them after Hitler, Hirohito, and Mussolini? And what was the preoccupation against Communism about, the political right pushing for national fear of an *ideology*, and for wars to protect peoples' civil rights while right here at home millions of people were denied them?

My father didn't want to talk about it. He cut off those conversations and seemed to think me a willful troublemaker for raising them. He said I was too independent. When I was a child, he'd engaged me in sarcastic banter, but now he considered it "disrespectful" and I should automatically drop it. The slang I was bringing home from school further disturbed him, and after all the years of living together, we had no communication. None. Suddenly he laid down restrictions and ultimatums. I balked. My mother was weak and helpless in the middle. One week she said I could go to a party, but moments before my friends arrived, my father threatened to leave her and the other kids if she allowed me to go. It was my turn to feel helpless.

My father stopped speaking to me when I chose to go to the beach with my older cousin rather than with the family. "You'll either go everywhere with us, or you'll go nowhere with us," he told me. I was thirteen. From that day, he forbade my presence in any room of the house he occupied, and instructed my mother to refuse me an allowance or travel money. He permitted her to set a plate for me in the kitchen, but, thenceforth, ignored any other arrangements, effectively blocking me out of his life. My mother supplied me the money she could, but advised that I could have avoided these hardships had I "just gone along with him."

As my school grades began a steady decline and a parent's signature was required on report cards, I signed my father's name, and neither of my parents missed the chore. Life for me was not that different. I had to drop out of the dance troupe, but when the family went on vacations, I had the house to myself, borrowed the car, and had a few friends over. Not every kid was so lucky. We drank a little to punctuate this freedom, but when the folks got home, the car was back in the garage, the booze back on the shelves. I liked to think myself mature. In that vein, I tried vodka with my orange juice for breakfasts, but arrived at class barely able to stay awake. I didn't want to be unconscious; I wanted experience.

One summer my mother, brother, sister and I took a Greyhound bus through the Midwest to a two-block alfalfa town and the farm where she grew up. For their parents' fiftieth wedding anniversary their nine children had planned a reunion of over one hundred relatives, most of whom I'd never met. The country was open, with long grasses and big, rich dirt clods under plows pulled by giant horses, and the air was so dense with life that breathing was like eating. My grandparents didn't even have running water. The farmhouse was small and wooden with a pot-bellied stove in the living room, a two-seater outhouse in back, and a pump in the shed. I thought it was beautiful.

The relatives had rented a meeting house in the next town and had dinner and cakes and liquor catered in. Grandma took off her apron and re-pinned her loose, high bun. Everyone was dressed up but Grandpa; he still wore overalls, and stubble on his face. He didn't want to go. All his little chicks who had grown into hens were around him flapping. His face was red and he wouldn't speak a word. Finally, someone explained to me that Grandpa had had a feud with a man in the next town. He didn't want to get dressed up, or to be honored at any celebration, and *he didn't want to go to Urbank.* I also found out that Urbank was only a block long, most of it shut down, and that the feud we were snagged on was ten years past; he hadn't been there since.

Grandpa waited until all his girls were anxious, mad, and tearful. Then he got up, shaved, and put on a suit that just barely buttoned. I felt as awkward as he apparently did at the party. The relatives seemed like strangers, except for my aunts who clucked and chuckled in clusters. My cousins and I managed to have a few drinks and take a rowboat out on the lake, where a comfortable companionship settled over us. I think we were all lonely. During the bus trip home, I fell so in awe of the land that I stared at the fields as far as I could see and cried.

We had moved into a more "modern" house in Redondo Beach, and it looked even worse to me upon our return. The walls were eggshell white plasterboard. Sometimes I would jump on any city bus just to see where it went. I'd look at the faces in the bus and imagine their lives. I'd see neighborhoods of black families sitting outside on crooked porches, eating, smoking, or playing music. They were in groups and it seemed they were always laughing. That looked like healthy family life to me. Then I'd go home to a concrete community, and face an uncomfortable blur of nervous stomachs and minds turning over the pages of the *Wall Street Journal*.

When my parents saw the Watts riots on TV they were scared. They didn't say so — my father just walked out of the room — but I could see it. What if those angry black people came to our community? A chill settled over the suburbs. My mother believed we should help people. She gave offerings of money and prayers at church for the poor, the sick, the crippled, the outcast, and I made sure to be nice to kids like that at school. I read books about such people and felt a personal responsibility.

During my fifteenth year, I told my mother that I wanted to get a job and move out. My friend, her sisters, and their alcoholic mother had offered me inexpensive room and board. My mother said, "You'll never make it," which apparently was all the pep talk I needed. I found a job the next week and moved. Our school gave academic credit for employment, so I could be a student *and* a sales clerk, fish scooper, and cage cleaner in the pet store down the street from my new home. I loved working with the animals, but they weren't themselves. The kittens, puppies, and guinea pigs were morose and sleepy, the capuchin monkey irritably hunched, and losing its hair. It flashed vampire teeth at cage-cleaning time. My boss hadn't thought to tell me how to bag fish. Customers were calling back to say that their pet fish were dead on arrival. Had I left a little air in the bag? No, I hadn't. Fish, my boss explained, need air. I suppose I should have known, but never in eleven years of schooling did I learn that *fish need air*.

I liked my job, and on weekends, my friend and I went around the corner for the carny atmosphere on the Hermosa pier, and to The Lighthouse, one of California's best little jazz clubs. We peeked in until invited by the manager, who warned that we would have to leave if we attempted to buy or accept drinks. We saw Dave Brubeck, Cal Tjader, Dizzy Gillespie, and others up close.

After several months at the pet store, I noticed that my boss and his only other employee were having a tiff. I never knew what started it, but one day my boss came to me and said, "You'll have to leave right now. She says she's going to report me to the IRS. I haven't declared you on my tax forms." I didn't understand the prospective penalties, and never knew the outcome. I just got a new job serving root beer and hamburgers. My friend was job-hunting too, so we felt we could pay rent on a big, old second-story place in Manhattan Beach. Our unfurnished apartment was windy and empty. Our imaginations had it comfortably decorated, but we never did the work. We played jazz, blues, and folk records, pretending to be beatniks, and became rapt students at coffee houses in Hollywood where live music was played, and educated adults discussed the world. A PhD took us to his beach home to experience LSD just months before the U.S. Congress pronounced it illegal. It was an exhilarating time.

On weekday evenings, I worked hard in the restaurant and didn't get home until after midnight to study, sleep, shower, dress, and run for the 7:25 a.m. bus to the high school. It was challenging. My friend, who had already graduated, was smart but did not have the nerve to keep a job on the rare occasion that she got one. We would have to find a cheaper apartment. Her timidity was biological and inherited. I didn't have time to think about it, nor the expertise to help her, but I knew not to hold it against her.

The restaurant where I worked was co-owned. Because I was quiet, each boss confided in me about the other. I kept their confidences, but division brought down the business and I was out of work again, until a friend at school got me a job stretching artists' canvas in his family's gallery by the harbor. I liked each of my jobs, and felt enhanced by the experiences.

After graduating from high school I turned down marriage proposals from three men who seemed pushed by age, and might have selected wives from a catalog were it an option. One of them finally married another of my friends, and I was sincerely happy for them as they drove off waving from their topless sports car. I wasn't much of a drinker, but sudden loneliness seemed a fair excuse for drinking the case of beer they left me.

To support myself without a roommate, I took a full-time job as a credit verifier in one of the fluorescent office cubicles of a furniture store. *Then*, I started drinking to get drunk. My stiff and bitchy boss was typically meticulous about all things trivial; I stayed off his radar. The job entailed fact-findings that could deny furniture to people who had applied to pay by installments. I disagreed with the company's policies, so I sometimes failed to record the condemning details, particularly when they involved charges of marijuana use.

One day, I went to see my father. He scorned me, but later had my brother invite me to dinner. I cried.

After five years, his silence had ended and I was welcomed home — with stipulations. I tried to respect the ways of my parents and the household, and to keep up a satisfied appearance, but at my desk job several months later, I felt compelled to struggle for my psychological life. I left work, closed my savings account, and flew to San Francisco, where long walks and cable car rides cleared my mind. I talked to people uptown, mid-town and downtown, improv entertainers, street musicians, one elderly accordionist with a tame monkey, and a tall black man in a suit selling newspapers stating that the Black Muslims of America wanted to go back to Africa. I didn't understand. I thought they wanted what white people had.

At the end of the day, I lay alone by the open window in a cheap hotel room, listening to the tick of the radiator, and the honking and roaring of traffic below. I was still the same me. The theater crowd across the street wore black velvet and diamonds; I'd felt like a child next to them. A few days later, out of money and the energy for adventure, I called my parents to give them my relative location, and was welcomed home with understanding, the kind that comes after whispers and before a visit to the nice psychologist. My parents tried, but I was so angry with them for being apathetic. They weren't curious about the world. I wanted someone who would be real with me, who would appreciate my hard work, and could spot and call my games.

At twenty-five desperate dollars an hour, the psychologist was pitifully shellacked with professional humility. He stuck out his hand as I left his office, and, like in a hundred movies I'd already seen, he said, "Trust me." I was furious and stomped off to do something self-destructive.

I drank all the wine that Christmas and took too many Excedrin. I was really just giving my family a big dose of my hate. Taken to the hospital doing commercial parodies ("Excedrin Headache Number 955"), I kicked the nurses and threw up voluntarily. My dad stood in the hallway listening to me. I loved my dad and he loved me. I recognized his unusual patience as we drove home, but both of us knew there was nothing to say. Our worlds were too far apart. The house was sterile, every one of my mother's coveted luxuries dust to me. Nobody played the piano. Nobody sang. It was a ghost town but for one lively little sister who was fast being subdued.

I had to do something, so I entered college. I was to make plans to pay room and board to my parents. They were not negligent in proper teaching of responsibility. There was just no bond between us. Nothing. The Beatles were singing of Strawberry Fields where nothing was real, and I idly considered a serious suicide. I didn't really want to die, but where had the living gone?

Charlie made love to me naturally — unlike the movies about moral frustration and the sudden manic-depressive mashing of mouths. He took his time. When I allowed it, he moved me. When I stopped it, he freed that energy, allowing me to feel beyond anything I had experienced. Mary was sitting on a tree stump crying when we came out. Charlie said something that made her streaked face break a shaky smile. I could see that she loved him more than any man in her life, save her father, and maybe even him. I was impressed by that love.

When Mary was upset, her lower lip protruded, her nostrils flared, she pointed her chin up and looked away. I thought of her as inwardly solid, but brittle. A man had once called her a "cold fish." Charlie told her she wasn't cold. He scoffed at the description and blamed the man who didn't know how to warm her. Charlie would make love to each of us and to both of us. He once asked us each to sit in a chair and watch him make love to the other. Beyond initial discomfort, I saw moving artwork and dance, tenderness and surrender.

One morning, he called to both of us from the bathroom. We halted at the door, but, from his seat on the toilet, he urged us to enter. Taking our hands, he motioned for us to sit, each of us on one of his knees. Then he grunted — loud, exaggerated grunts, devilishly obnoxious grunts, until we were so red-faced that we became embarrassed about being embarrassed. Later we stood at the doorway watching him shave. It was more like sculpting. Removing a spot of whiskers, the whole persona changed. Characters took face in the mirror, some with different voices and accents. His honest portrayals of human behavior were hilarious, his humor without sarcasm or guffaws, just ironies and paradoxes, a funny mug and an irresistible grin. He said, "Looky here," and "You dig?" From someone else it might have sounded artificial, but from him it was experience confided. He said so much I wanted to capture but couldn't recall right after he said it, because there was always something new. He said, "Words out of now are like fruit. The moment you pick them off the vine they start to die."

At night there were long drives through the woods, presenting a theatre of dark shapes and shadows. He said, "You can go up and down the same road and it's always different — at different angles, in different light — it's always different." He savored his moments but didn't hang on to them. He said, "It's all right now." The Beatles were singing of "Now." I thought that they must know the same.

Back in the cabin were candles, clean bedding, and the embrace of the stereo speakers. He settled down between us with an arm around each, made us comfortable, made us laugh, and appreciated the moment, sometimes dropping to sleep in the middle of a sentence. I lay awake in wonder of him. His view of the world was my earliest conscious dream.

The three of us caused speculation. We remained welcome visitors, but the conflicts of some couples kept us away. Men tended to think our arrangement ideal, not knowing that Mary and I could be moody and brooding. We were not satisfied with ourselves, each inwardly thinking the other was favored or better. I hear Charlie's voice, like honey, in deep, sliding tones. "So you feel inadequate. Are you adequately inadequate?" He comforted and cajoled, lampooning our nit-picking notions of self worth, our strivings to *become* something.

"Relax," he said. "You already are something. You were born perfect — you just forgot." We struggled with concepts of "ego."

"Ego," he said, "is made up of thoughts. It's a big collection of thoughts. *Whose* thoughts? Where'd you get those thoughts? Do you even know what you're thinking?" These were reasonable questions I'd never considered. At least some of my thoughts came from my parents, schools, and TV, but how much did they affect me? I expressed almost nothing of my thoughts while he spoke his aloud, as if walking around in his mind, as if the world was his mind. I got the feeling that he could quite literally read our minds. *But is it my mind?* Do I exclusively own the ghosts of thought that waver in and out of my brain? I exhausted myself exploring inner and outer landscapes, and only when Charlie made me laugh did I begin to release my grip on *insecurity.*

"It's ironic," he said. "People work hard for comfort and security, but security comes from within, and too much comfort smothers the soul of living free."

The soul of living free eventually ate Mary's bank account. One day we had only fifty cents and were hungry to the pit. We drove to the Sea Hill market and went in together. I was eyeing the fat potato chips but Charlie brought a pound of hamburger to the register. On the way out the door, he began unwrapping the meat, dividing it into sections. Then he put it all on the ground. He said, "Now we can get full just watching." Muffet's mouth was watering, Charlie laughing at her pleasure. Mary stood watching, her chin tucked into a grin and her eyes brimming with a flood of affection. I was helpless to resist.

Charlie said that dogs own their people rather than the other way around, because people have the responsibility of taking care of them. He said it was the same with all other possessions — that they own us as much as we own them. He joked that, in reality, he owned *all* the cars but allowed other people to drive them. (He was half-joking.) When Charlie was thirteen, he took a joy ride in a Packard hearse. Subsequently, he escaped a boys school, "hot-wired a 1948 Chevy, ran it at ninety-eight mph through a Standard Oil gas station, woke up with a wounded knee, and was sent back to boys school."

"I took a lot of cars in '48," he said, "and then the 1950 Studebaker. Sheriff Black of Beaver City, Utah put me in jail for that. I was in a band called 'Stark Nekid and the Car Thieves'." In 1954, it was a Cadillac, and from 1956 until late '58 he was imprisoned for stealing a 1951 Mercury. He said that he had been married to a girl named Rose who wanted to go to California. "I told her, 'I don't want to go to jail,' and she said, 'We won't go to jail.' So we took the car, and she was right. *We* didn't go to jail. *I* did."

Mary cashed in some kind of savings she had in Wisconsin and when the money arrived, we took a trip for supplies.

1967

San Francisco, The Priest

I first saw San Francisco from above — not a skyscraper city, nor a web of threaded freeways, but an open-faced picnic city spread on stuffed green hills — thick sandwich houses and frosted gingerbread houses neatly stacked on the heaping hills. Downtown was a surreal, wavering chessboard of colorful blocks and classy specialty shops up and down steep slopes tracked by click-clicking, ratchet-catching, chug-chugging, pull-pulling, tug-o-war-with-gravity cable cars ringing their arrival. And in the day-distance, from the hills you could see the chocolate factory on the wharf, the salt bay gleaming blue, the specks of colorful boats, and the deep orange, larger-than-I-thought Golden Gate Bridge.

On foggy mornings, it was a sedate city of Victorian houses that had not yet opened their eyes — long driftnets of mist still floating at their windows. But on clear mornings, crisp winds gusted scents to thrill your senses. I bet there wasn't a city in the world like it. Besides the open cable cars, and the panoramic views from humongous hills, besides at least seven ethnically distinct neighborhoods natural to The City since the rest of the world came to port, mission, and fort — with their garlic, fresh mint, olive oils, cayenne, curries, and soy sauces — besides the migratory flocks of long-necked tourists in ice cream parlors and red dragon restaurants, and the remnants of non-conforming North Beach beatniks (followers of the finicky shifting centers of art and fashion) in their musty book stores and galleries smelling of linseed oil, paint, clay, and leather — besides all of that was the Haight-Ashbury district, a crossroad around which were gathered the new beat, new hip, less proud, less isolated young hipsters, the "hippies" — a whole new culture. Here was a cohesive, mostly homogenous crowd, respectful of each others' rights to look at, talk about, worship, and wear as so moved, a young expanse of opening minds on the verge of adventure.

We entered "the Haight" through heavy traffic and throngs of people in vintage hats, sashes, vests, and every other costume stylized for presentation and customized for comfort. It was a time and place of unbound hair and bra-lessness. New in fashion were low-waisted, snug fitting, bellbottomed jeans that swayed at the feet, making a slender body look willowy. Music trickled and gushed from windows. Kids ran through crowds and never seemed lost. And everywhere, the words Love and Peace were unabashedly aired along with earnest belief in the ideals that went with them.

Mary knew a Catholic nun through whom we met an Irish-American priest who had just loosened his collar and let his hair grow for Christ. All of the years that I had been taught to revere the Catholic fathers put them at a distance from me and other mortals. Father Mike was young and bearded. He was smoking a joint. I could barely believe it. Before going out the door with his briefcase, Mike welcomed us to stay in the three-bedroom Haight-Ashbury apartment he co-rented with a theatrical homosexual and a hefty red-haired woman, both of whom worked during the day.

Charlie recalled that when he had first arrived in the city without friends or money, a sixteen-year-old had called him "brother," given him a blanket, and introduced him to the Diggers, a group of un-established philanthropists providing free food and clothing. He thought highly of the Diggers and went out to see them. I walked around the windy flat, awaiting my turn in a claw-foot bathtub, and, through the bay windows, watched a lively stream of people on the sidewalks below.

When Charlie returned, we buoyed ourselves with cannabis, and bobbed the mainstream to Golden Gate Park where paths narrowed and people meshed, spilling over the bright grass in the clearings. The air was spicy with oils and smoke, the spirit high. It spread through the gratefully live musicians, the laughing dancers, bands of merry men, and barefoot maidens, through childbearing family circles, curious observers, veterans, and vagabonds. Absent were hot dog and beer vendors, and money was not an issue. A sunny day in the Park was a Utopian dream. At the end of the day we were happy to have a place to stretch out our sleeping gear.

Father Mike and Charlie talked into the night about world changes, as reefer smoke curled between them. Mike seemed gleefully free of Church constraints, yet eager to air his personal theology. I fell asleep listening to the odd harmonies of Jefferson Airplane.

I was reading *Siddhartha* by Hermann Hesse about Siddhartha Gautama Buddha. Like Mike, I'd been raised in Roman Catholicism, but Buddhist practices of meditation and spiritual union with nature seemed more Christ-like to me than the rush of material production/consumption that Western life had become. Eastern beliefs in "karma" and "reincarnation" were common in hippie communities, loosely meaning a kind of universal report card and progression via rebirth, whether in this life or in a series of lifetimes. With these ideas, and in rejection of anything "Establishment," conventional employment was dismissed. Bartering became part of the new Renaissance, an active trade in wood and metal crafts, cotton clothing, raw wool and yarn, organic vegetables, marijuana, and LSD. The outcome would theoretically be a cleaner, more conscious, less violent world in communion with natural life. The underground Brotherhood of Love was even more invested in the transformation, distributing LSD as a "sacrament" to as many as could be reached.

The Beatles confirmed for me the correctness of our direction, musically tying all the tie-dyes and God's eyes in a philosophical whole. They were nothing short of a phenomenon. Charlie told Mike that while in prison he thought they were just another teeny bopper fad, but after listening to their words, he understood "what the kids are talking about." We would travel between San Francisco and Mendocino countless times, and on each visit Mike and Charlie exchanged supplies and information. On one trip Charlie ran into two ex-cons he'd met at McNeil Island, one of whom had taught himself to knit and sold sweaters as part of his living. He was short, stout, had very white teeth, and smiled a lot. The other one had a handgun. Charlie told us he had to take care of something and left with them for Berkeley where they were staying. On his return he told us that the short one would be back the following day, and that, by the way, he had talked them into giving him the gun and had tossed it off the Bay Bridge.

In Mike's communal kitchen we had to reassure the chubby red-haired tenant that we were not eating her food. Standing by the toaster, impatient to talk, she complained — it sounded more like boasting — that her parents would *just die* if they saw her with her new boyfriend, a black fellow named Earl. I didn't think anything of it, but Charlie later commented that this woman's parents had "programmed her in reverse," creating long-standing conflict with her, and then expressing their abhorrence for interracial relationships.

When, on Haight Street, a young black woman engaged Charlie in flirtatious banter, I didn't understand what he said to her, but it made her laugh, and I felt a sense of pride that she was interested in him. Then I heard him say, "I see you, woman, but I'm not your man." As we got into our car, I asked him what he meant by that. He said, "I see her beauty, but I'm not her man. Her man is black like she is." Simple. It wasn't simple to me. It was racist.

My parents had never said anything to me about race. They generally followed majority sympathies or said nothing at all. I had gathered my opinions from books and movies, seen racially diverse talents in Hollywood, and listened to Bob Dylan and Joan Baez records. Black suffering at the hands of white oppressors was one of the dialogues of the decade. Across the bay, the college at Berkeley was a boiling pot of pooled outrage against war and racial discrimination. I asked Charlie, "Are you prejudiced?"

He countered, "What do you mean?"

"Do you see black people as equal?" He eyed me skeptically.

"Equal to *what*?"

"To *white* people!" I said angrily.

He shook his head slowly and said, "Don't you like yourself? It's not that I dislike black people. I like *myself*. I accepted what I am a long time ago."

I wasn't sure *what* he was, or if I liked it at all.

He said, "I grew up shootin' dice with the black brothers in the joint, lived with them at the bottom all my life — some were like fathers to me — but that don't make me one of them. I knew it just as much as they did. I'm white; they're black. We're different."

I couldn't believe he thought like this. I was a quiet champion of the poor and oppressed, and prepared to feel sorry for his life in prison, but progressive people everywhere shunned even the word "difference."

I asked, "Well, do you think you're better than black people?"

He said, "Who's to compare? There's a beautiful tiger with stripes, a leopard with spots, and a lion with a mane — they're all cats, but they're *different* — not better or worse, just different." That sounded right to me but I didn't like it.

I said, "These aren't cats. They're people!"

He said, "To deny differences is to deny life and nature — and that's a lie."

I saw two little boys walking arm in arm, one black, one white. Charlie noticed and told me that those kids didn't realize what was pushing them. I didn't care what was pushing them. I was *comforted* by the sight of their contrasting colors. Black Americans had suffered and we had to make it up to them. They were ready to take vengeance to the streets. Only two years before, L.A. ghetto dwellers had burned down their own neighborhoods.

Charlie said, "Look, I have Mexican tattoos on my arms. I speak some Spanish, and I learned the Mexican songs — but I'm white. I'm what they call a 'paddy' — from a white mama and a white daddy..." he smiled, and then he became serious. "That's upfront. We were upfront about it and there's respect in that. It's your nice society that looks down on people. It's *you* who look down on *them* to think that they would want to be like you. The real black man don't want to be like anybody but *himself* — and then the word 'equal' is silly isn't it. Does the tiger say to the lion, 'I want to be equal'? No. To him there is no question of equal or not equal. He just is, and he serves life." He paused. "There is an order," he said. "Better or worse, up down, back forth got nothing to do with it. What people think does not even enter into the natural order." He was quiet for a moment. Finally he said, "It's your society that looks down on people and wants to *help them* into the misery, and the lack of love that drives all you kids away from home — you yourself."

I let the question about races rest. I had to admit that with all I'd had in society, and all I'd l learned, I was unhappy and confused. And it was true that I didn't want to spread my unhappiness to anyone else.

The scene near the university in Berkeley was almost military, the marchers dressed mostly in surplus khakis and army greens. American flags were on display — sewn on one guy's butt, upside-down on another's jacket. In Charlie's view, the emblems spoke loudest, and though the speakers said, "Down with U.S. foreign policy," the symbols said, "Down with the U.S.! Down with America!" He said it was like downing themselves.

On Telegraph Avenue by the university activists distributed political pamphlets. Black Panthers were selling Chinese Chairman Mao's "Little Red Book." It did seem like half the world was going Communist. I didn't feel qualified to hold an opinion. Having few facts about Communism to work with, I was either too dumb to understand, or our teachers and leaders hadn't adequately illustrated the pros and cons. By then I distrusted their opinions. Communist governments' motives were equally suspicious. But worldwide Communists verbally sided with Capitalism's poor and oppressed, an increasingly popular position amongst young people. Any difference between courage of conviction and criminal conviction was blurred. All prisoners were oppressed and therefore not only accepted but favored. Established institutions and material wealth were OUT, poverty IN. Suddenly it was popular to be ill-born and low down. People of no class had real credentials. In fact, if you hadn't lived a hard life, you might want to lean on, borrow, or steal the life of someone who had.

The Black Panthers and Black Muslims rallied on behalf of Black people with a capital B, incidentally raising white fear and guilt. They intoned hurt and anger few white kids had known, and it was commonly said that white people "have no soul." Charlie said, "No person, race, or religion owns soul. People may reflect it, but when you hook up, the soul has you. You don't have it."

I was fascinated with Charlie's perceptions. Before putting on my skate key, he wore no jewelry of any kind. On meeting a burly stranger with a penchant for ornamental chains, he asked, "Who's got you all locked up, man?" Catching his meaning, the man said he didn't know why he liked chains, but Charlie later speculated that the chains were "part of some woman's thought." His feelings about women seemed conflicted. He had said that he intended to visit his mother "up north," but he never called her, and showed no hurry in getting there. (He had also told me that in Haight-Ashbury he was called "The Gardener," but when I mentioned it later, he chuckled puckishly, and confessed that it was "just a pick up line.")

Before we left the city, Charlie stopped to talk to a man who was fixing a car. He said "I once knew a man who went to work to buy a car so that he could get to work and make enough money for gas and car payments!" The man with grease on his nose laughed and said, "Yeah, that's me." Charlie said, "Me, I'm gonna go look at the redwoods."

A century before, the entrepreneurial Henry Meiggs left San Francisco for refuge in South America. The errant creator of San Francisco's Philharmonic, "Fisherman's Wharf," and a saw mill in Mendocino took his wife, children, servant girls, and "a plentiful stock of fine wines" to Chile, where he lay down business and political tracks, until contracted by the Chilean government to build a railroad. With his success, the government of Peru requested his services for construction of two railroads over the Andes Mountains, resulting in *hundreds of miles of track built on millions of California redwood ties* shipped from Mendocino. At a train station in Lima, a bust of Meiggs was erected with a plaque that translated "Don Enrique Meiggs, Railroad King of the Andes."

As with most of history's wealthy and accomplished lawbreakers, public opinion couldn't decide whether to scorn or praise Meiggs. Before he died in Peru, the

California Legislature voted to completely absolve him for theft of San Francisco's city funds.

In a forest north of the city, we got out of the car and stood in the stillness. I wondered if his mother lived near. "She does live here," he said. Then a ghostly reverence for this forest came over me, raising the hair on my skin, and his voice was firm, as if I should already have known. He said, "You're standing on her."

Mendocino was fragrant in new life and decay. Odd prickly creatures bubbled in tide pools below waterlogged sod, wildflowers, and grasses. Apart from the strange afternoon fog, days were warmer, especially inland where woodlands enclosed sunny hills and meadows. We tripped.

Charlie's hair had grown down around his ears. A clean, burnished brown, it never seemed out of place. He had a trim goatee and often wore, without a shirt, a white sheepskin vest Father Mike had given him. It exposed his tattooed arms and a T-shape of chest hair that tapered to his navel. One day Mary came laughing with two white seashells that looked exactly like nubs of goat horns when placed high on the sides of his forehead. He allowed us to glue them on, but then insisted on twirling flower sprigs in our hair, and stripping us nearly bare. Grabbing Mary's flute, he played a few rough notes — to which his eyebrows did a dance — and commenced to chasing us through the woods, giving random campers a glimpse — of *who*? People came to investigate and we sneaked back home.

Charlie entertained with imitations, parodies, and characters he seemed to pull from creation. He could turn a rag into something classy and use anything for a prop. His humor was based in truth, recognition of which, paradoxically, sometimes came as a surprise to him. Mary and I were reluctant to participate in even some of our own schemes, but he enjoyed himself without fear, and sometimes without us.

By a hillside farm where sheep grazed, he stopped the car and said he would be back. He picked up a tall walking stick on the dirt road to the farmhouse, knocked on the door, and talked with the farmer for ten or fifteen minutes before he returned, chuckling to himself. All he said, as he started the car, was, "Man says they don't hire shepherds anymore."

From rock grottos to forest cathedrals, the northern coast is luxury to my memory. On the beach Charlie sang, "You must give to find love ..." with a tinge of tango and a mood shift from minor to major chords, somber to joyful, very cool. His voice grew in volume rather than loudness, and within the volume were dimensions in vibration. He was intensely handsome to me at these times, like a classical actor in an understated role. It wasn't the presence of seriousness so much as the absence of frivolity and everything else. It was the crashing of the incoming tide, the melting sun, and such feeling in his voice that it made me shiver. He made love in the same way, and although I couldn't entirely accept it, his sensuality communicated.

The Mendocino summer turned us beautiful colors. On a walk through the woods, Mary and I stopped by a friend's cabin and were amused to find the latest fashion magazines advertising cosmetics to make you "Look like you just walked out of the woods!"

The "Natural Look" was officially IN. I *felt* natural. For the first time in my adult life, laughter welled from deep inside me rather than politely from my throat, and I became so interested in the world around me that I forgot to doubt myself. Then I remembered.

We took trips for supplies, and for change. Mary and I *did* change, touching newness and retreating to the familiar discontent. It seemed that the happier we got, the more miserable we were on the rebound. It occurred to Charlie that we — and much of the world — were at war with *ourselves*. Little by little he conveyed his dawning notion that he was trapped; he couldn't be at peace until we were at peace. One day we heard him singing to himself, "Got a skate key on my neck. Got a million dollars in my shoes. Ain't got time to sing the blues."

When Charlie got depressed, Mary and I felt a little better. When he muttered, "I just want to be a dirt farmer," or "Maybe I'll be a truck driver," we smiled at each other. These childlike inclinations to be whatever and whoever he saw on the highways endeared him to us. In fear that he might actually go, we came around to a full recovery.

Charlie was changing too. There were times at night while he was driving, that he stared at the blacktop as though hypnotized by it. Not bug-eyed or weird, just serious and straight ahead in a very relaxed manner. And he talked. Some of what he said was beyond my understanding, but there were two distinct voices. One of them was wiser, the one that did the telling. The other was his ordinary voice asking things he sincerely wanted to know. Sometimes the things he learned in these "conversations" made him light up and turn to us to see if we had heard. At other times he drew into himself and was solemn for a long time.

I would attribute the advent of these dialogues to extended stays in a stark form of solitary confinement that may no longer exist in American prisons. He described it as follows:

"In solitary confinement it is dark. There is nothing but a cement floor and you. In darkness there are no bounds. Am I up from the floor? Or down from the ceiling? Am I right or left — of what? It's all relative. And if I could conceive of a question, surely I could conceive of the answer."

When Charlie was new to San Francisco someone had introduced him to a strong dose of LSD. He remembered it, laughing: "They took me to the Fillmore and I turned inside out. I became all the people dancing under the strobe lights and I panicked. I ran outside — and I was everyone on the streets! I tried to get away. I didn't want to see it. But I couldn't get away from it." Later, he said, he "lay on a beach and laughed with Timothy Leary," thinking that, as crazy as it seemed, in this fast and pharmaceutical age it made perfect sense for spiritual transcendence to come in a pill.

The LSD in San Francisco was rumored to have been created by a renowned yet mysterious man named "Owsley," a philanthropic genius, but Father Mike warned that the street market had been polluted with harsh varieties containing other drugs, and there was no way for a novice to know the difference. Mike was a reasonable constant in an anything-goes atmosphere. Each day he went to work with his briefcase, and each evening he and Charlie talked. Their conversations were sometimes debates, peppered with Charlie's old clever-isms and Mike's clichés and pedantry. (Mike offered, "By the same token..." Charlie dismissed with, "And you can get on the cable car.")

They laughed at being from such diverse backgrounds discussing the world's opening mind.

Mike's house on Cole Street branched off of Haight Street, and Haight was the place to be. It led to Golden Gate Park and to people from all over the country. At least half of all residents and travelers were barefoot. I cut my foot on a broken bottle and Charlie insisted on carrying me home. I was a bellbottomed newcomer, but plenty of hippies wore wild flourishes in beads, paint, and feathers. Tie dying had just made a splash and clothes were made to trip on. "Tripping" was not falling down, but waking up and enjoying the view. Marijuana was plentiful and inexpensive. It slowed the minds of our generation enough to realize that we were getting old *way* too fast, collecting worries instead of experiences. The consciousness it raised called for comfort. The caress of soft materials could be sensual, and early forms of polyester felt exactly like what they were: plastic. Breasts of all sizes bobbled beneath thin materials, and, with exceptions, the effect was more natural than vulgar. On the other hand, not everyone shared sensibilities. Some street people doused their clothes with petouli oil, as if to eliminate the need for washing, and today I can't smell petouli without thinking of sordid sweat. Behavior ran the gamut from creative to crass, but the majority of hippies were joyful, considerate beings. I heard Charlie tell someone that a true hippie would give you his shoes if you needed them, and be standing on the side of the highway playing his guitar with a smile on his face. I knew he had done it. I saw in his face the long, open road, highlighted by extraordinary experiences, and a little longing. Mary and I were like luggage he had to carry and store, yet we'd do something simple like find his socks and he'd say, "What would I do without yous?"

Charlie had a limited pass to travel. He was required to mail in a monthly written report to his parole officer; Mary always took care of the forms. He was *supposed* to be looking for a job, but he was a musician — anyone who heard him sing and play the guitar would agree. And he did play and sing for people who gave him money. Like Mary and I, for instance.

Roger Smith was a decent federal parole officer, both professionally and personally. Charlie took us to see him. Blond, brawny, and educated, he had a pert wife, and a twenty-two-foot sailboat. He offered to take us sailing in that "sometime" commonly understood as "never," but he liked the three of us, and he had no reason to believe that Charlie would ever do or be anything other than what Mary and I and his talent allowed. Soon we were traveling the length of the state.

Road Songs

Up and down California's highways, Charlie sang. He sang the fence posts, trees and mountains, songs made up on the spot, or old songs with new twists — and he seemed to know every gas station attendant, the old man with the bifocals behind the counter at the food outpost, even the cops. While other people feared and showed hostility toward police, he wasn't in the least defensive. Thus, the cop who rousted us was "granted his authority", and, rather than trying to bust us, directed us to local sites of interest. Charlie said that despite abuses of power and the ignorance of some, police had valid purpose. He said, "I got no argument with that." The part about "granting them their authority" was interesting, since one must have it to give it.

The road helped clear our minds of doldrums, co-nundrums, and other noisy drums. Charlie was full of characters who took our attention, among them a lounge singer, a cowboy crooner, and "Hyme Fein-schleister," a nebbish. Mary and I sometimes laughed so hard that our stomachs were vibrated to a lasting calm. Road time also helped us to get to know each other. We were talking about artwork when Char-lie said that his first grade teacher had criticized his painting. He looked dejected. Mary and I laughed.

"No, really," he said, half-really. "She put her nose in the air and said in front of the class, *'Now, Charlie, everyone knows that TURKEYS are NOT PURPLE.'*" He said that was the last time he tried to draw or paint. He joked about his lack of education. One time a guard had looked at a letter he was writing and read it out loud: "Dear Swart," it said, "You are my gril..." Charmed and armed with this new information, Mary and I could poke him with it. We were getting to know a little boy whose life was hard for us to imagine.

In Santa Barbara, we spent days on the beach, and nights with Paula, the smart and attractive wife of one of Charlie's "old cell partners." She made three strangers and a dog feel entirely welcome, even when she was at work. From another friend's house in Los Angeles, I left Mary and Charlie to visit my family, say-ing I would be back in a few hours.

My mother looked frightened when she opened the door. I embraced her, and she stiffened. Where had I been? Why did I look so different? In what I enthu-siastically described as a healthy life of camping and sightseeing she saw a depression of homelessness and poverty. Sickness and death would follow. No amount of reassurance could dispel these predictions. I smiled and said, "Mom, it's summer. I'm well and

I'm happy!" but I suddenly felt terrible. Divided, torn, contemptuous and sorrowful, I *loved* my mother but I couldn't stand to be around her.

Mary and Charlie found me at my boyfriend's house the following day. I insisted upon going back to my parents' house "to pick up a few things," but once there, I got stuck, nervously sorting my belongings. I couldn't stay, but I couldn't go. They waited, but only when they moved to leave did I grab a stack of my old writings and break free. Charlie didn't speak to me on the way to the car. He lay on the back seat and fell asleep while Mary took the wheel. I felt confused and delinquent, but as we got farther away, I felt relief.

At dusk we stopped for fast food. Charlie stirred, his hair mussed, his face puffy and like that of a petulant child. He ignored us, getting out of the car with Muffet, and going to the take-out window. From there he carried four hamburgers to a picnic table, sat on the table with his boots on the bench, and unwrapped the first hamburger for her, making sure that there were no pickles in it.

When Charlie spoke to me again, he said, "You don't seem to understand the meaning of your 'word.' Without 'word' there's no reality between people." He said, "Old men in prison taught me 'word is bond.' When you break your word, you break trust. When you break your word to yourself you lose your soul." Later he told me, "My mom was a liar so I learned to dislike lies."

On the road one night Charlie asked me what I was thinking and my instant reaction was to protect myself from ridicule. I said I wasn't thinking anything. He pressed me, and I refused to remember. Angered, he swerved the car to the roadside, alarming me. He said, "Why would you hide from me?" I shored up defiance. As he turned onto the road again, he asked, "Are your thoughts that terrible?" All I could think was how un-terrible, how insignificant they actually were. No longer sounding angry, he asked: "Are you afraid of being foolish? Maybe I'm foolish. Do I sound foolish to you?" I didn't answer him. He said, "What you withhold is from you, not me. I'm on my own trip. What you think is for you."

Confronted with my stubborn withdrawals, Charlie sometimes surprised me with U-turn sentences that began in ominous tones signaling the end of tolerance — a parent's ultimatum, a break-up or divorce — and cruised around a 180 corner toward lightweight suggestions I can only approximate here: "If, after all this time, you can't even let go of that... then you could just give yourself a break, and do what you can." In one arresting sentence I felt cornered, paralyzed, relieved, and open to a new idea. I was suspicious of psychological machinations, but these switchbacks, rather than being calculated, seemed to come naturally to him. In either case, they freed my mind from one pattern and gave me a choice as to how I wanted to proceed. I'd spent a big chunk of my life afraid to move or speak freely. I didn't want to live like that.

By Santa Barbara, the stack of my old poetry became a burden, a constant reminder of old, mostly miserable memories. Unbeknownst to anyone, I dumped it in a trash can, and that night, without warning, Charlie turned from inspecting the content of Paula's refrigerator, and delivered one of Shakespeare's soliloquies with more unaffected eloquence than from any actor I had ever heard.

Paula's husband was a talented jazz trumpeter who, in the unconventional style, had crossed a line that sent him to federal prison. Although I never asked,

I thought he might have been addicted to heroin. It is unfortunate that all illegal drugs and plants were lumped together in anti-drug propaganda. After marijuana was commonly discovered to be less harmful than alcohol, some people assumed that the negative hype about heroin was equally false. Paula's husband had years to do, maybe even a lifetime of addiction, while she lived alone, worked an office job, and visited him when she could.

Mary's parents were coming from Wisconsin, so we left Paula and traveled north to a friend's house in Berkeley to welcome them. When they got to the house, they wouldn't come inside. Charlie and I came out on the porch to be introduced, but after "hello" an ax of silence fell, so we left them to have words with their daughter. They took Mary away in their car, and, on return, stood talking with her beside it. Mary came through the screen door smiling with a red face and wounded eyes. Her mother had chastised her for giving up a good job, and her dad had called Charlie a "mooch." In no time, we were rolling north out of suburban traffic, past the surfers in Bodega Bay, to an unoccupied beach where we could take off our clothes. As Mary ran to the water, Charlie told me to look at how beautiful she was.

Intimacy between the three of us had seemed illicit at first, my mind constructing questions as barriers. Yet I could create nothing that didn't dissolve in reality. Our skin felt natural, our lips felt natural, and he felt natural between us. He moved us so that we didn't need to think about it — sensually, rather than with design — and we learned to relax into him. He wondered if Mary and I were sexually attracted to each other. He said that once while he was making love to a bisexual woman, she had blurted, "Not like that, stupid!" He had had the forbearance to request her instruction. But Mary and I were not bisexual. We were mutually sexually attracted to him.

In Mendocino we let our cabin go, and bartered for a red, pod-shaped trailer that we towed to a wide private beach. A contest of ownership had left this beach in legal limbo, incidentally opening it to the few who discovered it. Surrounded by dirt cliffs and a rock peninsula, it was island idyllic. In almost total isolation, we cooked on an open fire, bathed and washed dishes at the shore.

Charlie stayed up late and got up early. I didn't know how he did it. One morning Mary and I stayed in bed despite his efforts to rouse us. Two hours later, as we squatted beside the fire, cooking, he was still gone. When he showed, he had traces of the rust-colored cliffs on his clothes. He recounted being trapped on a ledge that was easy to reach, but dangerous to leave. For an hour he had clung to the jagged, unstable face of the cliff while picking a route to safety.

"You should have been there," he said enthusiastically. "You missed a good experience."

We took walks along the beach. Southern California's beaches were barren by comparison, and the only driftwood I had seen was on a pedestal in an art gallery. I could never have afforded it. Here driftwood was plentiful and free. I collected one piece after another. One was so big and heavy I had to stop and rest. Charlie helped me with my precious finds, hoisting the heavy log on his shoulder. As we spotted more and more objects d'art, he bent to inspect each piece and ask, "You want to take this too?" My arms were already full of shells, stones, and small, sea-whipped branches, each and every one a unique sculpture displayed across the earth as if tossed by... suddenly I snapped to what he was saying. Did I want to take the whole beach elsewhere? Could I personally own it? How blind am I not to see and leave this perfection? And there he was, silently carrying a tree trunk on one shoulder. I looked at him consciously. He understood, bending to lay down the load, and the face of an ancient wise man smiled.

When I was small, the beaches in Southern California were a perpetual treasury of starfish, sand dollars, and other beautifully shaped shells. Only a decade later, they were *gone*. I'm sorry to say we took them. I, my little brother, our parents, and similar bands of thieves. My father, on behalf of his family, carried the bucket containing at least one live starfish from each trip to the beach, as if we had some place to keep them or would be having them for dinner. In a week they would die, their fine pastel shells placed upon nails in the garage, or taken to school, then dropped, broken, and thrown away. But I think that the unconscious reason we took them was a longing to be closer to nature. The majority of shells from previous centuries were then scooped up for commercial sale, lest merchants miss out on an opportunity of a lifetime.

Infrequently, vacationers found the beach owned by no one. They stayed their distance, but when their vacations were spent, they waved goodbye, or dropped off leftovers. Children were sent with butter; teenagers came with grass. Encircling a night fire, we shared their smoke, and the conversation turned high school. A girl dropped the joint and one of the guys joked that she was clumsy. Another excused her, saying it was good weed, and a third countered that it wasn't as good as the stuff his brother had. It brought my mind to other nights on other beaches where kids chugged Coors and then told tales of other drunken times.

Charlie struck a guitar chord, and when everyone looked up, he said, "I've got an idea. When I say 'Now' everybody talk about when you were five years old." On his word, I began talking, but I could hear a mishmash of peanut butter sandwiches, fire engines, Santa Claus and mommy. Everyone cracked up. In psychiatric parody, Charlie crossed his leg and queried, "What does it all *mean*?" and leaning forward, "Do you really want to carry all that around with you?" Then he made up a clever song never sung before about "now" being endless, that all ever done in now is still being done, and that all nows make up one big now called forever. When he paused, I heard the ocean, as if for the first time. I felt the air around me and saw, above the mist, an astonishing display of stars and planets. This moment of silence is still in me.

With Owsley's latest we ventured into psychic space. Late in the shadowy trailer by the kerosene lamp, Charlie searched drawers and cupboards for something to quench his thirst, finding nothing but stale water and a neon envelope of powdered "space age" drink. After reading the instructions on the envelope aloud, he explained to it that he didn't want a quart, only a glassful, and then feigned helplessness when the package failed to give clue. Finally producing his own ratio of water and purple powder, he drank with satisfied thirst — but alarm crossed his face. Quickly he moved the glass down, pretending to pee, raised it to drink, back down to pee, to drink, to pee... His comical expressions had Mary and me rolling in bed. Later he stood naked at the open doorway, philosophizing while urinating into the darkness. He said many things I don't remember but, holding the sides of the door jamb, moving his pelvis in and out, he explained with glee, "I'm fucking the world!"

The Professor

By circumventing shoreline rocks, we reached another beach, and came upon a safari tent with boisterous noises inside. A statuesque young woman with one curler in her hair and a short stack of dishes was hurrying to the water. She ignored our greeting, but called for her husband, who bent as he came out of the tent, huffing because of his balloon shape and size. A serious beard failed to conceal his grin as he extended a hand and invited us inside. But first, he lifted a flap and said firmly, "Come out of there now. We have guests." There was loud rollicking and a sudden bulge of the tent before three small boys tumbled outside under his arm, and, after peeking at us, ran to be near their mother.

The man bade us sit around his squat coffee table. Sliding back the lid on a wooden box, he selected one of several dozen finely rolled joints, and lit it with a stick match.

"My wife rolls them," he said. "I'm sorry. I have no more hash." We settled on cushions and sleeping bags and a few cracker crumbs. "I can't control them," he said, passing us the joint.

Reentering the tent, the woman turned to bark, "Get out of here! Go over there and play now — I mean it."

Charlie said, "Just dropped out, huh?"

The man chuckled, coughing out smoke. "Couple months ago. Can you tell?"

He was a college professor on sabbatical, and she looked like a fashion model. After a second joint had gone around, Charlie asked him, "What do you know?" The professor hesitated. Charlie clarified, "What do you know *for sure*?"

The professor thought a moment and answered, "Well, one never really knows anything for sure — does one?"

Charlie echoed him. "Does one?" He said, "I never found schooled people sure. I went to school only three years. People say that's bad, but it left me open to see things most people are too busy to look at. Like, I know books are trees. Some would call that 'simple' but I read more in trees than in the books that are made from them." The professor nodded reflectively.

Charlie said, "Books ain't sure of what's true. Books don't change. But life is change, building and falling — like in a song."

The professor admitted that after years of teaching he'd begun to question his purpose. He'd found little inspiration and increasingly less fulfillment in his job, which was why they had come to the beach.

"You did right, man," Charlie lauded. "Nature teaches. It's your nature. Life teaches. I love this world. My love makes me happy. I *know* this."

The woman got up and straightened her clothes, rummaging their belongings to get to her purse. With her back to us, she brushed out her hair. Patiently, the man shrugged and explained, "I promised to take her to town."

As we walked back to our trailer, I was conflicted: millions of people attend colleges, honing their minds to cut through serious problems, finding cures for diseases and inventions that amaze. Why would we be so gifted with wisdom and knowledge beyond schooling — three nobodies?

Mary carried Charlie's wallet with all our money and IDs. On a blustery hilltop, Muffet jumped on her, and the wallet fell. There in the blasting wind, swirling notes, licenses, and dollar bills danced down the deep ravine. We headed south again, this time for new IDs, three nobodies indeed.

1967 - 1968

Kismet

In those days almost anyone could afford to drive. For better or worse, insurance was not required, and gas cost less than thirty-five cents a gallon. Half the cars on the road were clunkers. Mary's old sedan had a short circuit. Charlie used to get out, open the hood, and hocus-pocus it. He tinkered and tapped, explaining that you have to act like you know what you're doing and sometimes you get lucky. Incidentally, he believed in patience, sweet talk, and attention to water and oil. It kept the tread-worn tires rolling, and our minds traveling the past, present, and, rarely, the future. Being present for life was becoming real to me. But we wanted to know about *his* past, and it came out randomly. When we saw hobos in open box-cars, he said, "I left town in a boxcar out of Charleston at six or seven years old." I was skeptical. He said, "My grandmother got me back. Granddad was a WWI vet and a railroad man. All the family got a free pass to ride The Skunk — that's what they called the stinking train that hooked up to other farms."

"There used to be a difference," he said, "between hobos, tramps, and bums. The Depression was hard on people, and men rode the rails looking for work. Some carried hoes on their shoulders." He said a tramp was basically a traveler, no matter what condition the economy, and might work from time to time and place to place, and a bum was "pretty much always looking for a hand-out." These solitary individuals shared solidarity, he said, in codes and symbols they scratched on posts and the sides of old buildings to tell if a town was friendly or hostile, to watch out for police, railroad detectives, and so on.

We got off the main road one night in a dark industrial town of chain-link fences, smokestack factories, railroad tracks, and warehouses. A red lit guard rail and ringing bell stopped us at a crossing. While watching the passing train, Charlie said, "The cars are like thoughts. To know the *all* of thought you got to see between them." I darted my eyes between the rolling thoughts and got dizzy.

"You could look at the cars as lifetimes," he continued. "And the spaces between are called 'nowhere' and 'nothing,' and 'everywhere' and 'everything,' and you just ride in your own car, and the time track goes forever in both directions — yet it's always now."

Any understanding I have of Charlie came without my trying, and is my interpretation. He used the words "the all of thought" for what I'd call "the universe." He said, "Now is like thinking a parade of 5,000 years in a minute, a week, a year." And, "Most of the thoughts in your world were set years ago in prisons and nut houses." He said he had heard the expression "right on" in the 1950s, but that it didn't become common on the streets till the '60s. The word "hip," he said, "came from the old prisons in New York where dopers shot heroin in their hips. 'Are you hip?' meant 'Do you use junk?' Then it got mixed in with old whorehouse music, pimp and con games."

The significance of all this is up for grabs. We listened because it was interesting, and so much of the life we came from was not. He knew all kinds of languages and slangs. He sang us a song he'd written entirely in Australian Rhyme Slang, a language that originated in the rough Australian prisons of the 1800s. In the lingo, "dots and dies" were eyes; "I suppose" the nose; "north and south" the mouth; and so on. It seemed too obvious for obfuscation, but, when spoken fast enough, it must have by-passed somebody. ("That twist and twirl used a lady from Bristol to get in the jelly and jar.") Sometimes he used slang that is today an excuse to take offense. "Mick," "Mac," "Dago," and "Spade" were common amongst prisoners and hipsters. I heard no protest nor anyone offended by those terms. "Negro" was definitely out, like "Colored" before it, and "Nigger" was not one of Charlie's words. There was a Spanish word for blacks that he used right after he got out of prison. It sounded like my-ah-tay and I don't know what it meant.

The caboose came by, the guard rail raised, and there was the space between the thoughts. We drove off into nothingness. Indistinct roadside shapes became mammoth machinery, and blocks of factories soon surrounded us in a dark maze. I was hungry. Wheeling around the corners of empty streets, he seemed unconscious of the late hour and the fact that we hadn't eaten anything. He joked, "We couldn't have taken a wrong turn. We're not going anywhere." Then our headlights struck something. He swerved, opened his door, pulled in a brown paper bag, and handed it to me for inventory. I took out one quart of milk, corn chips, sliced cheese, bologna, and cupcakes. I was agape.

"Of course," Mary piped from the back seat. He grinned. How and who left this — no one was around to ask. It can't be over emphasized how remarkably often these perfect things happened with him, and increasingly it seemed to me we were exactly where we were supposed to be at all times. Even in the music.

Songs on the radio were tributes to the eccentric and free spirited, to wanderlust, and travelers with guitars who valued music more than money. The last time "folk music" was popular hardscrabble folks roamed the land, and owning a radio was a luxury. Charlie reminisced as though it was ridiculous to depart from the present, yet with droll affection, he remembered "Smilin' Jack" and "Orphan Annie" in the comic strips, and three decades of songs and singers of all genres. "Hank Williams," he said, "was called 'Luke the Drifter'. And Lefty Frizzel sang, 'We will travel far, just me and my guitar.'"

On a hot day we got out of the car to stretch our legs at a central California town park. Charlie brought his guitar onto an amphitheater stage and, within minutes, little kids were coming from all directions. It was surreal. They were climbing up on the stage and dancing. I'd never seen anything like it. After Charlie, himself, became overwhelmed, he crept down off the stage. We regrouped on the outskirts of the park, attracting three small boys who appeared to be brothers. Their initial excitement over the guitar quickly turned them inexplicably mean, and they began to hit each other. Charlie stopped playing, calling, "Hey, hey!" and they ran away. I thought the behavior typical, but he mulled it over. Later, on the road, out of a blue silence, he concluded, "That's the kind of love they were shown. That's the only way some people know how to touch each other." And, after another silence, "Kids pick up whatever you show them, even when they sleep."

Charlie was almost four when Kathleen Maddox turned twenty in the West Virginia state penitentiary at Moundsville. He remembered visiting her there and hearing her tell of having seen terrible things. When he was six and caught taking the train, he told his captors that it was okay because his grandfather was the conductor and he was allowed to ride. A conductor in life, his grandfather had actually died before he was born. The family lived by his legacy.

Charlie remembered his grandmother as a good woman, but so obsessively religious she had pushed her youngest daughter away from home. Living alternately with his grandmother and with relatives in Kentucky, he'd struggled to fit in "where kids were already living." He remembered "stealing" canned milk from a refrigerator and drinking it in a closet. And he remembered that when his mother got out of prison, she came for him.

Erratically, Kathleen kept Charlie and left him in the care of others, some of whom were not kin. She had once run out of money while playing poker and, on a lark, bet him. He recalled the other ladies laughing when he had to go home with the winner. He was sent to live with his grandmother one Christmas, and his cousins were there, receiving toys, including a dollhouse and bicycles. Because of his late arrival, the adults had only one gift for him, a Superman hairbrush. His grandmother found him crying in a closet and explained to him that he had gotten the best gift of all, because if he brushed his hair with that hairbrush, he might be able to fly. He said his tears dried up, his smile came out, "I brushed and brushed, caped a rag around my neck, and I was off to fly!"

Flying hadn't worked out for Charlie, as he would later tell, but his can-do attitude survived. His appreciation for our talents and abilities encouraged us. You could say that he played us, but it was to good effect. He asked me to do a little dance one day when we'd stopped for gas. A few leaps and a twirl in front of service station attendants and I felt like I'd choreographed a musical. He kept nudging us to sing and play instruments. That would be a long time coming. Shyness was called "cute" when I was a child, but it wasn't cute. It was just as he said — we were cheating ourselves of a simple pleasure.

They called them "boys schools" but the places Charlie was left for lack of stable parents sounded like jails. He was vulnerable, he said, because he had no one outside to speak up for him. A few of his relatives said they were coming to visit. Boys with visitors were made to dress in shirts and ties, and wait on a bench. Charlie said he got dressed up and waited, but they didn't come. His mother gave notice that she would be coming, and he waited expectantly, but she didn't come either. Too many times, he said, he waited on the bench watching other kids leave, and his people didn't come. When they finally came, and he was able, he took off running. Caught and returned to the school, he was punished and told he was ungrateful. He would later lament that most of his youth was spent "in a room with a bed, a table, and a locker." He imagined having a bicycle; he always wanted a kite; and at every opportunity he ran away.

Once he got stuck in a ventilator and had to be sawed out, and once he and a swarm of kids broke out and ran in different directions, believing that at least they *all* wouldn't get caught. At twelve or thirteen he escaped, robbed a gas station, and was picked up walking around town in a new cowboy shirt with three hundred dollars rolled in one pocket. Later, he was put with older kids and learned lock picking, pocket picking, and things like that. He and the kids in a gang pierced their foreskins and hung small phosphorescent skulls from their penises. Whenever a certain teacher walked by, they stood at the fence shaking their skulls at her. He said that her expressions were worth the possible punishments.

Charlie said he wouldn't wish his life on anyone, yet he was not sorry for any of it. He didn't say prison was a *good* place to be; he said it was the only home people like him have known, that there was heartache, but also soul. He used the word "soul" at different times in relation to feeling, knowing, and love. Describing newborn babies as soul, or "holes in the universe," he said, "In total helplessness and openness they absorb all they are shown."

Father Mike understood the contemplative life — theoretically. His exposure to prayer and solitude, Charlie suggested, might allow him to understand how one could come to know things he didn't realize he knew. Mike responded as he often did with a tight smile signaling bemusement and no understanding at all. Charlie said that in solitary confinement he'd begun to realize that he knew things without knowing how he knew them. He said he came to believe that "knowledge is available to anyone who wants to know." "Then I figured out," he went on, "there ain't nothin' to figure out." This tickled him, as though it were a joke played by the universe. He said, "Everything just *is* — no big mystical questions or answers." Mike wasn't sure he liked that. I think he had a penchant for doctrine. I didn't like it either. Figuring out stuff is one of the world's greatest pastimes. But Charlie said he wasn't talking about medical research. He was talking about questions like "the meaning of life." He complained to Mike, "A society built on fear and doubt teaches and preaches *away* from faith. In a world of faith, *knowing* comes first, then learning. Knowing first. *Faith* first. Then let the kids decide what they want to learn." Mike looked both hopeful and doubtful. His doubt was well founded. As Catholics, we were taught we were born dumb and sinful; the hierarchy of our church would enlighten us.

Charlie said, "I have never had anyone I could count on, outside myself — but I found out that's all I needed." It sounded like bragging, but he also said that he'd known many men who were like fathers to him. He said, "I looked into a lot of brains. Even Alvin Karpis was like a dad to me." He recounted to Mike his time in the Catholic boys school run by monks with straps and paddles. "Those monks drew a hard line, but they showed me unity of will and mind. It wasn't easy to get away because them guys could almost see what I was thinking, but I did." He'd also done time under ex-military men.

"In '49 I escaped, took the doctor's car, and got busted in Salt Lake City. They sent me to National Boys School in Washington, D.C. I worked in the dentist's office under MTAs who were all retired Navy. I raised myself, but the men in service taught me respect for the truth. Some of them were like dads, even though I thought men of school were dull-witted and slow to think."

He'd had to be fast. In Chicago, he said, you had to fight to keep food and a blanket. He'd seen a lot of kids whose mothers made them weak and subject to being overtaken by other men, but he said that almost always when a kid was willing to fight, other guys left him alone, that it was a matter of respect. He said he used to feel that being smaller than other guys was a bad thing, but that, while in the hole, he thought, "Well it's not the muscles that count, or how tall or short, but how much heart you got."

Muffet was often restricted to the car during our travels. Charlie said it wasn't fair. Mary's eyes watered and they talked about finding her a home. Then in Santa Barbara she wandered away, something she had never done before. Mary and Charlie walked the streets calling for her. The following day we spotted her by the hamburger stand eating handouts from kids. She came to the house another day but wasn't hungry, and that was the last we saw of her. At the time, it seemed that Muffet was prescient and resourceful, but I think now that we should have found her a home.

Muffet's departure is one of several reasons Santa Barbara is a milestone in my memory. Another is that Mary had learned she was pregnant. We were all happy about it, I think Charlie most of all. We applied for driver's licenses and we almost got married, all three of us. It was a lark — and illegal — but we would get licenses first in Santa Barbara, and then in San Francisco. The driver's licensing process would take several weeks, but we never went through with the marriages. We got word that Charlie's parole officer wanted to see him. He left, telling us he would hitchhike to San Francisco and return in two weeks.

I didn't want to be married. For the past decade, more and more people had opted to leave churches and governments out of their unions. I think that Charlie suggested the double marriage to secure our commitments. I also think that Mary would have liked to have been married, but after meeting Charlie, she'd begun to give up what she wanted, and, willful as she was, these were major sacrifices.

Charlie seemed to think it significant that he had never divorced his wife. The three of us could be married "in truth," he concluded, but he had been legally married to Rose, the girl he'd brought to California. She'd given birth to a son, and, as Charlie was in prison, she'd filed for divorce, changed the boy's name, and moved away. "I never divorced her," he said once. And later he added, "It would be better for a man to have a hundred wives than to divorce one."

The Fat Man and the Preacher

A fat man in a fat car sped down a highway in a hurry to get to the very place he didn't want to be. Passing a ragged hitchhiker, he surprised himself by braking and motioning for the hitchhiker to come. Driving, he introduced himself as Don, some sort of a salesman. He spoke of his unassuming wife, his three fine youngsters, his boring job, his uncontrollable appetite, the conflicts that troubled him, and as Charlie listened, the man's answers were in his questions: the Fat Man was talking to himself. When Charlie pointed this out to him, the man became elated. They spoke further of birth and death, and what of religion? He belonged to an obscure sect of Christianity, the Rosicrucian's. His best friend, Dean, was a traditional Methodist minister. Confidentially, both men had been looking to try LSD. Did Charlie know where they could get some?

Charlie went to see his parole officer, and returned to San Jose to fulfill The Fat Man's request, remaining with him while he experienced his first immediate sensations since childhood. Grateful for the chance to revisit perspicacity, the Fat Man had taken Charlie to meet Dean, the Methodist preacher, an uptight, compact "Mr. Clean," dressed all in black. Dean was not cheerful.

A man in a black raincoat was at the door of Paula's apartment in Santa Barbara and called me by name. It took me several moments to recognize him as Charlie, barbered and clean-shaven. He enthusiastically told about his visits with Don and Dean, two educated, suburban family men.

Don was of average height and weighed *at least* 300 pounds. His little wife probably didn't amount to a third of that. They owned a nice home in San Jose where their five-year-old son had told Charlie that his mother wouldn't let him sit on the couch. Charlie loved this story and told it often. The little boy said that he wanted his mother to put up a *picture* of the couch so that he could sit on the real one. Don had talked about religion, and moving away from the suburbs.

Dean was the Methodist preacher, already in the process of moving his family to a cabin in the Ukiah woods. He'd invited Charlie to bring Mary and me there to meet his wife and teenage daughter. Don and Dean were both taking a big step: they were *dropping out*. Dr. Timothy Leary's call for humanity to "turn on, tune in, and drop out" was not heeded by the American majority, but it seemed so in California. Dean had taken his first acid trip with Charlie in San Francisco.

He'd laughed about "superficial things" he once considered important, and, as tears rolled down his face, he'd said that he remembered "what it is to feel."

We left Paula's to visit these men after Charlie got his new driver's license. Stopping at a roadside motel, Mary and I met the fat Don. He said he would be moving his family out of San Jose, but had not yet collected the courage to tell his wife about a change in their lifestyle. That night as we sat around the motel room, talking, Charlie transformed. His voice, though not louder, filled the room with its magnitude, and his words were so powerful that my spine felt pulled through the top of my head. I couldn't take my eyes off him. Suddenly he noticed his own hand extended in an authoritative gesture, and he became still. Chuckling uneasily, he asked, "What am I talking about?" His assertive voice answered: "Don't question it," and instantly he returned to the previous expressions. My amazement was complete. When the meeker Charlie appeared again, he said, "I'm just listening to this for the first time myself."

The next day, as we drove north through evergreen forests, I wished that everyone could have seen and heard Charlie. I wished that we could have filmed and recorded him, because I couldn't recreate or even remember what I had witnessed. It was lost to the moments from which it had come.

The Preacher's fifteen-year-old daughter waved to us from the deck of their two-bedroom cabin above a rushing stream. Charlie had accurately likened Ruth to a dark-eyed fawn, her slender limbs sticking from loose shorts and a crop top. Her thick brunette hair had been attractively boy-bobbed, ex-

posing a decidedly girl neck. In the house, she sat listening to us talk with her father, and later, by the vanity mirror in her room, told Mary and me about a high school boyfriend, while opening bottles of perfume and offering us whiffs. "This is musk," she said. "It's deer cum — did you know it?"

During the next days, Mary, Ruth, and I walked the banks of the rapid creek below her cabin and became as close as we ever would. Ruth navigated the wet rocks like a wild girl, her feet as tough as her will, but she patiently waited for us to catch up. I began dwelling on my own shortcomings shortly after meeting her. Her skin was golden, and as smooth as a baby's. She was everything I wished to be, carelessly beautiful, and comfortably connected to nature. One day I felt like such a clumsy and speckled loser, I climbed a hill, sat down and cried, oblivious to all but myself until I heard dogs barking at the foot of the hill. Quickly I was flanked by Ruth's two dachshunds licking my face, and she came, rock to rock, like Tarzan's Jane, until she was sitting beside me. The dogs had come for her. The thought of those squat little animals leading her to my distress made me laugh. Ruth's communication with them and her regard for me gave me a stronger admiration for her than the personal comparisons I was making.

Ruth's father was going through his own changes. After preaching the Bible for more than twenty years, Dean wasn't sure about any of it. His personal life had become a schism. The more doubtful he had become, the more forceful his proclamations from the pulpit. He said that confessing this lifted a heavy weight from his mind, and he thanked us for being there to hear it.

Dean was not an atheist. He would continue to speak of God, but under no marquee of church or religion. He and Charlie reveled in history as put forth in the Bible, about Jesus, his people and times. But in a pensive moment, Charlie posed this question: "If you were God — and you loved your creation — would you want to be way up somewhere looking *down* on it? I wouldn't. I'd want to be right in the middle of it. I'd want to be living it." Later he said that "God, the father, and Jesus, the son, are in the nature of man." Dean smiled with great pleasure, but disagreed. He revealed *his* belief that Charlie was "Man's Son, Jesus Christ returned."

"Returned?" Charlie exclaimed gleefully. "Jesus Christ never went anywhere! Christ is a living consciousness. I may reflect it but *it's in you first or you wouldn't recognize it!*" But Dean was unready to believe he could harbor divinity.

The Fat Man hurried into the preacher's cabin, his big face flushed with fear. After taking LSD his furniture had spoken to him. It had begun innocently with a whisper from a stuffed chair. The coffee table had chimed in, and the couch was loudest of all: "Buy more of me! Get more of me! Me! Me! Me!" The cacophony was maddening. In a panic, he had tried unsuccessfully to hide under his covers. He'd retreated into the Bible, gaining a modicum of peace by construing its characters as living people. Mary and I were Biblical sisters, Manson, again, Christ, and Dean, he thought, might have a role as John the Baptist. But where did he, himself, fit in? Moses? Solomon? He'd spent the day looking for himself in the Book, probably to avoid being a man bullied by his furniture. The

111

message in the fantasy, however, was clear to him: he was addicted — desperately, unhealthily attached — to properties that could not sustain his life. We talked through the evening, providing camaraderie and some consolation, but his addictions were many, and none of them illegal.

Ruth's mother had gone home to the suburbs before we arrived, but one day she returned to retrieve her daughter and do battle with a husband who was no longer hers. Dean invited her to relax and take off her armor. He told her that he needed to start over, and he asked her to be patient with him. She was in an awkward position, older than the rest of us, more set in her ways. She argued and fumed and refused to say more than a few words to Dean's suspicious visitors. Finally he told her that he loved her but would not allow her to spread misery in his house. After failing to convince Ruth to go with her, she left angrily, and sent the county sheriffs to pick up her "runaway daughter."

Ruth's father was gone the day they came for her. She calmly told the two officers that she was not a runaway, and that she loved her mother, but was happy living with her father and didn't want to leave him. The sheriffs threatened to arrest her, but she held her ground. Charlie offered that she was not legally bound to live with her mother, and about twenty minutes later, twelve officers from the Sheriff's Department had the house surrounded.

Put into a squad car, Ruth told the officers that they should be stopping the lumber companies from robbing the forest. She was sent south to live with her mother. Charlie spent the week in jail for verbal "interference" with her arrest. When Dean returned, he was apologetic and quick to pay Charlie's fine. Far from being discouraged, he planned to visit his wife and daughter, and to see us again.

Heading toward San Francisco, Charlie told us he saw good reasons for marriage but that divorce had taken "the word" out of marriage.

"The husband and wife trip was to ensure everyone a chance for life and fulfillment. Then Kings and Queens played divorce. Marriage was lost in truth when King Henry VIII started that — a house divided."

1967 would be known in San Francisco as "The Summer of Love," coined in sincerity by hippies and repeated by "straight" commentators most of whom meant by it "rampant sex." ("Straight people" were separated from hippies only by the lines in their own minds, never venturing outside grids of habit.) Charlie said, "Do you realize some people get married, have kids, and die and never find out what sex is?"

Federal sanction of the contraceptive pill in the '60s was credited with relaxing fears of pregnancy and social prohibitions, but maybe ideas about sex have always been confused, the extreme being that sex is dirty, evil, an obligation in marriage and a perversion outside of it. Thoughts of nastiness coupled with innate physical pleasure created all manner of desperate behaviors and markets, but in every era some people have known sex as both an enjoyable and sacred expression.

Haight-Ashbury had its share of tawdry and random hookups, but there, if not throughout the modern world, sex in the latter '60s was considered natural and healthful. Even Father Mike disavowed celibacy for a live-in girlfriend, an oddly pedestrian arrangement of pleasantries and housekeeping duties. When

Mike and the other tenants were at work, we had the house to ourselves.

Charlie was smooth. He opened us with finesse. Clean and conscious, he enjoyed himself without shame, and seemed to embody a wholesome masculinity, the confluence of body, mind, and spirit. His touch was healing. It stirred in me regret at having slept most of my life and a longing to open up to the rest of it. His vitality renewed itself beyond what one woman could hold. He excused himself, saying he was making up for lost time, but it was more than that. He wanted children. He said, "I reach to reproduce myself in your likeness not only in the flesh, but in the soul." At times I thought of him as holy, even as he played upon my embarrassments with comic lechery. In love, I felt that he gave us everything he had. My resistance surrendered, and then he said something I thought profound:

"What you feel is what *you* give, not what I give. You feel your own love."

Runaways arrived in San Francisco, having hitchhiked from all parts of the country, some as young as thirteen, and some who would go to bed with anyone who asked them. Charlie could spot them at a glance. He said that without protection of the law, they were vulnerable. We brought some to Father Mike's, but our relationship with the paying tenants was already on shaky ground and Mike was too busy to take on the responsibility. Charlie talked to these kids like he knew them, and they were quick to respond. He smiled at me when the ingénues stared at him, wide-eyed and beguiling. Then he told them funny stories, or showed them crazy faces to put on "if anyone tries to run you with fear." We walked back to Mike's house talking about them. He said, "There should be a place where they can grow up to be themselves."

The City was really too much for Charlie and we never stayed long. Somewhere, on our way to the woods, we got out of the car for a walk down a country road, and he noticed a tree that had been hit by lightening or broken by the wind. Sap was running from it. Not far away we'd seen a rolling vat of tar in use to repair the highway. The connection was natural, and soon he was in the tree smearing tar on the wound. A stiff man with a large black dog approached, asking, "What are you doing?"

Without looking down, Charlie replied, "Fixing this tree …"

"Is that your tree?" the man demanded.

"No," Charlie responded, looking at him. "I thought it belonged to itself."

"Get off this land," the man ordered. I couldn't tell if he was angry or afraid. "This is private property. Get off this land now. I'll call the police." He went away.

Charlie finished tarring the trunk and we hurried back to the car so he wouldn't get arrested for aiding a tree. He said, "It's against the law to care."

"In prison," he said, "there was only one law I lived by: no snitching. And I didn't think much about it because it was the law I grew up with. My law was my word to myself." He used the word "word" like no one I had ever heard. He quoted Genesis to Father Mike: "First was the word, and the word was God," but he put more emphasis on the word "word" than on the word "God." "Breach of word," he said, "breaks people away from the God in themselves."

These traveling monologues most often related to situations at hand, but he talked a lot about being lied to and learning to lie, which seemed entirely about his own situation. He said, "As a kid, I lied, and I used to think I got away with it because no one else knew — but I knew. I learned that I'm worse on myself than on anyone. Others forgive and forget, but I got to live with my own lies forever."

While driving, Charlie recalled, "Here's a riddle: A traveler walking down a road comes to a fork, two unmarked roads. He knows that one road leads to Truthville and the other goes to Liarsville. He wants to go to Truthville. A local resident is standing at the fork offering direction. If he's from Truthville he's got to tell the truth, but if he's from Liarsville, he'll lie. The traveler is wise and asks just one question. What is the question?" I tried out several ideas before he told us the answer. (From which way did you come?)

Our little red trailer on the beach by Mendocino looked lonely but was unmolested, and as cozy as we'd left it. From the cove we took day trips to Fort Bragg, Ukiah, Willets, and the redwoods, passing lumber trucks and tough men whose lives and skills were bound to "forest management."

August 1967
Dear God,
We've been out admiring your artwork. Your redwoods are masterpieces. We just thought we'd turn them into picnic tables and trash bins. How do you like that idea?

A century before our arrival, Fort Bragg was militarily active. Among its tasks was the supervision of a Pomo Indian Reservation. The Pomo had been encamped inland until U.S. President Franklin Pierce

116

settled a property dispute in favor of American new-comers, ordering the Pomo off their home ground and onto a piece of land near Fort Bragg. The reservation had lasted less than ten years, its failure according to an official report, due to *"poor management, poor native adaptation, and white encroachment."*

The sky turned more frequently gray and a chill dampness filled the coves. Mary left us on such a morning. She didn't say why. I followed her down the beach, fitting my feet in the prints she left. We'd never talked much, but I'd learned her ways. Characteristically reserved, smart, stubborn, and capable of scorching sarcasm, her regard for him took down all barriers. I remember the amazement and amusement we shared in watching Charlie, her disappointment at having to share him, the way she could make me freeze from across a room, and the relief of finally seeing her laugh. And at the time I sympathized with Mary's chemical and emotional changes, because by then I, too, was pregnant.

Squinting, she stared out to sea, and when a squall blew back her hair, I saw her tears, and knew that the clouds had broken. She stopped beside a boulder the size of a boat, and got up on its deck. When I thought she wouldn't mind, I climbed up beside her, and we drifted for a long time. I don't know who spoke first, but by late afternoon we were hurrying home to make dinner.

It was blustery cold and time to move on. We fantasized baking on a beach in Mexico. Charlie had fled there in the 1950s after his parole officer issued a warrant for his arrest. He had sought what he called "the soul" in a Mexican park where he was learning to play flamenco guitar and sing Mexican songs. He translated a few but said it was not the same in English. He said that when the Triumph sports car he was driving broke down, he was sitting by the side of the road, and a Mexican woman — "short and sturdy with a husband who loved her and a houseful of kids" — welcomed him to a meal, washed his clothes, and hung them in the sun. "She showed me the giving of woman."

The Professor's wife appeared tense and disheveled. He was solemn. After she left the tent, Charlie apologized for our intrusion. He informed the professor that we would be leaving the beach. The Professor said that despite his love for it, he would probably have to leave it as well. His wife had married a man of income and social status, "not to be eroding on some vacant beach." Charlie suggested that maybe they could go on the road and see the land. He said that they could have our trailer, that his wife might be happier with a little stove and refrigerator. The man was smiling when we left him. He was a gentle man, brave in his own way, yet fragile in his love for his wife.

On the morning before we departed, I arose feeling wonderfully unencumbered. I leapt around the fire with my wings outstretched and my nose up to meet the gusts of cold wind. Suddenly we were running toward the ocean, Charlie and I, swallowing air until my lungs could hold no more, stopped abruptly, and breathless at the shore. He took the chain with the skate key off his neck and handed it to me. Without word or thought, I threw it as far as I could into the turbulent sea. Suddenly realizing what I'd done, I turned to see my reflection laughing in eyes knowing.

On the way to Mexico, in Santa Barbara we picked up Paula, taking her to visit her husband on Terminal Island. En route, we were conjuring up a vehicle we could sleep in. Along a private beach in Trancas, a wealthy section of Malibu, Charlie saw a dusty Volkswagen bus parked beside a big house that was surrounded by several other cars. He speculated that its owners didn't use the bus more than three weeks out of the year, so he got out of our car and went to their door to ask, "Could we use your VW bus now, and bring it back all shiny and in good working condition the three weeks you need it?"

A platinum woman freaked at the door, said she would call the police. Charlie had to talk her and her featherless husband and their little flock into coming out to our dented car to see that there were indeed three girls in it, and that he did play music for a living. Out came the guitar. The woman scowled. The capon cowered and the chicks clustered. Charlie sang a tender popular love song as the sun set over the ocean. The woman softened. "That's very pretty," she said. "You should try to get yourself recorded." Then she apologized, was very busy. They all smiled, waved goodbye, and followed her into the house.

Charlie said that he used to think that all the "good people" were outside of prison, but each time he got out he'd see people "stabbing each other in the back." "The only difference," he said, "was that the ones inside admitted to being cons. There were always a few guys in each penitentiary who told the truth — the ones doing fifty or eighty years for not snitching on their partners. They were the ones who said, 'Friday I'll give you what I owe you,' and Friday they brought what they owed. Their word was their bond, and you could find maybe four or five of them in each penitentiary, and they most often were in the hole."

Mary and I were not immune to the glamour surrounding the Italian-American Mafia, and Charlie was not shy about getting attention, so it surprises me that he was slow to mention even casual associations. He didn't use the word "mafia" but it was clear that some men he had met were connected to organized crime families.

"One of my prison dads was from Baltimore," he told us. "Frankie Carbo. His wife was the greatest. She would send him a box for Christmas — four pounds of candy each year — and he would always give me half, and we would walk the yard and talk. He used to run booze in the 1920s with the Rocco brothers from Philly. He was a grand old con man and I didn't miss a thought from him."

Despite his obvious respect for such people, I think now that Charlie's life had conditioned him against any attachments to persons, places, or things. His "home" had been wherever people put him, and anything he had could be taken away. It didn't exactly make him cold; it made him confident. He could ask for anything and give anything away. I don't think I ever heard him directly ask for money, but it seemed that people couldn't wait to give it to him. His conception of money was something to the effect that as long as it was kept in motion, there was bound to be enough of it to go around. It gave him personal freedom. "If you have to save it," he said, "it puts too much value on it. It only has real value when you don't have to worry about it." He played with clothes and instruments and passed them on. I saw him begin to give some things and pause to ask himself if he really wanted to part with them. He had some nice things, but he'd give them up if someone needed, or even looked like they'd like to have them. The feeling was not to have lost, but to have gained a new freedom: we had nothing, yet everything. It hadn't occurred to me that we had "everything" only because Charlie had no reservations about deserving or accepting it.

The Fat Man on the phone was worried. He told Charlie he had sold his home, but the new owners were due in five days, and he had yet to find a place for the grand concert piano he'd left in the living room. When Charlie mentioned that we were looking for a Volkswagen bus, Don said that if we could move that piano within five days, we could sell it and have the money for the bus. Energetically pursuing the task, we traveled to San Jose and found a suitable VW bus for just over $1,000. When local music stores were reluctant to take on the piano at real value, we offered it for little more than the cost of the bus, and made the five-day deadline.

Those few days in Don's empty house, Charlie talked about using the still-connected telephone to call his mother who he believed was living in Washington State. But, again, he let the opportunity pass.

Charlie's frayed address book provided us plenty of places to visit and stay. In Sacramento, Peter J. DeLeo opened his front door and grabbed Charlie by the back of the neck, welcoming him in like a son.

"Chahlie," he called him with a tight, glinting grin. "Chahlie, whadda you been doin'? Ah you kids hungry?" Pete lived in middleclass suburbia, but had a full bar in his living room, and a big, shiny well-equipped kitchen. He had grapes growing in his back yard, and lots of business visitors. While he cooked us omelets in olive oil, he and Charlie caught up. Yeah, the world had changed, Pete muttered, and he was none too happy about it. "Those girlies are out there givin' it away. Bad for business." He sounded worried, and I couldn't hide my amusement. Straight up, Pete was a high-end bartender and a professional pimp, unlike anyone I had ever met and a lot like gangsters in old movies. He sounded like Cagney and used Aussie Rhyme Slang more out of habit than to conceal his intentions. (He told Charlie he had to see Hank and Frank about some bees and honey.) We stayed only a few hours during which Charlie and Pete exchanged tough talk — short snaps and caps on former associates — and Charlie gave Pete his new outlook on the world at large: he didn't know about this "love stuff," he told Pete, but he thought he'd go along with it because he believed in "the kids." Later Charlie told us that Pete was old fashioned, but meant well and had done him right in the past. He said, "Pete don't like the new. In the old ways with women there was no sex before weddings, no nude bodies, no children out of wedlock. In Pete's line of work that was money. Tricks came to his place for what they couldn't get at home, or get at all. Now it's a new game."

Charlie knew a lot about working girls. I didn't know what the Mann Act was, but the charges were on his rap sheet. He explained that in his early twenties, while on parole, he'd taken the first job he could get. It was at a hot dog stand. Among the conditions of parole, he was not to associate with ex-felons. He said he didn't know anyone *but* ex-felons, and that the hot dog job put him to sleep. When an old-school con offered an alternative, he'd accepted training and went on to manage three women in L.A. who worked hotels and bars. He said the money was good, he wore expensive suits, drove a sports car, and flashed diamonds. He laughed. "I was MISERABLE! The women expected to be treated bad. I'd put on a show, get all riled up, go into a bar and order the best scotch." He laughed again. "I *hated* the taste of scotch."

I asked if he was saying that the women wanted to be hit. He said, "If you didn't act tough, the women thought you didn't care. With street girls, the way was if anyone tried to take your woman you were supposed to get mean and do bad. I always told the women, 'Go with them, get what they got, and bring it back to me.' Others said that was wrong and someone would take my women. I said, 'If you hold to a woman in fear, you show her doubt — that you don't trust her and ain't sure of yourself.' I felt if I showed myself unsure, the women would reflect that."

This indirectly hooks with something else he said about women that I thought funny and sad, but so true. He said, "I had a girlfriend. She said, 'I love you.' I said, 'I love you.' She said, 'I don't love you.' I was broken. Another said, "I love you.' I said, 'I don't love you,' and she said she loved me more. She said, "Please love me,' and I said, 'Okay, I love you.' And she said, 'Good. I don't love you.'"

Someone — it might have been Father Mike — gave Charlie a drum that he loved and decided to keep "until we're done playing with it." He said that the only other instrument he'd ever been attached to was the guitar he'd made in prison. His mother had offered to have it lacquered and strung for him. I asked if it was the one on the back seat.

"No," he said. "She never brought it back. I sent it out with her and she never brought it back." After a pause he said, "That's the last time I ever spoke to her. That's one thing about a guitar; it'll never lie to you." I thought I finally understood Charlie's animosity toward his mother, and I shared it, but days later, when I said something derisive about his mother, he surprised me with a fierce look.

"My mom was a fourteen-year-old runaway," he told me. "She was just a kid when she had me, and she had more love than anyone around her had the eyes to see."

Charlie

For a me to put words on paper, I myself must first understand them in a true light within the word "honest." Years of prison cells, as if in one large brain, I've heard, seen and watched my own thoughts turn a universe. I start, like life does, with moms in Ragtown, Ohio, as I was told by my earliest recollections of images calling themselves aunts, uncles, grandmothers and later, a woman came out of prison with a guy she called brother, and she looked like me and called herself mother, and all said I was to do the same. Uncle Luther and Kay did a nickel — that's five years in prison talk. He was a gambler and moms was like a bar maid, and the years of the depression was hard on them. Strong armed robbery carried five years. I remember going in the prison at Moundsville, West Virginia to see them, and how the big stones were like the temple of a solemn place. I never realized I would spend my life in such temples of suffering.

My other uncles and cousins were all hill people from Scotland, Ireland, and settled in the hills of

Kentucky and West Virginia right after Daniel Boone kicked the Indians out of their space. Jess was my first and foremost person. To wit of truth in my child's mind did he put himself with rage. Nothing short of a mean old mountain man, if words could touch him, with a wood shack from his own hands built upon stilts. He was known as a well digger, water finder and dog trainer, as wherever Jess was the town dogs tagged. He hated cars, schools, government men, or anyone that wasn't kind or kin to someone he already knew. His old lady had a big iron pot to cook apples, no shoes and four daughters in feed sack dresses would tend the fire and do their giggling. The state officials told Jess "get the children in school" but Jess vowed, "No youngens of mine will go to school. Can't take the kids from the land — the land is life. Leave the land and you all will die." And he would yell and beat everyone with a stick. He turned on me.

I had pushed a dog off the porch, ten feet or so, and I lied about it. They put a bucket over my head and beat it and yelled, "Never lie! Don't lie! Liars go to hell!" That bucket became my own. I was to carry the water, for it was time to kill the pig. I don't remember any money, for it was always "I'll dig your well and bring my cow to be bred," or "I'll trade a hand-stitched quilt for five jars of shine." The garden was income and Jess was always in the woods running possums, coons or whatever was plenty. He would get all the kin and with a big fire, the pot, jars, buckets, and the killing would begin. His knife was long and thin and he would cut the hog's throat and be on with it. With a fast move he'd cut its tail off and put it in my hand. Then he would yell, "Send this kid to the city and tell them people stay away and leave us alone —

no school, and I'm gonna make shine as long as there is a forever." Another uncle or some kin had just put dynamite under his house, under his still, in the yard, everywhere, and the U.S. government came in and he blew them, his wife, his kids, and himself up and the hills and hollows were rumbling with things I didn't realize.

Grandmom could get free tickets on the railroad cause granddad was a conductor and a WWI vet with medals and kind of a hero to everyone but Jess. Later I heard Jess had died in the nut house somewhere in Louisville, KY and my other cousin, Wormie — he was called Wormie because he dug fishing worms as a kid and sold them — saved his money, built a big market, got rich, never learned to read or write, and when he played big shot, he went east for a trip, came back with a fine class woman what in turn beat him for his money and left him back on the river bank digging worms and crying for his mother. I heard he died in the same nut house Jess did.

My mother was a bartender. She drank a lot and she used to come and get me out of bed so she and her Uncle John could go to bed. There would always be twenty or thirty dollars more and like she wasn't what they call a "flatback" but she was a hustling girl. I got sold for a pitcher of beer once but when I went up to the tall people of the attention, a dog hit me with his tail when the people wasn't looking and showed me big teeth as if to say "This is my people. Stay away. No space for you here." So I went on down the road and the grownups said "He don't like us and won't come to us." So I was sent to a place where people that got no one goes. I don't remember how I escaped but when they found me riding in a box car I told them "My

126

granddad runs this train!" And they said "What's his name?" and I remember grandmom getting me back.

Off to another aunt and uncle. Even as a child I knew they were not smart. Uncle Bill had no teeth and was always getting down on me and calling me stupid. I got to their pad on Christmas and their daughter was my first friend and love — Jo Ann. She kept the other kids from beating me up. Grandmom said it's a sin to fight and when Bill seen I didn't fight, he put a dress on me and sent me to school. Then Granny gave me a witches hat to wear in the cake walk, and for Christmas I got a hairbrush with Superman on it. Let down, because the other kids got dolls and buggies, little plates and doll houses, I ran to the ice box, got a can of Pet Milk with all the cows heads on it and hid and sucked the milk from the ice box I knowed as mom because I hadn't caught up to her. She was still in the pen. Grandmom caught me and said "Why you cry, boy?" And I said "A hairbrush is all I got." You got to know a hillbilly grandmom to understand. She read one book, the Bible. No movies, no makeup, no sex and she never lied. She said "Boy you got the best gift of all. That's the magic brush and who knows, if you brush your hair with that brush you may be able to fly just like Superman." Eyes dried up, rag around my neck, brush in hand, I'm off to fly. Off the porch, cars, for days I worked to fly. Then I almost did it. I leapt off the fender of a car, and the wind caught me just so, and I thought it was happening. I ran into the shack where moonshine jars were being passed around yelling, "I can almost do it! I can almost do it!" Uncle Bill was drunk. He said, "Almost do what?" "I can almost FLY!" He said, "You idiot, you can't fly. What's wrong with this damned kid?" and he went to knock me down. Back to the ice box, cry cry cry. The next day I got all the toys and dolls, put them in a pile in the doll house and I set it on fire, broke the piggy bank and was on the road again. Highway police caught me, gave me the ice cream and attention I had never known and for years I thought subconsciously that cops were like fathers and nice guys and the judge was like a god.

I've never had no one to hold to. The warden, the judge — they were God to me until I caught them lying. When I ran away and they got me back, this old black man in court was crying and begging the judge,

"Judge, I didn't steal that dog," and he looked at me and he said, "He just followed me home." I thought he was talking about me. Then I ran right into my aunt coming to take me back and on the train again out of Kentucky and to West Virginia to the prison where mom and Luther were.

McMechen, West Virginia, the town next to Moundsville where the prison was, I seen my first movie with Bing Crosby, got my ass beat, and ran away and lived with two river tramps that gave me a cup of coffee. Back to court and to a foster home where I met some honest, hard working people that had concern. Few I've met but I know there are some, and I would still be a part of them but some lady came and said "I'm your mother, let's go."

I started out learning Moms. Her life gave her little chance for happiness and little hope for choices. She was pushed out of the house at fourteen, got pregnant, had me, went to prison. Now she's out and a tough little girl behind the bar of a honky tonk, The Blue Moon. Other parts of the U.S. don't know hillbillies. They're not cowboys or Oakies. If you weren't dying in the coal mines you were lucky to work in the steel mills or on the railroad, and if the pad you lived in had a wood floor, that was uptown. Crime was crime and outlaw women were few. I lived in a room up over the Blue Moon with Mom and she came in on the run and said "Pack fast!" and out the back door we went. She'd hit a Beenie brother in the head with a fifth of Jim Beam whiskey and layed him out. He and another brother was out on bail on a murder trial for cutting a woman's head off. They put it on a pole and throwed her body in the river.

Me, Moms and a salesman for the Holland Furnace Company were off to Indianapolis, Indiana and she changed her name to Kathleen Deere. They drank a lot and that let me in the streets. Uncle Bill's dress had taught me to fight and I think I caused the invention of bicycle locks because when I started stealing bikes there were no locks. I had a paper corner selling papers until I seen you could put a rag up in the pay phones and come back later and pick up the nickels. I spent all my time at the movies, pool halls and bowling alleys where I set pins. I was too young and too little, but I got a job at the Mecca Theater where Hoppalong Cassidy and Bob Steel, Buster Crab, and Roy and Gene rode high in the saddle. Five dollars a week sweeping and running between two picture shows for the boss. But I got greedy and the telephones weren't paying off well so I moved into stamp machines. Two cent and one cent stamps. I had stolen some stamp dispensers and I got caught in a market with all the pennies and nickels, and then off to boys schools, and juvenile halls.

Moms would run her prison trip to me, how the food was so bad, and her job. Her job was sweeping and mopping the killing floor where men were hung. One day they came to hang a guy when she was still in the mop room, and she hid, and wasn't seen. They set the trap and the noose and something went wrong. The man was too big or the rope wasn't right and his head popped off. It came off his body and rolled down the steps to where she was hiding and she said it blinked at her. Her fear of that ran off onto me, and I took it and never realized until I was on death row for nine counts of murder and seven death sentences on a trip not my own.

I learnt to run early in this life. The cops would pick me up off the streets and some juvenile court would send me to a kids' place and I would hit the fence, never learning what friends were and never having anyone to ask what to do. To run was all I knew. Highway 40 went to California and I ran that road a lot.

My first bust came for the market and stealing stamp machines, and 25th and Keystone became my home and they had tall fences and running away became breaking out. After three tries I thought to play a different angle so I put a sob story on a priest and was sent to Boys' Town in Omaha, Nebraska. A ride on the train. I got there somewhere in the 1940's, '46 or '47, and three days later I was gone. Vern Black told me of his Uncle who was sharp, and we hit the road to Peoria, Illinois, walked through a snow storm and stole a hearse, a Packard, and kicked in the back windows of gas stations. I went to sleep at the wheel in Peoria, and we hit the streets on the run to end up at his uncle's pad where, a few burglaries later, I was in that hall again and shipped back to 25th and Keystone. That place was a curse to me and I was so sad to see it but I escaped four times.

I cut the wires on the back windows of the little boys' dormitory. Me and thirty-five kids broke out into the night. Newspaper, the Indianapolis Star, had just done a story about the new Indian blankets at the hall. Then they did another story showing the blankets out the back windows. They said I was the mind behind the mass break, and my first big jail stood in front of me at age thirteen. That was New Castle. The jail was an old castle in Indianapolis, an old Scottish castle given to the city, and they made a county jail out of it. It was big. Cellblocks with rows of cages. When I was taken inside, a bunch of people were outside carrying signs that said "The World is Coming to an End."

I was the youngest person ever to go to that jail. I would curse, spit, smoke, fight and no kid told me shit and all the grownups were fools to me. County jail cops said, "No — we can't take him — he's too young," but juvie cops said, "We can't hold him. He made thirty-five kids run away. He's no little boy. He only looks like one." So they made a place in County Jail outside of the B.R. (named for Bums' Row). I was kept on the cat walk that went around the Bums' Row cells. There were eighteen of us kids and each day was total madness. About eighty men set my young mind to much more than I realized. They were all like Uncle Jess but I was like their kid and each gave me something. Every day something new was jumping off and I loved it. The F.B.I. had just shot and killed someone on the ten-most-wanted list and they were all talking about the guy's gun moll had a butterfly tattooed on her puss. One of the winos was a nut and up for cutting the wombs from dead women and trying to buy wine with them. Another guy cut his wrist and put his arm and hand in a bucket of warm water. Another hung himself. They were running at the end of the road. I was just in training for my run through life.

Ten or so other kids had escaped with me, and they did what I said or I would kick their ass, and all the old men liked me and each one was setting my thoughts. I didn't realize until later. The monks were men but this was a different game. The cell doors opened on the inside where toilets and showers and games were played, and coffee was cooked and the older men roamed back and forth. The back side of the cells faced the outside catwalk and we could walk around and talk with each cell and each was a world I had never seen into. I learned to spit on my dick and stick it in this guy's ass. The guy that killed himself had gave me some head and told me how to fuck this other kid. Then he said "But don't ever let no one fuck you, kid, and never let anyone get away with whippin' your ass. Get a stick, a knife, a gun, whatever you must but NEVER let no one ever get away with playing any shit off on you."

To shower and shit we would raise the turnkey and he would key us in and give us time to do the three S's — shave, shower and shit. There were winos with DTs seeing snakes and fears of all kinds, and being a mean kid, I would torment and get off on them. One thought he was stuck in a grain elevator and I would tell him "I'm chopping the cables and you are about to die but suck my dick and I'll let you live." "No! No!" he cried, so I'd make him wash my shorts and shirts and he would fuck them up and I'd throw water on him. Another old man said, "Can I wash your socks?" and I gave him three pairs to do and someone said

"Watch him, kid, he's Klepto." I said "What's that?"
"A kleptomaniac. He steals anything and everything."
He came back with five socks and I said, "Where's my
other sock?" and he put his hand over his pocket and
said, "I don't know." I smacked him and got the sock
out of his pocket.

Each person that passed me set something in my
young, open mind and a lot of it I never realized until
years later. Like one night a big poker game was going
on and I played like I was going in to shower but it was
really to watch the game because this one guy was
teaching me how to deal and play cards. Everyone was
watching and Klepto was standing in the corner looking at the ceiling. The game peaked — all the money
was between two men. Tough, street men that didn't
smile and played hard. One said "Raise." The other
called and raised. "Called" was the cry that echoed off
the iron walls. Everyone was frozen. "Straight" was
the next voice. My eyes were wide. My heart pumped
and the other guy said, "Sorry, Full House, you lose."

He turned out his hand and the other guy said,
"That's only two pairs."

"Kings over tens, man, can't you see?"

"I see two kings and two tens — where's the other
king?" He reached for the money and his hand was
slammed to the table.

"Hold it — count the cards — I had the king of
hearts."

"Well it's not here now and that's sad shit."

And the money was taken and everyone watched
the loser. He looked under the table and yelled, "Who
got that king of hearts? I'm gonna kill! I WILL find it!"
Everyone looked at each other and one by one all eyes
went to Klepto.

"Klepto, you sorry dog, did you get that card?"

"No sir, I've been standing here all the time. How could I?" Everyone was watching. Then his face was busted. It just turned red. His head bounced off the wall and another punch caught him and turned him in a circle and he hit the floor begging and crying, "No, sir, I don't have it!"

He then was kicked and beat from one end to the other. Next to death he still swore he didn't steal the card, and the guy was tired of beating on him and said, "If I ever find out you took that card I'll kill you." The turnkey called and I went back outside the tank. I had never known such fear or seen such a thing. I was busy running it to all the other kids when the doctor brought the old man back all patched and bandaged up.

I was being sent to reform school, the judge said, until I was twenty-one. It was called Boys School but I got some wild stories about it. I was due to leave the jail. Everyone was saying goodbyes and giving advice when Klepto slid up beside me and the man took off his face and said, "Boy, one day all this will be yours. God gave me all of everything and I'm giving it to you because I'm gona go be god."

I said, "You're an old nut and a klepto.

He said, "When you're with god, you can't steal because it's all yours." He said, "I got a gift for you" and he pulled that king of hearts out of his pocket. My fear jumped up up up.

"You old dizzy fool – hide that! You'll get killed, sure."

"I did it for you, boy."

"No no no, not for me," but he give it to me and I hid it fast.

He said, "You must remember above all else: Trust a liar to lie, a cheat to cheat. Trust yourself and no one else but the old man, boy, because he trusts himself in you and you in him." I took it in my head but I didn't understand it until I was bitten by a snake and when the poison came up and through my heart it all became clear to me and the old man with the beaten face and bandages was standing in my head laughing and saying "See, see? My nows are in forever."

Yes, that time in that old castle of Indianapolis county jail was a trip and when it ended I was in handcuffs on my way once again. Put in with the little boys and rushed to a shower, a voice said, "Last one out gets a whack!" They rushed past by me on the run and I walked and stepped from the shower and pain hit me. I had picked up a razor blade in the shower to keep someone from being cut and when I looked at what hit me, a smiling face said, "You're last out!" I ran him behind the door. I whacked him with the razor blade and he started to bleed and yelled and he ran and so did I. I ran out the back door and was run down after about a four hour chase and taken and put with the bigger kids after the ass beating of my life. In them days they had large straps that could bust you up bad and fast.

On to new halls and a different kind of man, not like the monks or the drunks. Just as real but different. Service men retired from Navy, Army, Marines, and we marched. I was put in between four big guys and they were told if I ran out from under them they got their asses beat. I was smart enough to get out of school even if the law said school until sixteen years. I pulled all kinds of tricks, got a hacksaw and hit the bush, swiped a 1946 Chevy, ran it through a gas station at ninety miles an hour, got popped and put back in New Castle, Indiana jail, back to Plainfield, out again and back again, up and down that highway always the same. I had the record for escapes and the last one was three of us tunneled through the bakery into where the doctor kept his car, and away we went — highway all the way to Utah. Beaver City Jail was four cells and a nice enough Sheriff that wanted to give me a job on his ranch, but the judge said no. Back to Indiana where I got U.S. government time for taking the car over state lines.

Off to Washington, D.C. School for Boys. Kids from Detroit, Cleveland, New York, Kentucky and all over, still marching and fighting. Dr. Heartman was a pushover for a story so I got to go to Camp in 1950. Escape was my plan but I got caught punking another kid in the butt, and, at seventeen, I was sent to the first prison I was ever in, the U.S. prison at Petersburg, Virginia. The captain told them I was not a boy but the Irish devil himself.

I ran the food carts in the mess hall, got mad and ran everyone out of the mess hall and kitchen and bake shop and vegetable room, and I hit the lieutenant with a bucket of water and told him to clean the damned mess hall himself. I spent a whole year in the hole for that.

A Captain name of Bull Dog Edwards walked a line past the hole cells. A con told me "If you ever want out of here, you got to ask him." I'd hear others crying to him, "Please, Captain, can I get out?" and his ego would build. "Well, I don't know," he'd say, "Are you gonna be a good boy?" They would say yes and beg and he would swell up and feel big. The more they begged, the bigger he played.

Three months went by and I didn't ask him nothin'. One day he broke his line. He came to me and said, "How are you boy?"

I said, "Fine."

He got mad and walked. Seven months later he came over to me and said, "Son, do you have any problems you want to talk to me about?"

I said, "You would just laugh."

He said "No, no. I might be able to do something for you."

I said, "I can't shit." He looked bewildered. I said, "There is something you could do, but I hesitated to ask."

He said, "Go ahead."

I said, "I'm all out of toilet paper. Would you run down there and get me a roll?" The next bus out of there, I was on it, transferred from Petersburg, to Lewisburg in September, 1952.

The big walls were so high, the clouds seemed to touch and it looked like a movie. "Too young," they said. So I was put in a place away from the main flow where I met a guy named Big Frank from New York. Everyone respected him. Costello name meant nothing to me at the time. He talked to me like old friends about FDR and a guy named Dewey, a D.A. from NY, and two thirds of what he said I didn't understand until later. Being raised the way I was, I didn't understand that I was not under-standing. I just listened and moved and I had little to nothing in my head. The Nolan brothers escaped, and we listened on the radio as they made the run with all the cops after them. News said FBI gunned them down in a whore house in N.Y.

And then it was off to the baddest reform school in the U.S. at that time, Chillicothe, Ohio. When I got there they had the National Guard and the place was smoking. They had a lot of young men from the Korean War in for murder, and they were some tough guys. I was bad on my streets but I was no match for them heavies. That place put a hat on me and I lost my first fight and the guy got away with it. The lesson saved my life a lot of times and still sets heavy in my mind's brain. At this point in time no one but cops had ever whipped me and got away with it. I had built up an illusion in my own mind that I was bad and tough. I punched the bag best and ran best, best in handball, but in the real, like any coward trying to prove they're not afraid, I picked my shots. All the guys I thought I couldn't whip I was nice to and I was always catching fronts off the others that I thought I could whip.

I kept pushing this big clown because I thought he had snitched on me. He begged me to leave him alone but I touched him up a little and he said,

"I don't want to hurt you, Charlie," and that got me mad and I tore into him with right hands and left hooks but it didn't faze him. I punched him with everything I had again and still nothing on his face but "Well, now it's my turn." He hit me three times. Never had I known that feeling. I flashed as if I'd slipped on a melon in the fields on the run, for I had done that before and it was the only thing I could compare it to. Two black eyes, busted nose and mouth, blood running from both ears and a broken fist, laying in the hospital. He came to visit and I told him "I got to get you, guy."

He said, "I'm going out tomorrow and you'll never see me."

I said, "I'll follow you until I get you. It's in me to do so."

He said, "Man, you pushed me to hit you. You were trying to prove something to yourself. That's not my fault. Admit you're wrong." He told me, "A man will never push another man. It's always a boy or a punk that gets off on others. When you become a man you learn respect by giving respect. When you learn what you can do if you want to — I could've picked you up and thrown you off the tier. I don't like to be hurt and I don't like to hurt others."

But I didn't want to hear the truth at that stage of life. He left and to make this story complete I did meet him later. He was a taxi driver in Wheeling, West Virginia. I seen him and fear hit me. I had to get him, but I thought "No one will know if I don't." He said, "Let's go get a drink," and we did and talked about it.

I said, "Okay, it's over." He did me a favor.

I went out right after that fight in 1954, first time I had been out legally since the early 1940s, and I went back to Wheeling never realizing I was still nine years old. At the bus station I asked a black shoeshine man for change for a dime so I could make a nickel phone call and he looked at me funny and said, "Man, phone calls ain't been a nickel for years. Where you been, on the moon?" What a trip. I had never had a job and about three years of school. The big markets had so much I had never seen. Then I stole a car and took off for Dagoland in Cleveland, Ohio to see an ex-con who had fought with me in the joint. I sold the car to a gangster from Little Italy. I had fought for and with their kids. I was one of the Dukes and Bluebirds of the long ago.

In Cleveland I ran with a Dago-Mick named Murphy, running a half assed crap and card game and living with Murphy's girlfriend's mom. She had five daughters. I sat in the barbers' chairs and tipped a dollar, and the family took me into their hearts. I could've been someone, but I had a wife, and I had committed myself to her, so I gave that up. I was young and only on the ground floor but I could have been a good crook. A lot of my kin were small time hustlers and gamblers. I learned. It's no big thing to be a crook but to me it was in them days. I had met Big Frank in the pen and he raised his hand for me, he vouched for me. You got to be honest to be a big crook. Little crooks fake and lie. I didn't fake or snitch but I was still a hick.

When I married Rosie at twenty years old, I had never been around chicks. Rosie played me like the fool that I was. When I was in Cleveland with the Mafioso's daughter, Rosie gave me a story about her brother-in-law ripping her off. I got a gun and went back to her in Benwood, West Virginia. The gun wouldn't fire, and Rosie said to me, "Oh, he didn't DO it. He just tried."

I wanted a red '41 Cadillac. In 1940, '41 no cars were made. All was going all out for the war effort. GM was given permission to make 144,000 Cadillacs. I was told I could have the '41 if I stole a baby blue '52 and gave it to the barbershop people of Little Italy in Cleveland. They gave me some guns, some Frank Sinatra records and $300 bucks. I kept the blue Cadillac like a hole card, in case they didn't give me the red one. I went to Florida with the guns and to work on a tug going to Cuba but almost got killed when the hammers and triggers were discovered missing from the guns. So I went on a run out of Florida with the poker game out of the Jolly Roger Hotel, took the game with me to Fort Lauderdale, then back to me old wheel in Wheeling, West Virginia and to Georgia — hot but nice. I almost stayed. I left with a 1950 hot car, a shotgun and a straw hat full of dimes. I did three years for that.

One of my mom's husbands was a window washer at a U.S. courthouse. His name was Deere. They got me out of prison and she got me a 1954 Ford. I traded it for a 1952 Cadillac and used the name Charlie Deere.

After Rosie dumped me, I caught a rich chick and the world and all its treasures were mine, money, new cars, but that wasn't it. I ran some guns and got busted. I left three good girls standing on the corner, each with a dime. I left a Caddie, gave it all up and went to Mexico and started over to be a bull fighter. I had a big gun, a fast hot car — TR3, an American passport as William Sergeant Bartlett given to me by the woman secretary to the ex-president. Her husband was a general of the army. I was learning to "cape the horns" and playing music in the park each night where only the pure of heart smoked the good grass. I got caught and was put in Mexico City Prison and brought to the U.S. with some Africans being deported back to Kenya by Mexican Federales and F.B.I. After the feds got me that woman's daughter got 150,000 signatures on a paper to have me brought back from Texas where I was deported without trial, but the U.S. judge drove over it and sent me to McNeil Island in 1960. They still got my car and passport in Mexico.

— Charles Manson, letter from prison, c 1986

The Producer

Gary Stromberg, a record and film producer at Universal Studios in North Hollywood, had an incidental music scout inside the prison on Terminal Island. Phil Kaufman was doing time for international marijuana smuggling when he heard Charlie's music and referred him by letter to Stromberg. Charlie was just getting around to arranging that meeting. He called Stromberg from a pay phone in Los Angeles. On our way through the gate at Universal, I tucked in my shirt and tied my moccasins in bows. When Charlie got out of the bus, he took one look at me, laughed, and pulled out my shirttail. Walking toward Stromberg's office, I noticed that we were parked in a space reserved for Cary Grant.

Stromberg was young and well fed. Everything about him was glossy. In friendly small talk he referred to the letter he'd received from Phil and asked how Charlie was getting along. Charlie said that the world had changed a lot in seven years, and they laughed about the cultural transformations. In upshot, Stromberg seemed to like Charlie. He had another appointment but asked Charlie to return later in the week to use the recording studio. I was stoked.

We left the studio for Manhattan Beach to find Bill, another Terminal Island alumnus, and impose upon his lack of hospitality. I was surprised when he answered the door. Bill was eye-catching from his surfboard feet to his angular jaw, but his eyes were unwelcoming, and we could barely hear him introducing us to Patty, the modest brunette sitting on his couch. I could tell at a glance she didn't live there.

Charlie ignored Bill's cold shoulder, telling him of places we'd been and asking him about himself. Bill offered us a bit of nothing from his hollow refrigerator, took a beer for himself, and rocked back on two legs of his chair, while Charlie played guitar, and Patty listened intently. In contrast to her friend, she was pale, with deep brown Cleopatra hair, narrow shoulders and bare white arms that came to rest softly against her jeans. And unlike Bill, she gave us a great welcoming smile.

Charlie walked Patty to her apartment that night and didn't come back. Mary and I slept on Bill's two sofas. The next day Patty and I set out for a corner store, both of us barefoot and a little shy, and discovered that for part of our lives we had lived less than six blocks apart. She was half a grade ahead of me at Orville Wright Junior High School in Westchester. We'd probably passed each other in school dozens of times, and we nearly passed the store talking about it. Since high school, her life had been devoted to the downtown branch of an insurance company, an empty spot of beach, and her imagination, in which she said she had conjured us up.

Patricia

A time ago, but then it is always now, a disenchanted and frightened girl wandered aimlessly upon the sands of the Pacific shore, her mind filled with doubts and cares, knowing all is meaningless except the love of one another, but unwilling to extend her heart for fear of rejection. She might have ended as she had planned so often, a body swept upon the shore by the tide.

' Twas but a smile, a true smile, one which you could touch with the warmth of your heart, and a

143

glance — not like many you take, but one where you travel between two pairs of eyes, meet in the middle and know there is no beginning or end — a sudden load laid from your shoulders and a sureness of your faith — and to your own surprise you find someone who understands your every thought, a friend, ah, much more, a reflection of yourself, the hidden beauty that you find openly in another face looking into your own.

It was then, in that strange stillness of unspeakable aloneness and together, that brought me here to now. ' Twas but a few days before Charlie, Mary, Lyn and I began traveling the roads in a cozy VW bus, exchanging thoughts composed of all our fears, sorrows and loves, making of each other a family, strong by the bonds of understanding, experience of the road filling the longing of wants and making of us all one spirit of joy and laughter. For as long as you are together with each other, there is no moment of despair.

— Patricia Krenwinkel, Sybil Brand Institute
for Women   Los Angeles, CA., 1970

If that doesn't illustrate how florid and gentle Patricia Krenwinkel was, perhaps nothing could. Her parents had divorced when she was in high school, her mother returning to Mobile, Alabama while her father, an insurance broker, continued to live in Southern California. Her only sibling, an older half-sister whose beach apartment she shared, would go on to an untimely end, and she to, arguably, the most inexplicable mass homicide of its time.

During our second visit to Universal Studios we girls were permitted to sit with Charlie by the micro-

phones in the recording studio. Stromberg encouraged him over a speaker from the soundproof booth,
and played for us a tape of high beat African music
from a group he had recently produced. Then he suggested that Charlie tell some stories while playing the
songs he had written in prison. For some reason,
Charlie waned. He said that his prison songs were old
and there was "much more happening in the streets."
Stromberg assured him that people wanted to hear
about prison. So Charlie tuned the guitar, and unrav-
eled some stories, but he never seemed comfortable.
He said that while in prison he had considered a job
playing music, but "that was a hundred years past
and just an old ego."

"That's okay," Stromberg told him, "just play anything." So Charlie launched into the ego song, and a
few others. He was cordial and at times comedic, but
his heart wasn't in that studio, and I felt that even he
didn't know why.

> "Clang bang clang went the big iron door
> They put me in a cell with a concrete floor
> Nine other men in that cell with me
> Moanin' their date with destiny ... "

> — C. Manson, prison song, 1967

After the session, Stromberg told us he'd been kicking around a movie concept about what Jesus Christ
would be doing if he came back today. What with the
beards, the long hair and sandals, today's young generation could relate.

"Sure," Charlie said, "the kids aren't interested in
the money — they're interested in the spirit — they're
interested in life." Stromberg wanted Charlie to tell

him how we lived. Would Charlie be willing to spend time as a technical advisor on such a project? Charlie replied that he didn't want to get tied into anything long range because he never knew where he was going to be, but he agreed to call and to stop by when we were in town. As we left the lot, I was imagining success and fame, but Charlie wondered aloud, "What would they do with Christ?"

Patty left town with us, left her unhappy friend, her troubled sister, her job, her car in a lot, and her savings account still saving itself. Mary rolled over that night with tornado force, pulling the covers with her. It was one thing sleeping three in a VW bus, but four? We had no reason to complain; Charlie had asked us if Patty could come along and the truth was that she just fit. A stabilizer amongst women, a listener who demanded no attention for herself, an inspiration and conscience toward our own better attitudes, she was so easy to like that Mary couldn't stay mad.

We gave her the coastal tour to and through the Golden Gate. We went all around Haight-Ashbury, between the psychedelic banners, painted vehicles, and acres of hippies. People of like-spirit welcomed her, and she smiled, quietly thrilled. Patty deserved this vacation. Only in hindsight do I wonder, "At what cost?" But at that time in her life, and under those circumstances, could she have done otherwise?

Although a short distance apart in miles, the philosophical space between Haight-Ashbury and Berkeley was wide. The university collected and spawned opinionated, often political people. In

Berkeley, it seemed nearly everyone had something to proclaim. The feminist movement was gaining stride, a number of white women criticizing their male counterparts as either chauvinistic "pigs" or weaklings. Siding with minority men, they adopted the word "oppression" to say that they, too, had been enslaved. Ideological Black Muslims and Panthers rejected their advances, interested only in furthering their own causes and in African-American women. Charlie said that one reason he had not settled in society or married again was because he had seen men come to prison *for* women, and abused *by* women.

Charlie

The dope peddler asks his wife: "Do you want me to do this kind of thing for a living?" And she says, "Baby, I don't like to see you put your life on the line, but it's up to you." They go back and forth. He says, "Well, we've got a new home, new car, and money in the bank. Should I quit and get a square job? Will the kids make it on what we've got? I won't make this kind of money at a straight job, but then, if I keep on like this, I might get busted." She says, "You're right. Put the house and bank account in my name." And tears come to everyone's eyes when the judge says, "Fifty years."

Three years go by. Joe has come over to the house to help the lost wife of his best friend, and he's gonna sell a little dope so she can get her man out of jail. Joe just loves the kids, so what's wrong with him moving into the big empty room that no one uses? He can deal right from the heart of the leftover people his friend was dealing to. Wife can't understand why her husband's going crazy. After all, she tried to visit. So she decides to get a divorce. She had to sell the house

---

for her mom's doctor bills, but on the other side, her and Joe are gonna move into a new house.

Things I've seen all my life and didn't know right or wrong or judge — the man who took a shotgun and robbed banks because his dick was too small and his woman never happy, the man who shot someone a week before his wedding and lost his wife-to-be, but his mom comes every visiting day — I never thought of myself as thinking anything but I've seen it. I don't judge it or not judge it; I just see it.

— Charles Manson c.1976,
California State Prison

I said, "You can't blame everything on women."

He said, "Exactly. And you can't blame everything on men. Most men are doing what they were taught to do — by a woman. When the woman puts all the blame on the man, I just put it back. She's blaming part of herself. Then she runs to put her problems on the black man in the name of help. Maybe he thinks he's won a prize. He's been taught she's better than his woman, but in soul he knows. The real African man thinks white people look like bloodless turnips. You got years of TV and movies telling people what's good looking. How do you think that makes the black man feel? He's been taken away from himself."

The next time we saw Gary Stromberg at Universal Studios, he had moved into a larger office and his conversation was frequently interrupted. Between phone calls he explained that the Christ movie hadn't yet gelled in his mind but the one thing he had decided for sure was that Christ should be black. This did not

148

come as a surprise to Charlie. He told Stromberg that the important thing was not the color of Christ but the thought he was projecting. For over a thousand years, he said, Christian religious leaders have held up the cross purporting to speak for Christ. Christ, he contended, was misrepresented. He also told Stromberg that making Christ black was Stromberg's attempt to calm his fears and pay off feelings of guilt.

"Black people," he said, "should be allowed to make themselves in their own image instead of being manipulated by white people into images not their own." Stromberg wasn't sure he understood, but his mind was on more immediate productions. He said he would have more time to work on the Christ movie later, and that Charlie should "stay in touch."

A retired sociologist from the prison on McNeil Island had contacted Charlie's parole officer, extending an invitation for Charlie to visit his home in Washington State. The parole officer thought it would be a positive trip and granted permission for Charlie to leave California. We set off right away, but took our time. We camped in Oregon and Washington with all of the natural amenities: plush green carpets, songbird canopies, clear water and air. For brief interludes we heard the summer's symphony without one beep, whine, or groan from a machine, and were the only humans on earth. Charlie actively imagined being one of the first. Using a walking stick, he pretended to vault a river, make a tent, and spear food. He thought aloud about a world in which other animals walk around Man "because a true earth man can face his fellow animals and they naturally know to respect him."

"Man's dominion over animals," he said, "is natural dominance, not subjugation; it's a given, not something taken. Without doubt, people would know that."

The religious allegory about Adam and Eve's "original sin," he suggested, could be seen as "Adam doubting himself, permitting the woman to take him from his nature, his word, and the God in himself." But as much as he pointed up the gender divide, he wasn't cruel, or dismissive, or condescending, or disrespectful in any of the ways we had seen some men behave toward women in our lifetimes.

He made love to all of us together. He didn't encourage us to instigate the action, preferring instead to direct the moves, and expecting nothing from us but that we receive him. By earnestly working for our fulfillment, he held our attention and raised it. We became responsive to the slightest touch, and he was not overwhelmed by sensations until he had raised us above thought and brought us down gently, the sweat dripping from a curl over his brow. Tucked into woods at night, he said that all the money in the world was not worth the experience of being there with us.

And then he and Mary had a fight. We had driven off the highway to survey a possible campsite when they exchanged a few words, he braked the bus, she opened the door and got out. Charlie met her at the front of the bus. She swung at him, he took her arm, she grabbed his jacket, and they tugged, and wrenched, and scuffled. Inside the bus, Patty and I watched, wrestling worry and heartbreak, while mindlessly munching potato chips. As our hands collided going into the bag, we had the same funny thought of being at a drive-in movie. Returning to the action, we saw Mary take off toward the woods. Charlie was sweaty and somewhat torn up. He got into the bus, took some breaths and started driving slowly behind her until, hot and exhausted, she also gave up. Nothing more was said of it.

Each of us girls was a little stubborn and a little lazy. Charlie liked to take walks on what he called "the hard paths" between thorn bushes and fallen trees. At first I considered these walks an imposition, but we became thinner, stronger and more agile, and, without wanting to admit it, we began welcoming the opportunities to flex. On mornings when the bus wouldn't start, we got out to push it, grumbling silly one-liners, while the chauvinistic chauffeur steered and coasted, never missing an opportunity to show off "woman power."

It was as though we had never seen cows. We were hungry for the sight of any animal, and they were so close to the road that Charlie pulled the bus beside their fenced meadow, and we got out. In the stillness, accentuated by ticking insects and the calls of mourning doves, we ruminated on their lives. They had no ambitions or aspirations, no hopes of becoming horses or goats. They fulfilled their purposes, grazing, mating, giving birth, and nourishing not only their young but millions of the rest of us. Charlie said that despite our dominion over animals, he would rather see more alive than on plates. Did we really need to eat them?

I had been raised on two to three meals of beef, pork, lamb or fowl a day, and for all I knew, the rest of the world had as much. I liked meat; it was nourishing, but in a land of abundant alternatives, did I *need* it? In the following days I became aware of half eaten hamburgers stuffed into trash bins and on fast food parking lots. People had become bloated, thoughtless, wasteful and, ironically, unsatisfied. It was a habit we would break.

In a university town, needing money, Charlie said that he was headed for the student dining room to play music and "pass the hat." He repeated that we were welcome to join him, but, being too shy to sing, the three of us set out in broad daylight to ask strangers for money. Mary bolstered herself, saying, "We just gave away a $200 trailer, some bongo drums, and we almost gave away the grand piano." None of us had panhandled before but we'd heard the lingo in Haight-Ashbury: "Got any spare change?" I felt compelled to add lengthy explanations that proved less effective than getting to the point; nobody wanted to hear why we needed it. As a sideline, and maybe to feel normal, we stopped to chat with students. Patty was a natural at interviewing people. At the end of the day, sure we were called a few unflattering names, but we'd gone through our spare changes and were returning to the bus laughing with a whopping six bucks. With his guitar, Charlie had received more than fifteen dollars in less than twenty minutes. He'd had a crowd gathered in the Student Union when an administrator told him to leave. The rest of the afternoon he'd socialized, had lunch at some girl's house, and was invited to a fraternity party. The next day he talked a gas station owner into getting his plate glass windows washed for another six dollars and four ice cream bars. Lapping ice cream as he watched us, he mentioned that one day we might want to play tambourines and sing.

Passing through almost any town, Charlie noted the signs on commercial buildings. It was a curiosity to him that people aspired to have their names on laundromats and such. Not that he was against signs. Exiting a shop, he said, "Guy tells me business is bad. If he put up a better sign he'd have more customers. You can't see that sign where it is." He claimed that people didn't realize their potential. "If a guy wanted to go into the restaurant business he could start with a broom and be managing the place within a year." It sounded like hyperbole until he explained.

"Say he goes in that restaurant and starts sweeping the floor every day for an hour or so." He acted the happy sweeper. "The manager asks him what he's doing and the guy says, 'I just wanted something to do. I don't mind sweeping floors.' And the guy is harmless and he don't accept pay — maybe a cup of coffee or a bowl of soup. So pretty soon the people who run the place get used to him, get to know him and like him. He's useful. And he comes in and says with more authority, 'You know, if you move these tables over here, there'll be more room for people to walk,' or 'If you clear this window and hang some planters, people can sit in the sun and enjoy the plants.' You know, little improvements, and it brings in more customers and makes more money, and pretty soon the owner is asking the guy what to do, tossing him the keys, and saying, 'Lock up when you leave.'"

Charlie frequently had money-making ideas he mentioned only in passing. Then he'd say, "These people got me thinking about making money," or "That's my old self. It's all most cons can think about, the fastest way to the money." He said there wasn't much difference between legal and illegal cons, and he acted out a number of TV commercials, pointing out subliminal messages put together by highly paid psychologists whose intent was to target human weaknesses. The sexual innuendos he noticed were implausible to me. He gave as example a deodorant commercial in which a man and woman were running toward each other on a train platform, the man carrying a pink elephant. Just before they embraced, the elephant's trunk bobbed in her face to the announcer's words, "At the peak, the peak, the peak of your excitement!" Charlie said he once knew a bunco artist who talked wealthy middle-aged women into investments by off-handedly holding a rolled up magazine near his crotch and bobbing it now and then for emphasis. He said it sufficiently distracted some women to bamboozle their better judgments. These were the kind of psychology discussions I'd expected (but didn't get) in college.

The towns and counties of Washington State are rife with Native American names, most famously Seattle, chief of the Suquamish peoples. We crossed into the state just after dark, hungry and needing gas. Charlie spotted a coffeehouse where he thought he could sing for our dinner. It was the middle of the week, and more than half of the wooden tables were empty, so he talked the manager into letting him take his guitar on stage, and we three sat at different tables applauding. The place filled up in half an hour. Charlie proceeded to charm the crowd and, during a rousing applause, the manager walked across the stage and spoke in Charlie's ear. He then took the microphone and announced, "This is Charles Manson. He'll be here at the club every night for the next two weeks." We were surprised. So was Charlie. He later told us he'd only given the man his name. He was never asked, and hadn't agreed to anything. After we had our meal, we drove on.

The next afternoon, around Steilacoom, we stopped to see the father of one of Charlie's ex-cell partners.

Bent and gray, he was watering his flowerbed, and didn't even look up as Charlie approached to ask about his son. When the man finally did answer, it was in disjointed sentences, like a picture of a room in which all the furniture and appliances are floating, or in the wrong places. Just as natural as every day, Charlie spoke to that man in similar strange sentences, the man replied, and Charlie in turn, until the man began to communicate in an understandable way. When Charlie had the information he wanted, he respectfully said goodbye. Though Charlie said little about this bizarre exchange as we drove away, I got the impression that something had hurt that man so much that he preferred to live in a world apart.

McNeil Island Federal Penitentiary was opened in 1875 off the Washington coast and under the splendor of Mount Rainier. Washington was not yet a state but a U.S. Territory. Railroads had not reached the area, and ship was the fastest mode of transport, so the island site was perfect for prisoners. At the end of its first year, the prison's total population was just *nine* inmates and two guards. The first recorded inmate, Abraham Gervais, had been sentenced to twenty months for selling alcohol to Indians. By 1911 a second cell house briefly held Robert Stroud, sympathetically portrayed by movie actor Burt Lancaster in *The Bird Man of Alcatraz*. According to prison ledgers, Stroud had attacked and stabbed an inmate-orderly, receiving for the infraction a disciplinary transfer to Leavenworth, Kansas.

For about sixty years more, McNeil Island continued to confine convicted men from any U.S. state or protectorate. Charlie talked about some of them. Of interest to me were a Native American who had done fifteen years for stealing a pig — because he kept violating the conditions of his parole — and a cackling old lunatic who wrapped and hid small presents for guards to find on their typically shit-disturbing cell shakedowns.

"Before the other prisons opened," Charlie said, "there was a big cross-section of people here. I knew a Guam Island man with a face full of tattoos, and an Eskimo who fished through the ice and could live apart from the supermarket. There was Africans — the difference between an African and a U.S. Negro is night and day."

We found the Sociologist in a two-story house on the tree-lined outskirts of the city, and were met at the door by a trim woman in a shirtwaist dress. She was the lady of the house, but we'd barely said hello before the man was shaking Charlie's hand and inviting us into their living room. The house was spacious and orderly with polished wooden furniture, including a huge leather chair in the study where shelves were filled to the ceiling with books.

The Sociologist was eager to tell Charlie about his new job as a teacher. Glad to be out of the prison business, he seemed to align himself more with inmates than with staff. He wondered if Charlie was still playing the guitar and thinking of making a career of it. Charlie said that he'd been locked up so many years he was just out looking at life. He recounted some of the places we'd been, and talked about the "new music."

"The Beatles' music has a lot of the subliminal in it," he told the Sociologist. "You would know about that." The Sociologist said he hadn't really listened to it. Charlie sang a Beatles song about turning off the mind, relaxing and floating downstream. He laughed, saying, "You know, I learnt all that in the hole, but I didn't know I knew it. Man," he said, "you oughta see all the hippies in San Francisco. It's a new culture."

The Sociologist hadn't entirely caught up to the cultural changes, but said he was "one hundred percent in agreement" with the anti-war movement. He lamented at length the war and worldwide hunger. Charlie wondered what he had done to rectify his feelings, asking if he'd considered selling his furniture and sending them the money. The Sociologist caught himself mid-sputter. "Well, no," he said. "I don't think that would — we give in our own way. I don't want to argue, Charlie."

Charlie appealed, "I'm not arguing, man. I'm listening to what you say." The Sociologist's wife had disappeared and we heard pots and pans in the kitchen. After awhile we knew it was time to leave. The sociologist followed us out to the porch, telling Charlie how good it was to see him, and extending his best wishes. He said, "We may not be hippies, Charlie, but we want to end war, poverty, and hunger as much as anyone."

Charlie's next words were quiet but direct. He said, "You had four hungry people sitting in your living room and you offered them nothing." The Sociologist reached in his pocket, but Charlie said, "No, man, keep your money."

We drove to an area of smaller homes where a bearded man let us park for the night. The Sociologist found us the following day. He said, "Charlie, you're right. You really are right. I'm sorry. Please take this." Again he offered money.

"Look," Charlie said firmly, "I don't mean to make you feel bad."

"Not everyone is there yet, Charlie," the Sociologist said. "Not everyone can do what you do. I envy you, Charlie."

The Sociologist had much more property to lose than we did, and he had worked years for it. The fact that he felt guilty about having it was an underlying problem for him. Then again, he was passing that guilt on. As a teacher, his words about war and hunger would affect younger people into action. They could work out the problems. He would keep his furniture.

At late afternoon, Charlie turned the bus down a dirt road marked "DUMP" but instead of rubbish at its end we found a clearing in a clean wood on the banks of the Puget Sound. We explored, unloaded equipment, built a fire, and began cooking before Charlie asked, "Do you feel something?" I didn't, but Mary and Patty said they did. It was dusk. Charlie asked, "Do you sense somebody?" We looked around us. Nobody was coming. It seemed to him they were already there. He said we were trespassing, and he thought we should go. Without further discussion, we dumped the food, packed up the bus and drove out at nightfall. That was the second time I heard him allude to "spirits."

The next day we looked for a good place to camp. Most land was privately owned. Charlie said, "The Indians knew the land belongs to no one and everyone. But they were called "dumb savages." In the cool afternoon, Charlie sat against a tree, talking to a squirrel in a neighboring tree. I was thrilled to see the slinky little body move down the tree trunk and pause, staring at him. Holding down my breath and movement, I watched it cautiously cross the ground, coming so close to him that he could touch it, when into that silence a terrifying growl sent the squirrel into the underbrush. It was Charlie. When the blood returned to my brain, I was furious. I couldn't believe he had done that. He got up and passed us, saying with disgust, "The next human he trusts may blow his head off. It's not time."

It was at this point in my experience of him that the Charles Manson of court records began to display misanthropic ideology. More likely, a pre-existing condition was aggravated. When, on the most unused roads, in the deepest woods, and even in the streams we found wrappers, cans, and toilet paper, he said, "Animals are smarter than people. They don't shit and piss in the water they drink."

"You couldn't pay me to go to one of your schools," he said furiously. "I'd eat dirt first."

We were driving up a fire road when Charlie asked if we wanted the bus. He put on both brakes, turned off the engine and got out, telling Mary to hand him the pink slip. Placing it on the seat so that anyone could own the bus, he told us to take our things and come along if we were coming, or to take the bus and go.

We followed him up a steep wooded mountain in the heat of the day, but after thirty minutes, an hour, we dropped down, deciding not to go farther. From a distance, he turned to look at us, and slowly his face reflected our displeasure.

"I don't care," he told us, with no trace of feeling. "When you lay down your mind and die, you'll find me." He spoke to us as one woman, turned and continued up the mountain. We stayed put, defiant, angry, sad and at an impasse unprecedented in our lives. We loved him. Our tears came as a relief. After a time, I accepted myself as human and humanity as good, foibles and all. Mary and Patty must have experienced something similar, for we started up the mountain, laughing, and calling for him. A voice unlike his came back, mortally wounded. It said, "GO AWAY." I thought he was angry at us. Then I saw him higher on the mountain, not the Charlie we knew but an animal on the edge of a cliff, the sunset reflected in empty holes of his eyes. Looking across the fumes rising from the city below, I had the thought that some in its throngs would tramp to every hidden place on earth to destroy him. We had seen the crumpled cans, the trees stumped and burnt; we'd heard the silence after the shot. I thought I was facing "human nature," but I'd barely glimpsed it.

He disappeared. When we saw him again, he was absently drifting past us, looking through us, as if we were not. And then he paused to speak with a leaf in no words I had ever heard, and I thought he had gone insane.

A cool night was settling over the mountain. He lay on his back in a bed of leaves. We wouldn't leave without him, but we didn't want to stay. We were unready. So as darkness came, we lay down near him, crying, and after awhile, he reached out of his private world and drew us in. Together, we became a warm energy, he said something like the old Charlie would say, and he agreed, without words, to come down the mountain.

The 1960s busted out of the bland '50s, so radically changing the world it's surprising more ordinary adults didn't lose their minds. Homeless waifs roamed the cities. Marijuana was ubiquitous. Police were divided on the issue, some pursuing users with deadly force while others shrugged off recreational use as harmless. Cocaine and heroin were *not* popular amongst hippies, but marijuana and psychedelics were virtually in every patchwork pocket and satchel. One day I entered a room where Father Mike was standing over his open briefcase; in it were many plastic bags of marijuana and LSD. Beyond the startled second, he closed the case and behaved as though I'd seen nothing. I think now that Father Mike may have been a distributor for the Brotherhood of Love.

Each generation has its end-of-the-world scenario, and our end was imminent. All establishments and institutions seemed less stable. Communism, which seems to raise its head whenever the heads of other isms duck, appeared with several heads around the globe, shocking the capital holders into reactionary militarism and the tepidly religious to fundamentalist rebirth. Thousands of young men were drafted into military service, and few knew why they were fighting. People had burned themselves to death to protest the war, including a Quaker man who had poured gasoline over himself and his baby daughter below the office of the Secretary of Defense. Catholic priest brothers, Daniel and Phillip Berrigan, the latter a decorated WWII veteran, led draft card burnings and encouraged desertion. Repulsed politicians called these and other respected Americans "Communists," further confusing the definition.

On October 21, 1967 in Washington D.C., more than 100,000 anti-Vietnam War protesters gathered at the Lincoln Memorial. The next day in San Francisco was my nineteeth birthday and nobody even gave me a card. That's where my head was. Charlie finally answered my sullen disappointment by explaining that he didn't think of birthdays because they had always been like any other day to him. He consoled me with humor, and later suggested that we could be "born every morning, celebrate the day, and rest in peace at night." It was something to think about, a different perspective, a change of attitude.

Charlie

I have never in my life been able to look down on anybody because I've always been at the bottom. So my anger and frustrations I've always had to go to solitary confinement and take it out on who? You know. On me. And I'd stare at the wall and make music in my head.

But then it gets to a point to where solitary is peace. And when things got hectic in the yard, I'd just go up to the man and say 'You dirty so and so' so he'd put me in the hole. And I'd lay in the hole for two or three weeks and I'd hum.

So when I got out of prison, I take some acid that a young girl gave me on the street. I look at everybody and I see they don't know what they're doing. They all say, "Well so and so said this or maybe around the corner or ask him or it said in this book..." but nobody can say "I know."

So I look at it and I say: Wow, what an insane world you live in, Jerry Rubin. What a madhouse you live in. I just got a look at your world at thirty-three years old and the police are hitting the kids and they direct the kids to work off their karma for past debts, you know, all of their guilt for what's been done to the black man, to the Indians, and the kids get their heads beat for it. The kids have always gotten the world their parents left them.

> — C. Manson, 1970 from a visit with
> political activist Jerry Rubin

Father Mike and Charlie still talked ethics, religion and God, but Mike's reactions — alternately enthusiastic and doubtful — were more extreme. He seemed to be struggling to etch life into platitudes, and frustrated when, with a spirit of its own, it refused him. One night, psychedelically bouncing between the celestial firmament and subterranean fires, Mike's face contorted into demonic grimaces one moment, and glowed with beatific adoration the next. Charlie was telling him that "the church" needed to come to new understandings. "What God and Jesus conveyed two thousand years ago was for *that* time. The cross, like the pyramids, was put in the minds for reasons beyond common understandings. God always comes upon the earth to balance when needed. The earth nowadays is full of God on different levels." To Mike's training, this was blasphemy, but what it was to his sense caused him pause. Charlie said, "Even if churches try to put a monopoly on it, truth belongs to everyone, kings and sheep." He said, "The monks in Indiana said *they* had the real Christ, and since then I've heard hundreds of people say their Christ is the one. Who can own Christ? Christ is a thought. Coming into the brotherhood of Christ means giving up everything and starting over, and that's not easy. Rebirth is not easy. Churches buy and sell it, but it's not easy to leave a world and all you think you know. I was only smart enough to learn I was dumb. That left me with three years of school, a card game, a few jail games... not much else."

Mike stated, "You believe you're God."

Charlie said, "God and Jesus are in our nature, man. Father and son. The Indians knew everything is God — the sun, the moon, the river, the land — but you can only see God when you see you're his creation. Through you, all is his experience."

Mike ventured archly, "And what about Satan? Is Satan in our nature?"

Charlie replied, "If you insist. Sure, if that's what you want." He grinned. "But as God is all faith, the real devil would have to be doubt and anything that separates us from God."

San Francisco's philanthropic spirit blew minds — and then it was gone. From Mike's stereo, The Doors were singing "This is the end..." about the time that the Diggers were having a funeral. A casket with a large banner proclaiming the "Death of Hippie" was carried down Haight Street, and they left town. The atmosphere changed. On each of our visits, the Haight showed more signs of decay, rats and zombies gnawing at the sacred heart of it. Father Mike said that the LSD market had been flooded with everything from sugar to strychnine by people out to make a buck. The Free Clinic was getting poisoning cases and freak-outs. Every day we'd see gaunt, ashen creatures buying cheap poisons in dark doorways, someone stumbling down an alleyway, or in the back of some slick dick's car. Charlie returned to Mike's house one afternoon with wet, vacant eyes. He'd had no room to offer a couple of young runaways. So the next day we were headed north, out of a place where there weren't enough places, to find a bigger bus.

Happy Birthday Poem

Should I live a hundred lives
Be enslaved by foolish dreams of others
Wake and walk dead with no will
Knowing fear rules?
Rules. Not thoughts from church or schools —
Words used as tools running fools
Crying Why Mama? Why?

Music lie, babies cry
And run fast after their mothers
Preachers preach, teachers teach
As brothers kill brothers
I'm so dumb I ain't got a mouth
Or smart words to send
Went north and ended south –
How to begin — LOOK OUT! WRONG WAY!
I'm losing track of night and day
And say Why Mama? Why?

World of fatherless children
I know and say
AIN'T YOU GOT NO EYES, WORLD?
LOOK! LOOK! YOU'RE GOING THE WRONG WAY
It takes a fool to see a fool
And you know, fool, I see
Money's got your mind
Bread's got your head
Diamonds are glass, man
And gold's just lead

I said like your head's led.
And who's whose who
In Humpty Dumpty minds?
Bones are brittle
All's in the middle
And insane eyes do shine.
Can you see back through all your heads
Living forever in no time?
Whose thought are you stuck in?
Or can I explain there's nothing to teach
Where's the breached breach?
All is a part of the One
That we must die to reach,
Yet not reaching for another —
And giving on the sneak —
For who understands Why Mama Why?
Only your father

— C. Manson Letter from Los Angeles County Jail/
1971

.

1968 - 1969

The School Bus

In Sacramento we spotted it, a short, rusted, orange school bus beside a stucco house with a broken window and scattered evidence of kids. As we turned into a dirt driveway, a muscular man with the beginnings of a beard came out of the house, followed by a long line of whooping kids and their fat momma yelling for them to settle down. The man and Charlie hit it off right away and they began discussing a trade. He said his bus was worth about two hundred. Charlie told him we'd just paid a thousand for the VW bus but would be happy to trade straight across. The man said it didn't make sense to him, a thousand for two hundred. He worked at a local cannery and said he could really use the money, but, with six kids, he needed his bus. So he invited us inside for coffee, and to scan the phone book for bus retailers, and, then for supper, and then to park for the night.

The Van Deutches* became a part of our lives as we camped inside *their* bus for nearly a month while locating a small, retired yellow school bus, trading it for our VW, and refurbishing it in their back yard. Van and his sixteen-year-old son said that they "hobbied" at auto mechanics, and proceeded to rebuild our entire engine. The rest of us gutted the insides, unbolted and removed the heavy seats, laid carpet remnants, and built a partition between the driver's area and the back, including a door for complete privacy.

Evenings, we ate and sang with the family — canned beans and country-western mostly — and during that month the younger kids began to argue with their mother about going to school, the teenagers talked about going *with* us, and the mother seemed ready, at times, to tell us just to go. Mary suffered pregnancy blues and I suffered a miscarriage.

I was fairly sure I had caused it. I'd had a blow-up with Charlie during which I secretly wished that I wasn't pregnant. I'd cried on my way out of the bus — conspicuously reminiscent of leaving my father's house — then turned around, took off my shoes, and crawled into bed behind Mary. She'd kept quiet, but slid one of her hands behind her back into one of mine. That was how she consoled me, not with words but with rare gestures that meant much more. I would find consolation for losing the baby only after learning that one of my grandmothers had had four miscarriages in between nine healthy children.

It was a dry season in Sacramento. Work inside the bus was hot, and Mary and I were both irritable, but Patricia, the Lighthearted, decided that we should sing. The latest to our entourage, Patty usually yielded to our moods, but damned if she didn't assert herself at times, in this case dragging me kicking and snickering into a farcical opera. She and I were nailing down carpet at the back of the bus, while Mary worked at the front, hidden by the partition. Patty sang out,

> "Maarryy! We hear your hammer as you ding it —
> But don't say anything unless you siinngg it!"

168

For a moment it seemed that our levity hadn't traveled, until we heard two descending tuba tones:

"Fuckkk

yoouuuuu."

Patty was the backup singer that Charlie had wanted, but she wasn't interested in solo work. Ever the complement, she nudged and tugged the rest of us along. Mary might be the holdout, but physical hardships and recalcitrance were no match for the strength of her love.

The Van Deutches couldn't have been more hospitable, yet they were the poorest family I had ever met. Their poverty, however, had no affect on their fundamental character. The father was handsome, calm, steadfast, and strongly protective of his family. He drew lines, set an example, and had their respect.

The mother, with her hands full, had let her body go. More than a hundred pounds over a healthy weight, full of exasperation and complaint, she yelled at and swatted the kids, but they and her husband gave her purpose. Jealously, she clung to and wrestled her yoke.

The six kids were bright-eyed beautiful, full of unsophisticated wonder. Without the spoils of plenty, they were excited by small gifts and opportunities. Charlie gave the musically inclined six-year-old a downsized guitar and taught him chords. Mary and I listened to the dreams of the oldest girl, and made doing the dishes fun.

But I couldn't leave this story without mentioning one of our questionable influences. Van's oldest son came to the bus one night, and asked to try marijuana. Charlie warned that his father would be against it. But then he relented. When Van found out, he was ready to fight. I expected him to hit Charlie. But that didn't happen. Charlie talked him into coming inside the bus to smoke a joint so that he could at least speak with experience. To my knowledge, it was the only marijuana Van ever had, but the lasting result between him and Charlie was a funny and mellow peace.

With their hospitality, the Van Deutches gave us a rebuilt school bus, and a view from inside a loving, hard-working family. I hope that we gave them more than troubles.

We visited Peter DeLeo several times while we were in Sacramento, but we took a sharp detour after meeting his main girl, April.* She was a beauty with natural auburn hair and the freshness of a debutante. Pete was more than twenty years her senior and attractive in only the way that confidence can be, but I figured they must need each other in the business. We girls questioned Charlie about Pete's business. He teased that he could get us jobs if we were so interested. The prospect was both exciting and repellant. "The world's oldest profession" perhaps always has been equally romanticized and shunned. After talking it over, we said we would like to see for ourselves. He questioned us further. *Were we sure?* We considered it an opportunity and we were sure.

"You gotta have larceny in your heart to do this," Pete told me from one side of his mouth. "You got larceny in your heart?" I didn't know what the word meant, but I smiled and answered weakly in the affirmative. He sloughed off a laugh. He knew better, but we were available and worth a try. April was sisterly in preparing us for our first customer who would arrive at the house in less than an hour. She helped us scrub, shave, perfume, and dress, while instructing us in the art of seductive foreplay that was, in reality, a check for venereal disease. She explained that our first customer would be having "a party" — just him and the three of us.

The man I'll call "Roger" was thick around the middle and reminded me of a friendly rhinoceros, but he was a lug. He lay on his back while the three of us worked on him like lifeguards. It became clear that he was prolonging the session, so we upped the persuasion, feigned ecstasy, and finally closed the deal. April, who discreetly took care of the financial dealings, had listened to us on the intercom. She was pleased. Each of us cleaned up in the bathroom. I was glad to be done with Roger, only to learn that I would be accompanying him on an all-night "date."

April gave me a short green evening dress and matching heels, and I was off on a whirlwind tour of middleclass bars. Roger told me that I would be meeting people, but he wouldn't tell me who I was supposed to be. Inside the first bar he introduced me as Melanie Lane — his "secretary" — to a group of suited men who seemed jocularly un-fooled by my title. At each of three bars, he introduced me to men. Then he and I perched on barstools with highballs, pretending confidential conversation. Though two years below the legal drinking age, I was never carded, but not having had alcohol for months turned me giddy after the first gimlet. Soon, at my urging, we were whirling around a dance floor, me and Roger Rhinoceros.

Later, at a candlelit restaurant laid with red cloth napkins and tablecloths, we had oversized steaks with the fire marshal in an adjoining town.

"She looks young, doesn't she," Roger said, happily lifting a lock of hair from my shoulder, "but she *is* over twenty-one." Roger might have been an attorney, or an investigator. He had a police radio in his car and discussed "cases" with his cohorts. He'd ask, "What was his name, honey?" and I'd look like I was thinking through my filing cabinets. Then he'd throw out a name, and I'd chirp, "That's it!" So went the ad-libs through the night. There were more drinks I couldn't finish, along with most of the steak. When we finally retired to our hotel room, Roger was chortling. "You did very well tonight," he said, leering at me. I lumbered into bed, nauseated and not at all inclined to put up with his rhinoceros appendages.

The next day, as we drove back to Pete's house, Roger sang along with the radio: "Getting to know you, getting to know all about you..." I thought of the police radio. He told me he would see me again, that we would go golfing and bowling. I asked him where his wife lived. As soon as we got back to the house, I saw Charlie go in a side door, and I jumped out of the car with my shoes in my hand. This was not the life for me. Mary and Patty were not thrilled with it either. Contrary to April's assurances about her clients, Patty had been roughly treated. April was unapologetic. She rebuked Charlie for allowing himself to be seen coming into the house. She was furious that we had jeopardized her business simply so that we could have "an experience." Moralizing about the way we were living, without structure or regard for money, she made a point that she was sending her five-year-old daughter to a *conservative* Catholic school.

Initially standing up on our behalf, Charlie chose instead to leave our share of the evening's earnings with April. We would later understand that she considered us "spoiled" because she had *earned* her way up in this business, starting in migrant flophouses turning ten-dollar tricks at roughly *ten per hour.*

Sexy Susan was a stripper in a San Francisco cabaret. Stretched on the Persian rug in a big Victorian house on Lyon Street, propped on one elbow, she was barefoot and dressed in an orange sweatshirt, and jeans, staring at Charlie, not saying a word. He was strumming his guitar, and appeared unconscious of the six or eight people who had gathered to listen.

At least four people sublet rooms in the house. I spent some time talking with a thin blonde rolling her short wavy hair in curlers. That was Ella, an experienced woman on break from college. She looked like a 1930s actress, with a bright smile as ready as her conversation. Susan felined through the room with theatrical confidence, glancing, but not speaking. She reminded me of the girls called "cheap" in high school, the red wispy hair at her shoulders, the dark brunette on top, the way her back arched and she walked breasts first; yet beneath a few slivers of bangs was a face that looked almost holy, pale and subdued.

The Lyon street residents were between jobs or tired of school, and they had run out of rent money. They asked Charlie if they could travel with us on the bus. He passed the question to us. Patty smiled and shrugged, Mary was prepared for it, and I felt, like each of them, that the decision wasn't mine.

"I left the Establishment," Susan would say later, "the moment I stepped on the bus in San Francisco, and I never will become a part of the Establishment again."

Mary or Charlie usually drove the big bus by everyone's preference, the rest of us riding in back, feeling the wind through the open windows and the road beneath us. Susan opened up on the bus. She talked so much, and laughed so loud, I reconsidered the prospects of living with her. There was a haunted loneliness about her that she covered with careless flippancy and daring, with sly silences, and brash bombast. Charlie chuckled, telling me that Susan was not crazy but "coming from another side." I thought she was embarrassing. She talked too much, and said inappropriate things. She pushed herself to the center of attention, competing for anyone or anything at hand. When men were around, she waited to the side, watching for the best moment to come curling her tail, or, if necessary, to pounce.

It was rumored that Susan had watched her mother die in her arms, and grew up on the far side of the tracks, experimenting with boys on brown grass beds. She said she'd been to prison for armed robbery with two guys on a joyride, that she hadn't done the robbery, just waited in the car. She'd had "an affair" with a woman in prison, she said, and she seemed to hold that over us girls like a degree in experience and a show of nerve. As we lay resting in the moving bus, having stayed up late the night before, I felt her hand on mine, alerting caution. But it was not a sneaking or lustful hand, only a hand that wanted to be accepted, so I did, and we lay quiet, listening to the rattles and rumbles of the bus, watching shapes of sunlight slide through the windows onto the ceiling — not drugged, just relaxed, in touch and comfortable, like girls much younger — until we were both smiling conspiratorially with no real secret but the feeling of being a secret together.

Whenever we needed gas or a mechanic, Susan was the first to volunteer to get it. She'd come back in a pickup truck, her body brushed against some bare brawny arm, or in a station wagon beside a goggle-eyed guy who was gulping and loosening his tie. As she scooted from the seat, she couldn't wait to tell us how perfectly it had happened. That was Susan's forte, to go out and get everything without necessarily having to give up anything. Charlie collaborated in showing her off, one time even asking her to go to Rio for a coconut. Without hesitation, without pausing to ask directions or pack a bag, she started for South America. Had he not stopped her...

From collaboration, Susan advanced to competition. One night, as Charlie talked, she talked. I think it was her way of *being* him, but it looked like a challenge. She said exactly what he was saying a fraction of a second behind him. He laughed and played it, tripping her up only a few times, and using the game to entertain visitors with stereophonic conversation. The challenge she had foisted fell away, and for the moment she loved him beyond herself; there was nothing she could do about it.

Scattered along California's roads, streets, and highways, seekers of all generations were headed for the beaches, mountains, communes and farms, for San Francisco, Monterey, Malibu, and Southeast Asia. No matter how light, or high, or blasé the times, the distant, ugly, unpopular war ran undercurrent to the common consciousness. Even those not contesting the war seemed to carry an uneasy responsibility.

Charlie said that his responsibility began wherever he was.

We picked up hitchhikers, pulling to the curb and opening the folding doors like a city bus. They were hippies, migrant workers, soldiers, and lots of runaways. A slight fourteen-year-old boy was coming south to see his brother after four months of travel. We asked how he avoided the cops.

"Like if I'm on the street," he said, "I might point to a hippie-looking lady and say, 'That's my mom, officer,' and they'd leave me alone. One time I was ready to run. The cop went up to this lady, and I just knew she was gonna say, 'I don't have a son,' but she was cool! She looked at me and shook her head 'yes,' and he just walked away."

Plenty of kids had been kicked out, but few were expected to stay away. They were to beg back into their parents' favor, or be punished by juvenile authorities.

"My mother is *always* miserable," a teenage girl told us. "And she wants *me to be like her!*" Charlie said that some parents "hold on in reverse," fostering an ongoing conflict of misery and guilt from which their children rebel but can't escape.

Patricia

Did your parents seem to dislike you yet want you to depend upon them forever? Did they hold you down, pull your energy and leave you to your tears? (And when you left) did they make you feel guilty? Do they think you belong to them, mind, body and soul?

— Patricia Krenwinkel, 1970

A freckled runaway was sharp and blunt: "My parents act like I'm the cause of all their problems. Now they can argue with each other."

Patricia

My father wanted all my attention... I was the object in a wicked game of vengeance with my mother, bounced across the table, in the center of every argument. And then my parents would say "Where have we gone wrong?"

— Patricia Krenwinkel, 1970

Patty's parents had held together until she was seventeen, after which she had ping-ponged across the country to be with each of them. She loved them but had a healthy desire for independence. When we came along, she was self-motivated, self-supporting, and alone, even while sharing rent with her older sister. Patty's sister was involved in a dangerous lifestyle that Patty didn't share. Whether it was as easy as it appeared for her to leave Manhattan Beach, it almost certainly was essential to her well-being.

Susan said she'd felt alone in her family since the age of five. That's when her younger brother was born, and her parents were evidently clueless as to how to introduce him into the family. Her mother, she said, was always busy with the baby, while her father continued to do "boy stuff" with her older brother. She was not invited to join either of them. Rather than crying about it, she'd begun an emotionally independent life, challenging herself to do things that gave her a sense of accomplishment and identity. "By the third grade," she said, "I was the best shoplifter in the neighborhood."

Charlie said that rebelliousness and destructive drives could be "thought through" and "laid to rest in the mind." As much as I liked to consider him an ally against my own parents, he said he saw no reason for any of us to hold our parents in contempt. Our parents, he said, had done a good job in raising us "to this very moment." If we blamed them, we'd have to blame their parents, and *their* parents, and all the parents before them. And if we didn't blame them? We could more easily leave them behind. The socially irresponsible notion of walking away from our pasts was offset by the very real feeling that the present was all we could realistically be responsible for. Religious leaders would later point out to me that Jesus of Nazareth had done just that.

It wasn't long before all male passengers but Charlie found reasons to depart, leaving him with five women. Each of us took on small tasks, and together were a pale river in which he swam. There was jealousy. It didn't manifest outwardly as much as within: a wretched, harrying wraith wringing twisted hands inside our chests, stifling breath and spirit. It wrestled each one of us, and sometimes got us down. Mary was so afflicted she cried.

The paradox was in Charlie's transparency. He could have been an ordinary philanderer or bigamist. He could have taken each of us separately and told us nothing of the others. He might have said, "Honey, I'll be on the road with my music and if you want to do something for me, and stick by me, you should get a good job, and an apartment, and start putting money in the bank so we'll have something when I get back." He could have become an entertainer, a motivational speaker, a preacher, or any form of professional guru, and he *could've* had homes all over the country. Instead, he brought us together, witnessed our struggles, and sang.

"If I told you what I thought
Would it change your opinion?
If I told you how bright you are,
Could you make the change?
How can one compete with the ocean?
How can one compare the sun?"

— Road Song, C. Manson, 1967

He had quit singing standardized music months before, preferring to explore music of the moment. It was a loss to me. Standard arrangements were a great vehicle for his voice. But his spontaneity was interesting, the words and music always changing, and even when the words were scat, he connected with his audience rhythmically, bobbing and tapping, his face animate. He was a natural entertainer, but I think that conscientious objection kept him from an entertainment career. He said, "Soul in music is the expression of feeling, not an act of entertainment."

We struggled with ourselves. I bogged down in self-criticism. He encouraged us seriously, "Don't get down on yourself for getting down on yourself. We each do what we do because that's what we know to do," and humorously, "Learning to walk doesn't start with the first step. One must first stand. Walking doesn't work well unless one stands."

Charlie

You say how nice it is to offer someone "the best,"
and that is a nice thought illusion, but if you play best
then there must be a worst. You would probably feel
ashamed of me if I took a booger out of my nose and
put it on the Queen of England's hat. And if I gave you
a piece of candy with hair, sand, dirt, and tobacco on
it, you could wrinkle up your nose and say, "I take
only the best." All that is, is. So we can play it is
whatever, but we wink in knowing the universe has
always been perfect. I don't know how to make the
universe any better, do you?

— C. Manson, c 1973, letter to Lyn

He offered new views, new moves, and basic prob-
lem solving. "If it doesn't work one way, try another."
One time he told us a riddle. I call it An Impossible
Situation or How to Play Chess:

The captives of a conquering army were brought in
succession before its king and asked why they should
not be put to death. One man replied that he was but
a lowly rug maker.

"I will spare your life for one deed," said the king.
"Make me a rug to cover my entire kingdom. You have
until sunrise." Thus dismissed, the condemned man
was confined to ponder his fate. The rug maker would
survive. What did he do?

I'll give you the answer if you don't know it. I never
solved these riddles, but I loved that they that made us
figure. He didn't claim to have invented them. He said
he was telling us what others had told him. That was
important. He gave credit. He acknowledged others'

words and work. It wasn't flattery and it wasn't gratuitous. Everyone over the age of five knows the difference. I believe he'd seen people steal credit for other people's work, and that, to him, a boss stealing credit for ideas and accomplishments of employees would've been worse than stealing their worldly goods. His attitude bulldozed mental debris that had me stuck in yesterday. He said that he, himself, started over each day as if he'd never lived the day before. And in answer to the riddle, he said that the rug maker made the king a pair of shoes.

Recognition of truth is instant. I recognized it in Shakespeare, Moliere, and other writers. It may grab you, stun you, inform, or make you laugh. You want to see or hear or read it again. It's a gift, and you're grateful. That's what Charlie was to us. Words were meaningful to him. He once asked me, "Do you know how to keep from breaking promises?" And when I didn't respond, he said, "Don't make them." It was so simple.

He could talk in ways only understood by his target audience. The rare times I heard him make reference to this he called it "talking on the down low." It was a dodge of old outlaws and prisoners, and he was unconsciously fluent in it. He also communicated indirectly. One time in Sacramento he chastened me in front of Peter DeLeo for something I hadn't done. Later he told me he'd been talking *through* me to Pete. He said, "If it doesn't apply, pay it no mind."

So on the one hand, he acknowledged our works and our efforts, but on the other, he didn't coddle our egos. Once, after he lauded the feminine aspects of life, he said to me, "What makes you think I was talking about your little personality? My woman is the earth."

The ambivalence I had perceived in Charlie's view of women was not limited to two sides. As with men, he apparently had views from all women he had met, and he portrayed them, from the society gossips who begged, "Oh do tell..." to the nannies and servants who took care of their children. He didn't do imitations, but reverberations, and only in the context of the time and place and person(s) to whom he was speaking. Of servants, he said they are always more aware than the people they serve, and "the real master is the best servant." He knew country women. Whether describing his relatives or others, he didn't say, but in many ways his written description reminds me of my own country grandmother.

Charlie

    She was up at the sun and put fire in the stove, grabbed a bucket and was off to the barn, milked and fed the cows, came back put a meal on the table, homemade butter and bread, little if any store bought food, and I mean A MEAL. Then she slopped the hogs, fed chickens, turkeys, rabbits, got dressed for Sunday school, went to church, came home at 11:00 and at 12:00 or 1:00 had another meal on the table for six people. Tops, the best. She put on three a day, and worked seventeen hours a day to make ends meet. With little money, everything they needed they raised or grew themselves. Not a nail or board would go to waste, not a rag or string got trashed. In fact, the trash was little for everything was used and reused. There wasn't no scotch tape or paper clips, staples or ballpoints, no plastic, no waste. They was good, honest, and had not even a thought about it or knowing of the difference.

I've watched the progression of woman from wagons to space ships, from no smoking or bad words — and I don't know if it's progress or decline. I guess it all depends on what's wanted, what's the goal and reason. I was never schooled into judgments of it.

— C. Manson, c 1984, letter from prison

In the days of living closely together, we girls rebuffed, mirrored and embraced each other, exchanging random thoughts, and discovering that many of our unconscious thoughts worked against us. It was easy to see that if our minds had to climb over a clutter of negatives to access intuitive knowledge, our energy and potential were wasted. While now commonly understood, these introspections were new to us. We realized that we had accepted ideas about ourselves and the world as we toddled out of self-centeredness and learned to live in the thoughts of adults. We had mimicked them and fit in to our advantage, but we also had languished in their unconscious limitations of themselves. Superficially, we called it "negative programming," or "brainwashing," and it was roundly agreed that our brains could benefit from another washing.

The bus was a camp with sleeping bags and a Coleman stove. It was a modern cushioned living room, a sheik's lair, a think tank, a space capsule, whatever we wanted or needed. "Tripping" was therapeutic. Like psychotherapy, psychedelics provided inside info, the so-called hallucinations not mere distortions of the senses, but dreamlike states revealing subconscious thought in both a tactile and detached way. We didn't stop to fear these substances, but would learn to respect their potency, and limit use. Not all visions were pleasant. Charlie advised us to watch them pass without judgment. In my experience, the more natural the setting, the more universal the understandings, and accessible the peace.

About that time, the Beatles debuted a new album. They sang that "The Magical Mystery Tour" was dying to take us away. Death and dying took on new meanings. Someone aptly described a common psychedelic experience as the poignant sensation of life's resilience and its fragility, of its humor and sadness all at once. It blew our minds and brought us to the living present, an awareness common to the terminally ill — but who, after all, is not terminal?

Rational people who have concluded psychedelics to be nothing more than drug-induced insanity, unworthy of further study, might consider that sleep triggers the same fall into sub-realities, some more bizarre than we would consciously imagine. All the exact measurements and perfect formulas in the world do not explain dreaming, birth, death, or infinity. The realization that there is *no end* to the sky that surrounds us can be shocking. For those comforted by maxims and finite figures, the thought of infinity is completely insane.

Charlie said that "the soul" doesn't die or grow old. He didn't say that bodies would last forever, but we came to believe that we could "die" in thought so that *spirit* could live through our bodies for as long as we had them. Most of us got glimpses into this reality, but any attempt to capture and hold it erased the experience. We awoke from dreams of profound illumination knowing nothing but fleeting images and feelings. Beyond gradual understandings of our individual selves, and perhaps those of our ancestors, was a larger and lasting consciousness of oneness with all life. In that thought, we opened our minds to the discovery of intelligence and communication from *every living thing.*

People communicate on levels beneath their own awareness. Charlie said that, if we looked, we could see their communications in their eyes, their facial expressions, the movements of their hands and bodies. His understandings surfaced as both a courtesy, and a self-protection. One day he told us that our sense of freedom frightened some people, and that our happiness made unhappy people uncomfortable.

"People who can't dance and sing don't want to see other people dancing and singing unless it's on the radio or TV because it reminds them they're stuck." Those of us gleefully shedding inhibitions felt entitled to celebrate, but his read of other people seemed to produce in him both empathy and caution. It was more considerate and also wise at times to dim our enthusiasm. He called it "playing under."

As for the loudly touted ideal of "freedom," he was a realist. Once, as I watched a soaring seagull, he said to me, "You think that bird is free, but it's dictated by cold, heat, rain — and some days it don't eat."

In those days it was common to see buses and vans parked on the sides of roads so that the occupants could see the sights or sleep for a night. Nibbling raisins from workers behind a packing plant, or dining on camp grub overlooking the ocean, the thrill of travel, and the beauty of California got into us. On

185

massive breakwater cliffs beside Monterey Bay, wind-bent branches appeared to conduct sunset symphonies. Once a whaling town, Monterey was still home to a few scrimshaw artists carving tiny tableaux on whalebone. Locals said that at the turn of the century those shores had been heaped *fifteen feet high* with whale bones, and that a few might still be found. Most of us had never seen a whale, in whole or in part, except in books.

Seated on the carpet, after a meal, Charlie said that living with a harem was the stuff of prisoners' dreams. Then he added, "But it's not fair to you." We women smiled at each other, shrugging. He explained that his energy was limited, after which he was cheating us of both companionship and sexual love. He asked, "Where are all the guys?" and concluded, "They must be in prison, or at war." He said we should think about it.

Why would he want the complications of more men? Some of the girls may have liked the idea, but I think *all* of us wanted to be with *him*. Was his suggestion a tactical intention to recruit a malleable following? Was he plotting, even then, to send an army of young people against "The Establishment?"

The bus was stopped by curious police, and cited for its color. I think we got two traffic tickets for that. The salesman hadn't told us that, although the name of the school district had been removed, the yellow bus was legally still a school bus, and could not be privately operated as such. We would have to paint it. About that time we met Tony and Pancho. They were coming out of a house in one of the rundown suburbs of L.A., but it was the choppers that first caught Charlie's attention, custom motorcycles with high handlebars and long front ends. He got out of the bus to talk to their owners.

Tony could have been a pachuco, but he wasn't Mexican. Blond, green-eyed, muscular but lean, he was wearing jeans, and a white T-shirt under a plaid wool Pendleton. His mustache curled up at the corners, and he had small, straight teeth that showed when he saw five girls looking out the windows of the bus at him. His best buddy, Pancho, was also cute, but short, copper colored, and four legged — a Corgi. Tony took us inside the house where his biker buddies milled around, and one svelte young woman in curlers was putting on makeup, getting ready for work. After hearing our story, some of the bikers volunteered to paint the bus. The resulting beer-fueled extravaganza of provocative graffiti would have brought an endless chain of police, so we diplomatically blacked the whole thing, inside and out.

Unfortunately for Tony, the motorcycles around the house belonged to his friends. His bike was in pieces, literally a wreck, and he didn't have the money for another one. Furthermore, rent on the house had expired; everyone had to move. Charlie asked Tony if he'd ever driven a bus. He hesitated, but the outcome was predictable. Pancho jumped onto the box-heater beside the driver's window, as Tony sat down in the seat. It was a good fit. By his smile we knew he would agree.

Tony and Charlie spent the next several hundred miles talking guy stuff, generally apart from us women. Everyday dynamics in the bus changed, but rather than feeling excluded, we girls were lit with feminine energy. Tony was quiet with a dry sense of humor. Wherever we went, he attracted female attention, but he wasn't one to make the first move with a woman, and seemed clueless as to what to do with five. Charlie, goofing around in the back of the bus, took my hand, as he was talking to Tony, laid me down, and mischievously pretended that I was a motorcycle. He half stripped me, carefully examined and polished my parts, made sure that I was sufficiently oiled, and set about turning on my ignition, all while talking like he was checking out a new ride. He didn't do much more than rev me up, but I think he succeeded in showing Tony that we were no more difficult, and no less fun, than motorcycles.

We decorated and accessorized the bus a la hermit crab. Someone gave us the bleached skull of a goat that we mounted on the grill, and a friend built us a box about the size of a coffin to hold a water tank on the roof. In Sacramento Peter DeLeo introduced us to a "candy man" who loaded that box with every shape and flavor of his goods, and later in San Francisco, while checking the load, Charlie and Tony tossed packages of candy down to passersby, like beads at Mardi Gras.

Speaking of beads, I don't remember any of us wearing them. We were too active for beads. And we didn't say "groovy" either. We did say "wow" a lot. Charlie said things that the rest of us picked up: "All is one." "It's always now." They made as much sense as the rest of the world. He said there was no time, and no death, and "no such thing as no such thing." He asked, "Is there anything new? Does the earth weigh more than it did 100,000 years ago?"

> Charlie
>
> Nothing ended. Nothing began. People say "end" but that only means one change moving into another. The ball begins to bounce. It stops bouncing and begins to roll. It stops rolling and begins to decay. It stops rotting and blows away.

Hitchhikers asked us, "Where are you going?"

We said, "Nowhere."

They asked, "Where are you coming from?"

We laughed. "Nowhere."

They asked, "Well, what're you doing?"

And, of course, we said, "Nothing," explaining that we were doing whatever was "happening" at the moment, "being at home when the soul calls," "touring the planet," "group therapy" — whatever struck our fancy.

And people asked, "How do you live?"

We said, "Good! We give everything away and we still have everything."

So one day, a miserable malingering college boy stated, "I want the bus."

We said, "You have the bus — you're on it."

But he said, "You say you give everything away. I want the bus, and I want you all to leave." We were stunned.

Charlie asked, "Do you really want to do that to yourself?" He did.

So without further comment, everyone got a change of clothes, and left the bus. We decided on a meeting place, and hitchhiked in pairs to Malibu, where we resorted on a balmy beach under a bridge. By the time all had arrived, we'd found a wooden house across the highway, in a flowery hollow, down a sandy lane, and up a spiral staircase, a house reputedly "donated by an older hippie chick to be left open to whoever needs it."

The Spiral Staircase House

Dropping down off the busy coast high-way between sparse trees, Topanga Canyon Lane was a dirt road to maybe a dozen 1920s beach retreats secreted in plain sight. One house made of raw, dark wood, had spiraling wooden stairs to thick front doors. Inside was a meeting room such as kids might use at camp, with benches attached to surrounding walls, and a picnic table near the kitchen. Two rooms at the back of the house accommodated us for sleeping.

"The Lane" was outwardly sedate. However, "Hippie" was alive and well in Topanga Canyon Lane, where the garbage man not only took away grass, but delivered it. Then two weeks after we moved in, we received notice from a Northern California police department advising us to pick up our bus. It had been abandoned. Tony and Ella went to reclaim it. Good thing, because the Spiral Staircase House was a known inn for travelers.

Our next bus trip was just for the tripping. Charlie was always looking for warmer weather, Patty's mother lived in Alabama, and many of us had never been to Florida. Before departure we cast ourselves as "HOLLYWOOD PRODUCTIONS." The idea was to give the bus a pass, and Hollywood people seemed to have a pass to go anywhere. A pretty French artist living in The Lane needed something to do, and we needed professional-looking signs. We got her some white paint, and returned to see "HOLIWOOD PRODUCTIONS" in perfect six-inch block letters on both sides of the bus. Despite her French accent, none of us had thought to tell her how to spell it. Charlie said that we should add a number to the title, and chose the number 9 for no reason that I know of.

Our southern trip is abbreviated in both my memory and notes. We spent a night trekking barefoot through New Mexico's White Sands National Monument, leaving the bus parked by the perimeter fence. It was fortunate for us that the police arrived after we had re-tucked ourselves inside it, and that it was so late it was early, and that Charlie, by fluke in a long religious/theatrical robe, was able to quietly explain that the rest of our entourage were asleep in the back. We'd barely covered and hushed ourselves when he opened the partition door, allowing them to shine flashlights inside. Re-closing it, he assuaged their concerns about vagrancy and trespassing, asking if they hadn't seen the signs on the sides of the bus. They flash-lit "Holiwood Productions," cordially advised a better place to park, and left.

My next memory is of a small Texas college town where the bus broke down and the service station mechanic said something about a two-week wait for the necessary replacement part. Some college boys offered to share their apartment, rain kept us inside, I had a stomach sickness, and time dragged.

Patty got use of a car, deciding to travel with a few other girls to see her mother in Alabama. While gone, they had a potentially fatal collision. Patty was driving across a bridge when three dogs "seemed to come out of nowhere." She swerved the car, crashed the rail, and wound up over the edge of the bridge. Shaken and a little bruised, the girls were otherwise sound. Patty said later that she couldn't help her reaction because the dogs had "made eye contact" with her. In hindsight, if Patricia Krenwinkel had been killed or disabled in that crash, would Abigail Folger be alive today? That didn't happen.

When we got the bus back, Rob* and Deuce*, whose apartment we'd shared, asked to travel with us. As the weather was cold and the bus needy, Florida was out of reach. Heading back to California through higher elevations, we got snowed down in Winslow, Arizona. We had to leave the bus in a small service station, divide up and hitchhike on roads with seven-foot snow banks on either side. It was a cold 2:00 a.m. but I remember being warmed by a paper cup of coffee, and the heater in the cab of a semi rolling toward someplace warm like Bakersfield. Charlie traveled alone, naturally got picked up by a young woman, and later, with *un*characteristic amazement, reported seeing a *monkey* running around in the snow. He got out of the car to see if he could coax it inside but it ran away.

Once again grounded in Topanga Canyon Lane, we made ourselves at home, but more lodgers soon came up the Spiral Staircase: an uncombed six-foot-four-inch mountain man hoisting dirty outdoor gear, a wildly dark gypsy-looking woman in long skirts, and a cherubic young girl. As we adjusted accommodations, all eyes went to the girl. She was closer to twelve than twenty, with a freckled nose, thick, straight auburn hair, striking blue-green eyes, and luminous skin like pale fresh fruit. The two older people who brought her were not her parents. Later, I saw her surrounded by a small group of neighbors and figured that she was used to being stared at. There was no ignoring that Diane was pubescent, but she was also childlike. She was soon scooped into our social circles, while the black-haired woman with big bones and teeth, and the mountain man missing a few were entertained by others. Truth told, Diane was not happy with them, and they were not happy when she opted to stay with us. They tried very hard to talk her out of it. Later she told us that during the past year she had lived with different people, including one couple who shared her in rough sex with biting and pinching.

Diane's parents were middle-aged hippies who, a year before, when she was thirteen, had dropped out of conventional life to explore alternatives. Trusting, idealistic people, they had allowed her to travel with other hippies, and so it was that she came with us. Charlie knew that I was jealous of Diane. He finally stopped, looked me in the eyes, smiled, embraced me, shrugged, and said, "She's your sister." I loved my sister, but by then the words "sister" and "brother" had enlarged in popular meaning to include persons with backgrounds and identities like oneself. In that context, we women were a sisterhood, and Diane had become one of us.

Diane's parents and her own younger sister soon arrived in their van. They were attractive, arguably innocent people. The eight-year-old could roll a lid of weed quicker than any of the adults, and she never smoked it. They talked about going to see land their friends had purchased in the Nevada desert. Tony had regained our bus, so we made a group trip of it, their family, our "family," and another family with small children.

The most striking thing about the desert is the space. One Los Angeles mayor had suggested using the Mojave Desert as a repository for the city's massive quantities of garbage because he thought it was good for nothing else. We were just realizing that the space of the world was as important as the clutter, that a stretch for the eyes and mind could give new perspective.

For two days we drove down long empty roads. The rumble of the bus engine was mesmerizing. One night I spaced out until exclamations from the others drew me to the open windows. Some distance across that dark, flat landscape with its shady globs of brittle bushes was a phosphorescent green dome. It was big and looked alternately solid and translucent. It might have been a domed stadium or shopping center — but all around it was space, not even a road. We looked at each other in unspoken wonder as the green dome shrank into the distance, and we were just settling down when the bus engine died, abruptly engulfing us in loud silence.

The men got out to examine the engine. A flashlight beam bounced about the enveloping darkness. The bus door squeaked open, and one of the men got in to start it, but after half a dozen attempts, it was decided that we should wait until daylight.

People in the bus began nervously spreading blankets and expressing fears — half joking — of giant green insects staring in the windows. Their jocular fear made me smile involuntarily. When Charlie came to the door, I looked to include him in the humor, but was startled by his expression. He was absent. To no one in particular he said, "There's too much fear in here," and he took a sleeping bag outside. I lay down with questions, but my consciousness was extinguished with the light.

Bright sunshine poured through the open windows, people stirred, and we clambered out of the bus to find large bushes, awed by the pristine panorama. Tony pulled up one of the bus's old-fashioned hood flaps to probe the engine, but when another of the men got into the driver's seat and turned the key, it started. Grinning and shaking his head, Tony called everyone. We filed inside and were off. I had questions for Charlie that I forgot to ask.

After imaginary giant green insects, came a swarm of little red ones. They were all over the highway ahead of us. A closer view clarified: men in red uniforms carrying shotguns. They blocked the road with military efficiency, ordered us out, and, for nearly an hour, went in and out of our bus, rifling its contents. Before dismissing us, they begrudged an explanation: murder. There'd been a murder in the area and they were searching for a rifle.

Returning to Topanga Canyon Lane, Diane's parents waved goodbye to her, and to the happy group of what they thought were typical hippies. We would see them many times, but never once could they see what was ahead for their daughter. And more daughters would come.

Nancy and Didi were sunny, tanned beach kids ditching a Malibu high school when we met them in The Lane. Nancy was small and beautiful with ash-blond hair to her waist, and her chin held high. She was sixteen and savvy, an awarded amateur photographer. Her father, like mine, was an aeronautical engineer, but of a higher echelon, sometimes called in to work for the Pentagon.

Deirdre was taller, a wholesome, sandy-colored girl with freckles. Her parents were successful in the entertainment business, her mother then on Broadway playing the title role in the theatre version of *Auntie Mame.* Since her parents were in New York, the person Didi saw most at home, besides her teenage brother, and an often inebriated uncle, was the maid who let her get away with anything. Both girls began visiting us whenever they could.

Then came Melba, a trim fifty-ish woman with champagne hair and a Southern aristocratic manner. Melba came to The Lane looking for someone to clean her stables, figuring "some hippie kids might do it cheap." We took the job, three or four of us going on weekends into the Malibu hills where her stately white home on a private bluff distantly overlooked the ocean. Melba owned two thoroughbred horses kept in white stables, and, like her, they were high strung and unapproachable. It took a couple of hours to clean out the stalls and bed them with fresh straw. After conceding that we'd done a good job, Melba hesitated, putting probing words into the air about how much she would need to pay us. Her concern about money was unbefitting a woman of her dress. We told her not to worry about it. Then, testily, as if without her own consent, she invited us through the back door of her kitchen for lunch, directing us to wash in the bathroom, and, when we asked, to *go ahead and shower.* Meanwhile, she prepared, from dry ingredients and molasses, Boston baked beans and dark brown bread that we enjoyed with butter at a sunny, glass-topped table in her breakfast room. And, reluctantly, Melba caught herself enjoying our company.

As the weeks went by and the weekends came, Melba opened her back door smiling, and then pretended it was the stables that badly needed our attention, not her. Her home could have been featured in magazines, the elegantly shaped furniture and glass cases displaying artworks in a living room with a full ocean view. In reality, the house had two mortgages. Melba was not wealthy. Her Southern relatives were. She had been married and divorced, and then got into real estate, a job that hadn't worked out for her. She still had litigation in court over a man who had swindled her out of thousands of dollars. Melba said she couldn't bear for her friends and relatives to know it. She was now working in an executive position for a government social service, which enabled her to bring home surplus foods that she gave to us along with the secrets of her true financial status, and things she could divulge to no one else.

The "Cosmic Gathering" was what I heard someone call a night when a projected light show and live music drew to The Spiral Staircase House more people than would fit in it, and we danced down the hollow halls of the infinite. It might have been a New Year's Eve party to neighborhood hippies, but in cosmic perspective, putting lines between years would be trifling. Enter Bobby Beausoleil — "Cupid" to his former band — neither small nor baby-faced, but fine, according to us girls, in a top hat and cape, bobbing through the doorway blowing an instrument he called a kaliedesoon in trickling notes that ran up and down the spines of the dancers, faster and faster until I blanked out.

I awoke alone in our bus, hearing a rhythm that turned out to be rain on the metal roof. Far up The Lane, I heard a tremendous downpour coming. Anxiously, I listened to it approach, pummel the bus, and pass. After a moment came another deluge, and then another, the pattern sounding like sighs relieving the sky, or waves on the beach, or the pulsing of blood through my heart, releasing myself into myself to clean and redeem myself in cycles. The connections awed me.

The bus door cranked opened. Charlie stuck his boot on the stairs, asking me to grab a rag to wipe the mud from it before he got in. He was in good humor, talking with other people. As I cleaned his boot, cradling his foot like a rare treasure, I thought of Bible stories of devoted souls in the reverent act of washing others' feet. My reverie was broken only when he spoke. He didn't sound like Sunday school when he reminded me that I'd left the rest of him and several other people standing out in the rain.

The next day the Spiral Staircase House slept, as if we'd dreamt the night before. An older man named Zeb swept the porch, and dropped word that you could get good eats out of supermarket garbage bins. The treasure he left was to feed us for years.

We girls crept behind Malibu's markets, poking pinched fingers into the bins, and barely touching the piles of surplus food. Then we spied things worth a climb inside: crates of fresh fruits of which some, but not all, had bruises or spots, boxes of lettuce, onions, avocados, tomatoes, and peppers. It was good, nutritious food, and there was only one reason much of it had been tossed away: people didn't want to buy a small stalk of celery or a tomato with a bruise. They wanted picture-perfect goods and left the crooked carrots to us. Meat refuse was entirely avoidable as most markets kept it in separate dumpsters. We were continually surprised by what we found: sealed blocks cheese with a few tiny specks of mold; dented or misprinted packages of such things as crackers and pasta; dozens of *cartons* of cold, fresh eggs on ice, all but one or two intact, albeit a little sticky. We brought it all home, separated it, washed it thoroughly, and set about at different tables to pare it down for pizzas, spaghetti, and stews that fed dozens. We had real butter, bread, and bright, crisp salads, and we came to believe that you could have fed the world with just America's garbage.

One evening after dinner, the men were across The Lane playing music, and some of us girls were doing dishes, when a beefy, bald man with one earring and a heavy black mustache appeared at the kitchen entrance *demanding* to be fed. Two other men stood behind him. Ella coldly lit the flame under the leftovers, as some of us slid into the bedroom to put on more clothes, and Patty asked them where they were from, directing them to drop their bags in the front room. When our guys came in, the strangers were sitting at the picnic table waiting for food.

Charlie introduced himself and El Toro* did the same, maintaining a sneer and an attitude of confrontation. He seemed to believe that the house was his, and that we were intruders. Charlie engaged him in lightweight verbal sparring, after which the man conceded they would only be staying a couple of days. We didn't see them for that long, but the next time the bully came he was alone, and it was specifically for a woman. First he took hold of Patty. Susan challenged him, and someone ran to get Charlie. The ensuing exchange was brief. I didn't hear what Charlie said, but the Bull went straight to the front room where, sitting on a bench, he reached into his satchel. When he removed his hand, I saw the glint of a big blade. Then Charlie did something I never expected and will probably never forget: he went straight to the menacing man, sat down beside him, and turned his back to him. Suddenly the Bull rose, bellowing, and plunged the knife into a wall. Warning this would not be the last from him, he jacked out his knife, and left.

For a few moments, everyone was quiet. After Charlie went out, we girls began to talk, and then to laugh. Charlie had gambled the bully's bluff. It seemed a stunning display of strategy, but in the instant, he couldn't have thought much about it.

The prospect of conflict with the mixed up Toro put a shadow on us. If the police became involved, it could be worse. So, late that night, we gathered our things, boarded the bus, and left The Lane without destination. And there on the highway, hitchhiking, was Bobby Beausoleil, a seeming magician, who directed us high into the hills where he had rented the basement of a burned-down house. "This is Lucifer's place," he said, arching an eyebrow. We landed on the roof.

It was flat. I poked my head over the side and saw that we were standing on top of some rooms. The house had burned, leaving nothing but the basement. It had been renovated. A path led down to an atrium, a kitchen, a family room, a bathroom, and two bedrooms. The family room featured sliding glass doors with a view of the steeply terraced canyon. Bobby had considered fashioning a massive hollow skull on the flat roof, one large enough to live in. At night, he said, its eye socket windows would glow all over the canyon. Light leapt from his own eyes, bright blue glimmers of ideas too many for him, alone, to fulfill — and to what purpose beyond experience? He was nineteen or twenty, an artist by almost any means, with a masterpiece physique, and fair skin contrasted by dark hair. He offered us the basement for as long as we needed it.

Bobby was living in an apartment closer to town, and paid rent on both places with income from movies and rock bands I didn't know about till later. In the ensuing weeks, he dropped by the basement unannounced to spend time with girls. I'd find him in the kitchen at sunrise looking for food, or striding down the walk looking roguish, a role he seemed to relish. One afternoon he stopped by with his guitar, and few words later, he and Charlie were playing what became a long musical conversation. Charlie's rhythms were fundamental, while Bobby's music soared above and around those rhythms. In visual terms, Bobby's music was ornate. His superior ability was obvious, but he was impatient to air it fully, taking off on his own and losing fusion, an Icarus-like lapse. There were meetings and partings. Their styles were different. Yet when the music rose above them and meshed, they looked like they were listening, like *they* were the instruments, and the music was playing them. That was worth waiting for. The whole afternoon was entertaining, but Bobby and Charlie were not putting on a show. They were sounding each other out. At the end of the day, Bobby gave Charlie his top hat, an obvious sign of his respect.

I never realized what a partner or "brother" meant to Charlie before I saw him with Tony and Bobby. Tony didn't much relate to Bobby, or to the music, but he and Charlie were talking about getting motorcycles. They had Harley choppers in mind, but the first thing to come along, a gift to Charlie, was a nice BMW. When Charlie wasn't on it, Tony was. I think he felt more comfortable on a bike than on a woman.

Tony slept beside us, and showed us the utmost respect. We knew that he *liked* us, but he made no move to give anything but brotherly affection. Maybe, like a lot of people, he considered us "Charlie's girls." Maybe he wanted more privacy. Most likely, he wanted an exclusive relationship, but whatever the reason, it bothered him.

Ella was more like a buddy to Tony. She rode on the back of the bike, and carried the stash. They took off on the bike one day, saying they'd be back, but they didn't come back. The next day, Charlie went inside the bus and didn't come out. At late afternoon I went to the door, but it was locked. I knocked. He said, "Go away." There was nothing any of us could say or do to ease the loss of a brother.

Bobby Beausoleil was living up Old Topanga Road with a creamy-skinned older woman who was probably under thirty, but exuded sophistication and maternal tolerance for his uppances and rovings. He was virile and energetic, but took little time with women. When I stopped by their apartment one morning, and he summoned me inside, they appeared to be waking under floral sheets on a mattress in the living room. He stretched to his full length, and patted the woman's butt as she rose for her robe. Then he talked to me from the bathroom while splashing cold water on his face, and running his hands through his hair. He said he thought that I was his landlord, Gary, who lived upstairs. Gary had come earlier that morning while Bobby and the woman were corporally engaged. Bobby said he'd become aware that someone was watching them through the front window, and it turned out to be Gary.

A thin, pale individual, Gary Hinman was cradling a big cross-eyed cat the first time I met him. It vigorously needled and suckled his forearm, drawing specks of blood. Through a tickled grin, Gary explained that the cat had been weaned too early. This wouldn't be worthy of mention, except that within eighteen months Gary would die violently at Bobby's hand, and this is among the few uneasy recollections I have of him.

We had strange visitors to the Basement House. There was the guy Charlie good-humoredly deduced was a "narc," sending him sneaking out the door in the same way he'd tried to sneak in; there was a hairy schizophrenic mute with a young wife and baby; and maybe the strangest of all was the group that came looking for Bobby, a high strung band for whom he had done guitar work in the past. We were just beginning to feel the effects of some potent LSD when they filed into the basement — a noodley boy, and a thin, scowling man carrying a flute like a bludgeon — both dressed in white ballet tights and tunics — followed by two enormously fat, rat-haired women in pink tights, tutus, and mean gashes of makeup. The flautist, ironically uncomfortable being stared at, motioned Bobby aside to put forth his business. The rest stood over us, waiting. They might have been interesting, like a quirky carnival, had they not taken themselves so seriously, but the big women looked like they were hauled around to punch out the first person who laughed. After Bobby declined his proposition, the self-important stick man, followed by the others, left as he had come, bitch-angry.

Ella soon called to say she was coming home, but was concerned about leaving the bike. Charlie told her to tell Tony to keep it. Charlie got temporary use of another bike when we took a trip, the whole group of us in the bus again zonked on acid. I don't know who was driving, but I found myself on foot in a residential neighborhood touring an old man's garden — a luxuriant labor of love for which we showed appropriate appreciation. In another suburban neighborhood, the police stopped us and called for backup. More than a dozen of us stood beside the blaring police radios in bright daylight waiting for officers to process our IDs. Then it occurred to me that we had never paid the bus tickets, and that Charlie, in violation of this, might be subject to arrest. I glanced around the group but didn't see him. Nor was he in either of the police cars. Then I spied, at the end of the long residential block, a group of boys about twelve years old riding Sting Ray bicycles. He was among them.

The police returned our IDs, thanked us for our cooperation, and left. The boys on bikes rode up the street, leaning back to raise their front tires, shouting to Charlie, "That's a wheelie!" Charlie tried a wheelie and they hollered, "Yeah — yeah, like that!" One kid yelled, "Look at this!" Increasing speed, he skidded into a 180 turn. As the rest of us got into the bus, the boys circled and sat on their bikes, talking. A few minutes later, Charlie came walking up the street, separate and removed. I think I knew he always would be. As much as we liked to believe we were not alone, we each lived in separate worlds with different ideas, limitations, and problems. Yet, as in any union, each of our problems was all of our problems.

We still had *dozens* of boxes of bagged chocolates until a four-year-old boy took them. He was, by
definition, a brat, relentlessly whining at his mother's
skirts. His parents were conservatively dressed people, apparently well educated, and possibly affiliated
with the military. They didn't volunteer information
and we didn't ask. When we offered them a place to
rest, they were in a large shopping center, obviously
lost, tired, and traveling with two children, two cars,
and everything they owned. Something had caused
this couple to leave one home in search of another,
without a clue as to where they would land, and their
level of need was such that they were willing to leave
their two young children with hippie strangers for two
weeks while they looked for another place to live. They
also left their red sports car with permission for us to
use it, but Bobby and I spent nine hours in the Redwood City jail before the couple could be located to
verify the fact. It was my first arrest.

At the basement house, the ten-year-old girl fit in
right away, but her four-year-old brother could not be
satisfied. He was smart, and stubbornly determined
to do the opposite of what we were doing. If we were
sitting peacefully, he was stomping, pushing, and
pulling. When we were active, and urging him to come
along, he refused to budge. Charlie spent more time
with him than any of us did, and, one afternoon, summoned us to get out the candy. Someone brought a
single bag, but Charlie said, "No, all of it. He wants us
to throw it all in the swimming pool."

The dry, old stone swimming pool downhill was
half full of blackened debris from the fire. About ten
of us helped carry out the boxes, each containing forty
cellophane bags of chocolates. Charlie had to urge us

to open each bag before hurling them into the pool. Hundreds of chocolates went flying, caramels and stars and mints. Everyone was mute; nobody liked doing it. The boy stood stiff, rocking foot to foot, his eyes darting from one of us to the other. It took maybe ten minutes to complete the task. Then we went into the house without looking at him. From there I watched him sit down beside Charlie overlooking the pool, and I went about my business.

In the days that followed, the boy played by himself amongst us. We were never again awakened by whining, nor did he throw tantrums. Up early one morning, I followed him out the door to the paved road. Descending into the residential canyon, he knew that I was behind him, and he didn't wait for me, but every so often he said something. He pointed out a natural gas pipe and called it a dragon. After what seemed a long walk, I wondered if he was running away. The road became steep and busy with traffic. I decided to stop him. That's when he dropped out of sight. In a panic, I ran until I came to a mailbox. Looking down the mountain through treetops, I saw him standing on the landing of some long wooden stairs. Grinning. He was waiting for me. My relief was replaced by propriety. This was obviously the stairway to somebody's house. The boy's little body kicked around the landing, and he looked up at me again. "*Somebody's house*," I was thinking. With a clear expression of disgust, he continued downstairs without me. I followed.

Ten or twelve steps led to each of seven landings. At last I spotted a cottage and a creek with a miniature bridge across it. An old man in a hat came out to greet the boy, and they went inside together. They were friends! When I got to the open door, the old man looked at me without welcome. He had poured the boy a cup of cocoa from a pan on a pot-bellied stove, and he motioned for me to serve myself. The boy drank his chocolate and moved around the room freely. I tried to hold a conversation with the man, but he wasn't a talker. Soon, they both went outside and I followed. I started to comment on the wonderful bridge, but the man was across the yard, his back to me, tending his garden. After inspecting the bridge, I felt we should go. The boy had already started for the stairs.

We walked home as we had come, the boy allowing me to come closer but never beside him. I wondered how many mornings he had made this trip and gotten back to the basement before any of us knew.

After two weeks, the kids' parents returned, having found a place to live. The boy was playing when he heard his mother's voice. As soon as she had hugged and kissed him, he went right back to whining at her skirt. We laughed at him to say we knew this was a game, but he wouldn't look at us. It was something they had going between them.

Nancy and Deirdre came from Malibu, bringing food from their parents' cupboards. "They'll never miss it," Didi assured us. "They don't even know it's there." The girls also presented us with high quality cannabis and LSD. They knew all the best dealers at the high school.

Deirdre was of strong English-Irish stock, resilient, and good-natured. She wore jeans and soft blouses — too adventurous for dresses — and she looked like a child when she grinned. On a warm afternoon, she sat on our roof strumming a guitar and singing to herself, while below, Charlie and I listened, and he said tenderly, "Look at her. She's ten times the actress her mother is without even trying."

I looked up to Didi, and also to her mother, an Academy Award winning, internationally known actress who would languish awaiting another worthy role before accepting the part of a mystery writer in a watery American TV series beamed into millions of homes weekly.

When Didi expressed cynicism about her parents, I was surprised. She apologized in the same way, taking it back as if to dodge hurt feelings and keep from blaming people she loved. Her family was broken apart by the success of her parents, and she reflected it in her little cracks.

Nancy was tougher, more headstrong and feisty. She grew up the only girl in a large family of brothers. She was petite and pretty, but a scrapper, full of stick-to-it-ness, and the gut strings to do what she had never done before as if it were second nature. Of course, we didn't know this at the time.

One night we were rolling through Malibu in the bus when four sheriff's cars surrounded us. It looked like a drug raid, but the crux of the problem was a number of rookie deputies who needed experience. Twenty guinea pigs filed into the Sheriff's small substation and spent the night. The men were instantly locked up. We women sat in clusters around the questioning tables, giving ID information to the trainees. Superiors sauntered in and out of the room with comments like "No hanky-panky now, Ralph," and several of the older men gave us lectures on the perverted lives we were leading ("The men you're with are only after one thing.") No secret what was on their minds. Pencils fell on the floor. Crumpled papers went in the trash. The procedure took till dawn, and one young "Lorraine" was recognized by a local man as Nancy, wanted by Mom and Dad. Nancy went to juvenile hall.

On the day of Nancy's hearing, four of us girls went to court to meet her mother, a small, elegant woman at the end of her temper. She thought Nancy had been living with "speed freaks." She had intended to ask the court to take custody of her daughter, but by the time of the hearing, she was relaxed and smiling. To our relief, she asked for her daughter's release, and, so granted, the four of us were invited for dinner.

Nancy stayed in Malibu, tolerating her parents' rules, and talking with us on the phone Bobby had hooked up. Her father had her on restriction, and it wasn't but a few weeks before she called whispering: she'd overheard her father tell her mother that he could not accept her attitude; he was going to have her placed in a lock-up facility the next day. So she came to the basement to live in hiding.

With Nancy's illegality came a plague of police. They came using the black bus as an excuse, saying it was parked too far out in the street. We sarcastically guessed that it was blocking traffic *at the end of the road*. They came at all hours to check our IDs. One night I awoke as someone stepped on my sleeping bag. I saw the glint of a flashlight and the shadow of two large men on their way *out* the door. Seconds later came loud knocking, and the toneless announcement: "POLICE OFFICERS." Somebody turned on a light and they filed in, at guard and on point: "EVERYBODY STAY PUT. STAY RIGHT WHERE YOU ARE." They searched the house. What was the excuse for this early morning raid? People. How many people were living in the house, and how many toilets were available? Satisfied that our sanitation was up to par, they left.

Nancy knew that we could be charged for harboring her. Demonstrating a cool determination to stay out of custody, she slid between the house and the woods like a vapor, unnoticed even by many of us. When police came, she had the patience to wait in the bushes as long as was necessary, appearing later with foliage in her hair. Nancy was a light-hearted prankster, but she wasn't playing when it came to her freedom.

Donny Dinero* found us through a line of acquaintances he and Charlie had known at the McNeil Island Federal Penitentiary. He was short and drove an older model Cadillac with fins. Barbered hair and pressed slacks pretty much pegged him to the 1950s, and he looked like he'd swallowed a beach ball that challenged the buttons on his short-sleeved rayon shirt. But Donny had completed his prison time for making counterfeit money, and he was back on the streets to start a new life. In the trunk of his car he had a suitcase full of fresh twenties.

"What would we do with money?" Charlie asked, causing a round of chortles. Donny was offering us a substantial cut if we would help him pass the bills.

"No, no, no," Charlie said. "What we *need* are new IDs." Somehow he talked Donny into making the IDs without any recompense from us. Except Susan. Susan appealed to Donny in the raised-eyebrow way. So when Donny came again, Susan came out in her Chiquita blouse showing plenty of shoulder, hopped into his convertible, and they wheeled away like Frank Sinatra and Ava Gardner. He brought her back, but he was ID OK.

For the next week, while Donny set up, those of us opting for different identities considered new names. Ella, on a lark, chose the last name of Sinder. Others

210

were more ordinary, but Susan strolled the room pensively, coming up with something that sounded like a French whore.

Charlie said, "How about 'Sadie'?" Real country-like. "'Sadie Mae Glutz'."

Susan shrieked, "CHAR-LEE!" but she liked the laughter, and the name stuck. Nancy was to be Glenda but mistakenly became Brenda, and we paper-married young Diane to one of the Texans. What none of us knew about IDs was that there were seven distinguishable markings making them legitimate, including two sets of staple holes at the top of each card. When the police came looking for Nancy, the new IDs were scrutinized with doubt, but in the confusion of people rising and dressing, they sufficed. No, they didn't want any coffee. They split. After a repeat performance, we piled in the bus and took a trip. And so it was that we kept moving, circling back to the Spiral Staircase, and to Bobby's Basement, and forward to new places.

Charlie

Every time I get out of prison people are running faster, talking faster. The '40s were mellow. I got out in the '50s and things are going like ten mph. I go in and the world stops. I get out and it's twenty-five mph and I see a lumber truck a day. I go in and get out and I see more lumber trucks, new freeways, more smoke, more dead fish in the harbor, less birds. This last time I get out and it's all going 105 — lumber trucks twenty-four hours a day, kids all over the streets, and people going crazy.

So I think the answer is to pull away from it, get together with everything I missed, see it, and come back when it's burnt itself out. I look at it all, I say a few

211

> things, and pretty soon there's a bunch of us and all these kids whose parents don't want them and I say a little more, and pretty soon the police are after us and they've been chasing us all over L.A.
>
> — Charles Manson, L.A. Co Jail, 1970

The Condemned House

Nested in a crescent of trees, the "Topanga Shopping Center" was just a short block of mostly hippie-owned stores. It's where we first learned about the Condemned House and where I first saw Bruce. The house was to be torn down because it didn't meet the building codes. Its absentee owner could not legally rent it without making improvements, but locals said there was nothing wrong with it — if you didn't mind living without utilities. Topping another of Topanga's dead-end mountain roads, the property was wild grown and private. The house was clean, and it was wired for electricity but couldn't be legally hooked up. Worse, the only available water was from a spigot at roadside. But there was also no rent, so we took it, and set about making our own improvements. Buckets would have to be hauled from the road and kept in reserve to flush the downstairs toilet. Small carpentry projects were easy, and, in the interest of space, a platform mattress was suspended on heavy chains from the ceiling. Any do-it-yourselfer knows that challenge inspires creativity.

Down at the shopping center, I came out of the laundromat in time to see a stranger leaving our bus. I was suspicious until Charlie came out behind him.

Bruce McGregor Davis was as dignified as his Scot-English name, yet still befitting the Southern accent, the Brushy Mountain beard, the Levis, and the motorcycle. He accepted Charlie's invitation to park it on the road by our house, and for the next few days he tinkered with the engine, a smile, like a familiar song, playing on his face. A nice blend of verve and reserve, Bruce was not easily distracted, but his face colored when he was struck by Charlie's humor, or the eyes of one of us girls.

Lying in the last patch of March sunshine on the wild grown grass that fronted our house, I was dissatisfied and restless. Dinner was already made. Feet bobbed from the tree house. An expedition was trekking the back woods to plant the seeds of our stash. I wanted to spend more time with Charlie. Just then he walked out of the house, shaking something dusty. He paused only long enough to hand me a vest he'd found downstairs, asking if I'd fix it up for him. Then he was off down the walk with Bruce. It was all about motorcycles again. Half-heartedly, I inspected the material. Then I got an idea. I went to find the embroidery thread, and forgot about all else.

Brenda was the witch-handed girl who had brought us to the art of colored threads. Sitting on the lawn with five or six of us, she had pulled a wad of muslin from her pocket and, without breaking conversation, drew out an arm's length of thick embroidery thread. Separating the filaments by half, she'd dabbed an end on her tongue, threaded the needle, and continued an abstract doodle on the material, her face lifting to our curiosity.

"It's easy," she said modestly. "If you turn it and look at it in different ways, you can see creatures, and

213

faces, and stuff in the doodles. When I really like one, I fill it in." They were unusual, if not fantastic, forms, elongated and abbreviated creatures, caricatures, interconnected puzzles. They were tattoos in thread. Since being shown, the rest of us had been practicing stitches on muslin patches. The result was pure imagination. So it would be on the vests.

A sun-dark boy with a Cheshire cat grin and a nose for opportunity drifted through our doorway one evening on the aroma of dinner. Dressed to the teeth in ashram white, his dark hair and skin slickly oiled, he glided past each of us saying nothing more than "Hello," but with his eyes and eyebrows, "What have we here?" and "How about this!" Paul was seventeen and a runaway, but he quickly assured us that he'd been staying with people all over The Canyon and was a pro at avoiding the cops. He also announced that he'd been raised by American parents in Lebanon where marijuana and hashish were plentiful, and that he had learned about sex from the maid.

Speaking of maids, Stephanie, a new girl, was the medieval sort, the tavern wench, buxom and shy, with surprising bursts of hilarity. One evening in the kitchen, while we were cutting up the day's harvest, Stephanie said that her mother had told her if she took LSD she would turn into a vegetable. Ballooning her cheeks, she presented a convincing tomato, prompting rounds of vegetable mimicry. When we took up animals, Diane, often silent and separate, joined in with such a sincere and wonderfully wall-eyed snake that she broke everyone up and got a nickname.

Snake was prone to do-gooding as seen on TV. Someone on a garbage run picked up a whole case of

Tiger Shake, a sickly sweet powdered drink mix marketed to mothers "to make milk more nutritious." After finding that the powder reeked of old vitamins, we put it aside to return it to the dumpster, but Snake began *sneaking* it into our food. Each of her secret attempts to fortify us produced protests and puke faces at first bite, but she was incorrigible until somebody hauled the stuff away. Nothing is quite like the taste of spaghetti sauce made with Tiger Shake.

One night I was with Charlie in an older car on the coast highway. He picked up a couple of young hitchhikers, teenagers, a boy and a girl, carrying baggage. Climbing into the back seat, their faces were serious, and conversation sparse, avoiding any indication of where they were coming from or going. Charlie asked them if they needed a place to stay for the night, and the boy quickly said they had somewhere to go.

When we came to our turnoff, Charlie pulled the car off the highway and sat staring toward the ocean. The road was unpopulated but for an infrequent, swiftly passing car. He turned to me and said, "Come on." Following his lead, I got out of the car. The teens looked scared and confused. Holding the driver's door, Charlie said to them, "You can drive, can't you?"

"Well, yeah," the boy said.

"Come on then," Charlie told him. The two got into the front seat.

Through the driver's side window Charlie said, "The pink slip is signed in the glove box. That's your ownership paper. Here's fifty for gas. Now, it doesn't go too fast and you have to check the oil. It's got a leak — not bad, but check it." The boy nodded. They both thanked us, smiling. We walked a while, and then hitchhiked a ride back into the mountains.

Charlie was always giving things away, and just being there was worth the price of admission. I inherited a thousand dollars from a great aunt, and it took him over a week to get rid of that. He was driving a carful of us up the canyon from the beach and stopped for another hitchhiker. "Good afternoon," he said, pretending to be a British chauffeur, "this is Master Bruce, Princess Roopteedoo, Countess Diddydadd and ...uh....Lady Whatshername. And where may we take you today?" From the back seat, the hitchhiker, with noticeable discomfort, said something short and brittle, causing Charlie to toss out the accent and tone down to normal. But then he came up with an interesting proposal. "Tell you what," he said, "I'll trade you all the money I got in my pocket for all the money in yours." The hitchhiker's face wrinkled. He was in his teens or early twenties.

"It could be a very good trade for you," Charlie said frankly, looking into the rear view mirror. The hitchhiker touched his pocket and hesitated.

"Naw, I don't think so," he said, dodging a scam.

"Are you *sure*?" Charlie asked. "You'd better be sure. How do you know, I might have a thousand dollars in my pocket."

"Yeah, I'm sure," the hitchhiker said.

A couple of us asked him, "Well, how much you got?" Without looking, he estimated he had three or four dollars and change. Charlie pulled out the thousand dollars in small bills, fanned, and raised it so that the hitchhiker could see it. His jaw went slack.

"You were really gonna trade?"

"Sure," Charlie said, "If you hadn't been so afraid of losing your change. Ain't no security in this stuff. The security's in YOU. As long as you hold on to money — that's all you got."

216

It was a time of plenty. People were dropping out, and dropping in. One couple gave Charlie a beautiful new red Mustang and, at first, I could not pull from my memory any trace of what happened to it after all the enthusiastic excursions people found reason to take in it.

Melba buttoned her chiffon robe and fussed over her hair as she opened her back door on the mornings we came to clean her stables. Charlie and Bruce came along just to visit, and gave her a reason to look good because they always told her when she did. Habitually nonchalant, Melba still pretended that we were poor people she was helping, but when her Southern relatives were unexpectedly coming to see her, she fretted and worked herself up to asking Charlie if he might have extra money to lend, just until after their visit. I wasn't there that day, but I was told that he shook his head firmly in the negative. He said he wouldn't loan her money because it would tie him up having to keep track of what she owed. So he *gave* her two hundred dollars, and then he *gave* her the Mustang. He said it suited her. I was sorry to see that car go, but I would have loved to have seen Melba trying to be nonchalant about *that*.

Throughout 1967 and early '68, Mary had conscientiously kept herself healthy. Her experiences in the shades of her pregnancy were personal. Not one to complain about aches and pains, she sometimes climbed the hill across from the house carrying a sleeping bag. She'd sleep the afternoon on the grass under the trees, and return feeling better. I almost expected her to carry off the sleeping bag and return

with a baby, but she wouldn't deprive us of the event.
It was April. Sandra Good arrived at that time.

Sandy

Have babies! Are you kidding? How mundane.
Any animal can give birth. I'd rather develop my mind
than wash diapers, cook meals, and take care of a
house day after day. My mother wore a green apron
with black letters saying "To Hell with Housework,"
and she was very witty and very clever and children
were a burden. I went to college to learn to be witty
and clever, and to make the right allusions to the right
books and the right people at the right times. And I
was getting it down good. I thought women who had
children were trapped. The women on the college lawn
who circulated petitions to legalize abortions always
had my firm support. Illegal abortions were a fun "in
thing" to talk about with other girls, even if you barely
knew each other. Once I moved into an apartment in
San Francisco with three girls. One was the daughter
of the president of an airline, another's father was a
movie star, and the third was the granddaughter of
Karl Menninger, the noted psychiatrist. The girls were
all clever and neurotic. I felt I was in my element. We
discussed mutual experiences.
    "Well, in Juarez, all you do is call this number and
make an appointment. One by one you go into this
room, get on a cot and this woman puts a bunch of
cotton up you to begin the contractions. They give you
Pentothal and zap! — you wake up and it's gone."
    "They must run thirty girls through there a day.
They've got a big house and they give you some real
groovy orange spice tea when it's all done."
    "My father paid for mine. The bummer was I lost
my glasses coming home on the plane."

218

I carried this with me, along with my birth control pills, out of San Francisco on a break from work and school to Los Angeles where I first met Charlie. I had hoped to go surfing but my artist friend kept raving about Charlie and this bunch of girls who were always with him. He borrowed a small plane and we flew to L.A., rented a car, and drove to Topanga Canyon up a long winding road until we came to a dead end. The moon was out and I saw no house, just an old black school bus parked on a slightly sloped hill. It was quiet but for the sounds of crickets and frogs far below. As we got out a cat came to rub against my legs, and a blonde, very pregnant girl moved up the hill toward me.

"Mary! Hello!" my friend recognized her and they hugged. He made reference to her belly and she told him it wouldn't be long. My first thought upon seeing her huge belly was "what an unfortunate state to be in."

Mary picked up my suitcase and led us down a short path to a small house. She turned to me at the door. "You should see this when it's light out. It's really magic. There're little roses and vines growing all over the house." We went in. I needed to use the bathroom, so Mary set my bag down and led me down a steep flight of rickety stairs to a dark, cluttered basement. She struck a match as we turned into the bathroom and continued to burn matches as I fumbled for the toilet seat. She handed me the paper.

"Where are you going to have your baby?" I asked her.

"Right here in the house," she replied with all the enthusiasm of a child talking about Christmas. "The girls are gonna deliver it."

"What girls?"

"Oh, you'll meet them. They're upstairs." This stumped me. A hundred hows and what-ifs clogged my head.

"Are you married?" I questioned, "Or will your boyfriend take care of you?"

"Neither," she laughed. I felt awfully conventional and too embarrassed to ask any more questions. The toilet didn't flush. Mary dumped a bucket of water in it and led the way up the dark stairs.

"I'm going outside to wash some dishes," she said. We haven't got inside water so we wash under the hose. Did you see the bathtub in the front yard?" I hadn't. "Make yourself at home," she said. I went into the living room. Home? Christ, the house didn't fit into any category of anything I'd ever experienced — no shelves of books or electricity, just candle light and the glimmer of a dying fire in a pot-bellied stove. What kind of place was I in? There were no intellectual debates in the air. In fact, it seemed to be a place of timelessness. I uncomfortably shifted my body into various stances, removing my glasses then putting them on, untying and retying my hair.

A girl, Sadie, with snappy brown eyes and electric movements, motioned with her eyes to a guitar lying on a tapestry-covered mattress, saying simply, "Stephanie." Instantly the guitar was in Sadie's hands. Ah, something familiar that I could relate to. I walked over and sat cross-legged in front of Sadie, expecting to hear "peace and freedom" songs or something like that. A low, strong, eerie voice began swelling to the tone of a minor chord that her fingers flicked into ever-changing rhythms. I was afraid of her. I felt plastic.

"When did you start playing the guitar?" I interrupted.

"Since right now," she said simply, "...and the soul moves you. You don't need anyone to show you what someone else showed them. You just do it."

I looked over to the girl who had been standing in the entrance watching us. She was so young. A thick mane of auburn hair framed her small face and she had clear green eyes that looked right through you.

"That's Snake," Sadie sang. Snake kind of galumphed over to us, body loose, and knelt down beside me, saying nothing.

"Do you play guitar too?" I blurted.

"Yes," she replied in a soft, faraway voice. "I just haven't quite gotten around to it yet."

Sadie saw my puzzlement and said, "It's like you can do anything you want to do. Just know you can and you can." Now the eyes of two of these strange creatures were on me and I was uncomfortable. I went to the door of the kitchen where there were electric lights. Lots of crates and assorted food in boxes lay on the tables and floor. There were girls all over the place. Some were sitting on the floor cutting up vegetables, some were stirring food over a Coleman stove, others were crushing fruits into a strainer, getting the juice. One girl right out of a 1930s Broadway musical, her huge blue eyes and wavy blonde hair beneath an old top hat, looked up from her bread board. Shaking flour from her hands, she smiled, saying, "Ella," and everyone in the room looked up at me with cheery hellos. Ella said, "You wanna help us with the dinner? The guys'll be home soon." Just then, from the basement, came singing, louder and louder, and then giggles and more singing. A spontaneous madrigal!

"Oh Patty, my love, 'twas you, 'twas you
who stashed the weed, the precious weeeed."

And it got very loud.

> "Let us trip it trip it trip it round the room
> oh doooo!
> Be it Brenda, Lyn or Sue,
> She'll put it put it in the stew,
> And make of us another hue
> Dooo!"

Everyone laughed and the girls in the kitchen sang back. Ella handed me a knife and some celery sticks.

"Where did you guys get all this food?"

"We did a garbage run today. You oughta come the next time. It's really fun."

So many questions I wanted to ask but I couldn't. Somehow my questions didn't belong here. Yet these girls looked so familiar, freckled faces, brown, red, golden hair, straight teeth, small bodies — My old playmates? My sisters? And that Sadie in the living room; she was the girl I wasn't allowed to play with.

The madrigal quartet bearing the rolled grass bounded up the stairs into the kitchen. The room became electric with sound and movement. I was being inspected. A tiny, longhaired girl wearing a long ruffled skirt and no top began fondling my hair.

"Your hair's so pretty. Why don't you take out that rubber band and let it breathe?" she told me. Without thinking, I handed Brenda the rubber band and she said, "You know, Mary and Ella used to wear glasses but they threw them away. Can I see your glasses?" I handed them to her and she put them on, looking pretty crazy with her long hair flowing over her bare shoulders and breasts and my round, brown-framed glasses.

"Your eyes aren't so weak — and they're pretty," she told me. Whispers of "yeah, really" filled the room. Brenda left the kitchen with my glasses and rubber band. She returned with a long blue velvet dress, explaining, "I just made it today and I was waiting for the perfect person to come along to wear it. Put it on." At my hesitation, she said, "Ever heard of The Magical Mystery Tour? You know, the one the Beatles are singing about. Well, we're on it and it's fun. It's — you know — being different people every day." I put the dress on, reluctantly. It was beautiful and I didn't want to look beautiful. This little creature, Brenda, was stripping away my identity, making me into a Renaissance princess. All the girls got in on the act. Lace and ribbons were pulled out of boxes, a jewel tied around my neck, and an antique ring with tiny diamonds placed on my finger.

"I'd better take these things off," I told them, turning to find my striped pants suit.

"That's okay; you can have all this stuff. We just play with these things," they told me.

I was removing the ring with the diamonds, saying, "Here, this is valuable."

Stephanie held my hand still and said, "It was my grandmother's wedding ring. It's yours now and when you get tired of it, just pass it on."

This was too much. I slipped out of the kitchen, recovered my clothes, my glasses, and tied my hair back. A car door slammed outside.

Ella exclaimed, "The guys are home!" I crawled onto the couch in the shadows and watched five men come through the door. I had not hidden well enough. Charlie came into the living room straight to me and removed my glasses, saying, "Hello, pretty girl. Taking time off from college?" Before I could muster up a reply, he was back with all the bustling in the kitchen.

Candles were brought into the living room and set in the middle of the floor. A bunny-like girl moved next to me. More girls came, sitting next to her, and soon there was a circular conglomeration of — I wasn't sure what. The room became hushed; the girls brought the food and placed it down gently. I watched as Charlie tasted from a bowl and said, "Mmmmm, you witches are too much." He passed the bowl to Bruce and said, "You dig the love these girls put into their meals? Snake peeled the grapes, took the seeds out of the cherries, cracked the walnuts, and I saw her making that yogurt from scratch a few days ago." He looked at Snake and said, "Watch the nut shells, honey. These witches are tricky, too, brother," he said winking at Bruce. "Snake, I see what you do. You don't have to put nut shells in the salad to get my attention." Snake shrugged and laughed.

The way everyone talked, Bruce was a newcomer. He and Charlie looked like blood brothers. After the meal, Ella lit up joints, gave one to each of the guys and they sent them around the circle. I asked one of the girls how they paid for the weed and she said that people just gave it to them. Charlie took the guitar and began playing a song that made my loaded computer spark, fizzle, and die.

"There's a time for livin'
And the time keeps on flyin'
You think you're lovin', baby
But all you're doin' is cryin'
Can you feel? Are those feelin's real?
Look at your game, girl."

I felt very empty, lonely and confused in the midst of so many happy faces. The rhythm changed and he was singing,

"With your can cough medicines, and your wonder drugs
You got more sickness, than you got cures of Cancer of the mind
Take a look at yourself. Take yourself off the shelf.
You can belong to no one."

I felt like leaving the room right away. Charlie was in my head.

"No, you can't hide from intensified Tide," he sang, laughing. Suddenly he switched to a romantic fantasy song and I felt I was off the hook.

It made sense to me now. My artist friend wanted to be like Charlie. In San Francisco he lived in a comfortable home with four young children and a wife. Soon after meeting me, he'd suggested I meet her. The times were unconventional, but I found myself feeling very ill at ease sitting in their living room. She was a pleasant woman, but he was proposing a ménage a trois and I sensed her relief when I didn't agree. While I'd attended the University of Oregon, a college professor had shocked me with a similar proposal. I had never considered "kinky" sex, and going to bed with a husband and wife was out of the question.

In Topanga I slept in a room beside my friend, but he was asleep before I lay down. Routinely plagued by insomnia, I lay awake listening to the sighs and soft moans of people in the other rooms making love. When I awoke the next day, my friend was already up, having planned to fly back for work that afternoon.

He seemed neither surprised nor upset when I told him I'd decided to stay. I called San Francisco to tell my boss and my roommates that I wouldn't be back for awhile.

That night, after another circular gathering, Charlie asked if I'd like to go for a walk. He told me to ask one of the girls for a blanket. I started to ask why I needed a blanket, but felt he could see through my attempt at naiveté. We left the house, walking down the path and up a hill in the moonlight. He turned to look at me, and touched my throat, his fingers tracing a tracheotomy scar. I explained that I had been sick as a child, and even had most of one lung removed, and before I could go on, he told me to forget the past. He said he knew I was strong, just as the baby Mary would have would be strong.

"Those people in the house and you — you haven't even begun to see what super creatures you are. The babies you girls will have won't have to go through what you went through. They'll be like nothing anyone has ever seen." I was nervously poking my leg with a pencil.

"You don't like babies, do you?" he said, taking the pencil and tossing it.

"Well, it's like ... well, you know ..." I began running down about over population, finishing my education, and that an old psychiatrist of mine had once told me I wouldn't make a good mother because my mother wasn't a good mother, and that for me to have a baby would be unfair to the child. Charlie looked bored. I felt silly. He said,

"Jesus Christ, Sandy, I don't give a fuck about your mother, your psychiatrist or any of your other crazy problems. I see you, and I see you would make super babies. You take birth control pills, huh." I said he was right.

226

"Well, I'll be right here. You run back to the house and get them for me, would you?" I didn't really think about it. I just went and found my purse and pulled out the dial-a-pill plastic container of pink pills. When I came back, he was sitting on the blanket under a tree. I sat down, tucked my legs under me, and lit a cigarette. I handed him the pills and he looked them over in the moonlight, shaking his head.

"Here, give me a drag of that cigarette," he said, "... and take your clothes off."

"My clothes?" He sat there watching. I removed my jacket, tugged off my shirt, and then put the jacket back on. It was warm out.

"Go on," he said. I turned my back to him and took my pants off.

"Come on, Sandy," he said. "You know you're pretty." He slid me down to him and I closed my eyes. Gently, he removed the rubber band and ran his hands through my hair, massaging my temples and head along the way.

"Quit thinking," he said. He held my head in his lap, rubbing the muscles with his fingertips in continuous motion, stroking my neck and down my back.

He said, "Take off my shoes." I unlaced his moccasins while he continued caressing and feeling more and more of my body. He removed his shirt.

"Lie down," he said, pulling off his pants. I did and he covered my embarrassment with his small warm body.

"Relax," he whispered. "I'll do it. Just lie still and let me move you." My body responded while my mind was amazed. He kept moving in a gentle dance. He made love to me for a long, long time and when he sat up, he was still hard.

He said, "Sandy, you'll never make love until you quit thinking."

I said, "But I … I didn't know you could … how do you … wow, other girls are sure missing out."

He said, "The more I love — which is more every day — the more a man loves — the longer he can make love. It's guilt, doubts, and all that negative thinking that cuts them off. Your kids won't be stuck with that. If you hadn't been taking those pills I could've gotten you pregnant."

When we got back to the house, candles were lit. Mary was in labor. No shrieks of pain or fingernails digging into sweaty palms as I'd seen in the movies. She was making music, the most beautiful high, sweet panting sounds, and her skin was white and glowing. All the girls were smiling and calm around her. My mind was still with Charlie. I felt very strange. I crept over to sleep in the swinging bed.

I awoke at daylight to a moan that climbed to a high cry. Peeking from behind the tapestry, I saw Mary on a clean, sheet-covered mattress, the girls around her massaging her neck and holding up her legs. A fly buzzed. Then another moan, light panting, and Mary yelled, "It's coming!" Blood ran from her, but I didn't know what to think. What was emerging from her looked all wrong. Something was on top of the baby's head. It was purple, the size and shape of a walnut. Perspiring faces around her paled, and a silent fear solidified. Then a little penis appeared, and peed.

One of the girls exclaimed, "A boy! It's a boy!"

"What's happening?" Mary cried.

Patty said, "It's okay. He's breech but he's coming."

Mary struggled to rise, saying, "Help me up." The girls propped her at the foot of the bed as she instructed, supporting her back and elbows so that she could squat above the floor.

"NOOOWWW...OOHHH!" she yelled louder. The boy first inched then slid, unfolding from her body, but his head didn't come out. All was still. Mary was panting, beads of sweat all over her body. The room was hushed. The baby's body was long, narrow, and milky blue in color. I thought he was dead. I was waiting for someone to move to find a doctor.

Mary moaned and pushed to no avail, at last coaxing softly, "Come on, baby!" Water and blood poured from her... then bloop, the baby fell into Sadie's hands. He didn't move or cry. Brenda took him and held him upside down, patting him on the back. Mary put her mouth to his, drawing fluids from his mouth and nose. Finally, to everyone's great relief, he let out his first breath and a tiny cry.

I was in a state of mild shock. Charlie's lovemaking and the baby's birth began for me a mind blowing week that included my first acid trip. A day or two after the birth Charlie took me to a music club in Topanga where the band Buffalo Springfield played, and to Old Topanga Road where I was introduced to Bobby Beausoleil. He was good looking, but if someone had told me that by the end of the year I would be pregnant by him, I wouldn't have believed it. I met Bobby's landlord, Gary Hinman. On learning that I was going through a bout of insomnia, Gary offered me non-prescription sleeping pills. I wasn't sure I would use them, but I slipped them into the pocket of my jacket.

Back at the condemned house, I met Phil Kaufman, a sometime roadie who connected well known music people in Hollywood. What got my attention

229

was his humorous repartee with Charlie. In the early 1960s I was under twenty-one but had gotten into an adult nightclub in San Francisco to see Lenny Bruce, famous not only for his humor, but because he said "fuck" on stage before any other comedian. I'd also seen The Committee, a San Francisco improv group that was very funny and cool. But Charlie and Phil Kaufman topped all these guys.

Phil had been at Terminal Island federal prison for smuggling marijuana. After hearing Charlie play a guitar and sing on the prison yard, he wrote to his producer friend at Universal Studios that Charlie sounded like a young Frankie Laine. Frankie Laine was popular in the '40s and '50s and when I was very young he'd been a guest of my parents at their house in Del Mar. Phil would go on to be a road manager for the Rolling Stones and other popular groups. What impressed me was that he and Charlie didn't express bitterness or anger about their time in prison — just humor. They were imitating the ubiquitous radio communications between prison guards, including the static.

"Awrk we've got a 224 in progr — screech —."

"10-4 — squawk — two in custody — errk — 205 the bushes out side the Ad building."

Their parody of a totally alien way of life was hilarious. I wouldn't realize how right on it was until I did time in that same prison eight years later.

That week Charlie gave me my first tab of acid, assuring me that it would not make me go crazy as I feared it would. He drove me to a summit overlooking Los Angeles, and, unprovoked, I saw the scene below me in flames. I laughed and laughed until I cried. I don't remember what was so funny. It was like I was privy to some huge cosmic joke. I've never laughed so hard before that or since. Later, when I asked Charlie about the laughing, he said that I'd "seen the whole thing." He drove me to a more secluded place, and told me to get in the back seat of the car and take my clothes off. When I did, he told me I was beautiful but never to use my beauty. He made love to me, and when later I told him I didn't remember anything about it, he said, "Your soul got it."

Afterward, we went to a house where a few people were, and he started dancing with Lyn. Petite, with long red hair, she appeared bright and colorful. They seemed matched in size and energy. By this time the effects of the LSD were wearing off and I was feeling dull and inadequate, especially when I saw them dancing together, sparks of energy flying off their hair, hands, and bodies. It was almost like looking into a big bonfire. I felt that Charlie was showing me a mirror of the energy that was inside of me once I could let go of my past.

Next, he took me to a house in Malibu and introduced me to a woman named Melba. By then the acid was really wearing off, and I was feeling very ill at ease. I didn't know what their relationship was, or how to interact. My mind was blown. Part of me felt that he was trying to impress me, and maybe to impress Melba. What I wanted was the privacy and comfort of a warm shower to clean myself of all the intense experiences of the evening. As it turned out, he had brought me to the right place.

I believe that Charlie could see my and others' innate brightness layered over with our personal histories. He was smart to show me someone much like myself who was freer and happier and having fun, and then take me to the home of an older woman with all the trappings of wealth.

My parents were not rich, but certainly well off. They were comfortably uncomfortable. Both came from families of good social standing. They had two daughters before I came along. By then they were beginning to separate, and from that beginning I had breathing problems that put me in and out of the hospital, and later disrupted my schooling. Absence from school, but mostly extreme anxiety, fostered reading and learning difficulties, and I never felt comfortable anywhere until in high school when a group of girls and I were drawn together in camaraderie. They were the bright, popular girls, the cheerleaders and class officers, and no one suspected one of them of painting obscenities on the football bleachers. They had an enthusiasm for learning, but they also had a good healthy rebel side that I was always eager to aid and abet.

We called ourselves "The Nites," and in our times of nighttime roving, I felt a kinship and security I hadn't known before. There was also music. All of my friends could harmonize, and play instruments. One had composed pieces performed by the San Diego Symphony, beginning when she was nine years old. Sometimes The Nites would sneak onto the grounds of the San Diego Starlight Opera. One time during a performance by the New York Philharmonic with Leonard Bernstein conducting, I lost my footing on the hill, sliding noisily through brush, evoking "Shhhes" from the audience, and for a moment I thought I'd go tumbling into the orchestra pit.

Graduation, colleges, and careers split The Nites apart, and I was alone again, even with other people. When I entered San Francisco State College, after almost two years at the University of Oregon, while others were discovering the Beatles, I was listening to Gregorian Chants and madrigals. My sister, Ginny, had introduced me to Baroque musicians. She was dating the son of a conductor for the L.A. Philharmonic Orchestra, and also seeing a psychiatrist. Ginny was beautiful, talented, popular, and at the top of all of her classes. She had attended Sarah Lawrence College in New York. She had also been in two state psychiatric hospitals. I longed to be as cultured and informed as she was. I wanted to learn about every culture on earth, especially my own Northern European heritage. So after seeing the faces of Brenda, Lyn, and the other girls in Topanga, and hearing them sing, they, like my old friends, struck a deep chord. I thought, "These could be my people."

I had so many defense mechanisms that weren't needed here. There was no alcohol, no mood altering pharmaceuticals, or outward expressions of depression.

The police came as civil servants. Did everyone know that the house was condemned? They were told it was being fixed up, and they left, but returned to run identification checks. Then one day the girls had gone on a garbage run except for me, Snake, Brenda, and a few of the others. Mary and the baby were visiting friends. I hadn't slept a full night in weeks and was contemplating the Sleep-Eze pill I found in the pocket of my jacket.

Brenda said, "Every time I turn around the police are barging in. One time they came in the afternoon so I took some ivy and wrapped it around myself and just stood out in the backyard."

"Where do you sleep?" I asked her.

"Down the hill by the creek," she said. She got a slight grin on her face and added, "Amidst all the wild creatures that roam the hills at night. I watch the

233

flashlights go in and out of the house, and I hear the cops grumbling on the way to their cars about how many girls are living in this house, and that one guy's an ex-convict." She moved to the window. I heard two car doors slam.

"I knew it," she said. "They're here." She slid out the back just before three big cops stormed through the front door saying, "Jesus Christ, how do you live like this?" I told them I was visiting from San Francisco.

"How old are you?"

"Twenty-four."

"Bullshit, you're not over sixteen. Where's your ID?" I proceeded to show one of them my passport.

"Okay, empty your pockets." I dug around and handed him some Kleenex and four tablets — three yellow Sleep-Eze and one Quiet World.

"Where'd you get these pills?"

"A friend. They're sleeping pills you can buy in a store."

He said, "Hey Ed, this kid's got Nembutol on her." They rounded up the few of us and took us to jail, charging us with possession of my pills and some weed seeds they said they found outside the house. I think everyone was released but me. I kept telling them that you can get Sleep-Eze and Quiet World in any drugstore without a prescription, but they held me for six days until I made bail.

I'd attended two colleges. I'd been to Europe. I had never been in jail. In a word, jail was concrete, both sterile and dirty. Three fourths of the day was noisy, and the glaring fluorescent lights buzzed. After six days, the girls from Topanga picked me up at the gate and took me back to the condemned house. That night I was so exhausted I didn't need pills to sleep.

234

Sandra Good was like the faceless secretary in old movies who becomes stunning with the simple removal of hairpins and glasses. In real life, she clung to her reservations, and seemed to want to observe the rest of us rather than participate in what we were doing. At times she was so removed as not to be seen.

Perhaps due to the sheer numbers of us, the incriminating evidence found outside our house could not be pinned on anyone except Snake. Deputies found Snake's false ID with the weed seeds. She was then fifteen, but, in keeping with her new ID, she gave her age as twenty. At the women's jail she was taken out of her cell and questioned all night long, and each time they told her that they *knew* she was not twenty, and that she would *never* get out if she didn't tell them the truth, she stuck by her story. Finally they released her with her new name and age henceforth confirmed by her arrest record.

With continued police surveillance, it was time to move. The weather was warm, and all the bus windows were open as Charlie drove us to the beach, and then north, past the populated parts of Malibu, until the land opposite the beach was undeveloped. When he saw a road between two mountains, and no signs of ownership, we bumped inland on uneven flood-cratered dirt toward foliage and twisted scrub oak, until a rear tire lodged in a crevice, and the back right side of the bus sank six inches. Charlie and a couple of the guys were resigned to moving the bus because it was still within sight of the road, but everyone else seemed satisfied to consider this "fate," happily getting out, and trekking into the woods.

Several hundred yards inland was a round clearing close to a stream where birds and butterflies were plentiful, and there were no telephone wires. The guys wanted to hike around the stream, and most of the girls wanted to stay around Mary and the baby.

Charlie had named the baby "Sunstone" with Mary's agreement, but the men waiting out the birth on the porch said that a hawk flew over the house as they heard his first cry, so he became Sunstone Hawk. Soon after the birth, a neighbor who happened to be a medical doctor had examined Sunstone and, to no one's surprise, deemed him perfectly healthy. To us girls he was a source of wonder, especially to Mary who couldn't stop smiling or looking at him. At late afternoon, we made a circle of stones, and a fire. After a light meal, we laid sleeping bags and blankets around the embers and we all went to sleep.

I awoke hearing a crunch. Everyone's breathing sounded heavy in sleep. Then big beams of light strangely lit up enough woods so I could see two large animals — German Shepherds — emerging from the brush. My attention quickly shifted from the dogs to the ends of their taut chains.

"YOU ARE ALL UNDER ARREST. GET UP AND KEEP YOUR HANDS WHERE WE CAN SEE THEM."

Again? There must have been ten or twelve officers. Everyone got up, resigned to a procedure that would take all night. Marched out of the woods single file at gunpoint, we were ordered to sit on the ground at roadside where a paddy wagon and four blinking squad cars awaited us. Our IDs were collected, and after some official hubbub, names were read, four at a time, summoning each of us to a different car to be searched and probed for data.

Most of us had already been recorded when Johnny Bluestone's name came up. Coincidentally, Johnny was standing by another squad car, giving personal information about his other name. Whatever his logic or lack thereof, he had been carrying both his IDs.

"JOHN BLUESTONE," the officer called again.

"Here…" Charlie stepped forward, grinning and raising his hand.

The officer said, "We already got you, didn't we?"

Soon we were all laughing. The big shepherds were sitting beside us getting scratched behind the ears when, in sudden realization, their embarrassed handlers commanded, "Heel!" Snake recovered three tabs of acid, buried one, and swallowed two. She wasn't the only one deciding not to forfeit the treasured stash. Charlie took whatever he was holding, it ultimately becoming responsible for an iconic mug shot of him taken at the Ventura County sheriff's substation and later published on the cover of *Life* magazine.

Everyone was charged with Trespassing on Government Property, although there was no sign, and Grand Theft, on the assumption that the bus was stolen. Mary was charged with endangering the life of her child who'd been sleeping snugly beside her in her sleeping bag.

The next day, most of us were released without charges. Except Mary. The county wanted to prosecute her for child neglect. Their motivation was questionable and could have been fueled by gossip. A local newspaper had run a sensational story under this headline: NUDE HIPPIES FOUND STREWN IN WEEDS. Mary was quoted as saying as an afterthought, just before being driven to jail, "Oh, wait! My baby's in the bus!"

Melba, in her capacity as a social worker, intervened on Mary's behalf, getting Sunstone released and Mary probation, but the charge would make Mary's future life difficult.

We returned to the Condemned House for just a short time before its owner showed. Rather than being upset, she was impressed with the way the house looked. A couple of weeks later she decided to meet the housing codes so that she could legally rent it out. When we explained that we could not pay rent, she said she would like to let everybody stay, but she needed the money. Charlie gave her a new stereo to buy us some time, but as the deadline approached we didn't know where we were going to live.

The Hills On The Edge Of The Valley

Cocky Sadie, gallivantin' lady, see how she strut!
Always on the heel and toe,
Always puttin' on a show,
The smaller the pants,
The bigger the butt.
O, Sadie, Sadie Mae,
Who did you fall in love with today?
Will you tell us, or are you going away?
Sittin' cross-legged in your black silk scanties,
Evilest of all their aunties,
Braggin' bold and bare-faced,
Gettin' your high heeled boots laced.
Her mouth is puckered, her eyes are shady.
Got a booty full of acid, Sadie?
Got a head full of crazy schemes,
Wants to turn the world on.
Tellin' tales and makin' SCENES!
I always ignore you when you're here.
Out goes the thumb, and she's gone.
Got a bag full of tricks and pick-up sticks.
Wanna come? She's back at dawn,
Purrin' proud and talkin' loud.

(Been to London to frighten a mouse).
Well, just so happens we need a house
And Sadie rolls in like an avalanche –
Shoutin',
"HEY! YOU GUYS! I FOUND US A RANCH!!"

— L.F., c 1971

At the end of Topanga Canyon Boulevard, the Santa Susana Pass climbs the foothills between big boulders — the background scenes in old cowboy movies. A hairpin turn crosses the freight train tunnel, the tracks descending into a canyon, but the winding blacktop ascends to and past a big oval corral, dozens of horses, and a slope off the asphalt onto the dirt street of a Wild West movie town with hitching rails, a boardwalk, and a long row of wooden buildings with swaybacked roofs — Spahn's Movie Ranch.

Now, we'll go past the movie set, like we did when we first came, past the owner's grungy bungalow, and down a sandy road that can't be seen from the highway. It lumps along through territory thick with trees — dark, the pit of mystery at night, and bright in meadow clearings. Here's a fork, one road going down to a trickling creek, the other over a split log bridge barely safe enough to cross. And we cross it. Now, to your right is the car and truck bone yard, dull mechanical skeletons, and on the other side of the road near the mountains, is the Gypsy Wagon, a colorfully painted wood shack on big wagon wheels. About a quarter mile in, you can see a house near the end of the road. It has a kitchen wired with electricity, a stone fireplace in the front room, two bedrooms, and an unfinished bathroom. Opposite the house and up a hill are the skeletal frames of two "Outlaw Shacks" for movie use, crooked, holey, and two stories high, with open lofts.

Beyond these into the eucalyptus grove the road soon ends in deep gullies, giving way to twenty-seven acres of horse-hoof trails through grassland and mountain boulders. There are caves in those hills where runaway kids painted their names and left their old blue jeans. And on the other side of the mountain is a half-buried ghost town called the "Indian Mesa."

Longhairs were living in the house when we first came, and they told us where we might park our bus and stay a spell. And there were these wild animal boys, runaways from the suburbs, who lived in the hills half-naked, and came down just to hang around the corners of the buildings, and watch us, and run off again. Three or four of them came around the bus one day just after Charlie had left for town. They were skittish, but eager as young dogs. They wanted to see inside the bus, and they wanted to see girls. A moment later, Charlie came back to the bus for something, and when he got inside I heard fierce growls and sounds inhuman. Then I saw the boys leaping from the bus and scattering in the hills. (Charlie told me he got mad because they were sneaking behind his back, and that meant that they couldn't face him.)

The valley suffered a heat wave that summer, the metal bus becoming an oven at night. So we cleaned up the Outlaw Shacks, where night breezes blew between the warped boards. In the lofts we could drift to sleep under constellations we never thought of during the day — until a sharp splinter of sunlight forced us up, squinting and thirsty.

Towel and toothbrush in hand, I'd head down to the creek. I'd likely meet Brenda coming up, gripping the dry grass with her arched feet, her body damp beneath loose shorts and some relic of a soft blouse that always looked feminine on her. No matter how hot it was, Brenda looked cool. She'd start breakfast in the hippies' house. Sometimes I'd run red-head-on into the milk-made Snake, hauling a bucket of water for cooking. She'd been up early, ambling the woods. She was cub-like, cat cub, curious, near fearless, just a little clumsy.

Wading into the shallow creek, I'd wake more, my feet roused by spring water and cold stones. In a deeper crater, I'd strip and drop under, bolting from cold shock. If it happened that several of us were there together, we rippled around smiling, and not saying much. Sometimes we had to hide while horse-back riders passed. The owner of the ranch rented out his sixty-some horses.

Well, the drought persisted, the creek went down, and the hills for miles around turned bone dry and barren. On the brittle boardwalk fronting the shacks, we girls sat on wooden crates, embroidering patches for Charlie's vest. We concentrated deeply to keep from thinking of the heat, swiping at flies, and brushing back the sweat that trickled into our ears and eyes. Then one day Patty and Ella returned from a hitchhiking trip to the city and told us of a young man in a Rolls Royce who had stopped for them. He had taken them to the estate he rented near Beverly Hills where they spent the afternoon in his tree house talking about "coming to consciousness."

Dennis was a handsome musician, the drummer for a well-known West Coast music group. He had invited the girls to bring the rest of us to see him, so one evening a carfull of us went for a drive through the valley to the coast, and up Sunset Boulevard to Pacific Palisades. Finding Dennis' iron gates wide open, we followed his driveway around woods and well kept lawns to the carport of a wide-ranging ranch house, cabañas, and pool. A smaller version of the big house, a guesthouse, was lit. When no one answered at the big house, we went to the guesthouse and found the door open, but Dennis was not in. Patty and Ella had assured us that Dennis would have us make ourselves at home, so we entered to wait, resting ourselves on thick white rugs around a fireplace. We lit logs for ambiance; there was no kindling but the phone book, much of it already gone to the same purpose. The master of the house soon returned and was frightened. He did a quavering dance, mocking himself, as he did not even remember Patty and Ella at first. Then he smiled widely in firelight, inviting us to follow him through the patio into the main quarters, past a massive antique dining table, and into the living room where claw foot brocade couches faced a mantled stone fireplace in the style of nineteenth century hunting lodges. We talked back and forth, sang a little, and after the evening's exchange, Dennis outright invited us to stay. We told him about the black bus, and the many more of us, and he said to "bring them." Whoever claimed later that we had moved into Dennis' house uninvited was either untruthful or uninformed.

Hollywood

Dennis Wilson did not own the historic Sunset Boulevard estate. Rather, it was leased for him. There were, in the main house, at least four bedrooms off a hallway that led to a bath and a simple master bedroom containing his personal stone fireplace, white fur rugs, a low, wide bed, a high quality stereo system, and a large collection of the group's records. He

242

had been living in the house alone, paying thousands of dollars rent per month, and he was rarely ever at home. We filled it up, playing all of his records, the grand piano, and the antique harpsichord, swimming in the pool, and between the satin sheets. Alma, the maid, was aghast to find over a dozen houseguests, but we women were helpful, and listened to her stern instructions on how to clean and polish the good silverware. One day I saw Alma ruffling through the linen closet. Where were the blue satin sheets? Brenda was standing beside Alma in her newly sewn blue satin pants, and volunteered to look for the sheets elsewhere.

Brenda was slowly dressing us like genies. Dennis liked her billowy pants so much she made him a pair that he often wore around the house without a shirt — a chic sheik.

He was likable and funny without trying to be, loose, whimsical, and with few reservations, but his body was reserved under contract to the music group made up partly of his blood brothers. He said that he wanted to break those ties to go with us on the road or into the wilderness, so we waited between the bus and the house, exploring the short woods between fences. A high-pitched scream startled me one night just before sleep. It was the pet peacock that roamed the premises freely.

Dennis didn't feed the peacock. That was done by others. There was a man who came to clean the pool, and a gardener for the grounds. They showed up unexpectedly. The black bus loomed large in the yard, the gardener reported to the landlord that he'd seen a man swimming naked, and Alma probably put in her missing sheets report. After a couple of weeks it all got back to Dennis' band and advisors. They raised a ruff, but Dennis shrugged it off. He bopped into the house at the end of the day, humming, smiling, dancing a little, and stripping on his way to the shower. We were there, yet not there. And it was nice.

Still, we felt to be fewer during the day, so when Dennis was gone and others came around, half of us disappeared. Pretty soon we were spending as much time in shadow as in light, so a change was in order. Bruce had always wanted to travel and was considering a voyage overseas, so he took action on it. The two Texas college boys, Robb and Deuce, set off separately to see California. And Mary took the black bus with Sunstone, Ella, Patty, Stephanie, and Sadie to the Mendocino woods for a vacation that would last longer than expected. The rest of us remained at the estate.

Bounding through the kitchen one morning, Dennis told Charlie, "I'm falling in love with Brenda." Charlie laughed. Who wouldn't fall in love with Brenda? It was a nice thought, but Dennis was married to his company. It tied him down. It also gave him security. Before he rushed out the door in the mornings, he went down the kitchen counter unscrewing jars of vitamins, dumping the pills in his hand, and gulping them down with orange juice. That was breakfast. In the otherwise vacant cupboards I counted thirty-seven jars of vitamins. The refrigerator contained nothing but unprocessed orange juice and dairy products. Dennis told us to order what we wanted from the dairyman, and put it on his tab. He also offered to charge food, but we had other ideas.

We floated the Rolls Royce behind high-end supermarkets, and loaded it with Grade-A garbage, winking at box boys who pretended not to be looking. Then we spread big dinners on fine linen and china plates.

When Dennis' friends came to eat, we didn't tell them where we got the food until after they'd eaten it, then snickered to see their expressions of satisfaction sink. But Dennis ate heartily and always thanked us.

Ruth, the preacher's daughter, came from the north, fuller-bodied and fancifully dressed, lugging a big suitcase over the threshold, and barely pausing to say hello before asking to be shown the bathtub. Her father had permitted her a marriage of convenience, so she was legally free at sixteen. Ruth said she wouldn't be staying long because she was on her way to see a boyfriend, but she stayed for a week, then a month, until she was such a part, as a piece to a puzzle, that she apparently forgot she was going at all.

From the house on Sunset Boulevard a drive toward downtown Los Angeles passed the guard booths and gateways to the elegant neighborhoods of Bel Air and Beverly Hills. The real estate then descended in value all the way to the Sunset Strip, once the glamorous gold standard of talent and creativity, but by then just a hodge-podge of glitter and litter. Farther down, the boulevard was lined with junk yards, liquor stores, and little stucco Hispanic communities, before careening into the flat gray cement surfaces of downtown L.A.

But traveling in the *other* direction from Dennis' driveway, Sunset Boulevard was a clean breeze to the beach, bordered by quiet side streets of modest mansions. Those of us at the estate sampled lives of leisure, sipping orange juice by the pool, kicking our chlorine-clean feet onto brocade couches while embroidering, flopping on Dennis' bed, or dancing to all of his albums. "Good Vibrations" was still popular on the charts, and we heard the first version of *Smile* over forty years before the final recording was released. It seemed that Dennis and his brothers did not understand the physics of the "vibrations" they were singing about, but their music was catchy and their harmonies good. They had begun as teenagers fooling with guitars in their garage, then picked up and furthered a music wave that spread from California to the rest of the world: surfer music. By the time I'd hit high school, they were famous, financially successful musicians with a number of albums and yearly concert tours. They were not without problems.

The first time I saw the Beach Boys in person was at a big "Teenage Fair." They had short hair and wore pale, striped, short-sleeved shirts like the dozen or so in Dennis' closets. Most of the group was set to play on an outdoor stage at the appointed time, but the lead singer, Dennis' brother, Brian, was not there. A standing audience grew more and more impatient. Over half an hour later, when Brian did show, he was stumbling drunk, and had to sit down. Members of the crowd by then were rowdy and merciless. Some had bought raw eggs at the Orange Julius stand and the group got pelted. Watching the yellow yokes splash against their pressed shirts, I'd felt simultaneously embarrassed for them and glad. The words to their music had never meant anything to me.

Dennis and his brothers were not surfers by definition. Their music was commercially popular by design. The design was part of the business, which didn't necessarily have anything to do with the singers' lives or beliefs. In keeping with trends, they sang about vegetarianism and transcendental meditation, but most, if not all, ate meat, and Dennis couldn't sit down long enough to meditate. Brother Brian was seriously troubled. It was an accepted fact that he had been holed up in his bedroom for months.

Dennis was troubled too. The opinions of his fans were important to him, but he was seeing the public from a vantage few of its own ever get. They had raised him up to be an idol. In this position, a man might seek someone to look up to. The Christ of our culture was still on the cross, so Dennis and his partners, like the Beatles, had gone instead for a brief audience with India's most famous living guru, the Maharishi Mahesh Yogi. Dennis did not have a lot to say about the Maharishi. With a facial expression like the sheep in nativity scenes, he said only one word: "Beautiful."

Lots of Hollywood entertainers had been to India, and almost everyone we met had the albums of Ravi Shankar. Charlie said it was "music to the soul." Someone had lent us a sitar and a set of tabla drums that he learned to play. Each of the several circles of a tabla drum produces a different tone, and although Charlie didn't study traditional Indian music, he could play the circles individually or in combination. He didn't play the sitar much, and never spoke of an inclination to imitate East Indians in speech or dress.

We visited the shrine of Yogananda at the "Self Realization Fellowship" a couple of miles up the boulevard. Inside its gates, around a small lake and ornamental gardens, fair-haired Americans dressed in saris and nose rings wandered quietly in meditation. Though he said little at the time, Charlie thought it strange that so many Christians and Jews would migrate to other religions. To him, "religion" was indigenous; it was as unrealistic to wrap up in a sari and call oneself a Hindu as it was to put on feathers and call oneself an American Indian.

"My mom had a Christian name and spoke English," he said. "Good, bad, like it or not, I'm bound to be what I am."

Dennis spent a lot of time with Charlie, and I will never know all the things they talked about, but there was good blood between them. Charlie obviously got a kick out of Dennis, and Dennis routinely referred to him as a "wizard." After roaming the yard barefoot one morning, Dennis stepped into the living room through one of its tall windows, sat down at the piano, and, for the first time since we had arrived, played some of his own music. His music was beautiful when he put his heart into it, and that's what was attractive about him, not just his body and face, but the opening that showed heart.

Charlie made up a song for Dennis, and we wrote down the words. Part of it was from a man to a woman, and part from a man to his brothers. Dennis would later talk The Beach Boys into recording the song, but someone would talk him into changing the rhythm and words, and failing to even mention Charlie.

Dean, the preacher, left the Ukiah woods, heading south about the time that the girls in the Black Bus passed him going north. Since his daughter, Ruth, was living with us, Dean was welcomed by Dennis to use the guesthouse. Dean told us that Mary and the girls traveling in the black bus had gained a strange reputation. A hitchhiker had told him of "witches" and a baby goat in a "Black Pirate Bus." All I remember is that about a month after the girls left, we got a call. They were in jail. The way I heard it, Sadie had given LSD to some underage boys just before the boys were questioned by the neighborhood police. Small town. The police had come raiding and found the girls' weed, even though it wasn't in the house,

248

and they had a variety of charges from possession to contributing to the delinquency of minors. Sunstone was handed to Patty during the arrest, since Mary was already on probation. Patty had booked herself into jail as Cathran Smith and her son as Michael. The only potentially good news was that Sadie was at least two months pregnant by one of the young Texans.

I was cleaning the kitchen and Charlie was standing in the breakfast room talking to me when his sentence broke off and he looked like he was listening. Then his eyes watered. He went to a chair and sat down. After a silence he said, "It's Mary. I'm thinking of Mary." For the second time in the three months since Sunstone was born, Mary was separated from him, and Charlie knew her feelings about it. We had considered what we could do. None of them had sounded miserable, just a little put out at Sadie. Sadie had wanted to do all the talking: they'd been having a good time, magic things happening, "magic tuned-in people." Mary had been business-minded with a rundown of charges and legal procedures. She said they had a public defender, would wait, go to court, and let us know. Charlie's parole officer and his wife had offered to pick up Sunstone from foster care and keep him for the duration of their incarceration, so she was correcting the record, claiming him as her son, and releasing him into their care.

Charlie talked to Dennis about bailing the girls out. I caught only part of the conversation. It was a problem. Dennis' money was tied up in investments made by his advisors. He had specified charge accounts, but sometimes bummed pocket money from friends, and even from Charlie. I got the impression that Dennis' people considered him irresponsible and untrustworthy to handle his own finances. It would later be widely reported that we "took" Dennis for thousands of dollars, but we took only what he gave. We didn't press him or the girls would've been out on bail.

Terry Melcher drove his sleek foreign sports car through Dennis' carport and honked. Strawberry blond, with a big red mustache, Terry looked impeccable in pastel cotton sportswear. He was a young businessman, the producer of his mother's television show which we had never seen. Beside him was a naturally handsome actress, herself the daughter of a beloved TV entertainer. Terry and his girlfriend looked like print ads for expensive liquors and leisure vacations, but their expressions were serious and distracted. When he learned that Dennis was not at home, Terry continued around the circular driveway and zoomed away.

The sons and daughters of other movie, TV, and music entertainers came by the house, as well as some of Dennis' girlfriends from out of state. With the exception of a wholesome Irish girl, the girlfriends were stiffly jealous of other women, and tried to wedge as much distance between Dennis and the rest of us as they could. One high-heeled woman was so indignant she couldn't be in the same room with us. She'd flown into town with a wardrobe that jam-filled one of the big closets. Later, when she went away and left her clothes, we took them out and distributed them to people on the streets. She would call it stealing, but we never wanted her clothes. We just wanted to make sure that she wouldn't come back to stay unless she was willing to be naked in a sense.

No woman could possess Dennis. Each came and went with her own illusions of him, and each had him to herself, however briefly, long enough to sustain those illusions. One night Sandy, Dennis, and I were "camping" on his front lawn, when headlights came up the drive. The driver found her way from the front door across the lawn, and, within seconds of kissing him, was scooting her pants down. Dennis put himself into her like it was his duty. It was over in minutes. She got up without saying a word, straightened her clothes, went to her car, and drove away.

Dennis liked the *concept* of camping. When his music group scheduled a vacation at Lake Havasu, he took five of us girls in the Rolls Royce, and we lay sleeping bags on the sand within a circle of willows, while his band mates and their families parked large motor homes on the beach. It was a fun weekend of picnic food, sun, and water sports but, with the exception of Al Jardine's family, the entourage was inhospitable toward us.

Back in Bel Air, Dennis took us to Brian's home to swim and see his recording studio. It didn't seem to matter where we were; wives or girlfriends came to pull their guys away. I hadn't seen anything like it since high school. It was more than that our clothes didn't come from exclusive Wilshire or Rodeo Drive clothiers, or that we looked too young or too many or too much alike. Most of the women we saw in Beverly Hills were tense and unreceptive before they met us, and we didn't like going to places where catty women treated us like dogs. Increasingly we were perceived by Dennis' managers and advisors as a threat to them. Dennis said he told them he wanted time away from the business to camp and be inspired, and they pulled harder on him.

Dennis and Charlie walked the grounds, comrades of many moods. Charlie asked Dennis if he wanted us to leave, and Dennis insisted not, but each time he declared he was going to take a vacation to travel with us, he only got wound up tighter, and, in turning, looped himself into even more commitments.

"Okay, I'll see you at 5:00," I heard him tell someone on the phone.

I said, "Dennis, you already said you were going somewhere else at 5:00." He just shrugged and made a funny face. Wasn't he just in a big movie? He traveled the world, played before thousands who paid him for it, had girls in every state eager to lie with him or just get a scrap of paper he had touched. He meant well; what did it matter what he said? But it did, and he was perpetually agitated.

There was good reason for Dennis' dilemma. Popularity and wealth were not entirely satisfying ends to him. Surety and peace eluded him. And while most of us girls were ordinary, Charlie showed more faith in himself than even the most successful people Dennis knew. Dennis was beyond fame and money, but even in his youth he was already spent. He couldn't roam for more than a day. He was owned and operated. Peoples' investments rode upon him. He had signed the contracts long before, and he didn't have the will or the confidence to make the change. He had gained access to half the world through his company. It was a lot to give up for a soul he was unsure of.

Twice Dennis told us he would be home for dinner, and the rest of us waited, and he didn't come, so the next day we left the estate and went back to the valley, where the land is flat and wide, to the foothills above the smog line, to The Ranch.

1969

The Ranch

As we became, and have always become what is around us, The Ranch gave us texture. The sharp rocks and smooth stones, the sticks and grasses beneath our bare feet, the hoot of an owl, even the distant scent of a skunk all added dimension to our experience. The sun heated the mountain boulders above us by mid-morning, and rattlesnakes lay between them. In the deep, cooler places along the creek beneath thick-trunked oaks were shade and dark, moist dirt that felt and smelled good, but also insects, spiders, and poison oak to keep us aware. The medicinal scent of eucalyptus trees cut through the summer humidity, and their rattling signaled a welcome breeze to otherwise sweltering afternoons.

The five girls spending that summer five hundred miles north in jail had gotten so hot that they'd just quit wearing clothes. They were the only prisoners in the women's section, and all of their keepers were women, but Charlie's parole officer in San Francisco read a newspaper article about their "NUDE-IN," the reporter claiming that their cooling tactic was "a new kind of protest movement." Friends who had visited them stopped by The Ranch to tell us that they had lost weight, but "looked great," that Patricia was now an exuberant "Katie," whose song and humor filled the cellblock, and that, while facetiously called "a little crazy," they were well regarded by jailers and townsfolk alike. Listening, I was struck by the irony that this celebrative spirit was about a stint in the county jail.

The rest of us were spending nights in the jailhouse. Temporary arrangements had been made with The Ranch's owner for us to bed down on the movie set in the rooms with the black wooden bars. Then somebody brought the Black Bus back so that we could sleep in it.

A quarter mile from the ranch front, the "back ranch house" or "farmhouse" was still occupied by hippies who gave us use of their kitchen, so there was some intermingling and exchanges, including a quantity of grass and acid. One day a group of us was enjoying a walk down the road when I heard Charlie say, "Wasn't Snake wearing that blouse today?" Illogically, I knew that he was talking to me. Snake hadn't been wearing my blouse, but I understood that she was not among us.

"No," I said, "but she could be." I wheeled and ran back to the bus. Diane had been regressing — she was more of a child than she had been when we met her — but I hadn't realized that Charlie thought we needed to keep an eye on her. I found her inside the bus, sitting propped against one wall like a big blow-up doll, being manhandled by an unwholesome hippie known as Ratface. She appeared to be in a stupor. Had it been anyone else, I would have apologized for the intrusion, but I blurted something about our walk, and told Snake to come. Ratface was incensed, but he knew that I wasn't going without her, so he left the bus. Snake wasn't herself. She looked bloated.

"What are you doing?" I asked her.

"I don't know," she said, beginning to cry. "I feel like a dope."

"You're not a dope," I said, wondering where she got that idea, and we went down the road.

That night Snake's parents stopped by The Ranch. They were living across town at The Hog Farm with other hippies, and their infrequent visits were welcome, but always surprising. Telephones were rare to the disestablished; nobody called ahead, unless by telepathy. Snake's mother was pretty like her, but heavier. Cheerfully stepping into our bus, the first thing she said to her daughter was, "Hi dope!" Snake reflexively gave her mother a dopey little grin — then suddenly shot me a look to confirm her understanding.

LSD was cathartic. Our trips into other lives and lifetimes were awful and fantastic, but always interesting. Egos became visible not just as ideas but as physical beings, often in the forms of our parents and grandparents whose genes and thoughts we carried. In the extreme they might appear narcissistic, timid, stubborn, or arrogant — dripping off of us, or plastered on like armor. They might be racing toward winning a perpetual competition, or hanging back to avoid failure. Whatever the facades, these living sets of habit and thought blocked a soul we knew to be infinitely brighter. Most of us had glimpsed that soul and wanted to let it live in us. The want, paradoxically, was part of the ego that had to give up.

Eventually we gave the Black Bus to the hippies so that they could follow their dream to Oregon, and we could move into the farmhouse, paying the proprietor beside the movie set forty dollars a month for the rent of it. I wandered up the road one day to meet him.

George Spahn's "house" was a crude and cruddy bungalow with a row of filthy windows set to overlook the front yard, and flies going in and out the open door. Beyond the steps and the storm door I looked into a long, cluttered room with linoleum curling on an unvarnished hardwood floor. Mid-room, with his back to the opposite wall, an old man wearing a light cowboy hat and dark glasses sat in a saloon chair with arm rails — the kind movie cowboys use when playing poker. He was smooth faced and, despite the heat, dressed in a starched white shirt, suspenders, and grey work pants. Across from him, two ranch hands ate lunch at a table covered in red and white oilcloth.

In front of me were several old desks heaped with broken leather bridles and harnesses, and sitting on one of them, a gangly, long-nosed, pit-faced cowboy, clothed hat to boots in dusty black. One of his black-gloved hands didn't seem to have any life in it, but he used the wrist of that hand to prop a plate against his chest, while the other hand forked short greasy plugs of fried hot dog between his chomping jaws. After staring at me, he put down the plate, pulled a flask from his pocket, popped the top with his teeth, and took a swig before yelling, "WHAT THE HELL DO YOU WANT?" and laughing fiendishly at my surprise.

"Hello?" The old man spoke, as if searching the air with sound waves.

"Hello, Mr. Spahn?" I answered, but another cowboy, a short, dirty blond behind the counter in the kitchen, was rattling pots and pans and yelling, "GODDAMN IT! I CAN'T FIND A DAMN THING AROUND HERE!"

"Hush! Hush now!" the old man spat out, wincing with irritation. His voice settled when he asked,

"Who's here? Is somebody here?" It was as though no one had heard him.

I walked toward him, past a balding stuffed chair and said loudly, "Yes — I'm from down the road at the back."

"Here at our place?" he asked, still flinching at the noise.

"Uh huh. Yes."

"You're one of the ones who rented the farm-house."

"Right. My name's Lyn." One of his big hands extended and I took it. He nodded straight ahead and told me he was pleased to meet me. He had a solid speaking voice and proper manners, but he didn't seem pleased.

"I thought maybe you were one of our riders," he said. "We run a horse rental business here, you know." He shook his head once and complained to himself, "Some days you'd never know it." He felt the seat of the chair beside him, and with a twinge of disgust or regret, he said, "Excuse me. I'm blind as a bat," then offered me the seat. I sat down and was taken in by the action of the cowboys. They shouted back and forth, though the room was only about 14 feet wide and twice as long. A counter set apart the kitchen, which was greasy and full of flies. Scattered aluminum cake pans at its entrance contained water and a few pieces of dry dog food.

The two men sitting at the table got up, dusting crumbs off their hands, stuck their plates and forks on top of a pile of others in the kitchen sink, and continued their conversation out the door. Someone had dropped a chunk of hot dog on the table, and a cat in one of the chairs was reaching a paw to steal it.

"Now Randy ..." the old man said firmly, about to give instruction, but the darkly dressed cowboy with the gimp hand growled, "Larry, did you do what I told you?"

The short blond Larry came out of the kitchen, flaunting a fist and pouting, "Aw, shut up! You don't tell me what to do!" and he took a swat at the cat. Randy pretended to laugh loudly, and the old man wiped his sweating brow with a handkerchief, his bold jaw set in anger.

Then a pint-sized red lady with gnarled hands appeared in the doorway, her face flushed with heat. Dyed red hair, 1940s-style, bulged above her forehead from under a scarf tied at the back of her neck. She had a sharp nose, wore faded red lipstick, and was scowling like a bird. Her words were short in one raucous tone: "What are you boys doing?" Slack jeans and a snug cowgirl shirt showed her petite but aged body: five feet of embittered beauty with movements like a speedy chicken. Hurrying past me, she gave a curt, professional "howdy-do," slid the dog pans aside with one barely shod bunion, and seemed to scare the dirty blond Larry out of the kitchen.

"Pearl?" the old man asked. She didn't answer because she was drinking a glass of water.

"Yeah, it's me," she said, coming up for air. There was an undercurrent of resentment.

"Riders, Pearl?" he asked impatiently, like they would need his immediate attention.

"No. No riders," she obliged, turning around with her second glass of water, and delicately blotting the sweat from her forehead with the back of her cuff. "We haven't unsaddled from the last group. I had to come up here to see what was going on."

"We're *eating*. That's what's going on," Randy dared a battle.

She countered firmly, "Well I told you to get those horses unsaddled before you came up here to eat."

Before George Spahn could finish asking, Pearl told him that the horses were not lathered.

"It was a slow group," she said. "They walked most of the way." Still, he looked stricken with worry that compounded his anger. He asked what time it was but nobody answered. Pearl hurried out the door, sharply telling the cowboys not to "dillydally," and they got into a play fight, throwing something back and forth at each other. The old man asked again about the time, so I scanned the room and finally asked him where a clock was. He told me that behind me to the right was the door to his bedroom and an alarm clock on his dresser. I opened the door to an odd, sunny room, the windows without curtains. His bed was made and covered with a clean cotton quilt. It was lofty with old fashioned posts at its head and foot. The only other pieces of furniture were a bed stand and a dresser on which were the ticking alarm clock, a telephone, and a bottle of shaving lotion. To one side of the room a storage space contained two or three fancy saddles on pegs, and, nearer the floor, a cold-water faucet crooked over a half-gallon can. He had no hot water and no sink, just a hole in the floor. I could see dirt two feet below.

"Did you find it?" he sounded — I think to draw me out before I'd invaded too deeply. I closed the door behind me and reported to him the exact time, as I reseated myself beside him. I knew then that he had little left but time. I didn't know that he kept himself busy thinking about how much money the rental business was pulling in versus the cost of feed for horses and cowboys, or that he'd worked himself blind. He had a number of problems — two being that he couldn't take care of all the problems he thought of and people had quit listening to him.

I was impressed with George Spahn's hardiness. He was eighty years old and, although his blindness had for five or six years kept him in a world apart, he was mentally still present, living alone and working through all the frustrations of having lost authority in the running of his own business. I couldn't help but listen to him, and he gave me one of his problems. I took it to everyone at The Ranch.

There was a tractor-trailer size water tank on its side down a steep ravine in a creek bed. George figured that if we could haul that out of there, he could probably get a hundred and eighty dollars for it, and he was sure it looked an eyesore on his property. I thought that together we all could move it, but the tank was rusted, had holes in it, and had filled with silt — not the picture George had in mind. Nobody wanted to even try. I explained that to him, and it made him angry. What with all the people roaming around, there must be some able-bodied men — Christ, he'd do it himself if he could see! What was the matter with people today? I told him it would take a crane to haul it out and that the crane would cost more to rent than he could get for the tank. I also told him that trees had grown up and now concealed the tank from public view. The full truth was that the rest of his ranch fit quite well with the rusty old water tank.

Snake came up the road and sat with George. Ruth and Brenda and other girls came, and soon the water tank lost prominence in George's mind. He had visitors to entertain. I walked into his house as he was telling stories about old times, and in a brisk Irish brogue he said, "Top o' the marnin' to ya." He was smiling like a new man.

Much of Los Angeles was unpaved when George Spahn came to California from Pennsylvania. He bought land and built this ranch. It was one of several movie ranches in California, and the people from Hollywood rented it and his horses regularly. He told of Tom Mix, Gene Autry, and other movie heroes for whom he had wrangled.

"Autry," he said, "was a scoundrel. Most of his fans never knew it. He was mean to the hands and often came to work so drunk we could hardly get him on a horse. You can tell a lot about a man by the way he treats his help. Some fellas were real gentlemen ... and then there were the other kind..." We would always know when George Spahn disapproved of someone. He'd stop short, and substitute gravely, "My mother always told me: 'If you can't say something nice about somebody, don't say anything at all.'"

The five-room back ranch house was unevenly built, but the hand-hauled stones gave it rare distinction. George Spahn called it "the farmhouse." A modern bathroom had been plumbed but never connected so we employed the bucket method again. We furnished and decorated to our liking, but no matter how often we swept, fine sand crept into the house, along with a few cats, dogs, and even people.

There were usually a few well meaning, self-deprecating girls like Shirley* coming and going. If, when Shirley served you a meal, you said, "Hmmm looks good," Shirley confided that she had burned the rice, put too much oregano in it trying to cover the burnt taste, and then made it soggy trying to wash off the oregano. If you took that with good humor, she became serious. You really hadn't understood. With tongue-y grimaces and guttural sounds, Shirley confessed what she hadn't washed or had dropped on the floor — until you put down the plate, lest a morsel fill you with her negativity. Then, eyes watering, Shirley went away.

Bo was an excellent cook who came and went frequently. Petite and pale, with round dark eyes and dark frizzled hair, Bo seemed a shrinking violet, but she was something else. Charlie called her a "witch." I had never met Bo when we nearly bumped into each other one dark night on the movie set. I stepped back with a startled "Hello," but she moved closer, and taking one of my braids in her small hand, she yanked it — *hard*. Calmly her black eyes studied my surprise, and what I perceived as smugness turned into a bemused but warm smile. Although she said nothing, I felt afterward that Bo liked me.

Bo proved less predictable than a wildcat, which she sometimes resembled, bristling and yowling her displeasure. She both craved and hated attention, and she was into fighting with men. She'd been in a physically combative relationship with a hippie man at the farmhouse, but Charlie drew her out of it, and when the hippies left for Oregon, she stayed, silently moving to be near him, always in the shadows.

Dennis in Pacific Palisades said that he missed us. We visited, but didn't stay. Ranch life was rough, but active, with interesting characters and plenty of day-traffic. Despite his rundown surroundings, George Spahn always dressed for business. He bathed from a washbowl of cold, soapy water every morning, and shaved with a blade — he couldn't stand even the *thought* of a beard he could feel. Then

262

he put on clean underclothes, grey work pants, and a starched white shirt, and came out of his bedroom to sit in his chair for most of the day. On the days that we stopped in to see him we began cleaning his house, starting with the antique gas stove in his kitchen. It was so thick with grease it could barely be recognized. There was a modern refrigerator filthy with finger-prints, and two sinks of crusted dishes, pans, and cast iron skillets.

Frustrated, he told me, "It's hard to manage a place you can't even see." I told him we fixed up the farm-house, and that Brenda was cleaning his kitchen, top to bottom. He solemnly said, "I know it. She's a hard worker, and a good little gal." I could tell by his tone that, to him, the term "hard worker" was high praise.

George eventually allowed us to give him his meals, but he was very particular, feeling each plate, by hab-it, before we served the food. Almost everything, at first, had to come from a can. He told me that he used to have to feel his way around the kitchen which caused him to lose his appetite, and that there were times when he'd spent half an hour looking for a can opener before giving up and eating dry bread. He said that Pearl fed him, but not always when and what he wanted, and that she was always in a hurry, and he didn't like to argue. It made him mad just talking about it.

Ruby Pearl climbed into her dented green pickup every morning and drove from The Valley to run the horse rental business. Tough and shrewd, she super-vised all the horses, all the cowboys, and all the mon-ey. At evening, she took George into The Valley for din-ner at one of several hometown restaurants, and then shopping for a lot of coffee, hot dogs, pork 'n' beans, potatoes, eggs, and cinnamon rolls. They'd been doing this for years and knew each other well. The cowboys, for their work, earned little more than a bunk and the food and cigarettes that Pearl purchased with George's money. They were an odd set, Randy Starr being prominent as the bossiest and most cantankerous, and the others, simple down-and-outers, some who had found their roles at The Ranch years before and stayed.

After the day's hard work — and that could be any day — Brenda sat on the steps of George's house wearing a serious expression. Then she turned her chin up to the sun and she shined. Brenda had hair the colors of driftwood, and sea-grey eyes beneath long lashes. She was younger than most of us, but raised to be confident. Whether delivering babies, fashioning clothes, or driving Mack trucks, Brenda displayed the same calm confidence; and she was a giver, always doing something for somebody else. She was so endearing, able, and attractive that all of the guys wanted to be with her, and many of the girls just wanted to *be* her. It was the modesty with which she handled this that sustained it.

One day Brenda was ahead of four or five of us girls climbing onto a loading dock behind an upscale supermarket. She had just lowered herself from the ledge of the dock into one of the vegetable dumpsters when a little produce man burst through the market's swinging back doors carrying a big box of outer green cabbage leaves. At the edge of the dock he looked down, saw Brenda, and stopped. Then he spotted the rest of us and pointedly emptied the box on her head. I remember it in slow motion, the green cascade and her disappearance, and when most of the leaves had fallen away her small face reappeared, blinking up at the man under an elfin cap of curled cabbage leaves. After a stunned silence, the rest of us broke up laughing.

"Why don't you get jobs like the rest of us?" the man growled, marching his anger inside. His unhappiness was our answer to that. It wasn't the first or the last time we would be rebuffed, but there were then, and always would be, market employees who became our allies, putting food they were bound to throw away in boxes and bags for us. We would have a dairy connection, a fruit and vegetable man, a baker, and others with whom we might exchange words once, or talk to each time we came. And in some cases, as camaraderie became food, food became information, and information camaraderie in circles like that.

When the ranch creek was deep enough, we submerged ourselves in it. During hot summers, we sat beside it cooling our feet, the small, colored stones on its bottom making mosaics of our reflections. But rather than soap up the creek, we bathed in the shower shack near George's house. The shower shack reminded me of my grandparents' pump house. It was dark on entering. We could barely see the spigots over the big iron sink. Behind a wood partition, a bare pipe trickled cold water. If several of us girls were in there together, we sat on the bench below nails that held our clothes, and took turns soaping and rinsing. In dark wood and dim light we looked mysterious and beautiful. Shafts of sunlight streaked between the boards across part of a foot, an elbow, a breast, an eye, a strip of shiny hair. Sometimes we carried pots of heated water from George's kitchen and poured the warm water slowly over each other's heads, knowing the meaning of luxury.

At the end of each day, we gathered in the
back ranch house next to the stone fireplace. There
was noise until everyone settled down on the rug.
Then it was rare if we had more than one conversation going across the table. We didn't have a table, but
there was a level of respect above which we passed the
bowls and plates. Since we ate only one large meal together at sundown, most of us were hungry, the food
was good, and the only sounds were in response.

The house had space for all of us to sleep together
in a long room with a secret door. A stranger standing
in the front room might never know it was there. Some
people paired off to make love. Paul was a young go-
getter. I think Charlie liked that about him. He was
a good match for the younger girls. But half a dozen
women always awaited Charlie's touch, and every so
often he took his time, laying us out like delicacies to
be savored. He was also genuinely instructive to the
younger guys. One night in Dennis Wilson's bedroom,
as all of us lay naked on the white rugs beside the
fire, Paul was mechanically rubbing Brenda's leg, and
Charlie put a hand on Paul's arm.

"Easy," he said, "this isn't a piece of furniture. It's
a work of art."

The rumor of that congregation would travel as "the
orgy." When it began, Dennis was in our midst, but
some of his friends and band members were just sitting on his bed, watching us. As the caressing became
more intimate, and the sighs more intense, I was half
conscious of murmurs and snickering coming from
the bed. Then Charlie sat up, and said to the specta-
tors, "This isn't a joke. Have some respect. Get in or
get out." Three or four men jostled each other out of
the room, but one took off his clothes and joined us.

266

I didn't know his name until years later, when in prison I saw him on television receiving a music industry Grammy for having written "I Write The Songs," which had been deemed "Song of the Year."

We were always more women than men, and some of the men were still in their teens, but a few, like Bobby and Dennis, came and went, hurried by fate or fortune, and Charlie was inclined to spend time with them. His prosecutors would argue that he was "recruiting followers," but his inclination toward the company of more experienced, independent men doesn't support that contention. People of the day were calling "brothers and sisters" to stand up for causes, each kind of people gathered with and for their own. Ever since we had become a group of women-plus-Charlie, he had been seeking his brethren.

Charles Watson was sitting in Dennis' living room when we stopped by to visit. He reminded me of a tall sapling as he stood and called me "ma'am." I thought if he'd had a cowboy hat he would've tipped it. "I came to see this Hollywood I've always heard about," he said, grinning. No doubt he was keen. He'd come from rural Texas, seeking worldly experience on the fast track. While taking business courses at Cal State, he'd worked part time as a salesman, before quitting both to open his own businesses. Then, less than a year after leaving his two-block hometown, while driving up Sunset Boulevard, he had stopped to pick up a long-haired hitchhiker, and was wowed to learn that he was transporting a famous musician. Dennis had invited him into the house, and he'd been practically living there ever since.

I asked Charles about his businesses. "Wigs," he said. He sold hairpieces from a beach house in Malibu. He didn't tell me that he supplemented his income by dealing marijuana and lightweight drugs. I figured the wig business would be cut short. He was so personable he could have sold homes, cars, magazines, or *anything but wigs* on southern California beaches. He was politely aggressive, interested in girls, and ultra confident, even with the aw-shucks guffaw. He wore the thrill of victory like wings on his head. This Hollywood he'd always heard about was the destination of dreams — not that he wanted to be a celebrity. Just being in the same house with one was not much short of meeting God.

Charles at root was a church-nurtured Methodist from that wide strap of the Southern U.S. that used to be called "the Bible Belt." Imagine his surprise on meeting the weed-smoking, LSD-advocating Methodist minister who was living in Dennis' guest house.

Preacher Dean's new faith had blessed him with a beatific smile. His full white beard and ministerial history lent him influence as a psychedelic spiritual guide, but it was a reputation that had gotten him into trouble in Northern California where he had legal charges pending. During the next months he made several trips north to court, sometimes with Charles, and once brought back a carful of college-age kids, thinking that they might stay at the ranch. Since ranch visitors already included horseback riders, an ex-policeman, former ranch hands, and hippies, we directed his passengers to the Spiral Staircase House. One of them insisted upon returning and had to be accommodated. That was Brooks. He was quietly persistent, but he didn't quite fit in.

One day on the ranch, Charlie told Brenda and me that it might be a good time for the two of us to take a vacation. He said that we were "working too hard for people who were just along for the ride." I felt we were being cut adrift, but he borrowed an old convertible for us, and my sense of adventure was kindled. We took turns driving a lazy zigzag north, bumming gas at a quarter's worth a station. The convertible didn't actually convert, the top being permanently down, but the weather was warm so we often wore only bathing suits, stopping at public recreation areas to swim and sleep, and, somewhere, contacting poison ivy. I have never seen anyone swell up like Brenda did, her delicate face lumping like a monstrous potato head. The cause of this disfigurement was not obvious and it became difficult to talk attendants out of gas. For days under the hot sun, Brenda's skin wept. She shook herself to keep from scratching, and more than once I turned from the road to see tears rolling down her face, but she didn't complain.

North of Santa Rosa we realized where we were going. On the one hand, it was a "might-as-well" idea, but on the other, it seemed suddenly obvious this was what Charlie had in mind. We arrived in the wooded town of Ukiah just a day or two before Mary, Patty, Ella, Sadie, and Stephanie went to court and were released, trusted to return for another court date the following month. We had a happy reunion packed into the convertible, driving in the open air to San Francisco to pick up Sunstone. Susan exposed her belly to the sun; she couldn't stop talking about the baby boy she had dreamt was inside it. And thanks to Charlie's parole officer and his wife, Sunstone was as sturdy and cute as a bear cub. Charlie was disgruntled to hear us calling Sunstone "Pooh Bear" when we got back to the ranch. He later told me gravely that when Sunstone was born he saw an image of the moon eclipsing the sun. He said, "Women have been overshadowing their children for too long."

All of the girls came into George's house to meet him. He perked up, politely asking questions about our drive south, and listening to the sounds of their voices.

I could give you a tour of the movie set like I gave them. We'll walk out of George's house and to the right down this slope along a white picket fence to what George calls "The Rabbitories" — State Park-style wooden restrooms, each with a sink, mirror, and flush toilet. There's a big wash basin and a shower in the adjoining shack.

On downhill toward the back of the Western set, here's a red shack storeroom and, next door, Randy Starr's special and only trailer. Randy looks like a villain and he's always mad. We girls only saw his trailer from the doorway since we heard him yell, "Nobody better go messin' around in my trailer!" as well as, "Get in my trailer and take off your clothes!" Clever psychology, but we didn't go in — not until we had an excuse and he was gone. The inside is cluttered with everything he owns — tin-framed photos of himself, and posters advertising: "RANDY STARR FAMOUS MOVIE AND TV STUNT MAN SPECIALIZING IN DEATH-DEFYING NECK DRAG," and showing a fuzzy photo of Randy hanging from a noose. There are dusty rodeo awards, broken knick-knacks, and numerous pieces of larger junk on which to display the smaller junk. There's a rabbit-eared TV, a holey couch, and, in the cramped kitchen, a stack of dirty plates, and stashed in his closet, everything from his rhinestone-studded western costume to his former wife's wedding gown. Those are all the reasons we'd better stay the hell away from his trailer.

Next, around back, is a rusty freight car where Larry, the cowboy, lives. He's the small blond one. He's young for his age, and has a metal plate in his head. He'll go along with anything you say; one day he and Charlie saddled up to scout the territory in case we needed to move the wagon train. Larry keeps better care of the horses since we got here. Likes to show off. Ruby Pearl, the day-horse lady, has to keep after him to take his showers, and Benny looks after him too.

Benny's the dark-haired cowboy who sleeps in the Bunkhouse. He might be a little backward, but he's good at heart. He used to be a trapeze man for the circus until he fell wrong and wrecked his leg. He says it only bothers him when it's cold. Benny doesn't yell at the horses like Randy and Larry do, and he's gentle with the little kids who come to ride. He's gentle with Larry too. He and Larry are getting a big ranch in Texas some day, and they're talking about going back into rodeo. Larry has told me about it *many times*. Leaning against the sliding door of his boxcar, he says, "Yep... I got my Levi jacket in there packed right now."

Now we're in back of the movie set. We don't come back here much. This porch behind the saloon has been full of broken props and furniture since before we got here. To your right is the barn where about twenty-four of the horses stay in individual stalls. Fresh hay bales are stacked in there, and pleasantly pungent smells. And to your left is the Wagon Shed, housing two fine old buggies, a buckboard, a black-fringed funeral coach, and a *beautiful* full-sized replica of a Wells Fargo stagecoach. George doesn't want us messing with these, and they never get taken out of the shed except for parades and movies.

Across the saddling yard in that separate corral is George's prize year-old Appaloosa stud, Cody, "a Leopard Appy," he says proudly, "with perfect black spots big as your fist all over him." There are a number of horses George says are "marked like they came off a carousel," a few that are over thiry years old, but he makes sure they eat good because he says "they've worked hard for many a year."

Next to Cody are the tack room for saddles and bridles, a pen for mares in foal, and then the haystack — that's twenty feet high of baled hay. Behind it are the corral, the mule and donkey pen, and "the dump" — not for garbage but for junk.

To complete this circle tour, to your left is the little office where Pearl signs in the riders; here's the payphone; and, left again, rounding the corner, we'll step up and walk along the boardwalk in front of the movie set. Here's the Bunkhouse where Benny and some of the cowboys sleep. It's got one room with a table and chairs, and another with two beds, covered in clumpy mattresses and dog-haired blankets. Next is the boarded up wagon shed, and, then the jail with the black wooden bars. And this big log place with the thick double doors is The Longhorn Saloon. Look inside. See the stage? The whiskey bar, mirrors, and all those vintage bottles and props are true antiques. Over there is a huge potbelly stove, but Pearl says we can't light it.

The next room is the Rock City Cafe. It's just a facade and storage room. And across the sand, we're back at George's. Charlie says the soul of George is living in this tattered town. It's still alive in my imagination.

So much happened in such a short time, I was inclined to leave this telling in the present tense as I originally wrote it. People would later give legal testimony attributing months or even years to what in real time was much less. Time-altering supplements had something to do with it, but there were other variables, including the comings and goings of so many people, each affecting and acting upon the others.

Patricia Krenwinkel's bark-brown hair parted cleanly in the middle and draped to her elbows. Sometimes she seemed to duck under the weight of it. She was Patty to us before she used an alias at the sheriffs' booking desk up north and became Katie, and in my experience, Katie was a real heart lifter, a heavy-duty softy given to humble service, encouraging, giving right of way, yet not so shy as she might appear. Beneath quiet enthusiasm was a singer, an orator, an activist, and so on, but most often she listened, allowing each their hour and their stage. Everyone liked Katie. She was strong, but also delicate. Mucking out stalls, washing dishes or diapers, her slender hands remained milk white, and graceful as a harpist's.

Ella was a flashback to the 1920s if photographs and movies were the standard. She had the star-bright eyes, and the thin, wavy blonde hair, shorter than most of ours and parted to one side. Even her expressions were of another era. "What can I getcha, hon?" she'd ask, like a small town waitress. And she was one of those girls entirely comfortable in the company of "the fellas."

I don't remember any problems deciding what to do or who would do it. We didn't have job assignments or schedules. The obvious things to do were whatever was necessary, and someone usually stepped up to the need. Sunstone had full time supervision from any of his many admirers. Mary, Katie, and Ella often gathered the quilts and sheets, and all of the clothes that were not on our bodies, and took them to a coin-operated laundry in town. They brought everything home fresh and folded, then hung or stacked them in the closets, and made the beds. Another contingent hauled away our garbage, and came back with fresh food from the market dumpsters. Then a varying group of women prepared the meals. Almost *everyone* did almost *everything* at one time or another, but the women took care of ninety percent of the food, cleaning, and childcare. Charlie was no kingpin in our female drive toward cleanliness and sustenance, but he did influence us by noticing. He wiped his feet at the door, admired the decor, and cleaned up after himself, or else asked for help. In doing so, he set the behavior for the other guys.

In less than two years, county prosecutors would indict Charlie as a "mastermind" and "dictator," but Charlie didn't dictate by ordering or making rules. Most of us had had enough rules made by people who didn't follow them. He ruled by example. He still had the sharpest eyes and ears, and the most experience of anyone at the back of The Ranch. In the circle at night, we treated him as a kind of shaman, giving him sound space in exchange for his insights. They emerged not in sermons or elevated speeches, but in extemporary, often musical, *response*. And when his humor crept up on us, or we were amazed, or enlightened, or thrilled by what he said, he shrugged off personal attachment to the words. Once he said, "I just reflect thought as it goes by in the air." He could send a dart through the eye of an ego, yet his ability to target disease while leaving healthy thoughts and behaviors strengthened drew people to him. I never considered then that he had a unique and different relationship with each person, and only later did I learn others' interpretations of what he said. What I witnessed of his interactions were fostering discovery of the natural world, and a human unity I'd never seen or experienced. His leadership qualities were an unspoken fact, but, if you asked him, he was just living the time of his life.

Days at the ranch house were lit by unusual happenings, realizations, and observations of any wildlife. Learning the ways of wild creatures by coexistence was one of the thrills of our lives. A big spider web decorated our back bedroom, its mistress capturing stray insects, and showing no interest at all in any of us. Lizards sunned themselves on windowsills, honeybees zoomed around in the spring, and mice and wild rabbits crept about at crepuscular hours, keeping well hidden during daylight. Ranchers had killed or driven off the coyotes, but we could sometimes hear a pack of feral dogs in the hills, and always, at night, the owls.

Charlie and Bobby had a hawk and Pearl wanted it. Charlie had given her little things, like a vacuum cleaner when she hinted, but the hawk excited her so much that she outright begged to have it. The guys had never intended to keep it. They wanted to get to know it till its wing feathers grew back. Then they released it behind the ranch where they could see it flying over the hills and woods. One day Pearl complained to George that she didn't like a bird like that flying so close to the chickens. "It's a shame the boys let it go," she said. "I could've given it a nice home." The evidence is circumstantial, but when Charlie found hawk feathers on the ground in the foothills we wondered if Pearl had anything to do with it. Factually, we never knew afterward if the bird was alive or dead.

We had no radio or TV at the farmhouse, no games, clocks, calendars, and sometimes not even enough shoes to go around. George Spahn called us "mountain folk." He liked to play it.

George had appropriate manners conveyed in no-nonsense language when conducting business, but when alone with us girls, he used pet names, children's mispronunciations, and a variety of pretended accents, most often like he was "born in a cornfield." He said he would teach us "mountain talk" because it was "more high gaflutin" and, with his nose in the air, he bragged he was so loved in school, they kept him in kindergarten for nine years.

George Christian Spahn,
A gentleman, a mountain man, an Irish rogue,
And a German businessman —
A "Movin' Picture Man" since "Silents,"
Says he was "a big stock holder and a leading man,"
Says he don't tell people the rest, and he chuckles.
And we say "What?"
He says, "I hold the cows and lead the horses."
That's a wrangler.
You can see his life mapped in his muscled arms,
Red and blue vessels swelling.
Old times he drove a milk wagon.

Up at 3:00 a.m. to feed and harness,
Delivering by 6:00,
Running house to house in the snow,
Wanting to go inside by the fire
And eat a cinnamon roll.
He was eight when he started, since his Pa died,
And he says he used to cry,
Hurrying through that ice slush,
And say to himself, "When I'm a man,
I'm gonna have enough money
To eat a whole cinnamon roll
All my own
Every day."

— L. F. c 1971

George renamed all of us girls. We'd sit in the chair next to his and his hand would come to rest on our wrists or elbows or knees, and he'd say in his Irish accent, "Who bees it?" When his hand set down on my knee, I let out a small high pitch, being ticklish. He chuckled about it all day and started calling me "Squeaky." For Mary he employed the Italian (phonetically "Mahreeohcha"), and Ella was "Yellerstone." Bo became "Rainbow," Brenda, "Brindle," and Katie, "Katydid." Ruth he mish-mashed into "Ouish," the mispronunciation of a child he once knew, and too many for you to keep track of. Some of the girls were underage so he didn't need to know about them — and he wasn't asking either.

There were younger than legal guys — Paul Watkins for a time. Paul was archetypically California '60s — tan, boy-handsome, and flashing straight white teeth. Paul said "far out" to convey interest or surprise, and he said it often. A high school dropout, he was, in effect, a wandering poet-philosopher, but I more often saw in him the showoff, competitive brat. He watched the way Charlie walked and talked, and ran with it as though he had invented it. Most of us imitated Charlie to some degree, and Charlie was more tolerant, reminding us that the guys needed experience. In private, I heard him tell Paul: "If you think to prove, you got doubts." Charlie could compete and be challenging, but he had a distaste for division, and always encouraged us girls to give the young guys a chance, not just for sexual experience, but for the natural human interactions that allow boys to become men.

One day Paul was wandering around, looking for something to do, so Charlie suggested he go back to high school to check out what the other kids were doing. Paul liked that idea, so he picked a local high school and blended in every day for about two weeks. He had a good time, and, as usual, he scored. When he got back that first day, he reported, laughing, "Everyone's high in high school!"

I thought of Paul as a boasting loafer, a tripper, not inclined to work, and rarely without a pocketful of joints, but, as I recall, we always had a few to pass around the circle each night, and I just toked them for granted.

Chuck Grey* wasn't a bad kid — at over six feet tall, hardly a kid at all — but in the eyes of the law he was underage. He had lived with the law all his life. Both of his parents were police officers. He didn't say so until he realized we wouldn't hold it against him. Charlie told him that the cops had been running us all over the county, and we wondered if his dad could help to keep them off our backs. Chuck rolled his eyes.

"He's been on my back for seventeen years," he said.

"A bully?"

"You could say that. We hardly know each other. All he knows how to do is give orders. They're never at home much anyway, and when they're not at work, they're sleeping."

"Are they looking for you?"

"Not really. They don't care, but they put on a show 'cause they don't want people to think they're bad parents."

Chuck was man-some, with green eyes that looked hungry for acceptance. He shaded that look beneath a low brow and a "fuck it" attitude, spending most of his time at the farmhouse.

And then there was the legendary *Steve*. I had heard Randy Starr talk about a "youngster living in the hills," and when I asked about him, Randy said, "He's about sixteen, a runaway, and crazy as a loon — just your type."

The Malibu Sheriff's territory extended beyond George's property. They may have noticed more horseback riders than usual, or more beards on the Western set, or more girls going in and out of his house. Two deputies stopped in to visit him, "to see if everything's alright." He said he told them he had "a new bunch living in the back farmhouse, and quite a lot more help." The officers referred to us as "hippies." George told them he didn't think we were hippies. Upon leaving, they told him to be sure and call if he needed anything. When he told me about it, I said I didn't think they would come to clean the barn, and he laughed.

I found my niche with George. I have read and heard that Charlie assigned me to spend my days with George. That wasn't true; George and I had an easy rapport. But I wasn't the only one who visited George. Most of the girls stopped in to see him at least once a day. When the cowboys came cussing into the house to eat, some of us were there to keep the peace and clean up their debris. Incidentally, we heard their notions and stories in between their complaints. One day I heard Randy Starr talk about bandits. He seemed to believe that Mexican bandits inhabited the hills behind The Ranch. Then I realized that he was talking about dead people. Ghosts. They were rebel Mexican robbers of the 1800s, part of California lore. He was particularly interested in the outlaw Joaquin Murrietta. According to Randy, one of Murrietta's lifetime haunts had been in the hills near the Indian Mesa, and his ghost sometimes hovered up there over his stolen gold.

"I just might get serious one day and find it," Randy mumbled as he went out the door. I hoped he wouldn't go looking because we sometimes visited the Indian Mesa.

From George's house we girls could hear and see the cars of people coming to rent horses. George liked us to run to the rental office and get a look at the people, then run back to the house to tell him of their sizes and behaviors so that he could choose their horses. Panting, we stood before him, saying things like: "There's a man in his thirties, 'bout five-foot-eight, kinda stocky, says he has ridden a lot and wants a fast horse."

George might say, "Tell Pearl to give him Fred." So we'd run back to the office, knowing that Fred wasn't very fast, so George had a hunch that the guy was bragging. He had to protect the braggarts so that they didn't kill themselves, and the horses so the people didn't run them to death. One time a horse got so lathered it appeared to be covered in shaving cream, and Pearl was so mad she yelled at the rider and made him walk that horse for half an hour.

After telling Pearl of George's choices, she usually agreed, unless she was mad at him. Then, she either argued and did what she wanted, or skipped the argument.

We scrubbed down the walls in George's house, and put up old Western movie posters. He began calling it "The Hall of Fame" or "The Celebrity Room." We swept the narrow steps he theatrically called "The Stoops of the Veranda," and sometimes sat there with him, breathing the breeze, and shootin' it too.

One day Bobby Beausoleil blew into town in a '56 Ford truck with a dog named Beau and a quarter horse named Soleil. He gave the horse to George. Another day it was with two women and a Model T in tow. But this time he brought just one woman and a full-sized tipi. They were coming from the set of an independent movie where they'd been oddly cast as American Indians and living in tipis on the set. The woman had a polished look, olive skin, long, shiny dark hair, and plenty of cleavage at the V of her suede wrap dress. When I offered to help her gather her things, she introduced herself as "Gypsy," and, laughing, she confided her first meeting with Bobby.

"I had seen him on the set," she said, "and I invented an excuse to go to his tipi. But he was playing his guitar and he ignored me completely! So I talked to his girlfriend, Gayle — and suddenly Bobby stops playing. He looks at me and says, 'Do you play the violin?' I said, 'You must've heard me.' He said, 'No, no. I'm looking for a violin player.' So I went and got my violin, we played together, and I moved into his tipi that night!"

"What about the girlfriend?" I asked. "What about Gayle?"

She said, "Oh, we went through a lot of changes at first, but Bobby was always talking about Charlie and all you girls — and you know," she smiled, " I've been waiting to meet you."

Gypsy went inside the saloon to unpack, and something happened. She came to me saying that she had just met Charlie and he got mad, and now he was leaving the ranch. She wanted to know if she had done something wrong, and what she could do.

Charlie left the ranch often, but not usually on foot, and not usually mad. Finally I said, "Well, go after him then." By dinner they were back. Gypsy said that halfway down the mountain he had yelled for her to leave him alone, but before the bottom, he'd agreed to return. After dinner we hoisted Bobby's big tipi in the front yard and went in to smoke a pipe.

Randy Starr was fuming. We *goddamned sonofabitchin' hippies* had come *barrelin' in* and *TOOK OVER THE RANCH.* So some of the girls turned the jail into a Sheriff's Office, and stuck a sign reading: "RANDY STARR ★ SHERIFF" above the door, and he simmered down, and seemed to feel more important.

The most talented and physically attractive among us, Bobby was not one feather ready to settle down. I don't know how many times he came and went, bringing and leaving girlfriends, but eventually both Gypsy and a pretty brunette named Leslie Van Houten chose to settle on The Ranch. Leslie was a modest "doll," in 1920s parlance, with a slender neck and hair bobbed a la "flapper." Sweet and smart from the get-go, she proved to have a good, fast brain.

A couple of weeks after Gypsy arrived she told me that she had just seen a near-naked man in the hills above the ranch. She and Brenda had been taking afternoon hikes, *completely* naked, to a plateau above the ranch from where they could see the entire valley, and on this day she'd seen the man squatting on a boulder watching them. She said, "The instant I spotted him he uncoiled like a snake, sprang off the rock like a lion, and disappeared." Before she could alert Brenda, Brenda smiled and told her, "He always follows us."

"He" was Steve, the runaway Randy had told me about. I later spied him by the creek. He looked older than sixteen, tall and muscular, with wide shoulders, and a narrow waist. Another day I saw him on top of the haystack, just watching us. His hair was the color of the hay. Ella referred to him as "a fox" and approached him. I saw them running and laughing together. Then I saw him talking to Charlie, and after that he came closer to all of us girls. Some of us were shy of him because he had no pretense. He wanted to make love to all of us — not just to lie down, but to steal the moments when we stood on the boardwalk talking, to slide up, wrap his arms around us, and move us like Charlie did.

I saw Steve and Charlie shirtless one day, laughing in the hot sun. They were limbering up, rolling their shoulders and necks, letting their arms dangle. Charlie moved his pelvis, acting silly at first, then all around, smoothly. He said, "Come on, man, move your hips. How's a guy gonna fuck if he's afraid to move his hips?"

Steve came into our circle. He was learning to play the guitar. His singing voice was clear and of good quality. He came into our bed. It was a marriage of sorts. He was smart, tender, and funny. He picked up mountain talk from us girls, and put on a character we named "Clem." When nosy people came around asking too many questions, Clem was so dumb they walked away — sometimes in a hurry — thinking that he was demented.

Evenings when the farmhouse looked comfortably slumped, its crooked outlines etched by the setting sun or the moon in a dusky sky, we were drawn, tired and hungry, to the orange light through the screen door, and the simmering scents within. The front room filled, we ate, talked, and sang together. The music was the beginning of harmony.

The mutt that the hippies left behind surprised us with six puppies that quickly outgrew her. One evening, after all the dogs had been fed, Charlie came into the farmhouse saying that we would have to feed the mother dog separately. Taking another bowl of food outside, he showed us that her rib cage was visible under a thin layer of fur. It disturbed him that neither he nor the any of the rest of us had noticed her starving, while she allowed her wildly wagging offspring to eat *all* of her food.

Then one day I came to the ranch front and saw the county dog catcher's truck in front of the saloon. Pearl and Randy had conspired. The catcher was pulling one of our big, fluffy pups by a rope. Pearl scuttled around the truck ordering Randy to "grab that one!" but his arms were already full, heaving another puppy into a cage, and shoving it when it hedged. Vengeful satisfaction flushed his face when he saw me. The dogs had been up front too much.

"Pearl," I whined, close to tears. "Why are you doing this? They don't cause trouble." Pearl tried not to look at me.

"It's for the best," she finally said. It was her same testy tone with a fleeting sympathy. "We had to do something. We can't feed them all."

"But WE feed them!" I yelled.

"It'll be better for them," she declared.

"No," I said, "They'll be killed!"

"Somebody will adopt them," she contended. "That's what the pound is for. And besides," she added suddenly from the bowels of her contempt, "THEY'RE RUNNING WILD. WE CAN'T HAVE THAT HERE."

I admit Pearl was right. Loose dogs reproducing randomly leads to feral packs that can wreak havoc on domestic and wild life alike. But when she said THEY'RE RUNNING WILD, I think she was talking about US.

George had two dogs that Pearl fed before she left for the night, Tommy, a Border Collie mix he'd found as a starving puppy, and Wolf, who Larry said was part timber wolf. The dogs kept their distance when we first came, looking out the corners of their eyes at us. But soon they came to be petted, and to lope with us to and from the farmhouse.

Days, we spread out in all directions. I don't think anyone knew what everyone else was doing. I would later spend more time with Sandy than with any of the other girls, but at the time, I knew her only as a refined and self-conscious beauty. She had been scarred, but I didn't know how or why. Sandy wore fresh cotton skirts or dresses. In the shower I thought she would scrub her skin off. One day when she and Charlie and I were going into town, the closer we got to civilization, the more she straightened her clothes and rearranged her hair. Grinning, he told her, "Relax. Stop thinking of what you look like. I love for the love shown to me, not what TV says is nice looking. I loved my grandmom because she loved God, and told the truth, and made rice pudding." Sandy remained reclusive, yet familiar. I'd see her at a distance walking or riding a horse, a small figure against the blue sky and sandy hills, separate, but fitting. George called her "Sahndra," as if in the presence of a dignified lady.

Sandy

I was raised with what the English would call "form," but no soul or love, gentleness, or tenderness. Most of my life was never real to me except when I went exploring on my bike through nearby neighborhoods in San Diego. At the ranch, my bike became horses. I'd had little riding experience, but I think I shared a dream with millions of girls of having my own horse. TV Westerns were imprinted on my mind — the campfires, starry skies, and soft strumming of guitars — cowboys ambushed behind boulders, shooting their way to safety, riding triumphant and proud through the sagebrush. Exploring the hills around Spahn's Ranch on horseback was a dream come true. I didn't even know that many of the movies and TV shows I liked were filmed in those hills. The trails curved and climbed through chaparral, oak, and narrow passages that were sometimes bordered by giant lichen-covered boulders in colors of gold, bronze, browns, and greens. Tiny birds rustled in the brush, exploding out in a rush of air and sound as the horse came close. Sometimes I'd see tarantulas and horned toads.

I rode bareback or with western saddle. Bonnie and Queenie were my favorites, and I could only ride them if paying customers didn't, which wasn't that often, but as soon as I lifted myself onto the back of a horse, the thrill was on. I loved to gallop. I didn't know where I'd end up or who I would meet or if I'd get lost, so it was always an adventure.

I talked to my horse once we got on the trails. I'd tell her how much I appreciated her carrying me. I'd been told that you have to let a horse know who is boss. When I slowed to survey an area, the horses would often jerk their necks down to eat anything I let them eat. The more I gave in, the more they exerted their strength and will. Sometimes they tried to take over completely. The most dangerous part of the ride wasn't galloping on paths where a rattlesnake could spook the horse, but on the dirt road between George Spahn's house and the back ranch house, the road he called "Lovers Lane." Lovers Lane was bordered by a species of oak with small leaves having holly-like points that could hurt if brushed against. There were also branches at the level of my neck. If the horse veered off the road, it became a power struggle. I was thrown a few times, and once at dusk I rode while on LSD, exerting no will of my own, but surrendering to the will of the horse. She galloped free and didn't try to knock me off by moving under the low branches, or going far into the rocky hills. By nightfall, with just the smallest bit of prodding, she returned us both to the barn.

After exploring the hills, I'd pretend to come to a house where I'd be invited inside for a hearty meal. Food was major to my sense of security. Ever since I got to the house in Topanga, I'd been impressed with the amount of food that filled the kitchen three or four times a week. This abundance appealed to me on a deep level. How much human history has focused on this one basic need, obtaining food in snow, ice, drought, and during wars, on up to modern choices of what to select from the freezer, the supermarket, the comparing of prices and spending of money. With "garbage runs," cost and decision-making were done deals. Any food surprise might appear. I liked shopping outdoors, not having to make choices, not having to spend money, and most of all not letting this precious food be wasted. It was free, unconditional nurturance to be prepared in any ways one's culinary creativity could devise.

Throughout my life I'd had the fantasy of being a lone traveler coming upon a warm, hospitable place where she is heartily fed. The closest I came to realizing this fantasy was at the ranch, but I was the most remote person there. I had never wanted to sit inside and talk. At nightly gatherings, Charlie often observed that Sandy was absent, Sandy was hiding, and maybe someone should go find Sandy. I *was* hiding. One time I took LSD and went up to the Indian Mesa. When I returned to the back ranch house, a communal meal was underway. I stole into the group, furtively gathered food and retreated to some trees outside to quickly eat it. I had feral aspects, stealth, and fear. I wasn't a warm cuddly motherly female like some others at the ranch of whom I was extremely jealous, especially the younger, less complicated girls. As an older female, I was sizing up the competition and trying to determine my place and status in the group.

Despite the fact that I excluded myself, I didn't feel talked about or judged by the others, and I don't feel my opinions of them were based upon class. It was more like, "Does this person feel trustworthy and are they kind? Are they helpful, bright, good looking, and strong?" I did come with a prejudice that more education meant more intelligence, but Charlie quickly blew that concept out of my brain. But while education is equated with intelligence and the higher classes, ranch people exceeded my ingrained standards of qualities I sought in friends. I was the most broken, the most wounded, and the most in need of safety and kindness, and no one made me "sing for my supper."

They were "cowboys" to us, though The Ranch had no cows or cattle drives. Pearl and George just called them "the boys" or "the hands." Cowboys came and went, but three were fairly constant while we were there: Randy, Benny, and Larry.

Randy Starr was stellar in his own mind. He'd been a movie extra, a trick-rider, and occasionally, when drunk, sang "Your Cheatin' Heart" at a low-end lounge in The Valley. Weekends at the ranch, he and his rough-riding teenage girlfriend put on shows:

SLAM! The door. He'd come out of his trailer hollering, "Get your cock-suckin' mother-fuckin' ass outta here!" and he'd stride out to the middle of the yard.

CRASH! The dishes. She in her long-legged Levis would come out after him screaming, "You sonofabitch! You dirty motherfuckin' sonofabitch!" Boot to boot, teeth to teeth, they'd snarl at, kick at, and curse each other in a repeat performance, with variations on the fuckers and bitches. It happened almost every weekend, and Randy was such a good actor he convinced even himself. He could sulk for days.

Only audacity and access to horses had gotten Randy that girl to start with. He was twice and a half her age, had pocked, putty skin, a mangy moustache, a long nose with gaping nostrils, half bad teeth, and hair slicked flat under his cowboy hat, the only evidence of which were greasy spears of hair around his neck and ears. In addition to the black-gloved gimp hand, his body was bony and ill-put together. *And, he was a bully.* Yet Randy had a way about him that made us smile and wonder what he was up to, thinking that he *couldn't* be serious, and sometimes even liking him, all the ugly and disproportionate pieces aside.

One day Bobby Beausoleil was eager to go, but had given his truck to Charlie, and someone was using it. So they both approached Randy Starr about lending Bobby the "FAMOUS MOVIE AND TV STUNTMAN" truck in exchange for a new buckskin outfit and a diamond ring. It was just an old pickup, but the giant sideboards advertising Randy's peculiar claim to fame made it one of a kind. I never expected Randy to lend it, but I saw Bobby drive it away, the archetypical villain, grinning and twirling the ends of his moustache.

Cowboy Benny was older and scruffier, but he looked a little like Charlie. The similarity ended when he spoke. Benny was affably simple and shy. I saw him at night under a bare bulb in the Bunkhouse playing cards with another cowboy. In the dead silence between cricket chirps, he looked slow and thoughtful. The smile in his stubble might indicate a good hand, but Benny could smile win or lose, and just when I pegged him as clueless, he laid down the winning hand, his opponent groaned, and he laughed.

Benny courted a gal who came some Sundays. She was just his height and about his age, her long brown hair in tight braids to her jeans. They strolled Lovers Lane, hand in hand, looking twenty years younger,

Benny so modest and so proud. Then all of her children ran up behind her — eight of them under the age of ten — screaming, crying, and chasing each other. She swung at them, they ran a-ways, circled, and came back to bother her again.

In George's house, the ninth child lying in a plastic cradle was Benny's, a small, dark-haired, pale baby girl in diapers and an old pink dress. He came into the house to see her, holding her up carefully like he'd never seen her before. His face red and smiling, he looked at her again and again.

Cowboy Larry was blond, and shorter than Benny, and had suffered brain damage as a child. He had a metal plate in his head but you couldn't see it. Otherwise, he was not physically impaired, but impulsive. He could be ornery — occasionally on the verge of a tantrum — *especially* around Randy Starr. Larry compensated for his shortcomings by pretending. I could say that he outright lied, and sometimes he consciously did, but usually he was unconsciously imagining within the limits of his disability.

Sandy

One day Charlie took me for a stroll around the front of the ranch, pointing out colors, textures, construction anomalies, nails, wood slats, and knots. He said, "Look at the soul here." He showed me blue boards nailed to chipped peach two-by-fours where sections of wood had been salvaged from old doors and windows to build something new and functional. He opened my eyes to the fading beauty of old barns and bunk houses, rough hewn fences, horse stalls, and sheds.

Few people on the ranch fit into any classes and categories that I'd been conditioned to hold. The cowboys were characters as soulful as the ranch itself. Weathered, raised without television, and with little schooling, they were a different breed from anyone I'd been exposed to, and their presence added warmth and richness to the place. The exception was Randy Starr, who was a dark, even sinister presence. He wore black everything. Even his old, dusty Cadillac was black with his name emblazoned across the side in gold paint. He was sullen, and he yelled a lot. I ignored Randy, but the others were always friendly to me.

Charlie came sauntering across the yard one day, wearing a cowboy shirt, hat, and boots, and said that he and Larry had been to Abilene. Larry was from Abilene and Charlie wasn't joking or making fun of him. He had been in Larry's world for a few hours. He looked and talked like Larry, and Larry looked proud. I brought them both cups of coffee, and Brenda made victuals.

Slowly it dawned on me that I — we — were all characters, and we could invent new parts for ourselves every day. The cowboys didn't share that realization. Like most people, they were fixed in their roles. I was too uptight to play. I was in a tight trap of my history and I felt only Charlie could free me. If he saw me having fun, even if I was just pretending to, he might leave me alone thinking I was fine.

Sandra Good, a stockbroker's daughter, abandoned future financial security, cashed in her stocks and savings bonds, and invested the money in Charlie. He used it to buy a newer, bigger school bus that transported us all over California. It took the five girls and a supporting cast back to Ukiah for court, after which they were free to go with time served and warnings. It broke down in San Jose and was parked for several nights in a plum orchard where the passengers witnessed an uprising of drunken migrant workers on horseback, some of whom later dubiously explained that they were getting ready for a revolution in Mexico. And when all efforts failed to fix the bus, it was left in a parking lot until someone could get it, while its passengers hitchhiked back to the ranch.

Some bus people arrived with a dumpling blonde the likes of Mae West in the factory-new Dodge camper-van that her dad had just bought her. Her given name was Joan, but she called herself Juanita, and she was on her way to Mexico. Juanita had a sassy smile, a wink, and a way with innuendo, but she made no secret as to what she was after: "men who like *blondes*, tall, short, fat or skinny." Charlie headed her off at the pass, and she gave him her van.

We had a lot of cars at our disposal in those days. Dennis' Ferrari was parked by the Bunkhouse for awhile, but it was gone before I got a ride in it. I came out of George's house and saw Charlie walking across the yard toward Paul and Clem on the Pass Road. A bunch of interested people were coming out of the buildings, looking in their direction. Paul was grinning, Clem shrugging and looking sheepish. I got the story on relay: the two boys were returning from a test drive of Dennis' car when Clem mis-negotiated a curve around a mountain. It was a wonder they both walked away. I was told that the car looked like "a strip of bacon."

Charlie eventually gave Dennis the new van that we got from Juanita so that Dennis could go on the road. "Go see the Mendocino coast and the redwoods up north," Charlie told him, but Dennis only traveled to the home of his friend, Gregg, and parked in his driveway.

Preacher Dean and Charles Watson showed up at the ranch after Dennis gave up the lease on the estate. We couldn't have Ruth's father living in the same house with us, but Mary's father in Wisconsin owned a sporting goods store, and had sent her a full-sized tent that we'd set up in the woods, so Charles and Dean went to live in the tent. After Dean left for another court date and didn't return, Charles moved up the hill, offering George Spahn his service as a mechanic. George said he liked a worker, man to man, but couldn't pay more than the room — not even food. When Charles agreed, George asked if he could call him "Tex," and they shook on it. George had plenty of vehicles for Tex to work on — cars and trucks that would never run again, not because Tex didn't try, but because every movable part on them had been stolen or rusted shut long before we got there.

Tex went to San Jose to repair and bring home our bus, taking along TJ who had some experience working on old cars. TJ was a sometime visitor, older than most of us, balding, and missing front teeth for which he had loose replacements. He had already been through the military (demolitions), marriage and divorce (demolitions). Tex said that TJ was like a gypsy, and some would say more like a bum. However, with purpose, TJ was both resourceful and productive. He would later score not only marijuana and psychedelics, but transportation and weaponry.

There wasn't much hybridized marijuana back then. What we called "grass" and "weed" was nothing more than the leaves of a wild, unprocessed plant.

Probably a quarter of the population of California smoked it, but it was untaxed, illegal, and we didn't know how serious our local sheriffs or city police were about snagging people for having it.

Sandy

At night everybody gathered in a big circle in the saloon or at the back ranch house. The girls brought in dishes of food and Charlie regarded the presentation as would an experienced gourmand, commenting on the aroma and the artistry — maybe a sprinkling of flower petals on the salad, or sprigs of wild sage around the squash and rice — and the guys imitated his praise of the cooks. Slowly, too slowly for me, the dishes made their way around the circle. I wished I could have had the seeming lack of attachment to eating that Brenda, Pat, Lyn, and Leslie did. Sometimes I felt hostile toward anyone who held the bowls too long or took bigger bites.

After the girls took away the dishes and the few forks and spoons we shared, one of them handed rolled joints to each of the guys who lit them, taking a hit and passing them on. Someone handed Charlie his guitar, and at times he looked at it as if he were seeing it for the first time, like it was a new and sacred promise of pleasure. Tuning the strings, he might tap gently on the neck or body, while slightly cocking his head to hear the nuances of sound. This exploration could last minutes and some seemed rapt with curiosity and anticipation. Meanwhile Charlie was alert to outside sounds of voices, footsteps, and vehicles approaching or leaving. A sound we didn't hear could have him on his feet in a flash. He might step out into the night and be gone five or ten minutes while we sat waiting.

So much of my life had been waiting for something in the future — to go somewhere, to meet someone, to be seen, get asked out, go to college, and maybe get married. I was a little edgy waiting, but Charlie was out under the stars, likely petting Wolfer or Tommy and, like the dogs, sensing the environment. I wondered if he would encounter someone prowling around in the dark. Cops? Someone up to no good? And what would be the sound of his voice if he did run into someone? Would he sound warm and inviting, or sharp and loud, or stern with authority, or would he be laughing? Unlike anyone I'd ever encountered, Charlie wasn't waiting for life. Every moment in his world was alive and he was alive in it. His reflexes were quick and sure, lacking the hesitations of fear and doubt. He didn't have to think about how to respond; he just did.

I was filled with feelings from the past and with thoughts of the future, with how I looked, and how much Charlie could read about my present state. It seemed everyone had become conscious of themselves. Katie, leaning forward, her thick brown hair falling down the sides of her face, would softly chuckle and admit to a new insight about her conditioning. Steve, or Clem, was seventeen, agile, and handsome in a dusty, disheveled way that reflected his semi-wild surroundings, but he was self-aware enough to know he, too, had baggage to discard. As he shed his conditioning you could see him blowing his own mind with fresh insights and realizations, grinning and shaking his head, whispering "Whew!" Clem showed humility in the contrast between himself and Charlie, and made parody of the bashfulness he felt in the presence of so many pretty girls.

Mary, Lyn, Pat, Ella, Brenda, and even Leslie and Snake were lighter and happier than friends from my past, but all of us had a new standard for what it was to be human, and we compared ourselves and all the other guys to Charlie.

While Charlie was in Hollywood, he met a shiny new record producer who persuaded him to put some of his music on tape at a studio. When the producer invited him for second session, Charlie urged all of us to come along. Sixteen to twenty people in various styles of dress hustled into the bus, many of us silently coaxing and kicking away ideas of becoming a successful recording group. In reality, although all of us could sing, some of us had yet to find a corresponding key. Charlie, Bobby, and Clem could have become successful on their own, but when I suggested to Charlie he go alone, he said, "What fun would it be without all of us together?"

The studio technicians, a pair of balding men, were pissed. They were set up for a single musician. Charlie and the producer cajoled them in the sound proof booth, while the other guys positioned extra microphones for a circle like we had at home. Despite technical opposition, the tape ran.

It was a typical jam session, Clem and Charlie producing good instrumentals, Mary's flute and Gypsy's violin not half bad, and the elephant calls of Paul's French horn roaming a range between interesting and strange. But all of that in combination with Snake on a potato flute, several of us on knives and spoons, plus all of the voices created a cacophony only barely related to music. The technicians blanched, but Charlie joked the whole time. He suggested we relax like we did at home, taking deep breaths, letting them out slowly, and then with sound. Behind closed eyelids I saw the sounds take shape and color. They rose and wove around each other, branching and opening, then falling like leaves in the best harmony of the evening. Into the complete silence that followed, a technician's voice blasted, "Would you do that one again? We didn't have a level."

Cathy Gillies, the blue-eyed daughter of Mr. High School teacher, and Mrs. Entomologist, cantered by George's house on one of his best horses, her blonde hair flying. All of the guys were interested in her. The next time I saw her, she was lying on her stomach by the stone fireplace at the farmhouse with colored pens, paper, and drawings splayed around her. She paid me no mind as I examined her quickly penned — and I thought exquisite — caricatures. When she began talking, it was of books. She seemed nice enough for a know-it-all. I would come to love Cathy as a mildly rebellious teenager, a lovely tomboy, and a reliable, enthusiastic story teller, generous with details. George called her "Capistrano from Santa Susano," or just "Cappy."

George told me to be careful nobody saw us sleeping in the buildings on the Western set because it was against the law. With his fingers rubbing the stubble of a whisker he'd missed, his questions felt carefully around the real question of whether the "fellas and gals" were sleeping together. I told him that we all slept in different places. I might put a sleeping bag down in the saloon or go all the way back to the farmhouse. I think he decided that he really didn't want to know our sleeping habits, but I was aware that he was thinking of what he might do as a young man, and that it's not easy thinking like a young man in an old man's body.

The wide unpaved yard in front of the movie set provided space for trucks, horses, and customer parking. It was parenthesized by two driveways coming off of Santa Susana Pass, one near George's house, and one by the corral. This unintentionally allowed for road traffic to make drive-throughs and U-turns. The Malibu Sheriffs cruised the yard more than once a week. It seemed they were bored — "Let's see what those hippies are up to at Spahn's Ranch." They'd idle if we were willing to talk, maybe looking for information, maybe just to pass the time with barefoot girls in short dresses. We had to stay on our toes.

One time a lady from the State or County called asking cagey questions about kids.

"We run a horse rental business here, ma'am," I told her.

"But are children there now?"

"Riders I reckon."

"Are children living on the premises?"

"What do you mean 'the premises'?"

"Are children living on the property?"

"I don't see children, no." She didn't trust me but she ran out of questions. "Mr. Spahn isn't here right now," I said, "but if you want to call back..."

"Yes," she said she would do that, but she never did.

"You did right," George told me seriously. "Don't ever tell 'em there's kids here or they could shut me down, close the business, and condemn the ranch."

"They've got no reason to do that," I contended — but he was angry.

"Oh you think they don't. You don't know. They as much as told me they could. Right now the City wants me to hook up to their water. We have underground springs here, you know. City water would cost me over three hundred dollars just to start, and I don't have it."

Then one day a flat-topped government worker came to get a test tube of our water. He wanted the water from George's kitchen, and as he tiptoed through the house, he looked like he'd just eaten a lemon. George said that if they claimed they found bacteria in the water, they'd try to force him to hook up with city water. They didn't bother to tell him their findings, and for weeks he quietly worried about it. He said, "They'll leach a man dry if they can."

George didn't like to talk like that; he wanted to be good for the memory of his mother, and to respect the law. After the water question, though, he came up with a business proposal. Leaning toward me, he said confidentially, "I've got an idea to make us a lot of money."

"YOU DO?" I yelped.

"Now hesh," he rebuffed. "And don't be tellin' every Tom, Dick, and Harry before I get a patent. I've got the formula for Instant Water." After some verbal tussling, he spilled: "You jes put two of my little tablets in a jug. Then you add four quarts of regular, plain old water, shake it up — and you got a whole gallon of genu-wine *Instant Water.* Like that idear?"

Cowboys Benny and Larry got into a beat up car every Saturday night and drove into Box Canyon to The Fountain of the World, a quiet religious retreat by day that turned lively on Saturday nights.

"Y'oughta come!" Larry hollered. "I'll be on stage tonight!" Anyone who wanted to perform had their chance at The Fountain, and Larry was a storyteller who never got his fill of ears. He'd give pointers on rodeo and stunt fighting, or "Ridin' and Ropin' in the Southwest." Then, with the grandiose of a carnival barker, he'd leave word of where he'd be appearing next. But the following weekend, Larry would forego his Madison Square Garden appearance and return to The Fountain of the World.

We traveled in the bus to the religious community, parking beside the eponymous fountain that, by then, had gone dry. The buildings were reminiscent of Spanish Indian adobe, nestled between mountain boulders of near equal size. The only people living there were elderly women and few younger monks in long brown robes, working and wandering between gardens and buildings without speaking.

Inside the largest building, near an institutional kitchen, was a wide area filled with rows of chairs facing a curtained stage. They were soon filled by about forty folks of all ages and descriptions from the neighboring communities. We watched a brief morality play put on by the monks, and then were introduced to a teenage girl with flowing hair who played her guitar and sang a folk song. Next came Larry, of whom we were ridiculously proud, and a variety of others. The mundane appearance of these shows gave no clue as to the sect's history. Once part of a larger congregation, the people were acolytes of Krishna Venta, an Aryan Eastern spiritualist who had used catacomb-like caves on the grounds for gatherings of an unknown nature. In the 1950s Venta and about twenty people were blown to pieces inside the caves. Whether a conclusion was made as to the source of the explosives, no one was ever legally charged. Charlie speculated a sexual component to that story, but the oldest woman in the community would say nothing of the event, and of Krishna, only: "The master loved us."

We visited The Fountain of the World several times before offering our help with their programs and community charities in exchange for a safe place for Mary and Sunstone to stay. Katie soon joined them, specifically to work, and she ended up managing their kitchen.

Sandy

Katie had an aura of invitingness. She'd slightly bend forward as if to energetically scoop you up into her warmth and hospitality. She'd extend a cup of coffee with a smile and a twinkle in her eyes. She often seemed on the verge of laughing, as if everything was potentially amusing. Like Brenda, Katie liked to serve, and knew who was where, what they were doing, and about the time they might be wanting food and drink. She liked the company and conversation of the girls. I don't know which guys if any she was interested in, but since it was known Charlie made love with her I'm sure some of the guys approached her sexually.

Tex Watson was a problem solver with practical skills. At the farmhouse people were collecting truckloads of wood to send up the highway above The Pass for a project that was only whispered. One day I rode with the wood. We pulled to the side of the highway, got out, and waited for traffic to clear. Then we quickly tossed all the boards over the side of an embankment, got back in the truck, and left. We didn't see the results of Tex's work for over a month, and then only after a long walk in moonlight, wending through woods, over rocks and under the highway. There appeared a thicket between two concrete abutments, and the building was beneath it. Tex had labored to dig out a foundation in rocky ground for depth and height, and then built walls around the oddly shaped space. It was *nice* inside, big enough to hold all of us. We called it the In Case Place — in case we needed extra space, in case we needed to lie low, in case anything.

In one case there was sex, some luscious voluptuous sex. We were young and we learned from each other. There again, Charlie had cultivated nearly all of the women to yield to his motions, drawing us out of our minds and into our bodies so to move us weightlessly. Without thought, sex became a sensuous dance, later conveyed wordlessly from us to the other guys. I would describe the wet sheen of our healthy bodies, the softness and the muscle, but will suspend that tender tension. Not all of us could turn off our minds to experience ecstasy and peace, but we were on our way. Some nights we climbed the haystack and slept under the stars. Clem hollowed out beds by restacking the bales. We awoke with the sun, having been awake half the night.

When the cornfields in the valley were harvested, George and Pearl took several cowboys to dinner with them in an extra pickup truck with high wooden sides, and I got to ride along. After the meal, we drove to a big farm with acres of yellow corn. Most of it was being trucked to supermarkets, or reserved for sale at roadside stands, but some was deemed unmarketable due to superficial flaws, and George paid a flat fee for as much of it as the cowboys could fork into his two trucks.

On the way home, when corn bounced out of the trucks, George and Pearl blamed Randy and Larry for not tightening the tarps, Randy and Larry blamed each other, and I just rode along, feeling the dry September air through the open windows. We didn't get home until dusk.

After getting George and the groceries inside, Clem, Brenda, Ruth, and others of us climbed into the backs of the trucks on top of the corn. Under the stars, we ate a few of the sweet juicy ears raw, and separated the best into cardboard boxes for cooking. Randy opened the corral gate, and, as Pearl drove each truck around inside the corral, the rest of us pushed mounds of corn into bins for the horses. A thrilling rumble of hooves arose as they trotted to and crowded the bins, chomping into the corn, husks and all.

That week, everyone who wanted it ate fresh corn on the cob. We cooked big potfuls at the farmhouse and in George's kitchen. He had already told us that he would be generous, allowing us to have the more substantial middle cores, while he settled for the "lumpy side meat." (After we received a load of bananas, he was just as charitable, but it was the cobs he agreed to, while we could have the "tender outer strips.")

During autumn at the farmhouse deadwood smoke curled from the grey stone chimney, and pinpoint stars surrounded it. I met Clem and Cappy on my way one night, and the pupils of our eyes connected like long tunnels. Besides the attraction in the chemistry of our youth, we were excited by a belief in infinite possibility, on the edge of discoveries not only of our lifetime but any lifetime.

Charlie

There are more years in twenty-four hours than most brains can think. Think of all the heads that thought up art, music, mathematics. The cave man did not think up a cup or spoon or clock. Think of the hundreds of years it took numbers to come into play all the way to rocket ships and the all of all. It's as endless and vast as space and you could mind-travel it for a thousand lifetimes, or become it in now. The one big memory is now. It was now then, as it's now now.

We had enough LSD to take it about twice a month. Sadie said that Charlie was trying to talk her out of it. She understood his concern, she said, but she didn't believe acid did harm, even to unborn babies. I had no opinion to offer. Sadie always did what she wanted to do anyway. Cappy wrote a whole story about the night that Sadie let Zeezo in the house, but in the succeeding years, I lost most of the pages. The story began early one morning at the farmhouse.

Cappy

The Sun was up and already getting high as Sadie and I surveyed the cloak room for appropriate costumes, including a cowboy shirt that buttoned snugly around her belly. Then we danced up the dusty trail to visit George.

"Who bees it?" he inquired in his Irish mountain drawl. I landed a kiss on his cheek as Sadie called, "It bees 'Us Guys!'"

He chuckled. "I didn't know that was you walkin' in behind that belly. How bees 'Us Guys' this marnin'?" Standing in front of him, Sadie held one of his hands on the other guy.

"Maybe he wants outta thar," George suggested. "Why not leave him here? He'll be in good hahnds. Perhaps you could go dahncing or harseback ridin'."

Sadie said she found it impossible to go anywhere without him, to which George replied pouting, "Well how'm I s'posed ta know? Nobody ever tells me nuthin'."

We strolled on down to the office to sign up a few riders, but Sadie didn't want to stay. At the ranch house that evening, she sat in the circle with her hand on her belly. Suddenly she said, "Whoa! I'm gonna have this critter tonight!"

Nobody paid Sadie much mind because it was two months too early — and because it was Sadie. We passed the bowls, hungry and interested in other topics. When Sadie didn't want to eat, it raised a few eyebrows, and when she left to lie down in the next room, it wrinkled a few more. A couple of the girls went into the bedroom and came out looking expectant. Then everyone went into action, even the ones who didn't know what to do.

Someone brought fresh towels, soap, and a wash basin to Sadie's side. The men paced in and out of the room. The women washed their hands and arms with alcohol, and, discovering just half a bottle, sent three people to the store. Some of the girls wanted to change the bed sheets. Charlie asked for something clean to wear. Brenda handed him a patchwork shirt she had just finished making, and he suggested Sadie get up, and "go boil some water." Sadie got herself up and went straight to the task, the bed sheets got changed, and when she returned, carefully carrying the hot water, she laid herself down with a sigh, and another painful contraction. Her groans and the stillness between them were unsettling. No one was prepared for this. More sobering was Charlie's unfolding of a towel, revealing a razor blade like he'd used on Mary.

When Mary was far into labor, Charlie had made a small incision in her perineum. I don't know how he knew about the episiotomy. The procedure is sometimes done by obstetricians to prevent vaginal tearing because torn tissue, being jagged, heals unevenly, causing scar tissue, loss of elasticity, and further damage with subsequent births.

At the foot of Sadie's bed, Charlie poured alcohol over his hands and the blade. He folded a clean towel, and draped it around his neck. Then he inserted the blade into a hand razor, picked up a mirror, and, with the soap and hot water, began to shave. Tension broke into laughter all over the room.

It's fair to speculate that LSD had something to do with Sadie's early contractions. The fungus, ergot rye, is the source of LSD and believed by herbalists to induce labor. But this was not an issue. The birth held everyone's attention. Even Tommy, the dog, had sneaked in during the confusion, and sat alert in one corner of the room.

Sadie did not need an episiotomy. Very early the next morning Zeezo Z. C. Zadfrack came through the pass weighing little more than two pounds. Brenda caught him, and cleared his nose and mouth for his first breath. He was so small that his head looked transparent. A bed was made by the fire. A doctor's visit was arranged, and a few days later, Sadie and Zeezo moved to The Fountain of the World.

Witnessing human birth grounded us in reality, and raised our wonder about mystical mysteries. We all had come into the world thus, and we all would pass from it. Who in facing these facts is not awed?

Our experimentation with psychedelics

was brazen. We took them to learn, but lacked any

traditional rituals of preparation. Unadulterated LSD, while harmless to the body, could kill a personality. All of the thoughts that make up the you that you think you are might dissolve as you see yourself in the universe of worlds around you. But one of the drawbacks to this quick consciousness was that there was so much going through your brain that what came out of your mouth could sound like burble.

In the two years I'd seen Charlie take psychedelics, he was the sanest, most stable person in any group. His prosecutor would speculate, and then claim as fact that Charlie *issued* LSD to each of us, while secretly refraining from taking it so he could program and control us. We took acid separately and together so whoever had the stash "issued" it, and I don't think Charlie's ability to program and control would've been hindered by LSD, but here is what he said: "Spirit is a power that can't be controlled. I don't move it. The two ways to lose it are when I try to use it, and when I fear and fight against it."

I was prone to fearing and fighting against it. On some acid trips I was conscious of everything in and around me. On others I was unable to do anything but lie down and "die," tumbling into alternate realities and psychological black holes. The intense experiences were full of meaningful moments such as ordinary consciousness did not often perceive, but there were heights and depths that I didn't want to endure. Charlie's calm and confidence kept us above madness, except for one night when we shut him out, and tore the house apart. In the aftermath, almost no one spoke of it, but when we did we called it "The Freak Out."

It started with more and stronger acid than we usually took. There were a lot of us in the house that night, including a young surfer from Malibu, and a hippie or two left from the group that went to Oregon. Brenda had decorated with cushions and tapestries. Paul was playing a sitar. It seemed to set everyone off. The sound of its strings vibrated my view to eerie distortions, and I had to lie down. Apparently others did also. The surfer kid began to flinch and kick. His foot struck the side of my head and I went out of ordinary consciousness. I saw a lot of fire images that night. At one point I felt alarming combustion building. There was going to be an explosion! I thought it was atomic. A major dialog of the day concerned world leaders who threatened to bomb each others' civilizations into oblivion. I heard crackling and smelled smoke and burning hair. Suddenly I was in a 1940s style kitchen beside an open oven that had been blackened by fire. I was lying on my back looking up into the face of a policeman who was holding me. I was about three years old, and, by his expression, I was dead.

Sandy: I was sitting on a couch, feeling stiff. As I watched others unravel, I became more aware of my own inhibitions and "my calculating mind." I was wishing I too could let go, and scream or cry or go nuts like others were.

Lyn: The surfer was tromping around the house calling, "Grandfather! Grandfather!" and answering in the voice of an old man.

Sandy: I heard that Charlie had left. According to him, people dressed him in an old coat and sent him away.

Paul was trying to be sexy and macho. Kim was fighting the Vietnam War. Once, when I went outside, I saw the house dancing side to side, like in a cartoon, energy sparks shooting from the glowing house. It was alive!

Lyn: I remember different hells. One was between places, neither here nor there, an airport parking lot where strangers posing as friends, coming from somewhere they don't remember, fumble in pockets and purses for keys, undecided as to where they are going or why.

In another hell I was being thrown on my back against the four walls of a small, square room, each wall in succession. It was painfully jarring my head. The walls were giant playing cards. After what seemed like *years* I became conscious that I was living the same sequence over and over. It felt like some sort of breakthrough, but I didn't know what it meant or if I would ever get out of it.

Sandy: Lyn was outside in the wood pile next to the house flipping and flailing. I don't know who got her inside. I remember her lying somewhere, her lips nearly black, her hands and fingers curled up. She was gasping, "Water, water, water ..." but when Bo tried to give her water, she sat up and said plainly, "No, let me experience it." Kim came running through the house into the bathroom yelling, "I'm the devil!" We could hear banging and crashing as he destroyed the fixtures in there.

Lyn: Someone — they said it was Charlie — was outside the door saying that the police were coming. Instead of sobering up, I pictured comical movie police, the Keystone Cops. I saw the ranch dogs, and George and Randy, and felt we were real mountain folks. I had a southern Appalachian accent.

Paul walked across the room with his dick in his hand, asking, "Can we make love first?"

Snake began to chant, "Everybody make love. Everybody make love." I heard chatter about going to jail, and then,

"Jail? Look at us — we won't go to jail. They'll take us to the crazy ward!"

Gypsy laughed and interjected, "At least we'll all be together." I found that comforting.

When I opened my eyes I saw Clem and Leslie sitting cross-legged, seeming calm and happy. Leslie was rocking side to side saying, "Bloop...bloop...bloop..." in time to her rocking.

A small skittish cat, nearly a kitten, walked by. It usually stayed outside because it was afraid of people. In a routine manner, Ruth picked it up by the scruff and tossed it onto the embers of a low burning fire. A moment later, she plucked it out, dusted it off and set it on the floor.

Sandy: The next day, slowly putting the house back together, energy was scattered. A clump of people seemed to be in a semi-daze, not sure where they should be or what they should do. Lyn was lying on the floor with cuts and scratches and tangled hair. She was a mess.

Lyn: Every part of my body ached and appeared swollen to almost twice its normal size. Worse, I had a horrible feeling of emptiness. Brenda was clearing debris with typical efficiency, seeming indifferent, yet registering something just short of disgust when sweeping near me. Sandy came with a bowl of warm, soapy water and a washcloth, and without any greeting, inquiry, or explanation, she began washing my hands and face, and brushing my knotted hair. That was surreal.

Sandy

About visions — it's all one mind, collective unconscious. Some visions are traumas lodged in subconscious minds and pushing to come out. They may come out symbolically in visions. I think the shrink that came the closest to seeing that was Jung.

Did you ever see Hieronymus Bosch paintings of Hell and Purgatory? Those are visions in terms of medieval Christian culture like Dante's Inferno. In the 1900s, the Spanish artist, Dali, and the artist Magritte painted visions of machine sterility. In music, Beethoven painted his personal coming to One in his Ninth Symphony.

We're in Christian thought. Many cultures' depictions of monsters are just aspects of our human psyche. American Indian cultures have visions of one's life purpose, such as a warrior or shaman. It's hard for me to transcend my own conditioning. I don't know Muslim culture, haven't been to Egypt in thought, and don't understand Japan or China except that they are dying of pollution like the rest of the world that's in the money.

— Sandra Good, 1971,
Letter from L.A. Women's Jail

Charlie

One glance, one wave of a hand, one flash can hold your soul in forever. It only breaks and crumbles if

312

you withhold from it and yourself. If you run from it, it runs after you. If you run to it, it's faster and you can never reach it. It's there and it's not there, good, bad, the cries of a million lost souls, and the now of one. Few can live through it all to see it because it is all the hell of 2,000 years pushed in one grave, and everyone's afraid to face their own judgments of themselves.

After The Freak Out, ranch life resumed and the spirit came back, but I don't think anyone who was there forgot that trip. The cat Ruth had tossed in the fire was unhurt but totally changed. Overnight it became people-friendly, and it never grew. Half grown, it never got bigger. Most of us moderated our use of LSD and natural plant psychedelics, but we didn't stop taking them. Whatever they had to tell us — whatever they prompted our brains to tell us — we wanted to know. We were learning to walk with birth and death, to surrender the past in exchange for the present, to be spiritually renewed, like the body is healed by life's powerful will to survive.

Charlie

To face oneself in fear and death is to know one's true self in love and light. You can't have one without the other.

— 1973, excerpt, letter to Bo

One afternoon I caught sight of Brenda sewing in a field at the edge of the woods. She was so like her surroundings that I almost missed her. Brenda hand-sewed clothes — well fitting, artistic and functional clothes with pockets and patches. Ever since she had shown us her free-hand embroidery, we women had been stitching the pictures of our lives on Charlie's vest, each of us taking a turn. Then we began making separate patches to apply to the vest so that more of us could work together. Embroidering was relaxing, engendering focus. It led us from conscious thought into unconscious imagination, and back to conscious exactitude. Katie's work was delicate and florid. Cappy had exchanged her colored pens for threads. Passed through all of our hands and minds, the bland material became vibrant in waterways, plants, sky, land, symbols, animals, and people. It was one flowing work of ten or twelve women, and Charlie said he didn't miss a stitch. He called us witches. And as our visions became reality, reality became magical.

The wildwoods lifted spells cast by purveyors of merchandise and ideas. We were born every morning and died each night; our faces lost age; police suspected us of being minors; people couldn't tell some of us apart, and some thought we were natural born family. But in the era of hippies, there were hundreds of "families." That's what closely-knit communal groups were called.

A towering muscular figure, bare but for cut-off jeans, galloped a white horse past a group of us girls in George's front yard, raising the dust in our faces. Just short of the haystack, he reined the animal's neck around, and kicked it into a gallop past us again. Then he drew back the reins so far the horse reared like Silver under the Lone Ranger. The horse was big, but the rider dwarfed it, and though his eyes were blue and his bare skin freckled, he was deeply tanned and had high Indian cheekbones. In a mock show of caballero pride — back stiffened, nostrils flaring — he made the horse prance by tapping its flanks with his heels while reining it tightly. As it bucked and danced unpredictably, he sidled it toward us, forcing us to step back. Looking down on us, his mouth began to smirk and pucker, as if trying to contain a joke that finally burst into a cynical laugh. With a thick Spanish accent he introduced himself — a long string of names beginning with Juan. He said things only he understood, snickering with each cryptic quip. Then he said he would see us again, and galloped away.

Pearl had hired the new cowboy, and she would hire several others, taking them on at room and board, even when George questioned the cost and the need for more help. She argued that she needed extra hands to castrate the stallion, or that one of the other cowboys was in some way debilitated, or that, just out of human decency, some people should be helped until they got on their feet, and George always relented.

Dody was the withered woman Pearl installed in an old trailer out back of the movie set. When I first saw Dody, my inclination to speak was checked. Her fierce eyes narrowed and threatened: STAY AWAY. The next time I passed Dody's trailer, a rusty wire fence surrounded it. Nobody bothered her. She lived there two or three months, and was rarely seen. Her closest neighbor, Randy Starr, complained that her trailer smelled bad, and when the County finally took her out of it, they discovered something like twenty-nine cats and kittens confined inside with her.

Each time someone new came to live on the ranch, there was a little jostle of adjustment, a change in the overall balance of human relations. One day it would be clear that Pearl was recruiting forces to oppose us. At the time, though, it was simply more in the many, and everyone who stayed found a place and a purpose, even Brooks.

Brooks had insisted on staying without invitation. He was not unlikable; he was just physically and emotionally thin. Pale — almost transparent — he consisted of skin and bones which, together with a long pointed nose, gave him the exaggerated look of a caricature. Like the rest of us, Brooks needed to work himself out, and whether because Charlie suggested it, or because he found a place to volunteer, he pitched in, shoveling manure out of the barn. It was help of which the cowboys may have taken unfair advantage but certainly welcomed, and it's where Brooks got to know his physical opposite, Juan.

Juan Flynn was of Irish and Panamanian descent. I thought that he was bi-lingual but I never heard him speak Spanish. During the time that we knew him his English was both more *and* less broken, depending upon the subject matter and to whom he was speaking. And I didn't know if Juan had been in Vietnam, but he told Brenda that he had nightmares about the war. She told me only one thing about their conversations: she had asked him why he was so angry, and he'd told her that he was angry at *himself* and it had to do with the war.

"Post traumatic stress disorder," was a technical term back then. If it applied to Juan, his condition was not recognized by the military, nor would he ask for help. I thought he was probably caught in a cultural crossfire, taught both to sacrifice himself like Jesus, and to "fight like a man." I thought he would have been *ashamed* either to have participated in the war or to have avoided it. But that's just what I thought. Brenda sat and listened to him, and didn't judge him when he cried.

Our work at the front of The Ranch effectively paid rent on the farmhouse. The public restrooms got cleaned, fences mended, and barn chores done with less stress. Brooks' contribution alleviated some of the pressure on the other guys, but if others were like me, they didn't stop to thank him, and maybe we should have. We all could've thanked each other more, but at the time the words were unnecessary. Most of us were doing chores of our own.

Brooks was not timid, but he was quiet, and one day while on LSD he quietly tried to "die." That day stretched into four or five days during which he lay catatonic on a couch at the back farmhouse, and would not be stirred by coaxing, and not even by his own urinary and colonic emissions; the girls had to diaper him. Finally, as I heard it, Charlie told Brooks that it had to stop, and he instructed the girls to put the vest we were embroidering for him under Brooks.

"You been cleaning up shit for us," he reportedly said. "I guess we got to clean it up for you. But if you're gonna shit, you'll have to shit on my vest, and you know how much I love this vest."

This story has been satirized by strangers, but contrary to their assertions, I doubt that anybody considered what Charlie did to be a "miracle" as much as an example of his understanding of psychology. In any case, the vest remained unsoiled. Brooks was soon up, relieving and reconstituting himself like the rest of us.

Charlie

New starts now. We got to look at all the bad thoughts, fears and doubts, in order to pick out the good. When we see the worst in us then we can decide

> what we want to be like. Look at the mean and be willing to experience it. Then walk gently through it.

One sunny day I heard a commotion outside, and Pearl came into George's house looking traumatized. From the doorway I saw two sheriff's squad cars in the yard, and seventeen-year-old Chuck Grey in the back of one of them. A scatter of people who had stopped in the tracks of their daily routines looked stunned. Finally, someone explained to me that Chuck, the son of two police officers, had just been arrested for rape. A woman in the first squad car had identified him as the man who had hijacked her at knifepoint on Santa Susana Pass not a mile from The Ranch, and raped her on the back seat of her car. As shocking as the charge, the woman was almost sixty years old.

Murmurs of disbelief and denial failed to pick up momentum. The complacency on Chuck's face announced that he had done the deed. Those of us wondering why, based upon his good looks and access to girls, didn't understand rape. Chuck went away and didn't come back.

In less than four months, our numbers had increased by more than a dozen. I loved almost everything about living on the ranch, but suddenly everyone was talking about leaving it. Cappy said her grandmother had a cabin in the mountains above Death Valley, and her family didn't use it more than once a year. She had vacationed there since childhood, and said that for all the desert lacked, it had plenty of space for us to spread out, and explore. I didn't want to go.

Sandy

The day before a bunch of us left for the desert, I was on horseback by the back ranch house, and I volunteered to carry a big cardboard box full of dishes down Lovers Lane to George's house. Someone lifted the box up to me, and as I placed it on the saddle in front of me, the contents rattled, the horse spooked, and I fell to the ground with the box on top of me. The impact injured part of my lower back.

The next day, Halloween, we set out in the big green school bus. I was relieved to be able to lie down in the back and, as usual, I tried to get some sleep. I didn't know where we were going, except to Cappy's grandmother's, and Cappy seemed proud to be taking us there. After about two hours of travel she wanted us to see the spectacular view of the whole Panamint Valley as we drove over the pass between the Slate and Argus Mountain Ranges. When we got off the asphalt onto a dirt road, and came to a small collection of wood and adobe buildings, she introduced us to Ballarat, a once-booming mining town. Inside one its buildings was a little store and cafe counter, but many of the buildings had been whittled by high winds to nubs, and the permanent population of Ballarat was three. I think a few of us bought candy bars and then, as we continued on the uneven dirt road along the edge of the mountains, Cappy identified the canyons that sliced through the Panamint Range with names like Surprise Canyon, Happy Canyon, Coyote Canyon, and Jail Canyon.

At some point the ruggedness of the road really communicated to my sore body and I was relieved when we had to stop several times to check the gear that was starting to come loose from the top of the bus. I got out and wandered around an alluvial fan at the mouth of a canyon.

"You don't want to be in these canyons when it rains," Cappy warned, "...unless you want to die. There's a reason they're called 'washes.'" During brief torrential rains, water quickly rises and floods the canyons, carrying rocks, and even heavy boulders, with terrific speed, and splaying them fan-like at the bottom. I began picking up smaller rocks and showing them to Charlie. He showed me an ordinary brownish grey rock like thousands of others I wouldn't have noticed and said, "Look at the swirls of rust overlapping the browns. Look here on this side. See the blue? Beauty is where anyone can see it, but people learn not to look." Walking back to the bus, Charlie said, "Levels of life are without end, but if you rush through it, you miss it."

Finally the bus came to the base of a mountain cleaved by a jagged gorge, Goler Wash. It was too rocky and steep for the bus to go farther, so we got out for the seven-mile trek up the mountain through the wash, the first part of a long foot-journey to Cappy's grandmother's. Some of us carried bundles of bedding and clothing, pots and pans, heavy bags of dried grains and other food staples like coffee, salt, and peanut butter. Snake and I lagged behind the rag-tag procession as it staggered upward, Snake tootling on a little flute. I hung back even behind her, hoping Charlie would notice that I was hurting from the fall off the horse and give me some acknowledgement.

The desert was like being on another planet. As my mind adapted, I would see shapes, textures and colors I'd never known could exist in mineral form. At the top of the wash the land smoothed into valleys and rounded hills. After half an hour's walk between them, we passed the cluster of buildings Cappy said was the Barker Ranch, and a quarter mile farther, cottonwood and fig trees announced the Myers Ranch built by Cappy's grandfather in the 1930s. Near the house were outbuildings, and a stone and concrete swimming pool. Above it, a natural spring saturated the slopes, giving life to wild mint and alkaline-loving plants and bushes. The high mineral content of the water showed in crusty deposits all over the ground. In the purple dusk, the only sounds were of nature and the soft crunching of our footsteps. We heard owls but didn't see them. Cappy said they were burrowing owls, one of the smallest of all owls, and that instead of nesting in trees they make their nests beneath plant roots in the sand. I don't remember going into the cabin. I was sore and tired and I slept.

The next day Leslie, Gypsy, and I went back to explore the Barker Ranch, which consisted of a stone house and shed, a bunkhouse, outdoor enclosures for livestock, and a small stone swimming pool. The builder had brought in flat stones for the L-shaped porch around the house and different-colored desert rocks to make the exterior walls a naturally beautiful mosaic. All the buildings were framed and supported with wooden beams salvaged from an abandoned local railway. There was a big kitchen with cupboards, a sink with a trickle of cold running water, and a little pot-bellied stove. The house also had a rudimentary waterless bathroom, a bedroom, and a front room with a sleeping alcove and a stone fireplace. The place was a mess. We swept and got a rattlesnake out of the corner of the kitchen, and a dead lizard out of the sink. Then we washed windows and scores of gallon jars.

I was mesmerized by Leslie. Lean and lanky, with a dust rag in hand, she took each desert artifact off its shelf, dusted it and the shelf, and put it back. Leslie had style, and, like Brenda, she could design and make clothes. She was pretty, funny, intelligent, and always friendly. She had a slightly self-effacing manner. I thought it was because she was tall and pretty like a model and maybe was used to girls being jealous of her so she literally lowered herself. At the ranch, she became "Lulu," and fell right into mountain talk. It seemed Charlie thought of Leslie as Bobby's girl, and maybe that's why he didn't give her the attention she seemed to want from him. Anyway, she took good care of herself and others, and nearly always showed enthusiasm and a desire to please.

In the desert we had just a few items of clothing, including socks. Leslie went through each drawer of the old dressers rounding up clothes and dozens of socks, most of which didn't match. She mended some, washed and dried everything, and carefully refolded each item and put it back in the cleaned and freshly lined drawers. It gave me a good feeling to see her do that. Between Leslie and Brenda we always had fresh clean clothes. I loved watching these women get to work putting order and attractiveness into a place. Many of the girls did this every place we went. It's a trait passed down through generations, but some women never get it. I never wanted to be in the kitchen if my mother was there. Once she said to me, while clutching a knife, "Get out of here before I kill you."

Different ones of us traveled to and from the desert through the autumn and winter, at least one of us staying with George. Winter temperatures in the San Fernando Valley were in the 50s and 60s, but only a trickle of people came to rent horses. An unusually popular weekend might bring ten rentals, but ordinarily ten was a high number for the entire week, and some weeks there were no rentals at all.

George worried. I thought it was just a bad habit, but he finally told me that he owed three to five thousand dollars in back property taxes and penalty payments. He could lose the ranch. It shamed him. He said that even when the business was not paying for itself the horses had to eat.

Someone had brought George a modern trailer and set it up beside his house, advising him to move into it to avoid county intervention and "an old people's home." It was an answer to another of his deepest worries, but he didn't want to move out of his house. At his suggestion, I moved into the trailer. This worked for me because mornings, by George's time, started early. He had set ideas about people sleeping after six. After Pearl found Clem asleep in a pile of hay "in broad daylight," George didn't want to hear of him.

Before fixing George's breakfast, I made the rounds, getting the cowboys up to feed the horses. Randy and Larry had more grump and grouch than I could talk them out of, so I just beat on their doors with a stick. After feeding the horses, they'd come bickering back to the house to eat. Every morning was a cussing crisis and George was right in the middle of it. He hated their cigarette smoke that filled up the house. One day he got so mad he couldn't speak for an hour. Then he reiterated, "My mother always told me if you can't say something nice about somebody don't say anything at all — *goddamned sons of bitches!*"

When George was irritated, his jaw jutted forward and when he was frustrated his face got red. He wanted to WORK. He'd always worked. We worked on getting him to slow down and relax. One day he snapped at me, "I can't get much slower!" He fixed bridles at a workbench in the house, but sometimes that irked him more. Once I heard him cussing in his room so I knocked and opened his door to see him with shaving crème all over the front of his white sling undershirt, the broken aerosol can still spurting at his feet. Another day, while he was getting dressed and mentally giving somebody hell, he'd picked up a bottle of cough syrup instead of hair tonic. Boy was he mad. He *hated* anything sticky. I laughed, wiping his head with a wet cloth, and told him that's what he got for getting mad, but I hugged him, and pretty soon he considered the cough syrup incident funny himself.

That's how it was with him. That was typical of George's relationship with most of us girls, one of mutual fondness and respect — *despite* his bouts of cantankerousness. He was repulsed by our idea that he quit shaving. He joked that if he grew a beard, honey would get in it, and then bees would be attracted to build a hive. By the time he was done embellishing this story, large species of wildlife had taken up residence, so a beard for him was out of the question. His worries were many, but it usually didn't take much to reset his focus. He worried about the girls in the desert, and I told him what I was told about their adventure.

Sandy

The desert at dusk was magical, the mountains erupting in buff, pink, pale yellow, and mint green, with dramatic stripes of purple, blue, gold and red. It was awesome in the true meaning of the word. At Indian Ranch near sundown, I saw my first coyote. There weren't many tourists in the desert, but people passed through it on their way to Nevada or elsewhere, and older vehicles had water-cooled radiators that boiled over and needed refills. About thirty miles from Cappy's grandmother's, Indian Ranch was like an information center where travelers could get water, sodas, directions, and historical background. As the desert cooled, I walked out of the main building to take in the view, and I stopped. The coyote was in the brush just a few yards away. I felt surprise, and some fear. I think it did too. As maligned as the coyote is, it is actually a lithe, beautiful animal. After a moment's pause, it furtively trotted away. Charlie once said he was spiritually allied with the coyote, and Coyote in Native American mythology is a trickster, a very powerful god-like being. Many Indian gods were not flat cut outs, good or bad, but multi-sided, a concept that Christians find difficult to understand.

"A time ago," George told me, "...we had pumpkins growing on a hill out back. Then a hard rain loosed the soil around 'em and they commenced ta rollin' downhill."

"Oh no..."

"Yep, and there was a visitor in the little house with the quarter moon on it, and sure 'nough pumpkins hit the side o' that house and bowled it over." A second or two passed while I processed this. "One of these days," he said, "we ought to go down there an' see if that man needs any hep." George was shamelessly amused by the corniness of his own jokes. That's what made them funny.

I was surprised to learn that George had a wife. She arrived one afternoon carrying a covered casserole and George's shirts from the professional laundry. She was slight and seemed older than him, having short white curls and a disapproving expression. Barely speaking, she went straight into his room to tuck his clothes into dresser drawers. After reclosing his door, she picked up the casserole, and seemed hesitant to leave it. Quietly she told him where she would place it. They shared a few words out of my hearing. He stood up, reached in his pocket for some carefully folded money, gave it to her, and she left. This happened each time I was present when she visited, and that was maybe four or five times during the many months we were on The Ranch. George told me that they had separated because she had never agreed to stay on The Ranch and he didn't want to leave it.

I took in George's memories as they were offered. Had I been wiser, I'd have delved for details. He told me about movie making in old Hollywood, like about "trip wires" used to make horses and mules look drunk. They were long thin wires tied to the legs of the animals and stretched to where movie company men off camera could pull them side to side. He also told me about a legendary cowgirl performer who, while on her horse, dove from a high platform into a wooden vat of water. I asked if the horses in either of those situations could be injured or killed, and he said seriously that they could, but he hadn't heard of it happening.

Only a handful of George's horses were used for movies, but all were plump and healthy, many with people names like Bonnie and Fred and Sue. They were grain fed in winter, and hay fed all year round. The shoe smith came every six months, and the vet once a year. Beyond that, George counted on the cowboys to check their hooves and treat them for saddle sores.

"NEVER, NEVER LEAVE THIS GRAIN BIN OPEN!" Pearl scolded Larry, slamming it for emphasis. "You coulda killed one of 'em!" Each horse in winter got one can of oats per week. Given the chance to eat from the bin, they would bloat and founder. Pearl told Larry he'd be up all night forcing sick horses to drink castor oil, while Randy cursed him and plunged a gloved arm up to the elbow in equine behind. If a foundered horse didn't pass the grain within a day, it could go lame or die.

George said that some years before he had awakened at night sensing that a mare in the foaling pen needed help to deliver her colt. He called from his porch until his throat hurt, and beat the stair rail with his cane, but he could not arouse a single ranch hand. Then he was angry. He went back to his room, his heart hot, pulled his work pants over his pajamas, put on socks and shoes, wiped the sweat from his face, and wondered if the cowboys were already with the mare. But as he felt his way with his cane down the boardwalk to the foaling pen, he knew they were not there, and although he would have liked to have cussed and fired them then and there, as he imagined them out drinking or sleeping or hiding from him, he could hear the mare breathing heavily.

Leaving his cane parked by a fence, he felt along splintered wood to the gate latch and let himself in the pen, telling the mare to be steady. He could smell and hear her breathing below him. He told her that he would help her. He stooped and found a small set of hooves, and, listening to the cues from its mother, he pulled that little colt into the world. It was clear by the relief he expressed in telling this story that the success of his experience had softened his fury at the cowboys, but he reinstated it when he was through, just to keep stock of it.

Sandy

The desert was so quiet that we could hear breezes. One of us found a young owl and Charlie put it in what might have been a chicken's nesting box and checked on it until it could fly away. Lizards, rabbits, snakes, ground squirrels, birds, and all kinds of wildlife were moving in the brush, but it took weeks of getting used to the quiet for the chatter in our minds to be up-staged by nature. One time while Charlie and I drove out of the desert to pick up Lyn, he told me to look at objects and say out loud their names like bush, burro, boulder, rock, raven. I knew that the rapid naming of things was his attempt to bring me out and keep me from falling back into the morass of my mind.

Charlie

It is a self-truth to me that the little things of the mind and in the soul grind the rocks to sand and feed shellfish and that the snails carry the universe and the bugs are not fools and that ALL does communicate. But if you're ruled in your head, the wall school put up cuts your awareness down.

I don't remember leaving George in some-one else's care or the drive to the desert, but I recall that climbing into the mountains through Goler Wash was not easy. Besides the extra exertion, the stark-ness, after busy streets and towns, was a shock to my senses. From the numbing silence to our alternately muffled and echoed voices, it was a different experi-ence in perception.

The maze of the wash seemed never-ending, with no landmarks to note our progress, only more sand, more boulders, more dry brush, and the rock walls that flanked us looking like stern-faced American Indi-ans, indifferent to our small, struggling bodies. Once up and out of the wash, we could see miles of smooth hills, and distant mountains. The bare landscape was a clean pallet for the evening's soft watercolors — in reality, neither soft nor wet.

The desert is harsh. The rocks are hard, the plants prickly, and the need for water *startling.* It is so dry that rare rainwater reaching the earth rolls off its back downhill. Yet plants grow in the desert, and animals thrive. If you know where to look, there are potholes in stone that catch rain, covert waterholes, and sunny oases fed by freshwater springs. But you could search for days and die before finding any. Charlie had made it his priority to know them.

At last we reached the ranch left by the late Mr. Barker to his wife, who believed in making it available to prospectors and travelers needing temporary shelter. During our brief stays, we met and heard about people past and present who shared an affinity for the desert. Some were well educated; some never. Some had jobs and homes in cities, and some were among the most outlandish hermits in tarnation.

While out hiking, we met the bristle-bearded prospector known as "Ballarat Bob" on his way to Barker's. Bob traveled the desert with only his two burros, Billy and Jenny, for company, so maybe he wasn't accustomed to talking — especially to women. I couldn't tell if he was brusque or bashful. By appearances, Bob sought valuable ores, but I think it was as good an excuse as any for him to get away from the rest of civilization. While we slept in Barker's main house, he stayed in the nearby bunkhouse, the burros corralled just outside his door, braying to the answering mountains. They were especially suited to the terrain and climate, and may have once been part of a wild herd, but burros are not native to the California deserts, and conservationists would later try to remove all the wild ones from the landscape.

Throughout Barker's front yard, between cactus and rock gardens, were interesting pieces of junk — rusty wheels and mechanical parts, a dented fuselage from a plane crash, a box containing samples of minerals and ores. The guys were learning from the prospectors to recognize different ores. They had other more destructive recreations like a motor scooter, and a tin can target range for pellet guns, maybe a couple of .22s, but I'd say that they spent the majority of their time exploring what must be a geologist's dream. There are different types of rock layered together, and patterns in the cliffs showing that there once was water. In a nearby valley a mammoth butte (bigger than the town of Ballarat) has diagonal strata that may indicate its having been thrown upon its side during some cataclysm before our species arrived. While our parents' generation was looking to outer space, we were far from done exploring the earth. It seemed that the desert was on the edge of both.

Lying on our backs outside at night, we could see more stars and planets than we had ever seen at one time, shooting stars, meteors, and things to wonder about. On a distant dark hill a tiny light pinpointed the cabin where an astrophysicist engineer lived with his wife. Clem and Charlie had visited Clint and Stella Anderson, and Clem returned to see them several times. As I understood, Clint had invented a device for the United States military having something to do with the Laser (Light Amplification Stimulated Emission Radiation) and his invention had been patented by his employer. Whatever brought Clint and his wife to a lone cabin in this rough country, Clem said that they loved the desert — rattlesnakes, scorpions, coyotes and all. Clint told him that when they were nearly out of supplies, he took his rifle out to kill a rabbit, but when at last he saw one, "he couldn't shoot it because it looked like a friend of his."

Clem

I used to squat on Clint Anderson's kitchen floor while he ran down to me universal laws — celestial concepts that my mind could barely grasp. I was intoxicated with the wine of his wisdom and knowledge. He was gently humble, as if plugged into and talking for the whole magnificent universe. I walked out of his little desert cottage with the top of my head gone and my brain touching the heavens.

One time when I was leaving the Andersons, after bringing them a heap of goodies and supplies, they told me that if ever I feel a touch like a spring breeze on my shoulder, and soft whisperings, to know that it's them in the spirit visiting me. I've felt those feelings several times through the years, and one time found out that Clint had passed. They were magical beings.

Early mornings, before most of us were awake, Bo made cornmeal tortillas on the pot bellied stove, and hand fed the first batch to Ballarat Bob's two burros. One morning she didn't bring breakfast soon enough to suit them, so Billy or Jenny stepped up on the porch, turned the doorknob by use of teeth, and we awoke to see him or her standing in the kitchen.

Bo made the tortillas for us too. I would call them *burritos* but they weren't packing much. We ate them with ketchup, we ate them with syrup, we ate them with salt, and we ate them plain. If you don't see the pattern here, we were eating almost nothing *but* Bo's tortillas because the rest of the food was gone.

Five of us girls volunteered to go to Las Vegas. It was the closest city, and a straight shot on the back road through Shoshone. Dennis hadn't used Juanita's Dodge van, and now we had a use for it, but Dennis had already given it to a persistent groupie whose father could have bought her ten vans. I don't know how, but Charlie got it back.

"You know there's less than a quarter tank of gas in this thing," he said quietly when we were seated in the van. We did know. The closest mining camp was twenty miles away. We each had no more than a change of clothes, a toothbrush, towel, and maybe a knife. All the guys came out and stood around the van smiling at us with their hands in their pockets. Between them they provided us about a dollar and seventy cents. As an afterthought, they devilishly siphoned a gallon of gas from the tank to use for their scooter, and we were sent off with only one instruction: Have a good trip.

Not far from Barker's we got stuck on rocks, got out of the van, and struggled to free it. For nearly the entire dirt road out, we had to clear big rocks. At dusk, we rested. In one of the van's cupboards, we found a can of sweetened condensed milk. It was our only food until we reached Las Vegas. Ouish woke once during the night and saw a band of high tailed burros running and kicking under the stars.

Our next day was similar to the first, lifting rocks, shifting rocks, pulling and pushing rocks, pushing the van, breathing hard, sweating, and laughing. Finally we reached the mining camp. The people there gave us just a little gas since their supply was low. But beyond the dirt road, the going was easier. The asphalt looked like a wavy black banner up and down hills all the way to the main road to Las Vegas. To save gas, Brenda cut the engine at the crest of a hill, and we coasted down it and part way up the next. Rocking our bodies in unison further propelled us to another hilltop so we could coast down again. This tactic saved us enough gas to drive the long flat stretch into the electrified city.

In Las Vegas, Juanita traded her van for a Jeep at a car dealership, and we went to the big food warehouses where workers carted *cases* of canned, bottled, and dried foods to back docks, and loaded them into the Jeep. Some of the men broke cartons open so that they could account for the loss as "damaged goods." All we said was that we were feeding hungry people in the desert. We drove back to Barker's with hardly any space for us to sit.

Holiday season brought hunters, miners, campers, and even the military used the road that went by Barker's. When people came around, most of the younger girls stepped into the back room and closed the door, while the "adults" waved, spoke, or even served coffee around the kitchen table. Charlie had gotten permission from Mrs. Barker for Mary, himself, and their kids to stay at her ranch, but Mrs. B. didn't know how many kids they had. Some of us moved to "Grandma's" up the road, yet Cappy was half-expecting *to see* Grandma. What if her family had decided to take a vacation? Ouish was the fastest runner, so she stayed on point at Barker's to alert the people at Grandma's of possible company. She told me later she hadn't heard a Jeep's engine until it was nearly next to the house.

"Jeep!" she yelled to the people in Barker's kitchen. "You guys make a front. Stall 'em," and she swooshed away over the high path, while down below, Sandy flagged two men in the Jeep. It slowed, they waved and drove on. Leaping downhill to Grandma's Ouish yelled, "JEEP!" to Clem and Charlie, then dove head-first under a bush into what she called "an amazing world of spiders and their spinnings." She heard the blood pounding in her ears, and felt trickles of sweat on her face — or was it spiders? She was so close to the road that she couldn't move. The Jeep idled outside Granny's. She heard the bass voices of men. At last, the voices turned to bold, yet restrained, chuckles, and the men drove away.

Brenda, Gypsy, Mary, I, and at least one of the younger girls left Barker's Ranch on foot for Spahn's Ranch about mid-day, not packing much. Ballarat was a mere twenty-seven miles, but by sundown that twenty-seven seemed like a hundred. Seven miles down the wash, our feet hurt through our flimsy shoes, and the makeshift packs got to weighing more with every step as dusk settled over us in one cold blanket. On the dirt road to Ballarat we slowed to a trudge. Hours later, I lagged behind and saw dark robots without knee joints rocking foot to foot, inch by inch. We couldn't stop to spend the night. It was too cold. During one rest our blood slowed. We struggled to light matches that illuminated our fat purple fingers. Knowing the pain in getting up that time, and the deep temptation to sleep, we rested little afterward, and bend after bend after bend there was no sight of Ballarat until there was, around the curve of the foothills, a tiny light.

As we shuffled into town groaning, all appeared to be sleeping. We rang a buzzer. A hired hand came out and told us to follow him "to the Mrs.'s trailer." Waking and bundling, she appeared angry, a big-boned, gray-haired woman in a wool shirt and baggy pants. Sternly, she told us to follow. We tried, but we couldn't keep up. She stopped and turned around, looking at us. Then her stony expression lifted, and she laughed. She was a desert treasure, rough and rare. She put us up in a wood storage shack with two springy beds, plenty of wool blankets, two quarts of milk, cheese, crackers, and candy bars from her store. Then she went away. She seemed to know what we liked, and that we couldn't pay. Full and grateful, we dropped to sleep before finishing the meal.

In the morning, Ballarat was busy. Rugged miners were eating at the short counter inside the store. Our host was cooking. She barely said a word to us, set us up a breakfast of oatmeal and milk, and got us a ride out of town.

From Spahn's Ranch, we separated, each of us with tasks at The Fountain or in getting supplies for a return to the desert. I went back to the trailer beside George's house. I had discreetly passed on what George told me about his owing over three grand in taxes. Juanita had written home for money she had in trust or savings, and when it came she offered the entire amount for our use, over eleven thousand dollars. Charlie told me that he caught himself thinking he could triple the money by investing in cars, girls, or even horses. "But that was just an old ego," he said. Thanks to Juanita, George got the money to pay off his back taxes, penalties and all. And after Katie reported that The Fountain of the World badly needed to get their truck repaired, Juanita's money bought them a new truck.

I was sitting on George's steps when Cowboy Bill approached so I saw him from the ground up: scuffed cowboy boots, long legs, short hair. He was rough around the edges and looked older than he probably was, smiling down on me paternally like he already knew me. I was suspicious. Resting a boot on the stoop, he paused before going inside. "I haven't seen George in years," he told me, "...and, by the way, how's Charlie?" That cinched it. I figured him for a cop, but he lit a cigarette, and continued, "Charlie and I go way back. We were in the joint together down south. You know what we used to do in the hole?" Now he had my interest. "Whoever had smokes would tie a cigarette, a match, and a little piece of the striker to the backs of these thumb-size cockroaches, push 'em out the door, and send 'em down the tier." I didn't believe him.

"Really," he said convincingly, "we had some good times, me and Charlie, smokin' these thin little reefers..." Suddenly he took my face in his big hands, and kissed me on the forehead. I rose, pulled away, and went straight into the house.

It turned out that both George and Charlie did know Bill. What are the odds? And Bill had been filled in about Charlie and the rest of us by Pearl. And Bill wasn't moving in like I thought he was, but living somewhere in The Valley.

Charlie's explorations for desert water led him to difficult places. At least once, dry and exhausted, he lay down, knowing the possibility of bodily death. Sweat evaporates in desert heat before you know it's there. A remarkable number of people found dead of dehydration had water in their canteens. Fearful of using the last of it, they drifted off, not recognizing the seriousness of their condition. After a rest, Charlie got up and found his way back to Barker's.

> **Sandy**
>
> One day as Charlie, Mary, and I walked up the wash to hike the steep hills, I was ahead of him and felt competitive. I wondered why he was not moving faster and in front of me. I began feeling disappointed that he was not more athletic, and that I could out-do him. Eventually I ran out of steam and was afraid of going where the rocks were loose and dangerous. He then sprinted easily past me.

> **Charlie**
>
> Too much will is over-doing it. A body with a strong will fighting the hot desert would probably die. Like you're walking from one waterhole to another and fear of death is pushing you and your body is stiff and you're hard at work thinking and moving. Sweat comes from you and you think it's hell. But at peace, you enjoy a nice stroll. The willingness to die and give up, once you understand it, allows you to start over, strong as all life beyond death.

On one exploration for water, Charlie had a revelation he didn't talk about. Tex said he seemed to pull into himself, that there were things he couldn't or wouldn't say.

My mind was confused. It was night. I was asleep in George's trailer, dreaming of thunder and wind. I woke up. It was not thunder and wind. It was horses. I could hear them breathing heavily as they ran by the windows. The cowboys were too far behind to keep them from stampeding onto the road. Everyone was coming out to help, running, yelling, getting into cars to give chase, but the horses got all the way to the freeway before anyone could stop them, and it wasn't until just before dawn that they could be caught in a culvert, and the panic of the exhausted men be subsided.

I didn't wonder how the horses got out, or why they stampeded, and I heard no speculation on the subject, but the ranch had been coming to turmoil. One day Randy Starr ran into George's house like a demon. He began rummaging and slamming kitchen cupboards and drawers, daring George to say anything about it. He was thrilled to announce his discovery of a nest of pink baby mice in an unused bottom drawer. I don't know if my distress reached the air, only that Randy's face looked grotesque as over and over he plunged his fist down upon them.

George told Randy that was enough, to leave the house and come back when he was sober. Randy strode out firing threats about quitting, got into his Cadillac and drove away. Fortunately for George, he came back late at night, but for days he inflicted his torment on all within range, drinking to excess, yelling obscenities, and sealing in silence the things George most wanted to know. Benny left, Larry stunk of piss, and George began talking about selling The Ranch.

When Charlie returned from the desert it was only a stopover between trips. He put Randy in place, somehow relieving him of the compulsion to self de-struct. He checked with me and others of us, and then went back to the desert, but he seemed unsettled.

Sadie in the desert was restless. She decided that no one else should touch Zeezo. She would give instruction as to how he was to be held. I think people tolerated her directions but it didn't quiet her. She couldn't sit still. Finally, she went down the road in a huff, leaving Zeezo and everyone else. She spotted two men in a Jeep, took off her cap, unbuttoned her jacket, and put on an accent — "Southern dame in distress," she told me later. Her car was stuck and she was "just going to leave the damned thing." Pretty soon she showed up at The Ranch. She and I slept in the trailer beside George's house. She'd leave and come back from town every few days to excitedly tell me about "tuned in" people. Susan believed in signs — events and situations that gave direction if you paid attention. One day her eyes grew large as she told me, "The radio has been telling me to do things!"

In December of '68, George had me fire up the heater under the mantle. He fantasized a mountain-top Christmas. Someone brought him a little tree for the house, and he asked me to decorate it with dog biscuits.

Dennis Wilson and company had put the song Charlie had written for him on a .45 record, changing some of the words and the rhythm. It was a similar song in a different spirit with a different message. Dennis had put his own name to it, probably for convenience, but he hadn't told Charlie that they were going to record it. I think that Charlie found out about it in the desert. At some point I heard the record, but I don't remember Charlie saying anything about it.

The guys had been composing *new* music. Before the desert, our "music" had been, for the most part, a deep breathing exercise toward relaxation and release. We released words, but never wrote them down. What for? Suddenly they were writing down chords and words, employing Leslie, the business school graduate, to take shorthand. Suddenly, they had a message to send, and the message mattered.

"Pictures become words, if I use words to un-explain
the wide blue of the ocean in a tiny drop of rain.
Valleys green and amber – once were, and still could
be.
Our lives are in the water. It's time runs fast into the
sea."

— C. Manson, unfinished song, 1969

I cannot relate all the people who came and went where and when. I could not ever. Tex left one day to report to the draft board, and we didn't see or hear from him for three or four months. When almost everyone else was back on Spahn's Ranch, they seemed to be on a mission. One of the girls told me that while around an outdoor fire they'd had a sort of "hog calling." Selecting syllables to symbolize vehicles that could take us to and from the desert, they sent the sounds with the smoke into the universe. It was primitive style chanting, and not overly serious, but there was no doubt that these thoughts would manifest in physical form. Soon enough there would be shovelheads, knuckleheads, panheads, stock and chopped motorcycles in George's front yard. Most came with visitors, but TJ brought us a custom-made black, three-wheeled chariot with the word "Love" in red script across the back.

Charlie was driving the three-wheeler around The Valley one night with three of us girls in the back when, at a stoplight, we met Karate Dave on a rust-dusted Indian motorcycle — a nice old bike. Dave wasn't bad looking either. He was atypically clean-cut, blond, and masculine, and he came home with us after a few more stoplights. Charlie called him Karate Dave after learning he had a black belt.

The problem with Dave was that he wasn't done rebelling against authority figures. He was a military AWOL, and if he can be believed, he'd escaped the police twice *after being handcuffed.* Charlie told me that in order to respect his peers Dave needed to be beaten at his art and none of our guys was trained in the marshal arts. Charlie said this to him: "Challenge yourself, man, compete with yourself. You got more than twenty acres of hills, caves, and boulders to master. Can you run through here at night without breaking your foot or falling on your face? You can knock people down, but can you pass through a place without leaving a trace that you were there? Without disturbing a dog or a pebble? Challenge yourself, Man." Dave had a good false ID but he was another person who had to avoid the police.

Bobby Beausoleil had gotten Sandy Good pregnant in the desert. This was big news because their relationship was not exactly dovey. She wanted to be with Charlie and resented or ignored imitations. Bobby once asked Sandy to bring him a pair of scissors and she threw them at him.

Sandy

Charlie could say, "Honey, would you get me a shirt," and I'd feel privileged to be asked, but when

Paul or Bobby said it, it could come across like egotistic male insensitivity and I'd feel enraged.

Charlie paid mind to genetics. I remember him saying only a few things that led me to that conclusion. One was his assessment of himself as *not* being "top of the line reproductively," and another was about Bobby Beausoleil being the prospective progenitor of beautiful kids. Prosecutors, in seeking to bolster their case against Charlie, would call him a racist, but people have been breeding themselves and their animals with health, capacities, and appearance in mind for centuries. One thing that Charlie said that seemed significant to me with regard to different races: he said that he didn't want the earth to lose its colors. I think he said that with regard to colors of the sky, water, trees, plants and animals, but also the people. I never heard him express a desire to know his personal ancestry, but in the years since it has been traced all the way back to the seventeenth century and, through the father he never knew, he is a legitimate Son of the American Revolution.

Sunstone, a.k.a. "Bear," was blond and blue-eyed like Mary. Whatever characteristics he'd received from Charlie had yet to manifest. The biggest part of Sunstone's day was in the struggle to pull himself up on chairs, rocks, the porch, and, when tired, onto the hip of an available girl. At The Fountain of the World he'd been inadvertently given attention for crying. Pudgy older women had rushed to sweep him into their flesh, and feed him like a pet. At The Ranch when he dropped to the sand and cried, nobody came. It *infuriated* him. We encouraged him, but he wouldn't look us in the eyes. He cried as though we must be deaf, and then as if to curse us for this outrage, and inside we cried, but we still didn't come. And then one day I saw him stand and fall, reach for a pebble, and, after inspecting it, drop it, and move on. Soon he was walking, using us for balance. I remember him reaching to hold two of Katie's fingers, as she bent to allow him the lead.

Katie

To follow the child, the gate of heaven is opened, to follow his every move with empathy of spirit, knowing that he is the king of his world ... Without Man's madness he will fill his own mind with experience and, not given to doubts and fears, he will extend his all.

— Patricia Krenwinkel, c. 1970 letter from Sybil Brand Institute (L.A. County Women's Jail)

Charlie

I'm not of the school of the matriarch. I'm of the patriarch school of thought. I submit to intelligence and give up to the truth in all creatures but I've never surrendered and never will surrender spirit. Hundreds of years ago when I left Scotland, I said that I would never surrender. Wherever I stand is the Promised Land, the Holy Land to me. I got forever wherever I am.

You cannot be black or Japanese or any other than what you are. It is not a matter of one or the other being good or bad. It is not a matter of like or dislike. It is not a prejudgment. I love all and all is me but if there is no me I love nothing. I love me first and that's natural order. I know what I am, what was, is, and is before me.

Most of our fathers had little time for introspection or exploration, and little time with their families. They'd given the biggest part of themselves to businesses and industries. We'd grown up with amenities and accouterments far over and above mere food and good plumbing, but material goods were not the be all and end all for us. Modern society offered little purpose but earth-destroying jobs for money to buy substitutes for love, and guard against the risks of experience. Who wanted to live in a world where the most exciting and meaningful pastime was shopping?

Charlie once told Mary and me an old joke that had fostered a common experience. A traveler stopping in an unfamiliar town was taken to a poker game after which he said to his host, "You know they all cheat." The guy said, "Yeah, I know." The man asked, "Well then, why do you play?" And the guy replied, "It's the only game in town."

Our parents never thought to question the works of businesses and industries. Not until significant damage was done to natural life were voices raised to stop them. Masses of our generation grew up wary of the money rush, but to our parents it was the only game in town. Our generation was the first to even consider alternatives.

"The way people act, they don't really like their jobs Why don't they change the program to working four days a week and resting three?"

"Or rest half of every day."

"The time doesn't matter if you don't like your job."

"But how do you know unless you get experience?"

"You could train for different jobs like the old days when there were apprentices. And you'd work with an experienced person."

"And there could be places where you live and get training in necessary skills. Charlie said they had them during World War II."

"CCC camps."

"They could teach people to plant trees and make useful and beautiful things..."

"And be resourceful and grow food..."

"How're they gonna make money doing that?"

For over a hundred years, California's wealth had been tallied in precious metals, but its real fortune was in the variety of natural environments, from beaches to mountains to deserts, tidewater pools to freshwater lakes, pigmy forests to some of the tallest and largest trees in the world. Who would imagine these riches would need protection from the people they enrich and sustain? We loved California, and it was being ruined by too many cars, planes, factories, pesticides, herbicides, and whatever the industries could con people into buying. When Los Angeles' people finally admitted to smog so thick it could sicken, their answer was to cancel school recess and keep the kids inside.

Charlie

Air and water ain't worth much — after all, it's everywhere. How would it fit on the stock exchange?

We tried to keep our numbers down, but for every one who remained in the desert, or at The Fountain of the World, another person arrived on The Ranch. The person Pearl wanted there was not. Juan was in the desert.

Pearl could be curt, disagreeable, a real tyrant, but with certain people she was as perky as a professional performer. I saw this the first time Shorty Shea's car pulled up to the saloon. Pearl lit to such high wattage it raised our curiosity and some old ire in George. On their way past me into the house, Pearl informed me that Shorty was "a stuntman for the movies," but she didn't elaborate or invite me in, so I stayed outside.

Shorty Shea wasn't short. Next to me he was on the tall side, and burly. Something about him reminded me of a buffalo hunter. He seemed gregarious enough, another Irishman, but I could tell right away that George didn't like him. After the visit, George was tight lipped. "Talks big," he grunted. I wondered if it was jealousy at the way Pearl bustled around Shorty, but I came to think it was more. George didn't say what precipitated his opinion, and I felt it was not my place to ask. Anyway, Shorty left, and Pearl went back to being unhappy.

Some visitors, George enjoyed. When he had the funds and the opportunity to buy a horse and was led outside to determine its fitness by feel, he was in business. When the rare call came for horses to fulfill the needs of a movie, no matter how small, he was in charge, giving instructions, sending Randy and crew to wrangle. Both George and Pearl welcomed horse owners and ranchers from surrounding communities, so I left the house to allow them privacy. But there were other visitors who came to snoop and gossip, both male and female. They came as "old friends," but they were not really friendly, not to us, and not to him.

A ruddy ex-ranch hand with white-blond hair and calloused hands began visiting regularly in the evenings after Pearl had gone home. He sat across from

George making small talk and leaning back in his chair, putting his left ankle on his right knee, shifting his right ankle to his left knee, stretching out his muscular arms to glance at his watch, and, at sundown, reckoning he ought to get going. One evening in the half-light, Bobby and Charlie saw this man by the haystack loading bales of George's hay into a pickup truck, and they suspected it was not the result of a bona fide deal. Everyone knew George was barely getting by with sixty horses to feed, so when the guys confronted the man, offering him cash to pay George for the hay, he promptly put it back, and never came again to take it, so George didn't have to know about it. That was John Swartz. He would be back in several months for a job.

Sometime around January of 1969 we
moved to the suburbs. Charlie's friend, Bill, already had access to a two-story house where some of us were staying part time. But the reason we moved en mass was that George and I had an argument. Three or four times after he had visitors, he told me that someone had referred to us as "that bunch of hippies hanging around."

"A lot of your fellas have beards..." he told me. I told him it was the fashion. He said, "Makes a place look bad." I let it pass, but one day he got testy about it. He said, "I've seen plenty of beards in my time and they were usually on *BUMS.*" So I told all the guys, and the next day all who showed at the front of the ranch were clean-shaven. Still the negative prevailed, and George began to complain as if our guys were the cause of all his problems.

I said, "Is this any way to treat friends? How can you listen to a bunch of strangers?" He said they were not strangers. Then he told me something that stung, and I didn't repeat it to anyone. After asking me how we got our money when so many of the men did not have jobs, he let on that he thought Charlie was foolish for giving money away.

"Was he foolish for giving it to you?" I asked.

He said, "Yes."

This time I was furious. I yelled, "Well, do you want us all to leave?" and he was so stubborn, and so mad, he said yes.

We took three hours leaving, cleaning, packing, and petting the dogs, and as the three-wheeler roared out of the drive with the last of us, the wind hit my face and I saw the whole crazy, crooked ranch in wet bolts of color, and felt like I'd lost my world.

In January of 1969 the U.S. inaugurated a new president. I don't know that any of us paid attention to politics, but we knew that the Beatles had put out a new album. Down in The Valley, the two-story house that Bill leased had several bedrooms, two bathrooms, a fireplace, electricity, and hot water from the tap. A lot of coats and muddy boots cluttered the storm room near the back door, and the kitchen was scented with steaming food. It was a comfortable place, but the rain made me gloomy. I didn't know what to do with myself.

Most of the guys huddled over instruments in the furnished living room, working on the new music. At night, after eating, the rest of us joined them to learn words and develop harmonies. One night, tired of the repetition, I clammed up. I didn't feel like singing. I was sitting on a tall stool, watching Sunstone eat a piece of chocolate. He toddled toward my white capris holding out his hands, so I put a toe to his chest to block him, and he plopped down on his diapers. He was startled, but I felt like I was flying. Somehow I'd been catapulted eight or ten feet across the room and rolled against a wall. With a sideways view of the multiple eyes upon me, I heard Charlie say, "There. How do *you* like it?" I didn't feel hurt or defensive or contrite. I wasn't even embarrassed. I just got up, feeling cleared of an obstinate spirit, and, when the music resumed, I sang.

A tough east coast girl we called Little Patty (the shorter of two Patties) moved in with us. She had cropped dark hair and what someone described as a cookie-dough complexion, but a smooth voice, and a great smile that erased any doubt about her face. She was street smart and knew to listen before she spoke. But one day as we were about to pass in the hallway, she approached me with that smile, and spoke to me with that voice, and before I understood her intention, she pressed herself into me, tenderly kissing my mouth. I smiled into her eyes, shook my head, and Little Patty graciously understood. Although the guys, being fewer, received the attentions of more than one woman, and we women were comfortably physically affectionate, none of us who lived together demonstrated a desire for homosexuality. Not to my knowledge.

We had a makeshift bike shop in the garage and bikers came to talk shop. Some belonged to "outlaw clubs" with satanic names that really had nothing to do with good and evil or the occult. Some of these guys were at ease with themselves and with us; others hung back looking hostile. One day Charlie commented ironically, "Jesus Christ would have to be the devil to trick people out of their love." Another time he said, "Who would want to be with that stiff, sexless guy they got trapped in the church?" He and the guys eventually wrote a song that went in part like this:

"I found Jesus, and I locked him in my cellar.
(Repeat)
We was talkin' through a hole. Seems like a right nice feller.
He was locked up in the church house, locked up by the preachers' words.
(Repeat)
Ol' preachers dressed in black — you know, we see you, you silly birds.
Those are the birds that spread the words — that get down in your head.
(Repeat)
They'll dirty up your mind, and put you in your death bed.
Dominus Vobiscum —
If they don't pay, frisk 'em.
We need some more tanks to fight the Arabs."

— excerpt, song lyrics, C. Manson et al, 1969

Many of us believed that some "Churchian*" (*Robert Louis Stevenson) in the hundreds of years of Christianity had cut the manhood off of Jesus. I pictured Jesus as a kind of alternative-lifestyle guy who ran with a lot of other masculine guys, maybe like the bikers. After all, the Biblical Jesus was an alternative to the Scribes and Pharisees. He was bringing the people back not just to the pious words but to the spirit. He was bringing them back *to life.*

I don't think we had a Bible, but more than a few of us had been raised with one. After we heard the new Beatles album, someone got a Bible to check out passages that struck a chord (and accord). The new Beatles *White Album* was as appealing as their others, but also different, with specific sounds between songs, and the same sounds gathered in the piece called "Revolution 9." Most interesting were the sounds of gunfire, the grunts of pigs, the screams and moans of people dying, of people making love, a baby's babble, a black man yelling "Rise!" The album was timely. We believed that the song "Blackbird" was written for the Black race. We chuckled on hearing "Sexy Sadie," and wept with George Harrison's guitar. We acknowledged the genius that had created the album, *but we did not believe that the Beatles were talking to us, unless you included us in the soul of the world.* The album was just interesting.

There was a big oil spill off the coast of Santa Barbara. A pipe connected to a drilling platform broke, and before it was plugged, more oil spilled into "United States waters" than in any known emission before. Whitewater turned black rushing onto pristine beaches, and wildlife in the thousands were smothered or suffered prolonged deaths coated in thick crude oil. We had been to those beaches. People who loved the ocean and beaches and sea life were saddened and outraged. But the catastrophic results of human progress were not news to people who had been paying attention. We had already seen the factories vomiting chemicals into waterways, the oily fish and birds. For decades, the earth had been showing DAMAGE. We already knew that in the order of priorities for corporate and political leaders money was placed over life. *Who didn't?*

Sandy

For most of my life I've been sensitive to nature. I think I would have died if I couldn't ride my bike near trees, or swim in the ocean. I loved riding the waves and lying on the sand under the blue sky. Sewage in the ocean, however, was spoken of, and we saw the outlet pipes. But my starkest memory was as a much younger child swimming in the San Diego Bay while the adults chatted on shore, blind or unconcerned about the clumps of raw sewage that were floating around in the water. In my young mind I knew the water was not right. Later, measures were taken to clean the bay, but the problem just went elsewhere.

As the sky lost its blue my breathing problems got worse and I felt nervous and agitated in dirty air, particularly on drives to Los Angeles to visit relatives. They were wealthy and lived near the beaches and in wooded upscale neighborhoods away from the smog. But I remember the air getting worse the closer we got to L.A. And more and more land was being covered by buildings, even along the coast to where you couldn't see the ocean anymore.

Once, in early morning, I saw some owls trying to land in trees that had just been cut down and felt a seeping grief at the image of millions of birds without trees to live in and raise their babies. I was angry when vacant lots and canyons were paved over. Don't people see that kids need places to play in nature?

There was going to be a "revolution." Belief in this eventuality was written and talked about by some faction of almost every youth culture and minority population in the Western World. It was transmitted daily in popular music. The song "What About

Me?" popularized by Quick Silver Messenger Service described many of us. The world was on the Eve of Destruction, a Ball of Confusion; it was Helter Skelter. The Beatles were saying it in double entendre. I didn't think they meant a political revolt, and one song made it clear that they were not advocating Communism. I thought they were revolving in a spiritual way, aware of human greed and its assaults to the earth, and thereby to the self-esteem and mortal lives of all humanity. But I may have been seeing my own projections.

The music our guys were putting together spoke of alternatives to the chaos that would result if people chose to revolt rather than revolve. The need for change and the numbers of people calling for it, both "underground" and in world societies led us to prepare for either scenario.

For many people we met and heard of, the revolution couldn't come soon enough. Leftist politics aside, people feeling suppressed by laws that did not represent them were pumped by the prospect of revolutionary change, even if it had to be violent. Use of a natural plant had made *outlaws* of millions. Hippies and some of the college set touted "anarchy" in terms of a big celebration — freedom and perpetual fun at last — but the anarchy that Charlie envisioned was sad, and compellingly more realistic. Anarchy, he said, would go "from merriment to mayhem, rape, and the worst you can imagine." Without police, and, in our culture, without Christ, he said, "there is no sin that would *not* be committed." If fires were set, and everyone was doing anything they wanted to do, people, and especially kids who were otherwise unprotected would need a way out. He saw the desert as a natural refuge and bikers as potential defenders who could ferry them to safety.

Much contributed to our conspicuity in the suburbs. Our singing at night may have seeped outside the house. The sounds of bike engines drew attention to the vested individuals hanging around the garage. Clearly, we were the biggest family on the block. Parents came looking for their pets and teenagers. The Bank of America owned the house. When Bill suddenly learned that bank representatives were coming to view the property, he advised that we leave quickly. Sandy and I recall spending at least a day at the home of one or more members of Iron Butterfly, a rock band. Rock and blues bands were living throughout Topanga Canyon, and The Valley. Cappy had a boyfriend who was a promoter for Buffalo Springfield. She'd hung out with Neil Young who, incidentally, had taught Sandy guitar chords when he came to visit Dennis Wilson.

After the bank people had gone, we went back to Gresham Street and tribulations. Ruth broke up a street fight between Bobby's dog and one belonging to a neighbor, receiving painful puncture bites to her stomach for it. Sadie, on one of her independent outings, contracted the contagious skin disease, impetigo, returning home to infect a few others. Epsom salt baths and extra sanitizing were necessary to heal the affected and keep this from spreading. Some people were angry at Sadie and she was defensive. She came into the house after another of her trips and angrily told us she was leaving and taking Zeezo with her. This time, I thought she would really go. Several people were in a car waiting for her. As she moved around the house, gathering her things, the *White Album* was playing on the record player. No matter what the Beatles were singing about, the song "Sexy Sadie" loosely fit her, and on hearing it, she started to cry. Charlie shrugged in sympathetic resignation. "You can walk anywhere in the world," he told her, "but without your soul you're an empty shell." She wiped her face, and went to tell the people she came with that she was not leaving.

We were already fragmented. A handful of us remained in the desert and for some reason we couldn't go to them as planned. A letter from Mary written from jail two years later described their time there.

Mary

I'm thinking of the desert the winter when five of us were at Barker's — beautiful — raining and snowing, taking showers and washing our hair by the wash tubs and looking at the snow on the hills all around. Start out by drinking steaming cups of hot coffee 'round the kitchen table, thinking of how the water is going to feel, then going out, stripping quick, having the hose turned on your body, then your hair — and once the first coldness is over, it's all so alive — wet and naked in snow and mountain air, hosing each other — wow, I could dance now remembering it. God, we were so free and laughing. Clean and still wet, skittering barefoot over the stones to the house, fresh clothes, a fire in the stove, and maybe some hot chocolate, or else some tea with honey. Dishes, laundry, house-cleaning, bread baking started, we'd go gather firewood. Short mountain winter days, earlier lamps and dinner. Talk, music — music and words we didn't know were in us until they had a chance in the evening to come out — special sounds for the pack rat in the attic, and for Caspar, the baby skunk — watching for him to enter through his hole behind the food stash, sedately cross the kitchen floor, giving his attentive audience a

From the valley suburb we talked to the mad
George on the phone. He missed us, and vice versa.
We invited him for lunch, and led him around the
property. A day or two later he called to say we could
all come back to The Ranch — even the goddamned
guys.

Pearl accepted our return in stride; Randy pretended to pay us no mind; Larry and Benny were glad
to see us; and the dogs were all a-wag — Tom, Wolf,
and a white and buff fluffy mutt we called Muttsy.
Muttsy was the only pup from the litter at the farmhouse to escape the dog catcher during the Pearl and
Randy roundup. Now grown, he had the run of the
place with the others. After being cooped in the suburbs, that's what we needed — space and reasons to
stoop, reach, lift, climb, and *run.* We had privacy in
the little house at the end of the road. We had sun-
rises and sunsets, fires at night, and we were high
enough above city lights to ponder the galaxy. These
fortunes served us with age-old and future insights,
but, practically, we were just turning old shacks into
havens, wood nooks into forts, making meals, making
music, and making love. The Ranch still had restrictions, but we could fit between the routines of George,
Pearl, and the cowboys, who in their own ways were
misfits on the edges of society. A bunch of us were in
the house talking to George while Pearl prepared to

feed the dogs before she went home for the night. Hurrying across the linoleum with a dish of dog water, she spilled some, slipped, caught her fall, and slid a-ways on one knee without spilling another drop. To our cheering applause, Pearl displayed a blushing smile, and George said, "Pearl, would you do that one again? I didn't see it."

Mary, Juan, and others in the desert were picked up and came back to The Ranch. Juanita and Brooks had agreed to stay behind to more and less man the fort. We wanted to revisit the desert, and if violence came to the cities like so many people said it would, we wanted to be out of its way. We began collecting necessities were we no longer able to make runs into towns and stores. At the same time, we were living as if our ranch life would never end. The toilet at the back house got fixed, but the guys usually stepped out to the edge of the woods at night. Sometimes I'd see two or three of them out there quietly talking, chuckling, aiming at trees, and competing for distance.

Not all of us could ride George's horses. The Ranch, after all, wasn't a playground for "freeloaders." Discretion and timing were involved in knowing when and who to ask to saddle a horse. If Pearl and Randy were in a bad mood, they'd bitch about it. But Juan would do it. He was Pearl's best hand. He had the diplomacy to appease her, and the cajones to saddle a horse for whomever he damn well chose.

Many of my days didn't go past George's house. People who didn't know said later that I was imprisoned there by Charlie, but I was my own warden. I sensed and took on responsibilities that suited me and held my attention.

Lyn was vigilant to the comings and goings through George's house. George sat in his chair with his cane beside him and inquired, "Who's there?" or, in his hillbilly language, "Who bees it?" And we girls would announce ourselves using the names that he gave us. Brenda might come in soft as a breeze, and answer, "It bees Berrrrenda," greatly accenting and rolling the r's. Ruth would offer an enthusiastic, "Howdy George, it bees Ouish," and Cappy, "Top of the marnin' to ye, Garge , it bees Capistrano." When the guys other than the ranch hands came in, he became serious and suspicious, asking about chores. Juan might stride in, and with loud clear confidence declare what had been done or needed doing. Ruby Pearl with her flaming red hair and flushed face seemed driven in her work, always on the move, but her body language emanated her moods and intentions. Lyn would pick up each person's demeanor and the overall atmosphere, and she would let everyone at the back of the ranch know if there was anything they needed to do to keep balance with the front. Regarding the ranch, Lyn was about balance.

With George's approval, the whole ranch opened up to us. The movie set was my childhood fantasy. We could create sets, deconstruct them, and create new ones. The Longhorn Saloon had the most space for nightly gatherings, music and dancing. One night in the saloon, Bobby and Clem got into a fistfight that became stunning entertainment. It was in slow motion, their punches barely connecting but sending their jaws askew and their bodies buckling with such graduated precision that it knocked any lingering thought from my mind. Bobby's fist finally sent Clem exploding to the floor where he buoyantly rolled and bounced several times before coming to a stop and leaving the rest of us agape.

The next time visitors came up from The Valley, we let the weed go around and, on cue, slowed our movements to about a third normal speed. In a growling baritone, Bobby asked, "W o u l d   y o u   p a s s   m e   t h e   g u i t a r ?" It seemed to float forever to his hand. When the visitors were looking at each other, questioning their own perceptions, we increased speed and ran the game to them.

Bobby was a mover. I think he wanted to act, write, draw, paint, travel, play multiple instruments, compose and record his own music, and build whatever he imagined. Nearly everything was easy for him, and he attracted women without even noticing them. He spent as much time in The Valley, L.A., the Hollywood hills, Topanga Canyon, and other parts of California as he did at The Ranch. At times, Bobby seemed indifferent to all but himself, and, likewise, he could easily be ignored, but his self-interest was partly in keeping with his determination to be self-sufficient. Like most of us, he was barely out of his teens, still asserting his independence. I remember Bobby and Charlie walking together, enthusiastically trading info and banter, Bobby wearing a big smile, well-fitting jeans, and a knife in one boot. I never wanted to build conceit or give guys respect they hadn't earned, but, in hindsight, on occasion, Bobby was visually grand — a swashbuckling prince out to explore rough places, dine in finery, laugh with gusto, give women a tumble, and walk away to conquer more of the world.

Bobby was a peacock and Charlie loved him. He knew what he wanted and went for it without guilt or hesitation. He'd unashamedly stand in front of a mirror trying on shirt after shirt, checking himself from all angles. Of course, others of us might do the same in private but wouldn't do it in front of others because it looked vain. Bobby was brimming with energy and talent and creativity. He had interesting clothes, antique vehicles, and friends all over California. He had ideas, places to go, and people to meet, and he was eager to involve Charlie in his creative projects. So there was a time when the hustle and bustle was about getting Charlie and Bobby dressed to go into Los Angeles on one of Bobby's trips.

The "Parachute Room" behind the movie set was a cushy secluded place for afternoon naps and intimate mergers. It began as an abandoned trailer that, years before, had been backed to the edge of a cliff, its rear end entangled in the bramble of a tree that grew from the creek bank below. Brenda or Ruth conceived of covering the inside with billowing white parachutes so that it was like being in a cloud. Through the open back windows no earth could be seen, only sky, trees, roosters, and others of wings.

The parachutes came from military surplus. Brenda and Charlie were thinking to design lightweight capes that could be turned into personal tents. Drawstrings could shorten or lengthen the capes, and create a hood with little, if any, added stitching. Brenda would perfect the design, and experiment with dyes in desert colors. Like other animals, our survival might one day depend upon our ability to blend into our surroundings. We would also need shoes and clothes as near impervious to the harsh conditions as we could get.

Sandy

Once in the desert at Barker's, as many of us sat around a table in the kitchen by candlelight, Charlie showed us how to make patterns for clothes. He wanted clothes made for himself and, as usual, the girls were eager to learn. I thought and still think it was very cool that he was showing us this, but I was acutely aware of my separation from the group. As he cut out the paper patterns, I lost track and understanding of what he was doing, and I felt stupid and afraid that he could see my separation and the shame and guilt I felt for having fear and pain in my body — for, in short, being a wounded and scarred human being. I forget what precipitated this — it may have been because he did see my pain — but he brought me in front of everyone, and he started inspecting me. He looked at my teeth as if I were a horse. He was saying, as he turned me around, "Not bad." He pulled up my shirt and, pointing out the long curved scar that runs from my right mid-back to under my right arm, he said, "Been in the shop a few times, but we can use it." Rather than feel embarrassed or humiliated, I felt seen and acknowledged. I always appreciated Charlie's attention, but there were so many of us, and I think everyone wanted to be with him, and wanted any excuse to do something for him. One time at Barker's the girls were baking cookies and fruit turnovers on the wood stove. I ran outside with a cookie sheet of half- burnt ones to offer Charlie. He took a bite and said, "Hmm — I can taste the competition."

I was turning the front room of the Bunkhouse into a Victorian parlor when Danny DeCarlo and his chopper moved in. I'd put up a frame for a print of a 19th century nude, and ran to get the picture, but on return I found etched within the frame the head of a demon and the words "Straight Satans 1%."

Danny was a dark-haired outlaw biker who almost always wore black engineer boots and his club "colors," a denim jacket with the sleeves cut off and a patch across the back showing the club's name and caricature devil. They were some of the proud "one per-centers." (In the 1940s, public relation reps of the American Motorcycle Association had stated that 99% of all motorcyclists were law-abiding citizens.) Danny claimed the Bunkhouse for his bike, his gun collection, its display rack, and a bullet-making outfit. Most days he worked on his bike, playing jazz station 105 loud, and he got mad if anyone messed with the station. Some of the girls did, so he welded it on there. Straight Satans came to the ranch for afternoons, as did members of another club, Satan's Slaves, but only Danny moved in.

Each of the bikers was different. Joe was unmarried, with a light prison record and a steady job. L.A. George had a beautiful young wife and a bunch of blonde little kids. Droopy was a Satan's Slave. I think his dad was a biker. He had an old knucklehead that Charlie wanted to buy. Droopy was one of those gentle giants. What a casual guy. I never even heard him talk, but one time I saw him and Charlie and some other people kicked back in the saloon, talking all night, for so long that the candles on the wooden coffee table melted down and set it on fire. They didn't even break conversation. They just carried the table outside, and stood warming their hands over it as the sun was coming up and the mist was rising off the hills. There were other bikers, but these were the guys that I remember.

The sky turned gray. The wind kicked up tarps and sent stray hay flying. I saw Ruth and Danny in long coats like gangsters, trekking the hills carrying something, and later in the house George and I were tryin' to figure out where all that shootin' was comin' from ricocheting in the hollow. "Could it be thunder and lightening?" He said no. So I got up to find out JUST WHO WAS IN OUR WOODS!

"Check to see if there's riders," he told me, "...and see what the boys are up to, and..." Already out the door, I ran back.

"And what?"

"Don't forget to shut the storm door."

Checking on Larry was always a trip. He was usually grousing, or telling yarns to customers, like about his being a Blackfoot Indian and having to kill the whole cavalry with his "bare hands and only one knife." Checking on the others was a cursory exercise because George didn't want to hear that Randy was in his trailer, or that Juan was saddling horses when there were no paying customers, and surely not that an outlaw biker and the little Ouish were in the hills firing a machine gun. There were other things to speak of, and by the time I made it back to the house the subject had changed.

According to police reports, Danny had a modest arsenal, including rifles, shotguns, carbines, and a submachine gun. He was quoted later as saying that when he first brought guns to the ranch, Charlie had asked, *"What are we going to do with a machine gun?"*

And, when Danny told him it was for protection, Charlie laughed and said, "We don't need nothin' like that." But after a couple of months of his personal influence, Danny said, everyone had fun shooting his guns. His bullet-making set up was interesting. I watched him pour molten metal into the molds. He said that it took him about an hour to make several hundred rounds, and in a matter of minutes it was gone.

Cowboy Benny was staying with his girlfriend and only part time at The Ranch, but Pearl hired John Swartz, the ex-ranch hand that Bobby and Charlie had caught stealing hay. At Pearl's suggestion, "Johnny," she called him, was moving into the trailer beside George's house. I thought John Swartz was over forty. He still had the muscular arms of a farm-boy, but his white-blond hair was thin on top, his face perpetually crimson, and he looked like he never got enough sleep. He must have known that we hadn't told Pearl and George about his thefts, but whether that made him more amenable to us I don't know. I never saw him show feelings about anything one way or the other.

Cappy said that rattlesnakes have two penises, one on each side of their bodies.
"Each end?" I asked.
She laughed. "Not each end. Each side. But they can only use one at a time." Cappy knew interesting tidbits. She knew that "horned toads" are actually lizards.
"When confronted with danger," she said, "they speed-dig backwards until they're covered with sand. And if a predator threatens them, they can squirt blood from their eyes — and far! About six feet!" As

kids we called them "horny toads," and they were all over Southern California, but I never knew how remarkable they are, and now they are rare.

Cappy didn't presume to teach. Her enthusiasm just bubbled over. When George said he was "blind as a bat," she tactfully told him she'd heard that bats aren't really blind, and about their fine-tuned sonar detection, and that she really liked bats because they ate a ton of mosquitoes and other insects. And George thoughtfully nodded and told her he thought she was right.

Sandy

Cappy showed lots of personality but also feelings of inadequacy. She had creamy skin and fine white-gold hair, a full mouth and big china blue eyes. She didn't like her legs, so she never wore dresses or skirts, and she tended to gain weight. Cappy loved most everyone at the ranch, and saw each person's gifts and beauty, and often seemed humbled by what she saw. Overall she was exceptionally beautiful and didn't know it. She loved to talk and laugh and tell stories with the other girls, especially Mary and Ella.

Mary was as fair and blue-eyed as Cappy, but Mary was tall and lean and carried herself with surety and a sense of direction. I admired Mary's stamina, kindness, her competence, and her restraint in dealing with her jealousy of Lyn and the constant influx of new women that Lyn encouraged by her friendliness and warmth. I felt empathetic toward Mary, a strong, capable woman, expected by Charlie, it seemed, not to need reassurance or attention because she had a child and was strong.

Mary met a baker at one of the markets and made an immediate connection. She had done some baking, but after meeting him, she just drove to another town on certain days of the week and picked up a giant plastic-lined paper bag containing many loaves of bread, and a variety of pastries. I went with her once and busied myself finding food. She took her time; this baker was tall, and awesomely handsome. They stood at the back of the market talking and laughing like at a social event. Finally I went to help her with the bag and heard part of their conversation. It was all about kids. He was a new father, and they spent their time together trading anecdotes.

I remember Snake wandering alone down the ranch house road, tootling a little flute in the rain. Cherubic with her auburn hair and pale teal eyes, she'd return to the farmhouse at the end of the day, her face smudged with dirt, and a few wilting plants in one hand. Snake wandered physically and mentally. She didn't appear to be sad, or lonely, and she wasn't stupid. She could recite almost anything she had ever learned — not that she was talkative, but she seemed pleased with her brain and to enjoy its company. If she communicated with other people, it was only by accident. Into any conversation, or the absence thereof, she inserted things like, "I wonder if for every Bobcat car they sell that makes one less bobcat on earth." It was an interesting wonder. Nobody looked askance. That was Snake. I didn't take the time to know Snake or consider her age and aspirations at the time her family had pulled up roots to become hippies, but Sandy and I overheard Charlie asking her if she wanted to go back to school. He surmised that she had been an A-student, and she confirmed it, but she didn't express a desire to go anywhere.

Sandy

Snake was in a category by herself, the youngest of us and most eccentric. She didn't drink coffee or chat like Katie, Ella, and Mary did. Her eyes were often at half mast whether due to the weed she liked so much or to what looked to me to be near constant sexual arousal. It was by seeing her lip-licking attempts to draw Charlie that I learned that raw sex was not what attracted him. Snake had been weaned too young from a straight world to a hippie world, and then to the ranch. She had her sixteen-year-old libido and few social skills to navigate amongst more worldly people.

The dynamics between Charlie and each person were as numerous as the people and changed hour by hour. Often he was a blur to me because he was always moving, going somewhere with someone, or lying down with a girl. I could torture myself wondering who he was with, and I saw others, particularly Bo and Snake, hovering and inquiring, "Where's Charlie? Who is he with?"

Bo had a petite and nicely shaped body, but I never thought of her as pretty. Her nose curved downward, and she slunk around with her shoulders slouched and her fine curly hair obscuring much of her face. Under her dark cloud of hair you could see her big brown eyes darting. She was an enigma and seldom spoke. Sometimes she'd utter an unintelligible word under her breath along with a smile and a little laugh.

Bo was nine times more aware than me so I missed a lot of what she did, but once as she sat before Charlie I saw him massaging her head and shoulders, smoothing out her hair, bringing it back from her forehead and face. He gently pressed her forehead backward, straightening her neck. And Bo transformed before my eyes. When she stood up, her shoulders were straight, her head gracefully poised on top of her neck. She looked to me magnificent.

Ruth was then about seventeen. In my mental trove of snapshots is one of her standing on the hard-packed dirt in the front yard, somebody's baby on one hip, and a plumber's wrench thicker than her arm in the other hand. When the saloon roof leaked and nobody moved to fix it, Ruth borrowed a long extension ladder and patched it herself, looking to no one for direction or acknowledgement. Smooth, dark browed, and beautiful, she might brood over matters of consequence, but generally went for and got what she wanted. In town, she asked a stranger for his car. He said she couldn't have the one he was driving, but he had an older car at home that he never used. She told him to bring it back to the parking lot, and she came home in a well preserved 1949 Studebaker with the original beige flannel interior, and a signed pink slip.

Sandy

It was impossible to keep George Spahn's house clean with the constant traffic of ranch hands stomping in from barn and corral to report the day-to-day business. The whole house slanted because the ground had moved and settled. The counter where food got fixed was slanted, so cats easily slid when you brushed them off, but no sooner would it be wiped clean and the stove and cast iron pans scrubbed of bacon or hamburger grease, than another ranch hand would come in to cook, leaving another mess.

Ruth went after the kitchen cupboards with gusto. She removed every greasy glass jelly jar, restaurant coffee mug, and chipped teacup, and washed them in a big pot of sudsy boiled water. She tore out old shelf liners, put in new, and then proudly put back her sparkling assortment of glasses, pottery, and china, while selecting a favorite coffee cup and drinking glass for herself. Ruth was particular, and took good care of herself, and was selfish without guilt, selfish in a healthy out front way that said this is what I want, this is what I will take, and I'll have it with gusto and pleasure. This was with food, her coffee, her shower, her clothes, where she slept and who she slept with. She wasn't greedy and didn't step on anyone's toes, but her unabashed going for herself made her seem spoiled to me. Lyn and Charlie loved her.

One time Ruth and Lyn fell into what they called "the laughing pit" with me standing on the outside of their joy, their loose bodies rolling around on a mattress as they laughed and laughed with abandon. Lack of youthful exuberance and a relaxed body kept me from the magic inner circle of Ruth, Lyn, and the young loves Lyn escorted in and in and in. It ate at me, and Charlie would tell me the secret to happiness was in the giving, but I didn't understand that. I'd felt sore and uncomfortable my whole life and I was unable to relax with anyone. Growing up, I had not seen much giving. My mother was not the gentle, submissive, dutiful wife that was the model for so many women of my generation, and I couldn't and wouldn't pretend to be docile and pliable. At twenty-four I had been abused too much to be a doormat for any living creature. That Lyn showed no jealousy was supposed to be an indication of her love and lack of ego, but I thought and still think that jealousy is natural. In day-to-day dealings Lyn often seemed doubtful, but one thing was sure: her total love and devotion to Charlie. His obvious favoring of her put her in the position of being a kind of example for all the girls. I think this created conflict within us. I wanted a sure, safe mother bear and there was nothing approaching a strong matriarch to match Charlie's patriarch. I was envious of her position and her sheer luck in meeting him nearly a year before I did and having only a few other women around instead of over ten. I could sense though that if a person is full, happy, and brimming with love, then giving would naturally follow.

When we were out of money, bikers offered us stolen credit cards, but we didn't want them. Paul suggested that we could sell something.

"Well, we don't sell anything..." Charlie maintained seriously. His eyebrows rose, and he popped a grin. "...but we could trade it for money." It was a joke. We really didn't have a thing worth selling. Bill knew a club where girls who were so inclined might dance topless, but I don't know if anybody did. Despite what was later said to the contrary, we were a democracy, jokingly called an "Orwecouldjust." ("We could..." "Or we could..." "Or we could just..."). It was a consensus style government, everyone adding to the pool of thought. Charlie was both credited and blamed for having the most input, but anyone with ideas was welcome to toss them into the circle.

When it came to getting money Charlie went for what he knew. Her name was Charlene, a boot and whip-style girl with a curvy body. I read later that she was some kind of heiress, but he never mentioned it. He had met her at a party in Beverly Hills and invited her to The Ranch. She didn't come. *She* had invited *him* to *her* ranch in Nevada, and instead of going alone, he asked Sandy, Brenda, Paul, and me to go with him.

Charlene's Nevada ranch had an old-time hotel with a cowboy cafe at the front. Tired and hungry from the overnight drive, we went in for breakfast. Charlie sent one of the workers to let Charlene know that he had arrived. I almost missed seeing her. She was coming toward Charlie, but, after seeing the rest of us, she wheeled on her high heeled boots and let the screen door slam behind her. He went out to talk to her, and pretty soon an employee showed the rest of us to a bare rustic room with two beds, no telephone, and no TV. I don't know what gave me the impression that this ranch was more about women than horses, but I knew about Nevada's Mustang Ranch and I was beginning to think that Charlene might be running such an establishment. In any case, it was not an entertaining trip for us — we slept most of the time — and the next day Charlie returned to say we were leaving. As we drove away, he said that he had offered Charlene a place with us, but she didn't want it. I found out later that *she* had offered *him* a Cadillac, but he refused it. Apparently, this wasn't about stuff *or* money.

Charlie didn't talk about money. It wasn't a secret, but a non-issue. He said we never had to go out of our way to get money before and shouldn't have to now. With Bill and the bikers he pipe-dreamed fantasy schemes that ended in zuzus. One time he was walking away from a guy, shaking his head and saying, "If you offered some people a nickel to hit themselves on the head, they'd beat themselves to death."

For a while, a little trailer was parked down by the Bunkhouse. Entering it one afternoon, I saw glossy hair splayed across a pillow, and bare legs in the air. It was one of the Hollywood hopefuls with a beautiful body and straight teeth, murmuring and arching her back. Charlie leaned back on his haunches and called, "Cut!" He flashed me a grin and a wink. Then he rolled her over and called, "Action!" She never even opened her eyes, but if she could've seen herself in an old trailer beside a fake saloon where Buster Crabbe and Gabby Hayes tipped colored-water whiskeys, she might have thought it funny herself. Sandy walked in on a similar scene and didn't think it was funny at all.

> Sandy
>
> I left the ranch in a pique of jealousy. Holidays for me had traditionally been tumultuous and this one was no different. I had gone into the trailer looking for something and discovered Charlie about to make love to some aspiring Hollywood starlet. It was my twenty-fifth birthday and he hadn't so much as said hello to me. I opened and slammed every cupboard, and before he could get on his jeans, I slammed the trailer door behind me and was down the road.
>
> I hitchhiked to Topanga Canyon, the only place I knew in L.A., to the apartment of Bobby Beausoleil's former landlord, Gary Hinman. Gary greeted me at the door smiling, but I noticed that his eyes were cold. I asked if I could stay a few days, and he seemed to reflect both curiosity and calculations: Why had I left

the ranch and what would I give him if he allowed me to stay? He offered me the extra bed in his bedroom. I made it clear that I had nothing to give in return. I didn't have any money, and sex was out of the question. I think I even told him I was pregnant by Bobby. I didn't know then that Gary was homosexual and he had a crush on Bobby. When I sat down in his living room, Gary's cat, Suck-Suck, came to sit on my lap and knead my skin with his paws. It was interesting at first, but then it got weird and disturbing. There was something similar about Gary and his cat.

The next two days were awkward. Most of the time we spent apart. I roved around an L.A. suburb while he gave a boy piano lessons. He went out at night to sell LSD and chemicals I was not familiar with. I decided to go back to my old friends in San Francisco.

Tex returned after a three-month absence. He had reported to the draft board in December after receiving an official order, but a knee injury he'd received in a car accident before he met us won him a medical deferment. He said he'd gotten the attending doctor to hype his continuing disability. Afterward, he'd spent the winter in a comfortable Hollywood apartment, "dealing weed and speed" with his old girlfriend. He said they were a good team and made a lot of money, but the life seemed false and no longer satisfied him. Tex observed that we, like the Hollywood people, were collecting supplies and money, but I think that the nightclub had more to do with entertainment than profit.

One of the horseback riders, as she dismounted, said that she had to get cleaned up because she was going to a nightclub, which spurred one of us to joke

that we had our own nightclub in the saloon, causing someone else to imagine the saloon actually transformed into a place where people could come to hear
live music and dance. I think that's how the thing got
rolling.

The saloon had a stage with electric hookups for
instruments, a big hardwood dance floor, and even a
bar. When Charlie's friend, Bill, heard of it, he calculated a round dollar amount that might be profited —
Bill was always good for a money deal — and took the
proposal to George, offering him a part of any money
we took in at the door, and suggesting that, as a bo-
nus, nightclub customers might well come back to
ride horses.

George reined in his immediate interest by stating
his uncertainty about the legalities of running such
an establishment, but when Bill assured him that he'd
do the legal checking, George said yes, even agreeing
to let us enlarge the saloon by taking down a jailhouse
wall.

A cowboy saloon would've been cool for a club,
but back in the day it was all about fluorescence and
outer space. Our house band, consisting mainly of
Bobby, Charlie, and Steve, already called themselves
The Milky Way, so, in keeping with the theme, the saloon became infinitely dark with tiny phosphorescent
planets and stars speckled throughout. Brenda was
the decorating visionary, overseeing — or in this case
under-seeing — a ceiling covered in billowing parachutes, dyed in part to resemble clouds, and in part
the night sky. The stage walls were blacked, over-
lapped with day-glo freeform, and lit by black lights,
and the dance floor had several moods of lighting,
including the flashing strobes that appeared to frag-
ment moving bodies. The whole effect, if not Whiskey-

A-Go-Go, was nightclub enough. One end of the room we reserved as a comfortable hangout, with couches, lamps, candles, and a coffee table. When our San Francisco artist friend, John, and his family stopped by, he painted a spectacular mural above the couches, showing a city in flames as people on motorcycles fled to a clean land in the desert.

The Milky Way jammed electrically almost every night. When they wanted a break, we played .45 records that we'd paid to have professionally stocked in George's antique Wurlitzer jukebox. More people came to the nightclub than we had expected, and, predictably, we didn't charge them to enter. Some moments the place was a tornado of fragmented whirling bodies, and at others it settled into a serene den with kicked back conversation, the flicker of candles dancing across the mural in the living room. We put out popcorn, sold sodas, and stuck a sign for donations on a big water-cooler bottle, getting *up to* twenty dollars a night, which was just enough to give George a sense of success and buy more sodas.

Some of the bikers brought beer, and we girls were not above secretly pouring it out to keep them sober. One night a big guy mishandled one of the girls on the dance floor, and, seeing it from the stage, Charlie called the guy out in a pitch he once referred to as a "Tone Forty." He had explained to Mary and me that the "Tone Forty" was used by commanding officers in the military. It froze the room. The music stopped and he was the only one moving until he jumped from the stage, and the dance crowd parted. When the two men faced each other, their size disparity was alarming. It would've been a mismatched fight but was quickly resolved when the big guy swung. Charlie ducked under his arm and behind him, reached between his legs, took a grip, and escorted that guy out the door by the collar of his shirt and his balls. Events like that continued to reinforce our belief that Charlie would take care of everything. Another night in the club, someone came after Danny.

Danny possibly loved one thing more than his bike, a ten-month-old boy he said would "grow up to be a real motherfucker." He brought his son to live at the back of The Ranch with Sunstone and the other toddlers. Then late one night, a dark, wiry woman burst into the nightclub fully loaded and screaming that Danny had kidnapped her kid. From the time she hit the door she never stopped moving, jumping on tables and throwing anything she could grab. Danny shouted, "I swear ta God I'll kill you if you don't get down," and they tangled, she digging into his face and drawing blood with her nails, he pulling her long black hair until she was a crazy mess on the floor, kicking, punching, scratching, and *shrieking.* Charlie helped Danny drag her out the door, and the people who brought her took her away. About an hour later, the police came to charge both Danny and Charlie with assault. The woman was Danny's wife.

I didn't know Danny had a wife. She had cleaned up her words and actions for the police report, but it was clear that she was under the influence of something. Danny told police he wasn't about to leave his kid with a woman he considered *less responsible than himself,* a statement considered honestly funny by everybody who heard it. I don't know how or if this was resolved, but Charlie and Danny did not go to jail and his son remained with us. Of course, whenever attention was brought to the kids, they could go stay at The Fountain of the World.

One time Charlie was driving a carful of girls and babies down the narrow, winding Pass Road from The

Fountain back to The Ranch when the brakes went out, their speed increased, and he yelled to the girls, "ARE YOU ALL READY?" No choice. Faster and faster they sped, swoosh around one curve, screech around the next, to the edge of the cliff, and then straight for the rocks; he was zigzagging the car to slow it, brushing against the mountain, scraping, nearly rolling, at least a mile like this, and then down the north drive at the ranch to the haystack. No one was hurt, but Ruth came running into George's house to tell us about it, and I fell into the holes of her eyes.

The police began showing up at the nightclub, yelling for us to stop the music and stay where we were so they could check IDs. Because we were not a paying establishment, they took liberties without search warrants, at least once arresting someone who didn't take kindly to the harassment. After that, the nightclub itself was pretty much a bust. George didn't say much about it. He was resigned to the ups and downs of ne'er-do-wells. I didn't know that he considered *himself* a failure.

Sandy came back from San Francisco. She said that her old friends seemed stuck in the same routines and that no one even approached what she saw in Charlie.

Sandy

I came back to the ranch because I hadn't seen anything better thus far in my life. Charlie obviously loved making love to pretty women. Although anything of beauty caught his eye, all of nature was beautiful to him, and I learned that women who were most comfortable being close to nature, who didn't wear

---

make-up or try to look like magazine covers appealed to him way more than what he once called "plastic fantastics." Despite my constant frustration with the arrival of new girls, these were attractive, interesting, talented, and friendly people *on a horse ranch.* A group of resourceful women without jobs or income, living close to the ground away from streets and cars and noise, able to make beautiful clothes and find and prepare healthy, tasty meals from dumpsters, and be happy doing it all, was astonishing to me.

Sitting around the ranch-front drinking coffee, watching the parade of wranglers and riders, George Spahn taking his daily walk, Randy Starr yelling, chickens clucking, roosters crowing, the old goat, the dogs, the horses coming and going with new riders on their backs — even opportunities to ride a horse — might not have been enough to keep me at the ranch, but I held to the hope that I could spend more time with Charlie.

Charlie was all over Hollywood, meeting and playing music with talented and famous people. Gregg Jakobson was one of them. Gregg looked to me like the tall, handsome prince in fairytales. A longtime friend of both Dennis and producer Terry Melcher, he was employed by Terry to scout talent and movie projects. When we met him, Gregg was living with one of the daughters of an American comedy icon, and they had a child together, but there was talk of separation. Before he even visited The Ranch, Gregg and Charlie began philosophical discussions that lasted, on and off, for months. Gregg was more aware and far more curious than most of his colleagues. He was also more mystical. Another part of him figured finances and finagled business deals. He recommended that Terry come to hear us sing and consider us as subjects for a movie project. Later, he described what he saw at The Ranch for a jury:

"I remember the picture. I have a picture in my head of it all. It was very clear what my eyes took in as I stood there on the field out in back of the ranch with the motorcycles and the girls and the guys and the horses and the trucks and the brown grass and the green trees and the blue sky and the stream — would have made a very nice picture for other people to see as well as myself. The picture is still in my head. I could see it now when I just described it to you."

— Gregg Jakobson Testimony, Page 14,307, court transcripts, 1970, Tate/LaBianca Trial

Hearing about Gregg, Doris Day's son Terry, and the prospective music and movie project put George in a good mood. I was in the kitchen fixing jars of cold lemonade, and he was telling me about Corriganville, his competitor "Crash" Corrigan's big tourist and movie ranch just north of us. And he was envisioning our ranch like that, us girls in "cowgirl skirts, little white boots, and little white gloves," collecting money from the dozens of customers in the sunny yard, the serene sounds of baby ducks, chicks, and lambs, "a little School House with a bell," he said, "and a Hillbilly House with pokee-dot long-johns hangin' off the line." I told him I'd be right back, took a jar of lemonade outside, and, from the steps of the veranda, saw four motorcycles being worked on by the greasiest bearded ruffians George's mind could conjure, and thin, golden girls sitting in the dust with hardly a thing on, let alone little white gloves.

Most of the bikes that showed up at The Ranch were choppers, minimalist custom amalgamations of American and British bikes, and the guys they belonged to regularly honed and tuned them. Of the girls, Ruth and Leslie were probably most interested in motorcycle mechanics. They knew if Danny had a knucklehead, a shovelhead, or a panhead motor, and that he was so particular about his bike he wouldn't let anyone else touch it. After some weeks as on-lookers, though, they were given the honor of polishing parts. Once or twice they went with Danny and some of his club guys on "putts" — bike runs that took them a few days and many miles from The Ranch. They loved it. Bobby had asked Leslie to help him put a motorcycle together, and she was a quick study, but by the time she could have been a real asset to the build, he had decided to buy a boat and sail around the world.

Randy Starr sarcastically summoned me. He *knew* I didn't want to watch the castration of a young stallion, but I heard the struggles, and later heard Randy bray about eating "fried mountain oysters."

Charlie told me to keep an eye on Cowboy Larry around little kids. I didn't know what he was talking about, but sometime later, kids were running around the front of The Ranch while we relaxed with their parents, and I saw Larry teasing a barefoot little girl in a dress. She ran off giggling, and that's when I caught the shine in his eyes, the mischief in his grin. I never would have thought to notice, but just before Larry gave chase, I was able to casually head off a potential disaster. Larry wasn't a child molester. He was a child with grown-up parts.

"Wanna hear a stiry?" George was a grownup with child parts. I sat down beside him. "Once upon a time," he said, "there was a big, HUMONGOUS barn fulla wheat. Well, there were these little mice around the barn, so one little mouse went into the barn and got a grain of wheat, and he came out. Then another little mouse went in and got a grain of wheat, and he came out. Then another little mouse went in..."

About the third mouse, I protested, "Is that all?"

George suppressed a snicker. "... another little mouse went in and got a grain a wheat..."

"IS THAT ALL THAT HAPPENS UNTIL THEY EMPTY THE BARN?" He thought our complaints were hilarious. He said his kids used to say the same things.

George and his wife had *nine* grown children, some of whom lived in different states. His daughter, Toody, came one time in a shiny late model truck. She was a big-boned woman wearing pressed Western clothes and nice boots. His son, Jim, was a handsome man about forty. He was the first to visit while we were there, and the only one to visit more than once. Jim was also dressed in the boot and buckle style of ranchers, which he was. He had a ranch of his own. In fact, George told me, all but one of his kids were "prosperous."

Almost everyone was busy, but Paul was shuffling around after Charlie, saying he didn't really know what to do, and all of a sudden, Charlie sounded annoyed. He said seriously, "Why don't you go back to your mommy and daddy." Paul didn't like that. Later I heard that Charlie had asked him to take supplies to the desert for Brooks and Juanita, and he did.

Toughening a mass of people for hard times was a responsibility Charlie said he didn't want, but I believe that whether consciously or unconsciously, he accounted for everyone and everything on The Ranch. Late one night, after our gathering in the saloon, five or six of us girls huddled near George's house, shivering and talking. Charlie passed us, snarling, "Can't you hear them?!" I heard nothing but the other girls. He said, "Muttsy's chasing the baby chicks!" and he took off running down the dark, tangled ravine behind the house. None of us followed. Pretty soon, Muttsy, his eyes cast backward in terror, came streaking past us into George's house with Charlie close behind, and the night chill turned to fear. In the dim light through the open door we could see Muttsy cowering under Charlie's knife. Afterward he told me to clean up the floor. There was piss all over the linoleum.

Muttsy was a sweet-tempered dog. I didn't know he'd been eating the chicks. Charlie looked like a bully, but in the aftermath, Muttsy didn't chase chickens again, and seemed no worse for the terrifying experience.

George had a new dog he named Fritz, a tiny lap dog so small it more often slept on his shoulder. One day, after two sheriff's deputies visited and left the house, George told me he had mentioned to them that Fritz was tuckered out and had to take a nap. Pretty soon they'd wanted to know all about this "new fella, Fritz," if he was a ranch hand, or "with Charlie and his bunch." George thought this was funny. He'd had to identify Fritz. He said they'd been sitting across from him for fifteen minutes, close enough to reach out and touch him, and they admitted they hadn't seen that he had a dog on his shoulder.

Police were a constant in our lives. One time a young deputy was relaxing in one of the chairs on the boardwalk with some of the guys, and they were all laughing. I heard the cop say, "It looks like you guys have it made. I wouldn't mind living like this." Someone said he could and he asked how.

Charlie said, "You take off the badge and stick it in the hat. Put the hat on the front seat of the car, and walk away with faith in yourself."

"Sounds nice," the cop said, "but my wife would never go for it." It was a stale punch line, but the guys obliged a chuckle.

Un-established groups naturally raised curiosity, but in police that translated as suspicion that fostered adversity. When we talked to them, they came more often. When we ignored them, they got mad. Pretty soon they acted like they *wanted us to do wrong*, so they could bust in and find out "What's going on here?" And "How the hell can you do it when I can't?"

I stepped out of George's house just as sheriffs were cruising the yard. One of them was pointing his trigger finger at Brenda. Winking and grinning, he said to her, "Caught-cha!"

She said, "I'm not playing that game," and went about her work. Another day, I heard one of them call to Charlie, "We're gonna get you yet, Manson!" I didn't know if the man thought he was joking, or if he wanted us to think it, but I took it as a straight-up threat.

The next time we heard from Paul, we learned that Juanita would not be returning to The Ranch. In possibly the least populated wilderness of California, she had found her man. "They're getting married," Paul said of her and the miner she'd met at Barker's. We wouldn't see Juanita again, but last I heard, she and her husband were still together after decades.

Terry Melcher was blond and had the wide, freckled face of his actress mother, Doris Day. In the early 1960s she was the movie image of wholesome American womanhood, notably cast in several movies with Rock Hudson, the popular ladies' man, and one of the best kept secrets in Hollywood. Terry had a long collaborative association with the Beach Boys and other pop musicians. He'd produced an album for the Byrds, and was working on music for the upcoming motorcycle movie, *Easy Rider.* At twenty-seven, Terry was a busy man, but on Gregg Jakobson's recommendation, he'd agreed to come see us, and hear the music. Many of the girls prepared a place for his visit, but he didn't show. He could've called but he didn't do that either. I heard that this happened twice.

It seemed strange that both Dennis and Terry, while so polished in appearance, would display sloppy business habits. I don't remember us talking about this or Charlie saying anything about it, but I always liked something he once said to us: "When anyone lies to me, they tell me they lie, and that's the truth."

> "Everything has been here for you.
> It's all been at your hand
> Don't try to build a new world
> Just learn to live off the land"
>
> — C. Manson, song 1969

Brenda read aloud to herself the list of ingredients in a small bag of corn chips, including the then commonly added chemical preservatives BHA and BHT. In typical understatement with just a touch of amazement, she said, "Wow, now they embalm you before you die."

Each of us had food penchants and *nothing* was verboten, but every night we could, we ate vegetable dishes and sauces with rice or pasta. A garden would have been great for us, orchards, and milk animals, and chicken eggs. We could've learned what the soil would sustain, and if we didn't poison it, it wouldn't poison us. But we didn't even think to plant because one thing or another kept us moving. We took trips for exploration, to decrease our numbers, and to get out from under the ebbs and flows of negativity from people such as Pearl, Randy, and the police. I wouldn't have been comfortable leaving had someone not stayed with George, and one or more of us always did.

Camped under a giant oak on the land George referred to as "Iverson's," Karate Dave was bitten by a rattlesnake. For hours, he stood with his back against the tree, his glassy eyes reflecting the night fire. In the interest of keeping him calm, nobody said much to him about the bite, and within a day or two he didn't limp at all.

Rattlesnakes were all around The Ranch although I never saw one, but in a desert town some of us saw a coiled sidewinder under a truck. The truck owner had brought out a rifle to kill it, but Cappy and I asked him not to. We thought there must be a way to move it. The man had a wife and small child. Gruffly he told us, "You got five minutes." After about three, Sandy got mad.

"Oh, for God's sake," she said, "either move it, or move out of the way." The man shot once, hitting the snake near the head. Sandy walked over and picked it up. Then it moved. If the man hadn't rushed to knock it from her hand, it would have bitten her. It wasn't alive, but it was neurologically triggered to strike.

I was potentially afraid of any creature with which I was unfamiliar. At the same time, I think all of us believed that every species has an earthly purpose, and none is divinely assigned to chase around frightened people. Charlie was passionate about wildlife. Dennis and Gregg had gone out to the desert to see him and were astounded at his wrath when one of them drove over a spider. More than a year before, in a park, some teenage boys were chasing down a spider to kill it because some girls were afraid of it, and Charlie got to it before they did.

"It's natural to be aware of what bites you," he told them, "but I don't think little spiders eat people." The boys looked embarrassed. He said, "I would get something away from me if I wasn't sure — but I wouldn't *destroy* it because I wasn't sure. If you keep doing that you're gonna have *no life left*."

Living outdoors gave us a sense of the essential, and living covertly, closely together, was teaching us to function as parts of one body. About eight of us girls were camped near The Ranch when a large enough vehicle became available to take us on a reconnaissance run to the desert. We arose in the dark, quickly uprooted the tent, and, with strenuous effort, carried it and many supplies in a long, two-way shuttle through dark scratchy brambles, over a giant boulder, along a skimpy ledge, past a bush full of bees, over a deep gully, under arched branches, and up a sharp cliff to the Pass Road. I remember details because we made so many trips to and from the campsite. At dawn Karate Dave arrived in an old bread truck supplied by Danny. We were all girls, dressed bulgy warm, on our way to a land of new promise and no police — if they had just let us go. But that didn't happen.

On Highway 395, near the desert town of Lancaster we were stopped by the *Los Angeles County Sheriffs*, still within their vast jurisdiction. Before de-boarding, one of us suggested we pretend to be small groups of hitchhikers rather than what police might consider "a hippie commune." This seemed like a good idea, until I realized we looked undeniably similar. Then there was Dave transporting all these women to where and for what purpose? The whole thing was just too suspicious for them, especially when none of us could produce an owner's registration for the bread truck. It was impounded and we were all booked. This was my third arrest for "Grand Theft Auto," and I hadn't stolen as much as a Tonka toy.

Before we got to the sheriff's substation, Sandy, being pregnant, was allowed to use a gas station restroom, and this was the first of *several* times she was *forgotten* during an arrest. Soon she was at the sheriff's door asking to be taken in with the rest of us.

About a day later, charges were dismissed, and most of us were released. We had to leave Danny's bread truck for lack of funds to retrieve it, and I think this was the time that Ruth was kept in custody as a juvenile, her release contingent upon her legal marriage license, and her father's written permission for her to marry.

George Spahn was solemn as I explained the hitch to him, after which he resolutely said, "Let's go 'n get our Ouish," which we did. She was released into his guardianship. George was the understanding grandfather and a stern patriarch of The Ranch. Charlie was the new age, the visionary, the sage, and the wild one.

Some nights when it got warm, we went into the hills above The Ranch to the Indian Mesa, a flat space believed to have had spiritual significance for Native Indians. On the Indian Mesa we looked into the universe, the fire, and the mind of the world. One time Charlie told us, "The foundation of the will is locked up in graves of what we did hundreds of years ago."

Charlie

In Christ's grave are all the other Gods he put down. The Turkey is Mexican God of War. Indian Mexteka. The Spaniard who came with the cross was not of the land and its balances. He was more like a jackal, less gentle, less aware.

Birds, lizards, and others see two pictures. If you put your hands like praying and lay them on the bridge of your nose, you see two pictures. Indians would put on a beak and feathers and get in the bush and learn from the turkey who is God to himself in his Kingdom. Each of the sons or young men was like a feather and had to earn the right to fight, die, or be sacrificed to the different levels of awareness. When I met the Mexican Indian shaman awareness, he gave me a name and said I could live in his forever. He said he could have saved me a lot of time had the cross not killed him. He had told the Spanish that he was their God but he laid himself down for the cross because he knew it would only be a few minutes in the universe.

There's a whole lot more to it, but if you think I'm a fool because I can't spell, then go to school and make some more A-bombs. If you think the turkey is a fool, then try to outsmart him in the bush. Turkeys can't spell either. The dumb Turkey God built a lot of pyramids and lifted a 2,200 ton stone up over the mountains and placed it perfectly in a temple. Modern man can't lift it, much less move it.

On the Indian Mesa we primed ourselves for primal instincts, worshipped the trees, the earth, the sky, the sun, danced around the fire, and made love on altars of stone.

The facade on the roof nearest George's house read "ROCK CITY CAFE" but it was just a storeroom the size of a caboose before Bruce Davis plumbed and wired it for service. Bruce was from the South — Louisiana and Tennessee — but he was an explorer and seeker. He'd been exploring Topanga Canyon on his motorcycle when we met him the previous year, and he'd stayed with us a couple of months before resuming his travels. Since then, he'd been all over the U.S. and to Europe, but, if he found what he was looking for, he didn't settle until he found us on The Ranch. The only thing I remember Bruce saying about his travels is that while in England he had looked into the practice of Scientology. The attraction, he said, was their methodical "mind clearing" using a lie detector type device called an "E-meter." This was, to him, an interesting correlation to what we were doing without use of mechanical gadgets. Asked for details, Bruce said that he couldn't afford further exploration because Scientology's hierarchy was costly to ascend.

"What about the founder," I asked. "What is the founder doing now?"

Bruce grinned. "Making money," he said.

Bruce was a welder by trade, a part-time electrician, plumber, and mechanic. In response to us girls, he hooked up the Rock City Cafe with a gas stove, a refrigerator, and a coldwater sink. We put a table and chairs in one corner, a couple of stools along a counter, and we un-boarded the big screened windows facing the boardwalk. Then we opened our very own 1940s Route 66-style cafe.

Waitress jobs were always available at the Rock City Cafe. Passing down the boardwalk one morning, I saw Leslie Lu posed with a pretend pad and pencil in front of the table where Randy Starr sat splayed. She hollered toward the kitchen, "Two sausage, two legs, Mabel, and throw a biscuit on the side." A biscuit flew by the window, and Randy reached his good hand to grab it, yodeling "Gawd dayam!" amidst a swell of cowboy laughter. From then on, the cowboys chose to eat, smoke, and cuss in the cafe instead of in the house, and George was imperially pleased apart from the rabble.

On the café's back wall a mysterious panel was framed like a picture. We figured out how to remove the panel, revealing a pane-less window to a dark warehouse. The door to that warehouse was outside, around the corner. When Pearl saw Ruth open it, she warned her not to go in because George kept valuable movie props in there, but George had already told Ruth about that when she asked him if we could use the very valuable bathtub, and he'd told her to go ahead. After clearing and cleaning, we could heat water on the stove inside the cafe and pass it through the window into the warehouse for warm baths.

A cameraman arrived one day on behalf of Gregg and Terry to film preliminary footage for their prospective movie. George's signature was required, and all of us agreed to ignore the movie camera as we went about our day. George was alert and spry. A couple of us girls took him for a walk so he could be filmed, and then we sat in the house, pretending it was a day like any other, but nothing like this had happened on Spahn Ranch in a long time. Pearl was perky, Larry puffed, and Randy, as usual, wrestled himself, part of him acting angry, as if intruded upon, and another part wrangling for attention. At some point, George asked me how the filming was going, and I went out to the porch. I think Clem was the first one to come along and tell me that Mike, the cameraman, had taken acid and was freaking out. What was he going through?

"Death. His ego's afraid of dying. We tried to get him to go into the woods. He's been following Charlie around, begging Charlie *not to kill him.* Charlie don't want nothin' to do with him." Some of us had seen this sort of thing before when we were traveling in the black bus out of San Francisco. People told Mike to go home. Finally he left, taking the film with him, and we never saw either of them again.

George was in his own movie. "Them flat-land furiners," he complained, wagging his chin in the air. "They think they're so high gaflutin' fer havin' a canopy over the bed. Us mountain folk got 'em *under* the bed." He was referring to the tin can I had accidentally kicked when I went in to pull up his covers. On this day, he let on he'd been thinking up a song. He gave it to us in pieces. Brenda and Gypsy put a tune to it, and one night a bunch of us sang it to him in the house.

George's Song (Chorus)

"Livin' high high high on a mountain
Livin' high high high on the hog
Eatin' cornbread and taters
Side meat and maters
Coffee's bilin' in the pot
We likes to drink it good and hot ..."

In one verse Brenda was barefoot on the seat of a buckboard, wearing a gunny sack dress, a hat that looked like a flower pot, and driving a mule dressed the same way.

Most of us girls and some of the guys had picked up George's "mountain talk," and sometimes forgot to leave it in the mountains. A year in the future, Clem would be publicly disparaged with half a dozen words meaning "of low intelligence." People who never knew us would say anything about us in print and on film for decades, and were given what was, before the Internet, a rare platform.

Clem was actually classic as a country brother. He once gifted Sandy and me with a beautiful china teapot. Inside it was a beautiful live tarantula. The surprise was not left to chance. He stood by to supervise the discovery. Another time, he woke Ouish and me, telling us to "be still, and just watch" the snake he was putting into bed with us. His mischief and adept handling of creatures were parts of his charm, but Clem was no hick. Like Bobby, he came from a smart suburban family, and in some ways was a typical teenager, rejecting the past to form a world of his own.

Sandy

Like Sadie and Brenda, Clem would turn a question back at the questioner, or give pat answers as a way of "reprogramming" himself. In reply to, "How are you?" Clem would likely say "perfect." If asked when his birthday was, he'd say "today." I understood his meanings and reasons, but his refusal to give a straight answer could be exasperating. I sensed his rebelling at the conventionalities that hung on in my speech, but he was never sarcastic or mean-spirited.

Clem

Sparkling, glimmering, eyes shimmering
No matter what the tests may be
We bear them joyously
My Father's presence always in your heart
And all the Tragedies and Comedies of Life
Nothing but Dramas of ecstatic entertainment
Hating and fighting with a screech —
Each mosquito is an embodiment of someone's biting speech
Yes, it's true, Man guides Nature
Though he pretends he doesn't know
The children know. And they nurture
Light and sunshine days
Yes, Man guides nature in many ways . . .
You are to reflect the Divine image
Within your soul's dominion
You play whatever role he say
Whether yea or nay in public opinion
See the Soul's picture and roles it's casting
As keen as your sheen when not to be seen
You're throbbing with life

> Forever you're lasting
> No death, love knows time is not real
> Not the minutes, nor the hour
> Your smile is on the hill
> In the expression of a flower
>
> — Clem, California State Prison,
> c. 1973, letter to Sandy

Snake's face displayed a little smile as she remembered *Barbarella*, a surreal movie of the early 1960s. She identified with the title character, and, by transference, with Jane Fonda who played the role. I hadn't seen *Barbarella*. My references were from movies of the '30s and '40s. Sandy didn't relate much to actors or movies at all.

Sandy

I was never a fan of fame, and was too distracted to follow the plots of movies or TV shows. I noted things like good looks and sense of humor, but what impressed me were intellectual and artistic achievements, concert musicians, scientists, and doctors, not mass-culture celebrities.

My older sister, Ginny was paradoxically worldly and naive, and, like Snake, ethereal. Ginny had a tiny waist, a pretty face, pale blue eyes, and a brightness and curiosity that led her to excel in all of her classes. She won contests, was a song leader, was head of the student body, got lead roles in school plays, and, by the time she graduated from high school she had tried to kill herself three times. I looked up to Ginny, but the drama disgusted me, and I hated the way she drooled over the black and white photos of movie stars all over the walls of her room. The movie attraction for her had probably started with our parents.

Our oldest sister was born in 1936 so she remembers undeveloped Tigertail Road in Brentwood. Daddy's mother lived at the top of the road and the next house down belonged to his sister and her husband. They had chickens and horses, and their son kept a goat. The next house belonged to the actor, Henry Fonda, who was an avid gardener and grew prize-winning flowers. This knowledge was brought home to my aunt and uncle the first time Henry charged up the hill yelling, "You keep that goddamned goat out of my begonias!" But harmony existed; the Fonda kids rode my aunt and uncle's horses, and my big sister, closer in age to Jane, got to swim in their pool. The Fondas moved from Tigertail Road when I was just three, so I don't remember them or any but vague glimpses of Grandmother, but I always loved the country far more than anything on TV or at the movies.

Hollywood was big in my parents' world. Many films of the '30s and '40s showed sharp-witted sharp dressers who smoked and drank a lot, and women who liked careers and men way more than kids. People emulated them. My mother was a non-professional actress. Gregory Peck and Dorothy McGuire had started the La Jolla playhouse in San Diego, and my parents would drive there to act in the plays. My mother craved attention and organized community plays, fashion shows, and charity events to get it. On holidays and special occasions she had us kids all perfectly dressed and photographed for the society page, but in private, she didn't know how to get attention except by venting her frustrations on us, often violently. We were a burden and took time out of her social world where she could be the wittiest and most attractive.

We were living in Rancho Santa Fe near the Bing Crosbys — described by my sister as "another dysfunctional family" — and we had a beach house in Del Mar. My father co-owned the tiny Del Mar airport and came into contact with a lot of celebrities, some of whom flew into the airport to go to the race track. He described the ventriloquist, Edgar Bergen, as a small, funny man, who once deboarded his plane wearing a long coat belonging to his very tall pilot. Hidden beneath the coat, for surprise effect, was his dummy companion, Charlie McCarthy. Some entertainers who came through the airport also came to our house. Frankie Laine sang for my parents and their guests, such as Betty Grable, an actress and favorite "pin-up girl" for soldiers during the war. She and the musician Harry James lived down the way from us, as did actor Pat O'Brian and his eight kids.

I think my mother felt very rich and important then, with plenty to gossip about. When I came along, it really threatened her lifestyle because I needed frequent hospitalizations. For her that meant obligatory and time-consuming visits. My sister says although my mother was big into parties, my father was not. She continued to go out, leaving Daddy and the maid to give me the only human care I got at home.

We had moved from Rancho Santa Fe to Del Mar in 1949 when I was wrenched from my father. I was five but my sister was thirteen and the memory for her is clear. One early morning my mother came storming into the house with her brother. She told Daddy she was taking us kids. My uncle hit my father, who told my sister to run to the neighbors. She did, and hid out, but my mother took Ginny and me to her mother's big house in Westwood.

Bleak is not a strong enough word for how I felt. I wandered around Grandmother's house stunned. It was cold, but the top floor held her collections of *National Geographic* magazines, and minerals and artifacts from her travels with Granddaddy in the Southwest. She had a little black light to view the opened rocks, and I was amazed and thrilled to see the beauty inside. But at that time I was traumatized. I feared my mother and she was fearsome. She and her brother had virtually kidnapped Ginny and me, severing us from the only love and warmth we had.

My sisters and I fought viciously at vacation times visiting my father. Ginny and I clawed each others' arms bloody over a seat next to him in a movie theater. When I think of movies, I have bad memories. He loved movies and took us with him, but at five years old, I didn't understand the movies. I needed to connect with and feel loved by my father.

Jimmy Durante bought the beach house in Del Mar. My mother remarried and maintained control of us kids, and had two more. Daddy eventually got another wife and child. His sister, my aunt, was a Vedantist and opened part of her home in Laguna Beach overlooking the ocean to serve as an ashram. She was visited by Christopher Isherwood and other spiritual elite. When Ginny went to college and had mental and emotional breakdowns she would sometimes stay with my aunt, where she furthered her flights from pain into Eastern mysticism. Before accidentally killing herself with pills and alcohol in the 1980s, Ginny came into contact with a variety of known people.

The celebrities that brushed against my world did not impress me as lives fulfilled. Candice Bergen was the daughter of the ventriloquist my father had met thirty years earlier. She was an emerging actress and the girlfriend of Terry Melcher when she came to Dennis'. Dennis composed songs for me in his studio, and held me in his arms in his swimming pool, yet he held

> no charge or interest for me. Only Manson did, because he seemed to offer something that intimated peace, joy, and fulfillment.

There was a lot going on, and I didn't know the half of it. The music was coming together, and people were stopping by to exchange forecasts and offer supplies and vehicles. At various times we had a Cadillac, a 1929 Ford, a 1936 Dodge, the new Dodge Van, a 1948 dump truck, a Roadrunner, a WWII "Burma truck" Charlie said was made for long hauls into China, the Jeep, the Studebaker, a GTO, a Firebird, a 1941 Power Wagon, and some kind of camper we got from a retired cop who wanted to sell it quick because it had no papers. Charlie said it wasn't legal.

The Plymouth Road Runner was designed for speed, so it was no real surprise that Charlie got arrested in it for speeding. Brenda, Bruce, and Ella were with him, and all of them spent the night in jail. The girls told me they were out late in The Valley and saw two cops questioning a woman alongside the road. Charlie yelled out the window to the cops that they were "misusing their authority." He drove on, but circled the block, and seeing that the police hadn't moved, he yelled again, and sped away. This time they got in their car and went after him. The Road Runner lived up to its reputation. The girls said they were far ahead of the police when Charlie stopped the car and got out to wait for them. When the police approached, they were scared, and it made them mad, so they arrested everyone in the car. Charges were dropped the next day.

The Fountain of the World had an unlikely food connection deep downtown in one of L.A.'s black communities. Back then everyone called them "ghettos." At

398

least once a month someone from the Fountain took a pickup truck downtown to collect food for themselves and the needy people in Box Canyon. While working at The Fountain, Katie and Mary had picked up the job. That's where they met the black man we knew only as John, the overseer of the downtown operation. One of the girls told me that Charlie began going with them to see John, and that the two men talked about things other than food. It was through the surplus food distribution network also that Charlie met and had an on-going dialogue with a big American Indian who came to The Ranch.

Charlie

We talked of the world and far too much to relate. We talked about how the native peoples dreamed with animal people and earth, while white people's dreams were of cars, trucks, wagons and things to ride around in. He said he could see by all the cars and trucks I had that I had caught all the white people's dreams. I said yes, any car or truck you need? And he picked the little old German car that didn't even run and I seen no way of ever putting it in working order, but he had a truck come to take it away. I even offered him the silver Road Runner and he wasn't interested. I told him I was an Indian once in Scotland. He said I had a good heart and left.

Dune buggies were the way to go. That was the latest on desert transportation. Motorcycles could take us part way, used less gas, and were faster, but dune buggies were *made* for sand. I don't know where we got the money, but our first two buggies cost a couple thousand dollars, and came from a shop in

The Valley owned by a retired police officer. One didn't have a title. Tex and Bruce began examining and tuning up the engines.

Katie had purchased over two hundred dollars worth of topographical maps showing the land from the San Fernando Valley to Death Valley. When they were spread out over the entire saloon floor, we could walk on them and survey the terrain, much like in a low-flying airplane. Some of the guys were plotting routes through canyons and over mountains. I heard that one of them could get keys to the locks on the fire road gates, and when he couldn't, they'd just cut off the locks.

I may have mentioned that Charlie was a good driver. With off roads open, his abilities were sharpened.

Brenda

One time Charlie took me for a ride I'll never forget! We took off from the ranch and traveled back up through the hills and up the fire roads and we came to a ditch that was real wide and deep. So he circled back down the road, built up speed, and we flew over that ditch and up the road, up over a hill and way down into a valley at top speed — to the top of a mountain — to the edge — and the road dropped from there straight down. I was hoping he wouldn't but I knew he would and he did! The road disappeared and all to be seen was blue blue sky. I could feel ALL MY FEAR AT ONCE. Then I saw the road — straight down — we touched ground, and came to a big bump, slowed some, and caught on a rock.

Charlie stopped the engine, hopped out and looked at it from all angles, hopped back in, backed it up, and drove around it into some loose dirt. The buggy got hung up again, so we both hopped out and checked

---

the mountain for another way down, but this was the best way. Charlie got the jack and put it under the bumper and I got in the driver's seat and started the engine. The wheels spun and the buggy slid sideways. We moved the jack to the other side, and while I stood on the front bumper, he put the gas to the floor — and we flew over the bump! I got the jack and climbed in and we went on sliding down the mountain like that. Near the bottom was a plateau of rocks and boulders big as houses. Charlie asked for the binoculars and we climbed way up onto the rocks overlooking the whole city. As far as the eye stretched was cement, smoke, cars, construction, churches and graveyards.

The flavored aromas of buttered toast and grilled cheese brought congregations to the Rock City Cafe. Thanks to Mary and Katie, we always had butter, beans, rice, cheeses, and good breads. Then someone brought us a station wagon-load of pies, frosted cakes, donuts, and more in white bakery boxes with cellophane windows. It was the first of frequent deliveries and a mixed blessing: all the sugary gluten our minds ever craved, and far too much for our small bodies.

Cowboy Larry came into George's house talking about joining the circus; Randy said that Larry *was* a circus; Pearl reminded George that someone was coming about a horse; and *VAROOOM*, a motor was getting tuned LOUD out front. George frowned and told me we ought to move our mechanical operations to the dump.

The dump was on the far side of the corral where scrap wood and metal, fencing and baling wire were tossed for future use or just to get it out of the way. Cowboy Bill traded George something in exchange for a big cattle trailer he towed to the dump to hold motorcycle and dune buggy parts and tools, and the guys hooked up a generator for lights and equipment. There was even plenty of grease-free space at one end of the trailer for sleeping, so on some warm summer nights we hung out with the guys and the motorcycles and dune buggies below the insects flitting around the lights.

Mary

I just flashed on that crazy caravan we had moving up Devil's Canyon one afternoon — dune buggies, people and camping gear, tabla drums, and babies, sleeping bags sticking out everywhere, bouncing banging kettles and canteens, rice and honey, guitars, and a girl on horseback following. We had to lose her before the turn off.

When we first got the dune buggies, the sheriff's posse came for their regular check and one asked Clem where we got them, since none of us had the money for a pack of cigarettes. Clem ran down a rip-off that we'd pulled to get two of them and the cop just walked off looking like he figured Clem was out of his mind.

When I think of the dune buggies I think of Tex 'cause he got me to love motors, especially those running smoothly and really quietly. I think of us sitting out at the dump beyond the corral, getting hot and sweaty and dusty, cleaning parts and bleeding brakes, making perfection. He'd screw and unscrew, wrench and plier to get the engines as near silent as he could, and we'd take off for Devil's Canyon to test what he'd done, and just to have a stony ride. We'd go all over, winding in and out of washes and passes, finding places to stash people and things, sites to be checked further on foot, fences that could be avoided and where they needed to be cut. And just when we'd get up to places we figured none of us had ever been, we'd see tracks of the buggy Charlie drove.

We'd always stop at the creek. The water is so cold and good. We'd get enough to drink and wash up some, and fill the canteens 'cause Tex always kept Devil's Canyon creek water on his buggy. Usually he'd drive slow, looking all around, being as noiseless as he could, but times he'd cut loose to see what the machine would do, gunning it around curves and hitting the water as if it weren't there, sending it spraying over our faces, and the mud would splatter on our feet and legs, and I'd sit there and relax and laugh with that crazy motherfucker 'cause he was crazy as he could be, racing himself, all excited, a real rehearsal for a future flight. We were both so dead in our heads that we were flying. If the buggy had hit a tree head on we would have just kept on going and didn't care a bit. Tex said the dune buggy drove itself and it wasn't gonna do itself any harm. He'd zoom off the road and go nearly straight down either side of it. Damn those rides were so insane. I can laugh thinking about them — especially Tex and his laugh. He could go anywhere.

> — Mary, letter from Sybil Brand Institute,
> Women's L.A. County Jail

"How else did you think I could talk to you
except through the music?"

> — C. Manson, song, 1969

Charlie had been urging Gregg Jakobson to arrange the meeting with Terry Melcher, not because he wanted a recording contract — he had walked away from contracts — but because when we went to the desert, we wanted to leave behind a message.

Sandy

The cattle trailer at the dump was a rust-colored hulk that served as a place to hang out, play music, smoke pot, sleep, and probably make love. There was a raven that hung around the dump. I had a band-aid on my foot that the raven kept dexterously peeling off. He also stole cigarettes from shirt pockets. The dump was one gathering place where Terry Melcher and Greg Jakobson came to hear us sing. I wasn't interested, but I was aware that something important was going on. The excitement and tension were generated by Gypsy more than anyone. I also recall sometime later gathering on a sand clearing by the creek, and singing for people with sound equipment. I was conscious that we were being observed and evaluated, and that we were unrehearsed and unprofessional in talent and in dress. I could feel the tension in our group and knew it was a substandard performance. Other than the significance that Gypsy and a few others attached to these events, I don't recall any build up to them or conversation afterwards.

There exists a fuzzy photo of Charlie by the boardwalk with the raven on his forearm. I believe Pearl took it. He's wearing his embroidered vest, and an oddly cocked brown felt hat, and his upper lip is swollen, cut by a shard of wood that splintered off of some project he was working on. The raven was a

404

wonder to him and he spent a lot of time with it. He said it was the smartest bird he'd ever seen.

Charlie

That bird got into my head as if I was part of it. I didn't want it to be raised dependent on humans so I would take it far away and let it go. I'd drive miles back to the ranch and that bird would be sitting there. Part of me wanted to keep it but I wanted it to be free from humans because I wanted to be free from them also. You got to be careful for the wildlife. If you make friends with them, they run to other humans who are not friends. The raven flew to land on a guy's shoulder and he thought Alfred Hitchcock's bird movie was after him. He almost knocked the bird's head off before I got between them.

Randy Starr's heavy bullwhip came from behind me and, with a startling crack, splintered a corner of the barn. Turning, I saw in his eyes a wish that it could have been me. Randy was jealous of the attention we were getting. Greg Jakobson was still advocating for recording and filming us, but said that a scuffle between Randy and Charlie had unnerved Terry Melcher. Apparently on Terry's last visit, Randy had come out of his trailer blustering drunk with a gun. Charlie got mad, rushed Randy, struck or kicked him, took the gun away, and told him never to draw a gun on him again. The confrontation had made Terry nervous and he didn't want to come back to The Ranch.

A bunch of us took a ride in the bus across The Valley to The Hog Farm because Charlie wanted to talk to Snake's parents. One of the girls had found her sitting beside George, saying something like, "Walt Disney died for us." Afterward, George sounded concerned. He told me, "There's something wrong with that girl."

The Hog Farm was on steep, uneven ground. Rough corrals didn't enclose hogs or any other animals, only muddy dirt clods. One building was open, and people were around, but I don't remember anyone there to greet us. A birthday party had been celebrated. Curled ribbons, and plates smeared with cake frosting remained on the table. A few people and kids were involved in a game of tag. Other adults were scattered, and those we talked to appeared to have taken something psychedelic. Snake's parents were not at the farm and there was no word of where or when we could reach them. "Wavy Gravy" was not there either.

The Hog Farm was famous in the hippie world. It was formed by a coalition of people, including the tongue-in-cheek sage known as "Wavy Gravy." According to hippies, Wavy had a lot going for him; he got along with everybody, and lived his life by wisdom and whimsy. Beyond some interests and understandings, we didn't have much in common with the Hog Farm people we met. They got high and embraced a childlike state of being, but their child selves seemed stuck in re-plays of an idealized past. I don't know if Snake would have fit in, but she didn't want to go there. When we got into the bus to leave, Charlie went to a window and let loose with sound.

Charlie

The song I sang that night? From the new baby to the old and death and beyond, music hooks up all

406

we don't understand. It is a universe on a level all
its own. There are awarenesses hidden within sound
just like programs within your computer. I sang the
crucifixion, the music of suffering, dying, birth. And
the big circle of people froze and freaked out. The fear
was so heavy I left voluntarily. It was not me there,
but them in reflection.

Some people who say "love" keep it a weak baby
pissing on itself. How many times must I face all the
deaths of a world's fear of life? If no one hears my
song, it's okay because only one could hear it anyway.
Ain't no me, you or they in it. One Earth for itself and
survival of the world.

— Charles Manson, # B-33920, letter from prison

Summer heat and a plague of flies near the
horses literally browbeat our love of nature, but the
flies settled down with the sun, and the night air re-
suscitated scents and sounds from the amphitheatri-
cal hills. I think we all were seduced by natural surroundings, and by sensual, physical love. The sexual
contact I witnessed was smooth and amorous, the
kind that sheds ego along with clothes, leaving nothing but the giving. We spent a lot of our nights outdoors. On the Indian Mesa, and wherever we circled,
we were open for insights and visions. I thought we all
saw the structural and functional perfection of nature
on earth as a reflection of Divinity, and our own species systematically killing it.

Our survival while cities fell into chaos, and ma-
rauders roamed the land was a prospect based more
in optimism than knowledge or skill. The reverence
we had for each other was a soul-saving grace, but
the elements that sustain life were more valuable than
all the world's treasures. Without air we wouldn't live

more than minutes; without water, weeks or days; without food, maybe a couple of months. Charlie gave us insights as they came to him, options about dealing with extreme elements, animals, and people.

One moonless night, while walking from the farmhouse, Brenda felt a heavy creature with claws drop onto her shoulders from an overhanging tree. She said it screamed and bolted off of her toward the creek, but she never saw what it was. We had heard screams in the woods. George said that when it's extremely dry a mountain lion or bobcat might come down to drink. He said they'd been known to attack, "especially a she-cat with cubs," but it hadn't happened to anyone he knew. George was particularly fond of Brenda. I told him we would be careful, and I asked him not to tell Randy because Randy would like an excuse to kill something.

Charlie had seen desert waterholes where each type of wildlife came to drink. He said, "There is an order to this procession. The burro sees only one wolf. There may be thirty wolves but the burro sees only one. That's the one that will eat him if he falls. And the wolf only sees the burro that will kick his head off if he gets too close." He said he met each animal on its level, eyed down its fears, and was open to seeing into it *as if he lived in it.*

"Snakes," he said, "see and hear by vibration. A snake is everything he sees. When you walk up on a snake, you're walking into his mind." Brenda said she and other kids used to play in a field full of rattlesnakes, and none of them got bit. Charlie said, "All snakes don't bite, but all the snakes know reflections of the self." Tex later revealed he'd seen Charlie in the desert "glide through a gully full of rattlesnakes, touching them gently on the tails."

Snake, the girl, seldom came to the front of The Ranch during the day so I didn't keep up with her mental condition. Her father came in response to the message we left at The Hog Farm, but he didn't want to come inside. He stood in the yard talking to Charlie, and afterward we learned that Snake's parents were no longer a couple. I don't know how the news affected Snake, but responsibility for her care was left with us, and there were times when she had to be brought to the shower to bathe.

> Charlie
>
> You cannot get others' problems off you. You must learn to be free with them, as if you had eight legs and thirty-two arms and they keep getting in the way of each other until you learn to deal with them as if they were a part of a bigger self that you surely are as you grow.

Juan's bitter self-mocking was offensive. It was barely masked aggression. He'd reverted to making peculiar comments, and then snickering when people appeared to be trying to understand them. For awhile he amused himself by wearing cut-off jeans so threadbare his butt showed, and so short his penis protruded. Pearl appeared not to notice. Juan was never cited in town for indecent exposure, but a woman reported seeing Clem by the high school talking to girls. She said he had a hole in his pants.

The police found Clem, corroborated the hole, arrested, and charged him with "lewd and lascivious behavior." This might've been funny but a judge sent him for an indefinite stay at a State Mental Hospital in Camarillo. Clem wasn't mentally deranged or sexually perverse, just indiscreet and underage. I think all the girls on The Ranch were fond of him, and two set out to get him back. They didn't even have use of a car that day so they went to a local parking lot and found one with the keys in it. By dinner, he was home. Of course now he really had to lie low, being not just a runaway but an escaped lunatic.

Someone had given us an Army field phone for the desert, and we hooked it up between the Rock City Cafe and the back ranch house. We also used a little sign language, so barely there you'd miss it if you didn't know. It probably started when Charlie taught us some pimp signs, the tug of the collar to summon each other, the brush of the sleeve which meant *stay away*. These were beneficial in surreptitiously communicating from the haystack to the house, and to fugitives or runaways who needed to know if strangers might be dangerous. It was just one in several forms of communication, and others were evolving.

Rushing out of George's house with a big pair of scissors, I stopped. I had no use for them. I went back inside and left the scissors, but couldn't leave the house. After walking in circles, I grabbed the scissors and was halfway down the boardwalk when Brenda stepped out of the saloon, took them, thanked me, and went back inside. That's what was happening. People have been speculating about "extra sensory perception" for centuries. We called it "tuning in" or "channeling."

I was attuned to the friction between Pearl and George. Ella worked at the rental office one day, and

410

happened to be in the house at night when Pearl reported to George the number of riders and the day's take. She told me that Pearl shorted him by ten or twelve dollars. I didn't tell George, but sometime later I heard him and Pearl arguing after he caught her in a lie, and I got the impression he'd known she was skimming all along.

George needed Pearl. He never forgot it. She needed him too. He told me he would have liked to have reminded her of it, but she was so stubborn she'd have wanted to prove him wrong, and he said he was "in no position to test her."

When business was bad, George looked doubtful. It had nothing to do with us, he said, except maybe that he could hear us singing in the saloon at night, and it wasn't the singing that bothered him — he said we sounded "real talented." It was that "at a well run dude ranch folks don't stay up half the night." It may've been the way we girls sometimes got in a hurry to leave him and go with the others, and we had things on our minds that didn't include him, and he went back to worries and problems.

For a long time George had been trying to swallow a heart burning expression someone — he thought a city assessor — had used to describe The Ranch. They'd called it "an eyesore." Since he couldn't trust his own eyes or depend upon the hands, he felt helpless and enraged. He told me he felt "cornered" because if they were to leave him for even a day, the horses would go hungry, and the business would be lost. The humiliation of needing people he often despised was enough to make him wish to be done with it, to have the satisfaction of wielding the final stroke rather than succumbing to impotence. He could sell. I thought it would take years to get a buyer, and meanwhile something would work out.

In my mind, The Ranch would always be ours. In revolutionary times, it would be a safe place to rest and refuel before moving on. The Fountain of the World would be another. A prosecutor would allege that we were leveraging George for the deed, but who needs a deed in the midst of lawlessness?

The saloon was cooler than anywhere else, with big open doors to catch breezes. At night we usually closed the front doors so as not to attract the attention of people driving by on the road. Coming up the pass in his dune buggy one night, Charlie met the tail end of a two-car contingent of sheriff's deputies on their way to The Ranch. Accelerating, he passed them. They sped to pull up beside him in front of the saloon. Then they went casual: "Hi, Charlie, where is everybody tonight?" Nodding toward the saloon, Charlie said they were probably inside. He gunned the engine, zoomed around the squad cars out of the yard, around the corral, and into the dump. The sheriffs followed, but while they were cautiously tripping through baling wire with their flashlights, he had abandoned the buggy, and was running across the corral back to the saloon where he warned us, and someone got on the field phone to the kids at the back. Charlie was honest like that.

Of all the influences in my life, Charlie and LSD stand out, but TV programming was at the beginning, and lasted more than ten years. People of our generation believed in love, God, and country, in loyalty, and honor of dying for what we believed, and then we watched all those words merchandized into meaninglessness along with our trust.

Charlie

That's all anybody is — a long reel of tape, TV, movies, past experiences — until you stop, turn around, and start new thought, new time, new reason. All minds are held together with reason, cause, purpose. The Godhead is like a room and you can only get out of it what you put there. Life, love, trust, faith are just sounds. Without truth it's only change for a dollar, or what time is it, or meaningless garbage. Feeling in truth makes majesty. We must find a way to make the words real again.

Galloping down Lovers Lane, Ruth believed that a trust was developing between her and Silver until he veered straight for the low hanging branch of a big oak that would have knocked her off if she hadn't jumped first. Silver was a strong white horse marred by a soot-like pall, but the real marring was behind his eyes. We thought he must have been abused before coming to The Ranch, especially about the face.

Silver had a brown eye and a blue eye, the blue one having a dart-hole pupil that made him look unearthly. He was never rented to customers, but they could see him when he held his head over a gate near the saddling yard, and some were attracted by his different-colored eyes. Pearl said that people had no business going back there, but some did, especially those who hadn't been around horses much and wanted to cool their fears or impress their companions. Silver seemed to anticipate these people. He awaited their touch on his muzzle, neck, or forehead before he lunged. Then, as their faces fell and they screamed or cursed, struggling to wrench their arms or shoulders from his teeth, Silver jerked back his head defiantly as if expecting, even relishing, reprisal. He was a lawsuit on hooves.

I only saw one lawsuit coming, and it wasn't Silver's doing. Johnny Swartz kept an untrained German Sheppard on a choke chain attached to the bottom of his trailer. I think he got it to guard his possessions; I never saw him pet it or heard him call it by name. When we objected, he just put it on a longer chain that stretched taut as the dog ran frantically side to side, barking at people almost continually. It was not a mean dog, but agitated, fearful, and totally out of control.

One day John's dog got loose and ran all over the front of The Ranch. Down by the rental office Pearl and I had just watched a big-bellied man haul himself into the saddle of one of the tallest horses. The berserk dog ran up to the horse, barking, and the horse got dancy. The man, who had claimed to be an "experienced rider," grabbed the reins to catch his balance. The taut reins brought the horse to its hind legs, tossing the man backward, causing him to pull harder, and the horse to rise higher. At the pinnacle, both horse and rider struggled for balance, and the poor animal, with its mouth stretched open and terror in its eyes, fell straight back on top of the man. Only a few yards away, I saw the man's stomach squash outward like a tomato, and I broke into a cold sweat. I was sure he was dead. The horse squirmed, rolled, and stood, and, to my astonishment, so did the man.

Pearl ran up to take the reins, her face drained of color. She told the man to sit on the office bench. He was badly shaken. He said "No", while jerking unsteadily toward his car. He seemed angry, maybe to cover his fear. Pearl wanted to call an ambulance, but the man said, "NO." Angry. That's all, just NO. As soon as he had recovered enough breath, he got into his car and drove away.

Meanwhile John Swartz's dog had gone after the goat, and I don't know how Charlie got the dog back on the chain but I suspect he scared it half to death. The lawsuit came later from a lawyer claiming that George was responsible for his client's back injuries. George couldn't afford a lawyer, and the case remained suspended over his worried mind.

A little radio in George's house played country music and short blurts of world news every half hour, the U.S. casualty counts, riots, rallies, politics and business as usual. The previous year the army was revealed to have tested a "nerve gas" near farmland in the Midwest, inadvertently killing a lot of sheep. In 1969 the Defense Department acknowledged that unbeknownst to citizens, they had been transporting the gas and other lethal chemicals across the U.S. by railroad.

Another report said that NASA was getting ready to land a spaceship on the moon, and had plans to send one to Mars. Couldn't they apply that level of intelligence to protecting the planet we already had? Were they preparing to escape if the earth got too polluted or were they mentally already gone?

Katie

    If people would trash this planet, they'd do the same to another one.

— Patricia Krenwinkel, c.1973, letter from prison

Some of the public were campaigning to "give the land back to the Indians." Charlie asked, "You gonna shit on a plate and act like you're serving a good thing? I'll tell you like the Indian told me: 'I don't want it. Clean it up and I may change my mind.'"

A few months later amalgamated native tribes under the banner of the American Indian Movement would move onto Alcatraz Island in San Francisco Bay to stay for nearly eighteen months. The island had been abandoned since the federal prison was closed and the government listed it as "surplus property," part of thousands of acres they no longer needed, but it was not the Indians' intention to steal it. They would offer the U.S. government $24 in glass beads and red cloth as payment, a symbolic representation of what was given to early American Indians for the New York island of Manhattan.

"Say the burros came within fifty yards of me in the past," Charlie said, "but some man gets ahold of them, beats them and the lets them go. The one mind of all burros runs together. Their fear of humans goes up. It's the same with people. The level of trust disappears slowly until no one knows who and what to believe."

Who could we trust when for decades political and business leaders had been dealing the earth's resources for personal profit, leaving nothing but plastic and chemical concoctions that cannot recycle back into it? Some of their creations will lay like slime on the soil, in the water, and in our own bodies for longer than we live, and some will kill not only us but future generations. The progression of consequences did not require scientific study: as land, air, and water became more polluted, more people would be sick, and more would go crazy without knowing why. Wouldn't the world's militaries naturally protect our planet, the armies for the land, navies for oceans, and air guards... of course. Instead, they were part of a long chain of command owned and operated by corporate Earth eaters.

That was the year George got a stomach sickness that he took hard. Brenda, Ruth, and I took turns sleeping in the big stuffed chair in his house, one of us in the house at all times to put cool cloths on his face, neck and chest, and get anything he asked for. He refused a doctor. For three nights and days he was nearly delirious with fever, but managed repeatedly to lean from his bed over a big tin can to disgorge the sparse remains from his spastic stomach. Afterward he rinsed his mouth, wiped his face, and fell on his side, exhausted. Sometimes when we folded the sheet or blanket over him, he gently patted our hands. On the third day, he asked us to prepare warm water in his wash pan and lay out a clean set of pajamas and undershorts before we left his room. On the fourth day he asked for tomato juice. Then we knew he was on his way to being well. For months afterward, George talked about our care of him as though we had done a great thing. In our youthful invulnerability, we didn't fully understand.

I think that Ruth met herself in Sherri, both long legged teenagers drawn to horses and motorcycles. Sherri had owned a horse, but had to sell it when her parents divorced, so she came to The Ranch to take care of horses in exchange for the privilege of riding them. She was fifteen and came across as shy, but she had run away before, and told Ruth she wanted to do it again. Ruth advised against it, but Sherri explained that her father had left her and her little brother with their mother, and their mother had remarried. Their new father was Chinese, with a different orientation toward parenting. Her attitudes inflamed his temper. She believed that he and her mother wanted her out of the house. All they needed, she said, was something to tell the neighbors. This turned out to be remarkably true.

Ruth enlisted me in creating a scenario about my grandparents' farm in Oregon where the three of us could live in the country, taking care of animals. Sherri told her mother of the opportunity. Responsibly, her mother invited Ruth and me to dinner, where we apparently pleased her and her husband with the proposal. Sitting around the dinner table, we were prepared to give them an alleged address where Sherri would be living, the name of a high school she would be attending, and a number of other details, but they *never asked*. Soon after our dinner, Sherri's mother dropped her at The Ranch with two large suitcases, and said goodbye to her daughter who was going to live in another state with unknown people. And she *never returned* to even ask about her.

Cappy's mother had so severely spooked her in trying to kill her spirit that it's a wonder she could trust any other woman. Leslie confided that when she was pregnant at seventeen and wanted to have the baby, her socially conscious mother had forced her to abort, pushing on Leslie's stomach herself to expel the fetus.

Sandy

My mother didn't have a maternal bone in her body. On my first day of kindergarten she dropped me off at the school and drove away. If she'd stayed long enough to see that I found the right classroom, she would have seen that the school wasn't even open. She had brought me on the wrong day. A policeman found me wandering around, totally disoriented and crying hysterically.

I think that I began to feel the tensions of my parents' relationship even before I was born, and later to show the extreme physical effects of a child who has formed no attachment with the mother. Mostly it played out in respiratory issues. In infancy I had two tracheotomies and in childhood countless painful exploratory procedures. Doctors back then did not know much about the correlation between parental neglect and abuse and childhood and adult illness. I was in and out of the hospital and oxygen tents. When I was ten a surgeon removed most of my right lung. I still wonder if that was really necessary.

Charlie

You are a woman. Whatever that is or is not is of little difference for the man-woman games set by Queens that destroyed their Kings and Kings that played their own parts poorly, reflecting self destruction into the mirrors of their own wives, daughters, mothers, and children. If woman don't hold herself in love for herself the children won't reflect her in love and this is what falls hard on the earth — because that is what woman is.

We thought we'd left our parents, but they were in us, with a long line of ancestors, like the lineup you see by holding a mirror in front of a mirror. Charlie could see these people. I don't think it was in his control to avoid them. To understand him you'd have to acknowledge the weaves and warps of twenty *centuries* of Christianity, and the Sanskrit word "karma."

His prosecutor, in building the case against him, would broadcast, "Charles Manson claimed to be the second coming of Jesus Christ." But Charlie didn't say that. He said a fair amount about God, Christ, and religion, the most succinct of which I remember being: "Religion is God's biggest problem."

He said, "Christ was not a Christian. He would be anti-Christian because Christians don't believe in him." He said, "Without the cross Christians got no will. Without the Pharaoh, the Egyptians would've been blobs. Without the will and word, there is no reason to live." He said, "All things that give us life are God. The Christian woman's still trying to put Christ in Sunday school. She's drained the life out of everything, including herself. As long as Christians keep God dead that's where their minds are going."

Charlie

I can remember the sun's explosion, the ocean life, the pyramids, dying on the cross, and on and on, as all time is now's mind in waves of karma. Beyond time's mind I am a coyote and a rubber shoe and the swing on the back porch on a farm in Arkansas.

Pearl was almost always professionally polite. Enthused when we girls talked about costumes, she told about her own costumes while working in a circus, and of her days as a dancehall girl for bit parts in old movies. She had a class of voice and manner like movie characters of the '30s and '40s. You could see she used to be pretty. I found out she used to be George's lover too, but got old, and seemed to hate even the thought of it, so she treated him like a guilty memory, tugging him around by the sleeve of his coat instead of his hand, running him into doors and other things. George didn't speak of it. When Pearl brought him back from dinner with a scrape or a scratch, he said he had caught his sleeve on something, and brushed off further concern about it. But when he came home one night with a bleeding gash on his forehead, a few of us girls conspired to get an invitation to go with them.

We took turns going, sitting in the truck between George and Pearl, serving as mediators when the tension got jagged. Neither of them wished to be thought impolite. At the tables in cowboy restaurants where varnished wagon wheels were on display, we moved light conversation, and made sure that George had a cloth napkin to tuck under his chin. He always urged us to order more food, worried that we'd get "puny." After the meal, while Pearl paid the tab with George's money, he quietly consulted us to be sure he had no spots of food on his coat or tie. One time he had run into an old business associate, and, after a fine conversation, had returned home to feel food on his tie. He was still mortified.

In the fluorescently lit supermarkets, while Pearl scurried to fill her list, George stood straight and tall, holding the handle of the shopping cart. Pearl pulled the cart from the front and he marched behind, sometimes picking up his large feet higher than was necessary, much like a horse. And, too, like a horse, when Pearl pulled the cart too suddenly or stopped too abruptly, George's head jerked back in a start. If he bumped into anyone or they bumped into him, he apologized promptly, never meekly but as a gentleman, but when his mind was elsewhere or he and Pearl were at odds, a scrape with someone made him look furious, frustrated, and humiliated.

When Pearl got busy and left George standing by himself, he marked time, slowly shifting his weight from one foot to the other. One night as I returned to the cart with a sack of potatoes, I saw him from a distance, looking completely out of place, a fine old tree in artificial light surrounded by tin and plastic. After watching him get bumped by and show deference to an overfed stranger in curlers, I dropped the potatoes in the cart, put my arm through his, and we went to find Pearl. Like this we often strolled the supermarket aisles, me telling him whatever the sounds didn't say, and he, in a low voice, chuckling and talking mountain talk. He said he once got mixed up and took hold of some other lady's cart. I told him not to worry what people thought because a lot of those bulldozers on legs had eyes and didn't use them. I could tell he blamed Pearl. They could've filled a barn with the grudges they had stacked up between them, but their arguments were a part of George's world and, despite the frequent friction, they were beholden to each other in ways I didn't know. Pearl was, on occasion, gracious or feisty, depending upon how badly she wanted to get home. She appreciated our help, and sometimes even treated us like kin. She never mentioned having a husband or kids of her own.

Frank Retz braked his pale yellow Lincoln Continental at George's porch, and stepped into the sun frowning. He was about sixty, bald under a flat golf cap, and stood rigidly erect about an inch shorter than me. Not many rich people came to Spahn's Ranch. I thought "rich" because of the car, and his clothes, a smooth polo shirt tucked into Bermuda shorts showing tanned, athletic legs. I went inside to tell George, but George was expecting him. He stood, extending his hand when he heard Frank come into the house. I'd never seen him do that before.

Frank had a thick German accent and didn't bother with small talk. George introduced me to him as "one of the good little gals who give me some help around the place." Frank begrudged me a grunt before asking George if there was someplace they could talk in private. Apologetically, George offered his room. Frank eyed me as he shut the door.

George told me later that Frank was gruff because he was a very busy man and only stopped by on business. I felt that George didn't want to lie to me, but, in keeping Frank's confidence, he didn't want to disclose too much. I kept my wonderings to myself, but soon George told me that Frank had a lot of wealthy German-American friends who were looking to build a German club.

"Here?" I asked.

"Maybe," he conceded.

"You wouldn't sell the ranch, would you?"

"I haven't decided one way or the other," he told me.

One Saturday, German Frank arrived, wearing knee-high riding boots. George met with him again in his bedroom, and later told me that the planned German Club would have a restaurant, a spa, lodges, gardens, tennis courts, and a hotel. He was so impressed with the plans he couldn't hide his enthusiasm. He said he liked Frank's solid handshake. He was unconsciously imitating Frank's clipped speech. It embarrassed me that he felt so honored to be in Frank's company. I knew he believed he was finally getting a chance to share the prosperity and association of men he considered respectable, but I could see that Frank didn't respect him. I told him I didn't trust Frank Retz. He said that Frank didn't trust us either.

The daughter of a world famous American entertainer was seated at a baby grand piano in Terry Melcher's Malibu house where we went to pick up Dennis. She was in her twenties, pale and petite, with a bubble of platinum hair that flipped up at her shoulders, and a black evening mini-dress featuring high, pointed breast cones and plenty of leg. I was star-struck. Her father was one of the first voices I'd heard from my parents' radio before we saw him on our first TV. Passing the piano, I tried not to stare, but Deana Martin didn't even glance at us.

I sat on a couch beside a man wearing granny glasses and a long Nehru robe. He didn't acknowledge me either, but continued to elucidate the fine points of something he was writing. I was the only person close enough to hear him, and I had no idea what he was talking about. He concluded his monologue by standing, parting glass doors to the balcony, and disappearing into the night. Likewise, a few people drifted through the rooms like ghosts.

I headed upstairs to find a bathroom. Opening a door, I was startled by a movie-like scene. Dennis was poised over a beautiful woman on a bed. Before I could apologize, I realized they hadn't noticed me, and I reclosed the door.

Downstairs, Charlie had paused to see Deana Martin play the piano and sing. Incongruent with her surroundings, she chose an old blues song about cocaine. I watched her eyes, below tarantula lashes, slide sidelong to Charlie, and her lips mimic a sexy come-on. I never knew what Charlie was going to say or do. Meeting her gaze, he suavely propped himself against the piano like her father had done in countless movies and public appearances. After her last tragic note, she paused, looking up at him. "Well," she asked, "what do you think?"

He said softly, "I think you should go wash your face." To her expression of disbelief, he smiled and said, "I can't see you through all that plaster."

Dennis descended the stairs, telling us that he wasn't ready to leave, and we would need to come back later. Then he went back upstairs. It was a brush off. From my vantage, Charlie and Dennis were once connected in a brotherhood known to men since ancient times. There was love and honor between them. And then it was gone.

We left Terry's house and didn't come back. If Charlie had wanted a recording contract, he could have been more restrained. I once heard him answer Dennis by saying, "How do I feel? I feel that you can't spend 500 years fucking up the earth, air, and water and then pay a Hindu to get you to forget it."

Being near or just seeing Charlie gave me a sense of being in the right place at the right time. I always latched onto the upbeat and humorous things he said, but one night he stopped mid-sentence, as though snagged on a nagging thought.

"You know," he finally said seriously, "not everyone can live off the land. Two hundred million people living off the land would strip the bark off the trees." After another pause he said, "When we got to the mountains and desert, most of the wildlife was gone. Mountain goats, deer, big-horned sheep, big cats — *gone.* I looked in the spring above Barker's and seen a dead rat, and I could see through that water all the way to the ocean all the shit and garbage being put in it." None of us spoke. I was thinking of the desert as one of the last places we could get away from pollution. He said, "It's not water here or there. It's ALL WATER. It's connected."

For years I didn't realize he was saying that we *couldn't* get away. *It's connected. There's no getting away from it.* But we were already on our way.

Brenda

Once the first dune buggy was together, Charlie and a couple of us girls took it out into the hills and lived in it. To me, it was a very serious practice run, and I spent the whole time going through the saddlebags and tool box to make sure everything we needed was there. When Charlie first asked for the binoculars, I found out what was there: soap, toothbrushes, toothpaste, combs, towels, extra underwear and clothes – all the things we girls packed. We could hardly get to the tools and binoculars. So, we fast found out what we could use and got rid of the rest.

We were testing the best ways to camouflage clothing, and considering the most durable foods like whole grains, dried fruits and vegetables, oil, honey, and nuts.

The need to travel unseen inspired fine-tuning of our senses and muscles, and melding with the vibrations of any environment. Clem could so thoroughly absent himself that even the dogs didn't hear him coming.

Charlie said, "A bird can make a sound you can't hear five feet away, but at twenty-five feet you can. Bush men use sticks and logs to do much the same thing. A drum or flute can be set to go over and around some people yet others can hear it clear." I had experienced sound as a vibration, but I'd never considered the possibility of bouncing it over and around things.

What each of us envisioned of our future in the desert came to light only after we were arrested. Scenarios varied from the need for basic survival skills and supplies to a phantasmagorical world beneath the surface of the earth where chocolate trees grew without sunlight. Charlie was wont to fantasize, and often in jest, but underground chocolate trees were not what I had in mind. Cappy, with scintillating zest, had told us a legend about Montezuma and his peoples' descent into the earth, and also of the Aztec's use of the cacao bean. Chocolate. To her it was an allegory, but in others' versions, we would meet the people already living underground. Prosecutors would inflate the ideas, claiming that our plan was to emerge like cicadas years later without having physically aged. In their story, Charlie intended to rise as king, Jesus, God. Hogwash. Charlie was looking at underground tunnels and caves to hide from the insane people who would destroy their own planet in pursuit of gold and oil. He inspired in me a sense of adventure that supplanted paralyzing dread. If chaos was inevitable, we would ride it out on top of our fears rather than cringing beneath them. We would do what was needed to survive.

Pearl got a phone call from her former ranch hand, Shorty Shea, and she was strangely nervous telling George about the call. Shorty would be coming to visit, she said, with his new bride, "a showgirl" he'd met in Las Vegas where he was working as a bouncer. Pearl didn't know how long Shorty had known the girl, but he hadn't mentioned anything to her about marriage before.

The couple arrived late one afternoon. There was a lot of rushing and blushing on Pearl's part, as she got George into the passenger seat of her truck, and they all went out for dinner. They didn't return until after dark. Then, in the shallow light from the bunkhouse, before their departure, Shorty introduced his wife all around. The following morning, George whispered to me, "Didja see Black Beauty?"

She was a smiling black woman in a wig, and everyone was cordial with her, but Shorty seemed to be showing off an exaggerated notion of his own magnanimity. In other words, it was all about him. My opinion may've been tainted by George's view of Shorty as a swaggering braggart, but George wasn't hateful and didn't elaborate on the subject.

In my teens I'd come to think that all black people needed help. Obviously, I didn't know there were whole towns with black doctors, teachers, and other self-sufficient people. I thought that the pursuit of human rights grew organically, whereas integration was an engineered arrangement, and resistance to it was not exclusive to white people.

Sandy

In the early '60s I was at a huge rally in Berkeley where Stokely Carmichael was haranguing the American government and white folks in general. I clapped along with thousands of other white people. When blacks talked about poverty, I felt angry that people let it go on. I had the makings of a crusader — intellectual curiosity, discontent, and rebellion against the status quo. Black oppression movies were released when I was in my teens, romantic, powerful movies. A direction and purpose were programmed into me and millions of others.

I enrolled in the tutorial program at San Francisco State College because I wanted to help. Organizers of the program sent me to the ghetto to tutor three little black girls about nine years old, Deborah and a set of twins whose parents I assumed had a sense of humor in naming them Marijuana and Tijuana. The twins lived in a flat in the part of San Francisco called "the Fillmore" after one of the major streets. I went one day to get them and picked up a cacophony and medley of images. The twins were among several children playing around two central features in the room, the mother and a big table covered with the remains of breakfast, dishes, boxes of cereal, ketch-up, ashtrays, packs of cigarettes, and, since the mom was doing the kids' hair, an area of the table was cleared off for combs, rubber bands, ribbons and rag strips. The mom gently shoved one little one from between her knees and replaced her with Marijuana, braided her hair, and then did Tijuana's. Some big guys were near the front door, probably older brothers and friends, digging in their pants pockets, producing money, dialing the phone, and getting things together to go somewhere. It was a warm atmosphere.

Deborah, on the other hand, lived in a nearly empty apartment in the projects with only her mother. In the bleak living room were just a chair and a couch on which Deborah's mother sat bleary-eyed, telling me over and over how nice it was for me to take her daughter out. She was an alcoholic.

The church where the kids were tutored was a big old wooden one story building that had lots of room for the kids to run around. The coordinator of the tutorial program, a black guy in his twenties, was brotherly to the kids, and the black women tutors were motherly. I felt awkward. It was hard for me to even understand what the kids were saying.

We all went into a smaller room and let the kids read and helped them when they didn't know the words. The books had pictures of white children. One day, after a tutoring session, we were all standing around the big room and the children were playing. I said that we should get books that pictured black people instead of white people. I said that when a book has the word "hair" and a child sees only light straight hair instead of black kinky hair, it could be confusing for them. The black dude looked at me, his expression full of hatred. He said with deliberation, "The word is nappy, baby, NAPPY, NOT KINKY, AND DON'T YOU FORGET IT."

I was embarrassed and confused. Later, the white people in the tutorial program were told that only blacks would be allowed to tutor the children, and it was only a matter of months before the black student union rioted on campus. For a long time I didn't understand why this black man had been so angry over my use of words. I had the right idea. I knew that those kids should be looking at images like themselves. It was the beginning of a period of overt black militancy in the country, and they, more than I, understood that I didn't belong amongst them.

Nation of Islam Black Muslims presented as religious and racial separatists. In periodic publications sold by bow-tied members on city streets, their leader, Elijah Mohammed, asked why black Christians would worship a God that allowed himself to be nailed to a cross. Allah, he said, would not sacrifice himself or his people. There were differences, Elijah Mohammed said, between white and black people; white people even smelled different. He said that overthrow of white rule was in Muslim scripture, and he told of a time when "the white devil" would be "wiped off the face of the earth."

Black Panthers showed solidarity with their Afros, their black berets and jackets, and their *guns.* Gathered for the stated purpose of defending black communities from police brutality, they were self-disciplined, and they had cause, supervising police while displaying legal firearms openly according to California law. The City of Oakland's police force enlisted a congressman to change that law, and Panthers made a trip to Sacramento to argue that the proposed bill would render them defenseless.

News people filming then Governor Ronald Reagan in Capitol Park turned from him to record about thirty *armed Black Panthers entering* the State Capitol Building. Some, if not, all were arrested, but the boldness of their action attracted many more to their ranks. The public was divided on whether to view Panthers as freedom fighters or criminals. Left to the discretion of individual police, treatment ranged from a hands-off respect, to a reinvigorated effort to assert the upper hand. In response to the latter, Panthers rallied big crowds chanting, "Revolution has come!" "Off the pigs!" "Pick up the gun and put the pig on the ground!" There were open clashes with police, and alleged clandestine murders on both sides.

To some people the word "Pigs" referred only to police; to others, moneyed establishment types; and to still others, all white people. A babysitter for a family of black children told me that after she saw an automatic weapon in the case their father carried, he candidly told her that the time was coming when he would have to kill white people.

"You would kill me?" she asked him.

Nodding in the affirmative, he said, "It's nothing personal."

There were fundraisers for the Panthers all over Hollywood.

Gypsy was ripe for revolution. Her parents had been active in the French resistance during WWII, and had given her up for the cause. She was raised by other people in France and later in the U.S. She said that her foster mother had died of cancer, and her foster father was blind. I never heard more about her past. In the present, she was playful, lusty, busty, and, when she gained weight, mothering. Each of us had personal struggles and conflicts, but recurring were those between Sadie and Charlie, Snake and Charlie, and Gypsy and Charlie. With rare disregard of discretion, he once told me he'd seen some of the girls working all day in the kitchen, and Gypsy glide in at the last moment to deliver the meal. Things like that set him off.

Sandy

Gypsy liked to be where the food was and where
the guys were, so she'd often be carrying mugs of coffee and plates of food to the guys. She was an accomplished violinist and she could sing well, but despite
her musical ability and smooth talk and hustle, she
seemed to me heavy and indolent. One time in a nomad
phase between the ranch and Devil's Canyon, we were
struggling to carry equipment from one campsite to
another. Instead of carrying the conga drums, Gypsy
rolled them downhill. When Charlie saw the drums he
threw her down and knocked her around like he said
she had done the drums. Then he hacked up lot of the
recording equipment. I'd never seen him so angry.
The incident caused us all to be careful with regard to
any equipment, but it also furthered stories — some
false, some true — about his treatment of women.

Outlaw bike clubs, interestingly, had bylaws
and elected officials. Danny was the treasurer of his
club's chapter, and word came that some members
didn't like him spending so much time at The Ranch.
I couldn't tell that this had any effect on Danny. He
looked fairly content with his bike, and his guns, and
the frequent company of both Ruth and Sherri.

The girls had chosen to spend time with Danny.
Allegations that Charlie had "ordered" girls to go to
bed with men came as a surprise to me. I never got
an order. He did have a thing about respecting the
relationships of the other guys. When Leslie was new
to The Ranch, he asked me if I would spend the night
with Bobby so that he could be with Leslie. I didn't understand his reasons, and I declined. I said, "He's not
you." Charlie sounded angry as he walked away.

He said, "Maybe you're not me." If the other girls reluctantly acquiesced to other partners, or were happy to experience and give experience to the other guys, I never questioned. I think now it may have been a point of contention.

Hell's Angels and Flying Tigers were legendary, but just two of the rogue names fighting men gave their units during the world wars. After the wars some who missed the camaraderie of military brotherhood, and others who had yet to know it, formed their own rolling squadrons unbound by civilian moral laws, or anything but each other. That was a core value of the early bikers, and Charlie was a believer. He said, "War is not murder," and "What you do for a brother is not a sin or a crime."

Outlaw bikers demonstrated both traditional patriotism and insolent rebellion. Some members of the Oakland chapter of the Hell's Angels once barged into a crowd of anti-war marchers to stomp heads, their president, a military veteran, offering the U.S. president their service as guerrilla fighters in Vietnam. Some of the same guys wore German helmets, swastikas, Iron Crosses, and death's heads because they were imbued with a warrior spirit, because they looked "cool," and because they obviously made conventional U.S. citizens feel uncomfortable. Charlie was not the only one to think these rebels could be a force in protection of life. The Merry Pranksters, Grateful Dead, and Rolling Stones, among others, strategized them as allies; the U.S. government did not.

Charlie took bikers on some wild dune buggy rides. He composed a song with them in mind, and interacted as if he lived in them, but despite their outlaw leanings, many of them were traditional in their thinking.

Our ideas were new and strange to them, and if they saw a revolution coming, they didn't envision hiding in the desert. They seemed to be more about illicit ways to make money. "Cowboy Bill" was like that. He liked the rock 'n' roll of robbing with no pesky ideological attachments.

Sandy

Motorcycle parts, tools and greasy rags lay in unorganized disarray all over the Longhorn Saloon. In a corner sat witch Brenda sewing amongst her reams and scraps of velvet and satin. The rest of us sat in a circle near the long bar, passing around a joint. It was dark and quiet, except for the shuffling and snorting of horses in the barn. The heavy door of the saloon creaked open, and, quickly, three people slid in. Their eyes were large and the sweat on their bodies dampened their leather vests. One dug a hand into a Levi pocket and tossed some clinking clattering silver onto the dusty hardwood floor. From another pocket came a wad of bills.

"Wow! How much didja get?"

"Oh, just a couple hundred. We had some trouble and had to split."

Ella pulled a paper bag out of her purse, removed a Colt .45 from it, and began wiping it with one of the rags. "Whew," she said, "That was something else. Someone stash this for me." Sadie took the gun from Ella. It was the first time they had robbed. Ella said, "It was nothing. I was calm as a rock." She took off her cowboy boots and with a big sigh, lay back against the bar. Lulu, Katie, Mary, and Cap were making a list of the things we needed — like bolt cutters, entrenching tools, binoculars, knives, water bags, can-

vas, down sleeping bags and many hides of leather for
our last and only set of clothing.

Charlie

The drawback about the money game is fear and
violence. For love, for family or cause that's justified
in honest and right, yes, but to give a life for money
is total BS. I, myself, wouldn't sell one drop of blood,
but the people in the money would buy and sell the
lives of a whole people, a country, and a lot of people
would give their own daughters for a goat, two mules,
and a barrel of wheat.

I liked to think of Charlie as all good. He said,
"Come on real, I'm kind to kindness, I'm love to love,
and a fool to a fool. Like you and all humans I love my
own selfish self and now that's all of you." He said, "I
can reflect mean, bad, and death and fear as easy as
I can reflect gentleness, life, and love, for in truth I'm
one with both sides. That's where I find my own glory
in knowing I am just as good as bad, and I am free to
make up my own mind without worrying about the
opinions of the past. You can't do much if you need
everyone to think good of you. Most only think good of
you if you die. After you're dead everyone will cry and
say how good you were. Some people are raised to do
right and don't know right from wrong because it's
all just programming. Right and wrong for who and
what? On what level of honor, grace, or survival? Do
you think a momma lion evil when she downs a deer
to feed her baby? Good and evil is related to balance
for survival."

Frank Retz came one afternoon and took George
and Pearl to dinner. George looked pleased and very

important upon returning, and Pearl talked about the wonderful rich food. She was full of kind things to say to George too. The next day George was quiet, but he was so thrilled with Frank's proposal he couldn't be quiet about the doctors, lawyers, and other professionals who were invested in the club. They were of German stock like himself. Frank had told him if he sold the ranch, he would naturally be an honorary *member* of the club without paying dues, and could live on the property and be taken care of for the rest of his life.

I thought George was naive to think he was to benefit from the sale of the ranch in any but a minimal monetary way. He didn't see that Frank looked at him with contempt. Frank never came to visit socially. He behaved as though the property was already his, coming and going without even telling George he was there.

Just beyond the back ranch house, George's property adjoined land belonging to a woman named Mary who had for years allowed him use of it for horse trails. One day George told me that Mary had already sold her land to Frank Retz.

I said, "You wouldn't, would you? We love the ranch just the way it is."

He said, "I haven't yet."

One day Frank Retz went to the back farmhouse and said we were trespassing. But the back ranch house and the land under it belonged to George. We were in the right. Frank's contempt exploded: "People like you should hahve no rights." When he got to his car, he turned to look at Charlie and called, "I hahve more macheen guns dan you, Charlie. I vill raze dis place and all ov you vill be gone."

437

We called them "cops," "sheriffs," "The Man," and, Gypsy called them "Blue Meanies" referencing characters in a Beatles' movie, but I do not recall anyone on The Ranch calling the police "pigs" before Linda Kasabian came to stay. Gypsy, who liked to tell people she lived with kings, brought Linda and her toddler daughter after finding her unhappy with her hippie husband. She was short and sturdy, fundamentally pretty, with sandy blonde hair, a hard mouth, and a snarling vernacular. I didn't know if, like Susan, her aim was to shock, or if she had been roughened by a hard life. Charlie's prosecutor would tout Linda, to his advantage, as "a gentle little hippie girl," but he didn't know her when we did. She dished revolutionary rhetoric and personal vengeance toward "the pigs," and was as disgusted or dismissive of her husband. Apparently unsuspecting the depth of her disaffection, he kept a stash of five thousand dollars that he and a partner had saved for a trip to South America in a place where she could get it, and she did.

No one was more primed or persistent in the effort to get wheels and supplies for our last run than Tex. This is what TJ told me: He was driving to town when Tex jumped into the car, asking if he could ride along. En route, Tex asked to be dropped off in Hollywood, and to be picked up later, which TJ did. On their way back to The Ranch, Tex pulled nearly $3,000 from his pocket, saying that a guy had just given it to him. TJ was impressed. After they got home, Tex told other people about the money, as did TJ, and they went their separate ways. An hour or so later, the phone at the end of the boardwalk rang; whoever answered it said it was a guy wanting to talk to Charlie.

When Charlie got to the phone, the man on the other end was talking about killing a girl if Charlie didn't get back with money or "the dope." From the boardwalk, TJ heard Charlie asking questions. Charlie tipped the phone so they both could hear a woman in the background yelling, "Tex! — ask for Tex!" Charlie said Tex wasn't there, but the caller continued to threaten.

The man on the phone was Bernard Crowe and he had just given Tex money to buy twenty-five kilos of marijuana. The woman was Tex's Hollywood girlfriend who had vouched for him, but Crowe had decided to keep her as collateral until Tex returned with the kilos. TJ said that Charlie believed the woman was in trouble. He indicated to Charlie that he knew where Crowe lived, so Charlie told Crowe there was no need to get excited and that he'd be right over. Before leaving The Ranch, Charlie told TJ to grab a revolver from the Bunkhouse.

When they got to Crowe's place, Charlie asked TJ if he *would* use the gun if he *had* to. TJ hesitated. So Charlie took the gun from him, spun the cylinder, and slid the barrel in the back of his own waistband. TJ said that Charlie was trusting chance, since the gun was not fully loaded.

Inside the apartment were two or three men sitting on a couch, and a young woman tied up with cord or rope. Then Crowe came into view. He was a big black guy and he was mad. He told Charlie that Tex had burned him for nearly $3,000. Charlie told Crowe he had no dope and nothing approaching that much money, but he could pay him off a little at a time, but Crowe refused to settle. He had other people to answer to, he said, and then he began talking about killing everyone on The Ranch and burning it down.

Charlie asked, "Does it take a life?" and Crowe said yes, so Charlie took the gun from his waistband and offered it to Crowe, saying, "I stand in my brother's place. If it takes a life, take mine, and leave my people alone." Crowe looked at the gun, but refused to take it. So, according to TJ, Charlie pointed the gun at Crowe and pulled the trigger. It clicked but didn't fire. This happened three times, after which Crowe and his partners started to laugh, and then boom! — a bullet entered Crowe's body and he fell.

TJ ran for the door, but he said that when another man got up, his military training kicked in. He caught the man by the throat, threatening to crush his larynx if he moved. In the midst of this drama, he heard Charlie admiring someone's shirt.

Through astonishment and laughter, TJ said that a man wearing a leather shirt stripped it off and handed it to Charlie, and that Charlie had put the gun down to put on the shirt. While holding one man by the throat, keeping an eye on the others, *and on the gun,* TJ heard muffled laughter and a comical call for help. He could barely believe it; Charlie was *stuck inside the shirt,* his arms straight up in the air. Nobody moved. Finally, TJ gave up his guard, pulled the shirt down over Charlie's head, Charlie thanked the man, and they left without further incident.

The following day, a woman called The Ranch to say that Crowe's body had been "dumped in the park." That afternoon one of us heard on a car radio that "the Black Panthers' Minister of Defense" had been found dead on a lawn near UCLA. Word spread quickly around The Ranch. There were three witnesses to the killing. The police might arrive to arrest Charlie and TJ. But the police did not come, so we figured the witnesses to be outlaws who took care of their own business.

For a few days, maybe a week, we were hyper alert. And then something extraordinary happened.

440

The Ranch was visited by its first black customers since we began living there — not two, or four, or eight men and women but *forty* of them. The entire yard filled with cars. They asked to rent horses. Pearl almost didn't have enough horses to give them. Clem sprinted into the hills to watch them during their ride. At the end of the day, although he reported no unusual behavior, precautions were in order. For a week or two, the little sleeping we did at night was on the roof of the Rock City Cafe, covered by the big sign and an armed watchman. Charlie told me that if retaliation came while I was in George's house to disregard George and protect myself. "Don't think about being a hero," he told me.

I never learned more about the forty people who came to ride horses, and little about Bernard Crowe, except that his body was not dumped in a park. He had survived the bullet that went into his body, and kept it because a surgeon said it was too risky to remove it. The Ranch was quiet. We settled into a new norm.

Barbara was one of those girls who came to ride a horse and then, after meeting one of the guys by the stables, came back for the attention. As far as I could gather, nobody really knew Barbara, but on the night she called to beg protection from her father, one of the guys remembered a thick-set, albeit shapely, seventeen year old in coke bottle glasses. Since her character was unknown, it was suggested to Barbara that she call a friend or relative who might take her in, but she said that there was no one, she had no transportation, and nowhere to go.

"Please come and get me," she said, crying. "He's beating me up."

I met Barbara as Ruth was shepherding her around the ranch, instructing her to move fast and lie low at the first sign of police, to understand the risk to the rest of us, and to know she was responsible for herself. What Ruth knew then about Barbara would prove true, but at the time we tacitly agreed to give her the benefit of the clueless.

Barbara could not see to any degree of clarity without her glasses, and of course she broke them when she needed them most, so one of the girls had to look after her. We surely would have sent her home had she not hooked up with Karate Dave. Then we couldn't send her anywhere.

I didn't see much of Snake or Katie, Leslie, Mary, or Sadie. We were all doing different things. No one was more surprised than me when Snake remarked that she had been in Randy Starr's trailer (and he had been in hers.) In that faraway voice with the slightest irony, she said, "He didn't even take down his pants."

Everyone who lived on The Ranch owns a piece of this story, and each has different recollections about any event, but I think all would agree that we were living not only on the edge of society, but of something that was about to jump off. While maintaining a façade of normalcy, some of the girls became bulimic and anorexic, some people took drugs not normally used by any of us, and a lot of people were over-eating *donuts*.

Mary, Ella, and Tex took acid before a trip to the city for supplies. At evening when they returned, the girls looked haggard. Everything was fine, they

1969

said, until they were about to come home, and Tex began literally picking up children, saying he had to get them to the desert before sundown. The girls had to disengage him from a child and get him into the car. They were exhausted. A few months earlier Tex had gone out after drinking a tea brewed from the roots of belladonna or jimson weed. The medicinal plant was suggested to one of us as a route to psychedelic effects, but, unlike LSD, it produced no clarity. I don't know how far Tex drove before he had to pull over. How could he drive? He said, "Little green men were all over the dashboard." A bright, handsome former athlete, Tex didn't have a police record, but the goofy booking photo from that arrest would later be the most widely disseminated public image of him.

It was late at The Ranch when four Sheriff's cars jammed into the yard, flashing. Most of the girls and kids were at the back farmhouse. Somebody stepped in the cafe and called them on the field phone. I was asleep in the stuffed chair in George's house. When I sensed the light and commotion, I leapt up to warn Sherri. Danny could've been jailed if caught sleeping with her. Sherri had already gone for the woods. Ruth and I sat on the porch and shivered, watching the sheriffs roust out all the men at gunpoint. Tension was high. Every ranch vehicle was being sequentially lit up and examined. A flashing squad car came bumping up Lovers Lane from the farmhouse to rejoin others in the yard. "We found the field phone," a hefty deputy growled. "No," he continued, "Nobody there."

The cops in the yard were questioning Bruce, Danny, Tex, Charlie, and Bobby. They were looking for stolen cars. Danny looked groggy-eyed but smirking as the conversation turned funny. Finally everything checked out to their satisfaction. They had no intention of pursuing the rest of us in the hills, but they did flood the woods with lights, providing a hair-raising, perfectly frozen moment for half a dozen teenagers. They left and we all went back to sleep.

Next morning in George's kitchen, before going out the door with a pan of hot cinnamon rolls, one of the girls told me that Gary Hinman was "floatin' in the cosmos."

The news about Gary shot through my brain both quickly and slowly, lodging on the edge of my spine. I chose not to ask questions. People said later that Gary had sold some bad psychedelics, and then failed to reimburse the buyers. Bobby Beausoleil, on the road to see one of his girlfriends, was arrested for Gary's murder. He wrote to us from the county jail. I don't recall what the letter said, but he wasn't whining, or crying for help. For the first time in months I thought about Bobby. He had good will. He was honest, and generous. I never knew him to lie, bogart, hide, or hoard anything for himself. But no matter what was happening to him or anywhere in the world, The Ranch needed routine and order. It's what I needed. It would be years before I heard Bobby explain that he had bought the drugs from Gary for some bikers, and they wanted their money back. Bobby was just the middle man, but the bikers had a reputation for retaliation, creating the potential for war. Gary either didn't have the money or wouldn't give it.

Curly Bailey*, all elbows and knees, got out of a car on the Pass Road, showing more teeth than the law allowed, kind of be-bopped down the hill straight into the saloon, put down his suitcase, and started to dance. I thought he must be a police plant, but Charlie and Clem connected with him right away.

People came and went all the time. Ella left, and a Valley girl named Sue started coming. She was a horseback riding customer who stayed to hang out, and then wanted to live with us. But first, she told Charlie, she wanted to get her high school diploma. He told her to go for it. After she graduated she was back to stay. At The Ranch she was "Country Sue." She said she was drawn to our music and loved to sing with Brenda and harmonize with Gypsy. She and Cappy got close, but the person Sue said she connected with right away, and who became her "friend and best buddy for adventures" was Sadie.

Sandy

Sadie was the only person I didn't like. She was arrogant, bossy, and condescending towards many of us. And she was man-hungry and didn't seem clean.

Susan "Sadie" Atkins you see, was quirky, eliciting mixed feelings. Brassy. Provocative. Competitive. One guy noted that Sadie and Gypsy competed over who was most feared and who had the biggest breasts. On introduction, Sadie could be seductive, only to challenge and blast her captive audience with proclamations. To me she seemed caught in a sad circle, so hungry for attention she drove it away.

Charlie

True, I let Susan do anything she wanted to do so she could find herself as each and all were free to do. How about the time she stole three or four hundred dollars worth of hashish, gave me a hundred dollars worth, and left right before a bunch of tough guys came in and asked me if I knew Susan and told me she ripped them off. Did she want to see if I would lie to save myself, or snitch and tell where she was? They said, "You know her," and I lit the hash pipe and said, "Name sounds familiar, but there are a lot of women around this ranch."

One guy said, "That looks like our hash." He looked me in the eye and said, "Is this our hash?"

I said, "It is if you want to sit down and smoke some. And you can tell me more about who it was that tricked you out of your stash." We smoked and had a three hundred dollar laugh.

— Charles Manson, c. 1981, Ca State Prison

George didn't go to church but he generally respected the clergy. A big preacher in a black Cadillac kept coming around to see old-buddy-buddy George as an excuse to eyeball "all these little round rumps," muttering asides as if George were as deaf as he was blind. The man weighed over three hundred pounds and was an eligible bachelor, he made sure to tell, a strutting cock and cornball to boot, sticking sex jokes meant for us into conversations about horses.

"Well, I can take the hint," he finally said after the girls fixing food in the kitchen started doing knife tricks. "These girls just don't like me." George would've said he didn't either, but he kept his mouth shut.

A retired police officer came often just to sit in a chair on the boardwalk. He was an alcoholic, his body wracked and hacking like a crow. He seemed to be looking for a place to rest, and The Ranch was some comfort to him. Pearl said he was dying of cancer.

One day Pearl asked me to go with her on an errand. On our way through The Valley she said she had to make a quick stop at her house, and, after hastily pouring each of us a glass of lemonade in her kitchen, she grabbed bowls, saying she had to feed some of her animals. I looked out the kitchen window into a big back yard crowded with rows and rows of slapdash wood and wire cages, thirty or more of them of different sizes, many on stilts. When Pearl returned, I asked about the animals. She said they were not only cats and dogs but birds and other wildlife. I asked to see them, but she said we were in a hurry. As we drove away, it got through my head that the animals Pearl acquired for her collection *never* got out of those cages.

The next time Pearl's friend, Shorty, showed up he was alone and living out of his car between bent cardboard grocery boxes of plastic-ware he had bought to sell for a profit. He opened the trunk to show Pearl a heavy load of chalk-white plaster lawn statues he'd bought for the same purpose. In the house, Pearl told George that Shorty was waiting for an insurance settlement for a back injury, but the money hadn't come in yet. She didn't say what had happened to Shorty's marriage, at least not in front of me. She said he needed a job, and she could find plenty for him to do. George didn't say anything.

I don't think Shorty slept at The Ranch, but during the days he was handy for Pearl. Whenever not doing something she asked him to do, he hung around the office or sat in one of the chairs on the boardwalk. He was talkative and seemed friendly, but I didn't trust him, largely because I didn't trust Pearl.

The timid, tabby-colored girl on the board-walk was Kitty, one of Bobby's girlfriends. At least four women were then pregnant with Bobby's children — Kitty, Gayle, Sandy, and Linda Kasabian — and he was in jail for murder.

At the back ranch house people were taking a lot of acid. Tex said later that he, Susan, and maybe a few others were "secretly taking speed." While walking down the boardwalk, I saw Katie and some of the other girls near the Rock City Cafe. They seemed to be deep in conversation. Maybe that's where they discussed ideas for getting Bobby out or maybe not. They didn't acknowledge me and I was not moved to question or include myself in their discussions.

From Transcripts: Katie/Fitzgerald Vol. 78:

Katie: That was completely my brother... we wanted to get him back... the system arrested him, a system that we were trying to get away from... it was like the system was eating him up, and the only thing we could think of was to in some way affect the system, to get back at the system. We put a lot of thoughts around.

Leslie/Keith Vol. 81:

Leslie: We took an acid trip... and we discussed it in many different ways.
Q: Did you ever reach any conclusion as to what you could do to best serve Bobby Beausoleil's interests?
A: No, not a conclusion. We just kept all the thoughts in our minds.
Q: And one of the thoughts was, as you put it, a copy-cat killing?

A: Yeah, they do that on TV and stuff.
Q: But nothing ever jelled in any of your minds about that kind of operation I take it?
A: Well, just say it this way: the thought was in our mind... but we did not ponder upon it or plan anything.

Charlie seemed frustrated or depressed. Walking down the farmhouse road, he said to me, "It seems I have to hide from people to keep from breaking their law. I keep thinking I want to stay out of prison. I didn't want responsibility. That's why I've always told you: You do for yourself. It's your world. The only thing I want, if I can have a want, is to be left alone to walk on it." I thought he was planning to leave us. He said, "You have to be with yourselves. I'm just an animal raised up in a cage. I'm mean, and I'm a killer when the need comes up. That's not what I want. I see God in a drop of water, but others want him to come out of the sky with lightening bolts in both hands. They want fear. Fear locks the mind. To unlock it, you need a bigger fear, but without love, you got dogs eating dogs." There were pauses and I didn't know what to say.

He said, "If a guy feels guilty and sees that I know the truth about him, and tries to get me to kill him, what do I do? If I don't want to go back to prison, I hide. Why doesn't he kill himself? He can't bring himself to do that, so he tries to get some fool to do it for him. I could straighten all that out quick if I had the control but I don't want the control. Yet I got to live under anyone who has it." "I'm nothing," he said angrily. "And I like being nothing — but that can't be explained in a mad world of people trying to be something." When we got back to the farmhouse he went inside to sleep.

Charlie left alone in the bread truck and traveled a few hundred miles north along the Coast Highway, then back, making a pit stop at The Ranch before heading south with his passenger, another pregnant seventeen-year-old. Right away I saw the change in him. He was weightless. I hadn't seen him that light since our old traveling days. He was taking the girl to her parents' home near San Diego. I don't know how long he was gone, but when he came back, she was still with him.

Stephanie was a good girl who walked into a mad dash. Her boyfriend had abandoned her pregnant in Big Sur when Charlie was out on his own. He told me he'd considered leaving with her and not looking back. He couldn't do it, but still, he said, everybody needed to fend for themselves.

Sandy

It was muggy hot to where I didn't feel like doing much more than lying on my back with my eight month pregnant belly to the sun. All the activity had moved from the back ranch house up front, but I stayed in back where there weren't so many pesky flies. August 8th it was just too hot to even lie down and I was restless, so I found a fresh dress and walked up Lovers Lane with nothing much in mind except taking a cold shower. When I came out of the shower shack, the milk truck was in the yard, and so was Mary. As I was just wandering around looking very pregnant, she asked if I'd like to go with her to the city to get some tools. It had been months since I'd been to a city, let alone in a store, so I was game.

While I meandered around Sears looking at nuts and bolts, Mary was lifting a few small items and

---

collecting others which she presented to the cashier along with a credit card. Then we headed home in the milk truck. While breezing through San Fernando, the police pulled us over. Mary quickly ditched the credit card. "It's stolen," she whispered. They jacked us up along the side of the road, rummaged through the truck, and took us off to the police station. I was charged with burglary and forgery — forgery because there was a letter in the truck that their experts swore was incriminating and in my handwriting. To this day, I don't know what the letter pertained to, who wrote it, or its significance, but I learned right then that those experts don't know what they are talking about (or do, and it's all in how they want to look at it). That night, Mary and I were transported from the valley substation to Sybil Brand Institute, the main Los Angeles county jail for women, and put into different cellblocks.

The next day was uneventful, but that evening when the inmates went to the front of the cell block to see if they had mail, I heard a minor commotion and saw a woman holding her newspaper while others leaned over her shoulder exclaiming words like "how horrible," and "I can't believe it." Curious, I walked over and saw bold headlines announcing that a movie actress "and four others" had been killed. I asked someone who, and although they said her name I had never heard it before. It bothered me that the death of people connected with movies could command so much emotion. I stepped back, looking at the gaggle of emoting women, and said, "Every day the news reports deaths of troops killed in Vietnam and their grieving families, and you're practically hysterical over the death of an actress you don't even know?" I doubt any of them heard me. As I returned to my cell, they were turning pages, seeking the gory details.

The next day Mary and I were brought out of our cellblocks and put in a holding tank to await transportation to the San Fernando courthouse. I told her about the newspaper story. I had a strange feeling, and then out of my mouth came the words, "Do you think we did it?" Matrons called us to board the transport bus, and she didn't say anything.

After a long wait at the courthouse and a short hearing, Mary was kept in custody, but charges against me were dropped due to "insufficient evidence," and I was released. I hitchhiked partway, got an ice cream cone, and then a good ride all the way to the ranch. Several visitors were out in the yard talking to Charlie, and Leslie was polishing a motorcycle. I walked over to her real quick and asked if anything unusual had gone on in the past few nights.

"Nope," she replied. "Everything's been purt near regular."

There was some ongoing problem with members of Danny's bike club. At the time, I didn't know about the drug deal. The thought I caught was that Danny appeared to have joined Charlie rather than Charlie seeking to join them. When Danny was late or absent from his club meetings, it threatened their order. If Danny could disregard club rules, everyone could, and they reacted by threatening him with sanctions, and eventually threatening us.

Gypsy

Danny's brothers were talking rape, kill, and burn if he wasn't with them in the city "by sundown." The bikers left, but one came back sober and apologized. He said they were just trying to keep their club together.

In the saloon I lay melting into the arms and one-ness of myself. Charlie stirred and tucked me to him, saying, half consciously, "We're being raided in the morning," and he instantly fell asleep.

I woke to the voice of Ouish at the foot of the bed. "Someone needs a bed," she told me. "You know — the biker who came to visit — he's been up all night." Charlie was up and sitting at the edge of the bed as I sleepily reached for his shirt. He grinned and asked how long the sun had been up.

Sherri appeared. "Just peeked over the mountain," she said.

We got our clothes on, Sherri opened the door, and she ran back whispering loudly, "POLICE! ALL OVER THE PLACE!" With that, she and Ouish ran out the back door, leapt off the porch, and disappeared into the woods. Harsh sounds crashed through the silence, out of place and time. Within seconds, Charlie was gone. I slipped out the back, walking toward George's house, a shiver running through me. The air was muggy and permeated with a nauseous smell. Paranoia. It brought me to a tiny peasant town in wartime. I heard breaking glass and then I saw helmets and men with weapons — HUNDREDS of them swarming — shoving boots into doors, smashing guitars and our record player, dragging sleepy-eyed bodies out of beds. I was spotted by a young cop who ran at me with an M-16 and in a shaking voice told me to put my hands behind my head and not to move because he'd have to shoot me if I did. We stood eye to eye, both shaking. He motioned me with his gun to the front of the ranch. A helicopter chopped the air above us, passing so low that I could see the pilot clearly, then another helicopter, both sweeping the early dawn woods with beams of light.

At the front of the ranch my eyes widened to the sight of about a hundred radio vehicles. There were enough paddy wagons to hold ten times our number. The TV people were there, a Red Cross truck, even a catering truck. They were ready to see blood, drink coffee, and make a TV spectacular. It was the Special Enforcement Bureau and the Riot squad with knee boots, snake bite kits, and other equipment hanging from their belts. Squeaky was pulled from the house hollering, "What about George? Who's gonna give him his breakfast?" And from the hills came Ruth and Sherri, rudely shoved by four armed men who huffed and puffed in their heavy hip boots. Those girls must've given them quite a chase.

I joined the others in the dragnet, a cluster almost entirely of girls seated on the ground in front of the saloon, some holding babies, shivering in the morning chill. Armed men in green uniforms stood around us. Then word rippled through the troops, one to another: "Manson... we got Manson. We got Charlie..."

"What is all this for?!" I demanded.

"G.T.A." said the gunman over me.

"So what did we steal?"

"You know damn well," he said, glancing across the yard. There were our super custom dune buggies rolling out behind tow trucks.

I said, "Those buggies aren't stolen! We *bought* those!" I was explaining all the stocks and bonds, savings accounts and inheritances, not to mention all the work that went into those buggies when he gave me a jab with his rifle saying, "Keep your mouth shut."

By this time, four of the men were forcing Charlie to walk with his hands cuffed behind his back and held high so that he had to bend over. Instead of bringing him to the front, they took him around back of the saloon, where they kicked and kneed him, breaking three of his ribs. When they returned his bent body, they pushed him face down on the ground before us girls, putting a foot on his back. The gesture was not lost on us. Danny, too, was brought to the front with one purple eye swelling shut.

Only George, Pearl and Randy were not present in the yard. The rest of the cowboys and any hapless visitors stood handcuffed with us, as the violent screeching, cracking, and smashing continued. Rooms were torn apart and searched over and over by different crews. Open doors were kicked in, and boards ripped from walls. George's old Wurlizer jukebox in the saloon was bludgeoned and shattered along with sections of the antique mirrors behind the bar. It was apparent that these men had been given permission not only to search but destroy. Sacks of flour and corn meal were slashed, their contents spread from one end of the kitchen to the other. In the shack, baby oil was squirted all over the walls and on the baby clothes. It was a free for all. Larry couldn't understand why they stomped in his hamster cage *with the hamsters in it.*

As we were loaded into paddy wagons, Tommy and Wolf tried to get in with us. Squeaky complained that George needed his breakfast, and Sherri asked, "What about the horses? Who's gonna feed the horses?" One of the superiors told us that all would be taken care of.

As it turned out, George was kept hungry for hours while the men checked out all his medicines, and confiscated a giant hypodermic needle and serum used for horses. The horses themselves were entirely neglected. A welding machine was taken, some of Danny's guns, and two dune buggies that we bought from a retired police officer who lived and worked out of an auto shop in the valley. It was for those we were all charged with Grand Theft Auto.

"How're you gonna explain this machine gun?" a sergeant asked.

"Well, I was in the woods one day," Brenda said reasonably, "and I came across this violin case and I thought it was Gypsy's. So I opened it up, and there it was — right out of the '20s. I brought it home, and we put it in George's house in the prop room. He could use it in the movies. What's against the law about that?"

After hours of waiting in the Malibu Sheriff's station, we were transported in buses to the jail downtown. A sense of calm and well-being washed over me in the bus because we were all together. I gazed out the window, took a swim in the ocean and a run through the trees, and Leslie took my hand.

Inside the big women's jail, after being searched, fingerprinted, stripped, showered, and sprayed with insecticide, it was evening. We were escorted in a double line to a large "Day Room," and given mattresses and blankets. We stretched out our bedding around an imaginary fire, made ourselves comfortable, and sang. The night nurse with a cart of pills stopped by to sarcastically ask if we'd all had our milk, and later our response to the piped radio music brought a matron to tell us, "THERE WILL BE NO DANCING. DANCING IS NOT ALLOWED."

The Los Angeles newspapers reported that a VW theft ring and chop shop operated by a motorcycle gang had been busted up at Spahn's Ranch. They said drugs and drug paraphernalia were confiscated. But four days later, aside from a biker or two kept for outstanding warrants, the "detainees" were released. When queried about the expensive and time-consuming raid, the seizure of people and property, officials stated that charges had to be tossed out because one of their own had typed an incorrect date on the search warrant. We believed it had more to do with the ex-cop who sold us a dune buggy he had never legally owned. It was not returned. Worse, the kids were now in state custody. Most would be sent to live with relatives, but Zeezo was placed in a foster home. At the time, even that seemed like a minor glitch.

George welcomed us back, we assessed the demolition, cleaned up, and ranch life resumed. The raid had exhausted the unspoken apprehension in us. I didn't ask how Charlie knew it was coming, but a couple of years later he said something to the effect that he had orchestrated it.

Preparations for the desert were in overdrive. I don't know where we got the next three VWs, but they were being transformed into better dune buggies than two we'd lost. We bought whole elk and deer hides downtown. Some of the women soaked them in pans of water and olive oil, stretched and tacked them on boards to dry in the sun. They bore holes in their fingers in days and nights sewing leather pants and shirts with sinew-like thread. The same tough, painful work went into making the canvas coverings for the dune buggies, and an unwitting mother or two contributed a fox stole, an ocelot coat, and a mink to the covering detail.

Brenda

I took the furs apart and nailed them all over the dune buggies for camouflage, and rubbed some dust in them so they wouldn't shine. I spray-painted all the metal that showed on the buggies with greens, browns and golds. Months of work went into those dune buggies, nights and days of sanding, painting, welding, and fitting. Bruce took care of the engines and new frames. Bruce is a welder and spent night upon night welding custom designs, all perfect.

We stretched hides from one end of the frames to the other. The seats and floors were covered with canvas, furs, and soft cushions. We made cases for machetes on one side, and hung saddle bags on both sides to hold tools, flashlights, food, and rope. We built cushioned platforms that unfolded into beds. One gear shift on Charlie's buggy was a skull's head. Fully equipped, the buggies carried an extra tank of gas, full or partial skid plates, a front wench, a set of VW tools, a heavy duty rope, two water bags or canteens, binoculars, maps, gun and/or sword sheaths, and anything else anyone wanted to carry with them.

Essential for the trip we were taking were good knives. Each of us got a new Buck knife of our choosing. I had a nice folding Buck. The knives assisted us in work with rope, leather, wires, wood, food, and for sport. Some of the guys got good at hitting targets on the haystack.

Sandy

Ruth was proud of how proficient she was at sharpening her knife. She had gotten the knack before any of us, and loved to teach it. I can see her in her jeans and skimpy top, squatting on the ground over a line of variously sized knives, whetstones, honing oil, and a tin of soft yellowish cloths. She'd oil a whetstone and, dexterously angling the blade, pull each side across the stone. She'd wipe the blade clean with a cloth, and then, with a big smile, demonstrate its sharpness by removing tiny down-like hairs from her forearm.

Sandy

Lyn could absorb and respond to expressions of complex emotions, lending a sympathetic ear if and when she had time, but she didn't have or didn't make much time. She had a big pile of sewing in George's house, projects that I don't recall her ever completing. Mostly she worked on Charlie's vest.

Brenda's movements in whatever she did were quick and sure. If she decided to make a shirt for one of the guys, she'd find fabric, cut it, and sometimes within a few hours she'd have a whole new shirt, and later embroider it. She looked out for all the guys and was sensitive to their feelings for wanting a little of the attention that Charlie was getting, and she treated them all with equal care and consideration. She was also aware of and giving to the girls. We all admired Brenda, and without jealousy as far as I knew. She was blunt in her speech, simple and straightforward, which could be off-putting. Complicated thoughts and feelings fraught with doubt and confusion might be met with a clear-eyed look, a shrug, and a word like "So?" Or she might just say, "It's all perfect." Brenda was quite simply a magic witch too busy doing to take time for introspection. She loved taking care of babies and wanted to have children herself.

One time I was on acid in the hills. As I looked down in the fading light I saw the entire ranch enveloped in what I can only call love. It was an exquisitely fine and soft, nearly translucent blanket COVERED WITH TINY ROSES. There was a wholeness and security there, like what a mother would use to cover a new baby. I had a small backpack with clothes in it. I pulled out a pair of blue jeans and could tell by the almost baby softness of them that Brenda had worn them. I could feel Brenda's love in those jeans even before I saw them, and I could see Lyn's love blanketing the whole ranch.

Brenda

I had some bolt cutters I used to cut locks off gates. I really got a big charge out of it too cause I used to get locked in rooms when I was little. It took me a few times to get the hang of this bolt cutting. You have to put all your weight on the cutters at once and the lock breaks in half. At night we'd go out, four and five dune buggies at a time. The guys drove, five or six girls in, on, and hanging off of each buggy. One at a time, the buggies would creep out of the ranch with no lights... and then tear up Santa Susana Pass, up under the freeway and onto the dirt roads above Devil's Canyon. When all were there, we'd take off down curving roads in a line by the light of the stars... or the moon might be out, casting our shadows over the hills... another world. Going downhill, we'd turn the engines off, drifting silently to the night symphony of crickets by the creeks and coyotes singing on the mountains. When we came to the locked gates, I'd hop out and cut the locks.

Brenda also cut most of our locks, originating a style by leaving one long braid wherever on our heads we chose. She laid out the rest to sew with leather into a mantle Charlie could wear around his shoulders, or fly from the back of his dune buggy.

George had a new "idear." He was gonna pump out and fence off about two thousand acres of Ocean — a chain-link fence, he said, to keep the rest of the Ocean out — and there we'd have our new

460

ranch complete with seaweed for the horses and sunken ships for houses and barns. He said other people were so dumb "they never thought of that afore." I asked how a chain link fence was supposed to hold back the whole Ocean, and he snapped, "Oh, don't be so technical."

Late that summer someone gave Randy Starr something to smoke besides Camels. It blew his cap. Randy always wore his hat around his eyebrows. He strolled into George's house laughing, his hat tipped way back, sat down, shook his head, and laughed again. I said, "Randy, you loaded?"

He said, "That goddamned Charlie blew my whole image."

Tex was a live wire, munching mushrooms, acid, and things I didn't know about. Some of the girls referred to him as The Mad Hatter. They were crazy about him. One night I listened as he tuned into a truck driver sitting high on the spring seat of a heavy hauler on the new freeway that we could see from the farmhouse. Brandishing an imaginary CB radio and a smooth, fast drawl, he said something like: "Breaker One this is Ringtail on the forty-four — is anyone looping the ribbon?" "This is Okefenokee Bob, smokin' and locamotin'. Can I get an echo?" And he went on like that in a string of lingo that left me laughing and amazed. I never before knew that Tex was that crazy or that smart or so clear a channel, but for just a moment, I thought he was talking on a real CB instead of merely responding to the sounds of a semi passing in the small dark distance.

Sandy

So much energy there was around the ranch in those days! Everywhere clothes and vehicles being camouflaged, dusty brown bodies zinging with energy. Leslie danced almost in a frenzy one night, all night long until she collapsed, sweating, upon the floor. Katie was radiant; I'd never seen her so bright.

One golden dusk several of us sat on the steps of the veranda having coffee. The horses in the corral lazily munched their hay, and the ducks pecked bread we had scattered round the house. Katie was laughing, her eyes shining. She was talking about how to scare the life out of people who have enough guilt that they could have the life scared out of them. It was some of the people at The Fountain Of The World she had in mind. They spoke of peace and brotherhood but, as she had lived with them, she saw the backbiting, jealousies and money grubbing.

She acted out her fantasies. "How about a long flowing white robe with sleeves like wings, a robe to be worn atop the biggest rock behind the buildings — a figure at dusk, arms outstretched, wailing unearthly sounds." Katie laughed, pulling her long hair down over her shoulders on each side.

"Or how 'bout John and the trap door in his bedroom. That door leads down to a tunnel running under the buildings — down under the dining hall, the kitchen, the dormitories, the gardens, and finally to a secret cave in back. No one knows where that trap door is. I do. This apparition in white could make its appearance at any time during the night. And after the guilty, frightened people are gone, the children could come. That's what the place is for — hills and caves and animals and beautiful kids. And directly over those hills is the desert."

"Where the eagle flies we will lie under the sun
Where the eagle flies, we will die, die to be one"

— C. Manson, song, 1969

Two weeks after the ranch raid, Frank Retz called
police to arrest Charlie for trespassing. They found
him asleep in the farmhouse, a marijuana roach and
one of the girls nearby. I think it was Gypsy because
she went to the station and claimed the roach. She
was not charged, and Charlie was released.

Frank said he thought the police raid had taken
care of the job he wanted done, but now he would
have to do it himself. He openly announced that he
would hire and arm a man to watch over the property.
Pearl suggested Shorty Shea, and he made no secret
of his intention to take the job.

Sandy

Almost a month after the police raid, all the underage girls had left the ranch and gone to the Mojave
Desert. Brenda was driving the big flatbed truck back
and forth with people and supplies. Lulu, Katie, Little
Patti, Gypsy and some of the guys were driving dune
buggies to and from Death Valley. Sadie was tripping
between the ranch and Hollywood, Lyn was caring for
George, and Mary and Bobby were still in jail.

All I knew was that I was going to have a baby. I had
chosen the little red shack, cleaned and re-cleaned it,
and had all supplies for delivery in place. The day I
felt the baby moving down, I filled all the ranch pots
and pans with hot water. One by one I carried them
to the shower room and took a long, thorough bath,
pouring cups of water over my body. One last sweep

of the shack, and then I made the rounds of the ranch to let everyone know I was ready.

By evening I was in fairly hard labor and had thrown up all the peach and licorice ice cream the girls had gotten at my request. By nightfall, it was Brenda, Katie, Leslie, and Sadie who surrounded me on the mattress, waiting for the baby to show. I moaned and yelled in increasingly hard labor while the girls in their all-night vigil massaged my neck and shoulders while others wiped my face with cool, damp cloths. It was hot in there, and it seemed all the chickens and cats were on the roof trying to get in. Wolf and Muttsy, and, especially, Tommy had to be blocked at the door.

Charlie was in desert and must have sensed that I was in labor. He called the ranch and Lyn told him that I was. The next evening, semi-delirious and in the middle of a yell, I felt his firm, cool hands on my face, and heard his rich voice telling me to relax. He took one of my fingers, bent it back slightly, and said, "Look at all the faces around you and turn up all the love you have for these girls." I looked at Katie — face soft in the candlelight, eyes huge with love and expectation as if the baby were coming from her own body. Sadie had gone, and it was Cappy's face I saw next. She had been massaging my legs and feet for hours. Charlie bent my finger back more and said, "Now turn on all your love and there will be no pain." I looked at Brenda, serene and watching. Ever patient love, it was Brenda I counted on to do the actual delivery, tying the cord, cutting it, cleaning the baby's nose, eyes, and mouth with her delicate, sensitive hands. She hadn't slept for several nights and was visibly tired, but she wouldn't let me down. The bending finger didn't hurt, and the contractions not as much. Charlie then left, taking Cappy with him.

I felt confident. I didn't want to go to a hospital or take pharmaceuticals, but the next evening I accepted the pill a biker had dropped off a for me, and it did nothing to ease the pain. Charlie called from Ballarat to ask if the baby had come. Lyn told him no and he said, "That's what I thought. I think you need to get her to a hospital." This time I was ready to go.

The ambulance arrived with the fire department and the police. Someone was using an ax to get a stretcher through the doorway, and I was carried away, sirens blaring. The fire and police crews departed and the ambulance crew took me to a small quiet hospital. It was so small it didn't have a baby ward or an obstetrician on call. The front rooms had been completely torn apart in the process of a major remodeling. Ambulance attendants left me lying literally on a wooden plank stretched between two sawhorses. When I finally saw a person walking by, I managed to speak and said I needed to be on a bed, but she said she couldn't help me and left.

I heard Lyn in another room emphasizing that I'd already been in labor for two days. A woman was on the phone with police who said there was some kind of red tape they had to go through before they'd be allowed to transfer me to a hospital with an obstetrics ward. I was out of it.

It was early the next morning before I was finally taken to the right hospital, hollering like a banshee. The nurses told me to *be quiet* — and to *quit pushing*. The doctor came in, asking who was going to pay for his services, and he left. After one big contraction, a form was put in front of me, a pen placed in my hand, and I signed. Then to the delivery room I went, a cut was made, the doctor put a hand inside me and turned the baby around. I pushed like I'd been pushing for the last two days and this time a baby popped

465

out and was dangled upside down in front of me. Happily I acknowledged, "A boy!" and fell asleep.

When I awoke the nurses wanted a name for him. The name I chose was the very one George Spahn was suggesting to Lyn at about the same time, and we had never discussed it. Sadie arrived to take me home, dressed all in black. She warned that the police had been nosing about the ranch. She had been trying, without success, to find me a house, so the girls had converted Randy Starr's abandoned trailer into a nursery. The fridge and heater worked, so the Health Department wouldn't object, but everyone felt that Cho and I should stay indoors, away from the eyes of snoopy cops.

Cappy

Headed for refreshment from a hot desert day — a day spent close to the ground motionless as lizards, motionless as the air that let the Sun's heat turn the earth's crumbled rock to blazing dust, the same dust we had all become — two dune buggies of nude night bodies flew over the hills along the ridges and down the banks into the beds of forgotten rivers. This night had no moon but freedom was a-rise. The dune buggy engines hummed into the vast darkness. We neared the opening to a canyon that gave birth to a hot spring. Our heavenly hot springs popped into view — but SOMETHING of huge and grotesque proportions loomed out of the darkness beside it. A ruthless monster had invaded our unblemished desert home, a thing that had leveled a nearby hill and had stopped just short of shoving it into the pool of steaming water. A U.S. Government monster. Ouish's loud exclamations rebounded off the mountain walls. Then sparks lit within our eyes. We all laughed and charged to the dune buggies, lugging out gasoline and all the matches we had stashed. What a beautiful picture it would make exploding in huge tongues of flame to return to the earth it was trying to destroy! We doused the tires and the seat with gasoline. Lit matches found their places. POOF! POOF! POOF! THE FLAMES WERE TITANIC. THE WHOLE MACHINE WAS ON FIRE... until the gas evaporated. Just how much of a Michigan loader burns? More gasoline — everything saturated once more — more matches — ah! And finally the seat caught a-blaze.

We slid into our pool beside the fire. And after a long bath, dawn came creeping. Goosepimply and wet we stood in the chill air, viewing the remains of the monster. There it stood unscathed — only a few patches of blistered paint and a gorged seat on melted rubber feet. We left our mark and sped off laughing into the morning.

Sandy

I think I was the last to know about the murders. It was mid-September. Candles were lit in the trailer where I stayed with my newborn son. Katie and Sadie slipped through the door, talking quietly so as not to disturb the nursing infant. The police had taken Bear when he was just five days old so the girls were on constant lookout so they could alert me to head down to the creek. Sadie's attention wandered from the baby, and in a low voice she remarked to Katie, "Every time I go down to Hollywood, someone always mentions the name Tate."

I flashed: that sounds like a rich boy's name. Who does Sadie know named Tate? Then I caught Katie giving Sadie a knitted brow shut-up look and I said, "All right you guys, what is it?" Both were quiet, adding fuel to my curiosity. I said, "I have a feeling about something and I want to know right now." The baby nursed contentedly. I gave my word not to say anything and Sadie couldn't wait to spill her story.

Between shock and curiosity, I was eager for details. She told me how much adrenalin shoots through your body when you are fighting for your life. A big man had her by the hair and was pulling with all his might as she stabbed at him with her knife. She called for Katie to help her but Katie was trying to subdue someone else. Linda was becoming frantic as death became a reality to her, a reality she had thought she could face. Her panic generated more energy and haste to get out and leave no one alive to call police. I asked what it was like to be killing people. Katie said that each stab was herself coming closer to death till she felt nothing but total peace when it was done. She said she could not have taken lives unless she was totally willing to face her own death. I asked "What about the baby?" Without a thought Katie said, "You have him in your arms." I understood and I asked them if others knew about this. They told me they didn't know. Their move was for Bobby and there was really no need to say anything to anyone. After the girls left the trailer, I thought about what they told me. I could not judge them.

A week later, when I wasn't so sore from the stitches, I packed bags for the desert. The VW, with Tex driving, was filled to the top with baby things. On our way to Death Valley, we made a brief stop at the house where Zeezo was kept. Sadie looked in windows until she saw him asleep in a crib. A few nights later, she went to the window, cut the screen to get in, and took him away to the desert.

The Desert

We traveled from Spahn Ranch in different vehicles. Some were purchased and customized, and others procured at the last minute. Memorable is the clean-cut visiting college boy who, in wanting to help, went to a car dealership to price VWs. He returned to The Ranch only briefly to tell us that the dealer, eager to make a sale, had hastily offered him a test drive and tossed him the keys, saying, "It's all yours!" So he took it.

Sandy

When we arrived at the mouth of Goler Wash, I was proud to present my two-week- old son to Charlie. Still very sore, I rode with him in the Jeep, the baby tucked under my breast. A week later I would walk miles with the rest of the girls, sometimes carrying him on my lower back in a hunting sack designed to carry ducks. It was just the right size.

Lying by the fire nursing my son, I imagined seeing the world through his new eyes and I felt gratitude that these were among his first impressions. He was being washed in the light of millions of stars, clean air, soft breezes, deep quietude, and the love and care of my friends.

Barker's Ranch was now occupied by more permanent squatters. A gray-haired erstwhile prospector named Paul, tall, swarthy, and weathered, blocked the doorframe. Behind him, around the kitchen table, the Paul we knew, Juan, and Brooks sat in self conscious postures. After the elder Paul stepped aside and we entered the house, the young Paul sat upright and forced his over-proud smile, but Juan and Brooks leaned back in their chairs, staring at the center of the table. The older man with alternately self-righteous and suspicious expressions, had claimed the space, and commanded the order. We would hear rumors that he'd once been a military "deprogrammer," and that the three younger men were under his tutelage. Whether he was the product of the military or a free-lance philosopher was unclear, but we could tell that he did not want these men distracted by women. After a brief, awkward visit, we left, and thenceforth referred to Barker's Ranch as "Man's Camp," and to Paul Watkins as "Little Paul," to distinguish him from the older, taller one.

Tex, Gypsy, and I, were crossing the desert in a dune buggy, and had paused in a gully to rest when two rangers came over a ridge above us. Cutting their engine, they parked their Jeep on a hill, and walked down the slope to meet us. After cordial small talk, they asked to see our IDs. I don't recall how many of us had IDs, but Tex was very cool, relaxing the atmosphere.

One of the men asked, "Where's Charlie?"

Tex spoke up. He said, "I'm Charlie."

"The other Charlie," they clarified, smiling.

I believe it was Gypsy who answered next, also smiling. "I'm Charlie."

Tex shrugged, with his big affable grin, and said, "We're all Charlies." This banter was cut short when the men saw another man on the hill near their Jeep. They rushed to catch up to him, their hands on their holstered guns, but when they reached the top of the hill, the Charlie they were looking for was gone, and when they jumped into their Jeep to give chase, they couldn't start the engine. The doors flew open, and they got out. We took this as a cue to get in our dune buggy and hightail it.

Sandy

Several of us were walking leisurely on a dirt road when we heard vehicles and walkie talkie radios. Little Patty grabbed me, pulling me and Cho into the bushes where I crouched with my hand covering his mouth. We witnessed sheriffs searching our dune buggy. After the badges left, we knew the heat was on. When Charlie saw the white comforter and baby things I was carrying, he said, "Too much white. It needs to be camouflaged." Reluctantly I dragged the diapers and quilt thru the desert dirt until they blended in.

From then on, our days were spent on the cliffs being still and aware of planes, and taking only one sip of our small supply of water per day. We had way too much in our packs, so we stashed some of it in pocket caverns. At night we could stretch, and sneak down to the water hole.

Sandy

There was a tiny shack at Willow Springs in Butte Valley where we drank and bathed in water pouring from a large pipe. One dusk, as we were gathered in front of the shack Charlie spoke to a bunch of us about the need to defend ourselves. He said he couldn't be everywhere for everyone. He demonstrated martial arts moves as well as some motions that he had evolved for his own survival. Hefty Gypsy lolling in the doorway, wearing a wool plaid shirt over a long skirt and holding a shotgun looked tough enough to scare anyone.

A group of us girls set out on a journey. Charlie said he and Clem would meet us on the opposite side of a distant mountain. It was hard to tell how far. We walked toward that mountain for some days, stopping at night to make small fires, cook oatmeal or rice, and lay blankets on the ground.

Upon reaching the mountain, we began the long difficult ascent up sharp rocks. It was then I felt the baby wasn't safe enough in my arms, so I traded him for the sack of brown rice Ruth was carrying. She was sure-footed, and eight years younger than me. I'd been so jealous of her that I couldn't see her, and now I completely trusted her to carry my infant son up a craggy treacherous mountain at night. We climbed for hours, and settled on a sandy plateau with sheer high cliffs on either side. Exhausted, we laid out our gear, and I fell asleep nursing my baby.

The next morning Charlie found us and gave us the "all clear" so we could make the descent into Butte Valley. Food was in short supply and people were looking thin, but because I was nursing, I was given first consideration, and ate half a can of fruit cocktail. I "washed" the wet and soiled diapers in the dirt, shook them out and got ready for the climb down the mountain to a Jeep and several dune buggies.

As many of us as could piled into the jeep, and Charlie sped through the Valley. The wind was whipping my face, and the valley floor with its surrounding mountains was brilliantly lit by the red glow of the setting sun. These wild rides in dune buggies or Jeeps with Charlie driving and the baby and I tucked in safely beside him were exhilarating. He stopped where the ground was more densely covered with bushes.

We quickly unloaded and stretched our camouflaged parachutes over vehicles and between bushes, then placed bushes on top of everything, and climbed inside our bushy cavern just as the airplanes arrived to canvass our area. They didn't see us.

Ruth

We moved camp. The moon was out. As the Jeep headed slowly into the desert, a long line of dancing witches swept away the tracks behind it with desert brooms. We were disappearing, leaving no track or squashed down plant to let anyone know that we had headed in any direction.

The Jeep stopped after a long, long way, and soon all the witches caught up. Here was our new home. Now someone had to go to Barker Ranch and let Tex and Brindle know where we were. It was a ten-mile walk — the straightest route, over hills. I decided to stop thinkin', walk out in the night, and have a good time on me way.

The desert has so many voices and moans and groans and whistles. It has everything imaginable, and that's what I did; I let my imagination go and died a thousand million deaths every second, right on the point. But at last I arrived at the Barker Ranch in time to see the dune buggy fixed, and ride in it to the Jeep. It was getting light mighty fast, so we found a good stash place for the buggy. We covered it with bushes and rocks and all the desert things that stash dune buggies nicely. Just as we were finishing, we spotted a green Jeep far in the distance. Early morning made it clearer. And behind it was another one, and another one... all official green. If they had spotted us already, we knew to lead them away from the Jeep and the family of elves and witches.

Tex picked out a white shale mountain to lead us up... and up. Tex is like a lean, keen mountain goat, so we managed most beautifully. We had no shade, so there we lay on a white mountain, watching a bunch of green Jeeps race around with little stiff gray men looking for us and yelling, "We know you're here — come out!" ("Come down," they didn't say.)

The sun gets hot fast in the desert, and quickly we had peeled off our night clothes. The little men bored us into sleep, as the sun browned us and dried our tongues. At nightfall we awoke to the sound of an engine. It was a dune buggy with messengers of our new camp high in the hills.

We usually traveled only at night. One time we were caught in a shallow arroyo at dawn. The day was too hot to travel, and we needed sleep. Charlie suggested the parachutes for cover. Minutes later, we were about fifteen people and at least one baby lying side by side in a dry riverbed beneath a camouflaged parachute.

I awoke perspiring, hearing noises on the bank above us. It was a vehicle. It stopped. Almost everyone was either sleeping or listening. Two men were edging the embankment less than six feet above us, discussing their weekend plans. It was so quiet we could hear their words. Then Zeezo woke up, making small sounds. I grabbed a bottle of milk or water, desperately hoping he would accept it. He did. I think that I have never been as tense as listening to these men come terribly close to us, so it was a huge relief to hear them conclude that we were not there, turn, walk back to their vehicle, and drive away.

The next time I saw Man's Camp, it had been vacated. I didn't know where Juan, Brooks and the two Pauls had gone. Seven or eight of us girls came in at dusk, meeting up with Charlie and some of the guys. Before all else, we savored the taste and feel of *water*. Then we ate a small meal, and put on extra clothes. It was the season of hot days and cold nights. Some of us wore knit hats. Each of us downed a tab of acid, and headed out the door, picking up several shovels and a pick-axe. Across the road, halfway up a steep hill, Katie built a small fire. It allowed us to see a roughly twelve-foot-square bunker dug into the slope, about three feet deep at the front and five feet deep at the rear. Some of the guys had spent hours digging, and part of the hillside was solid rock. One of the last things they did was to carry a thick double mattress up the hill and place it in the bunker. Now it was up to us girls. Katie tended the fire, her face radiating joy and light.

All night long we worked, searching the landscape for materials to complete the bunker. Remnants of shacks and mine shafts were around, and I recalled seeing some thick beams for the roof. More surprising to me than finding them in the dark, was that I could carry a ten-foot beam up a hill on my shoulder simply by keeping it balanced. Once the beams were across the bunker, we found corrugated sheet metal to place over them. A gigantic canvas tarp had been left for us to cover the tin. Then we piled shovelfuls of sand on top of the tarp, and dug up dry bushes to "plant" in the sand. We selected a big piece of desert brush for the entrance, and many of us tried it, dropping down into the bunker and pulling the bush behind us. At some point one of the girls — I think it was Leslie —

was sitting inside fitting together small stones in a gap between the roof and the walls. The result was invisibility. Even at night, when the bunker was lit inside, it could not be seen from the outside.

Charlie and I think Bruce had gone to the city for supplies. Clem and the rest of the guys had gone off exploring. It was early morning. Little Patty and I were taking shovels back to Granny's. Sadie in a bright red shirt came out of the bunker to take a leak, and several hills over, the Inyo County Sheriffs were watching through binoculars.

From behind the house I heard the crackle of police radios. A man in khaki uniform with a bayonet appeared on the hill above us, shouting. Several more came at us from the front, giving commands: "STOP, KEEP YOUR HANDS UP — DON'T MOVE." Two came toward me but as soon as they reached to put their hands on me, I backed away, telling them, "You're not supposed to..." Smash! I was punched in the face and went down. They searched me.

From distant hills, girls and babies were brought to Barker's at rifle point. Brenda lay half naked, asleep in the sand. When a rock hit her back, she awoke hearing strange male voices. She grabbed her shirt and ran. They shouted their intentions to shoot her, but she kept running, swooping down to stash some acid. She made it over another hill before meeting more bayonets.

A loud shot sounded, a bullet piercing the tin roof of the bunker. The big bush in front of the door moved. Katie, Sadie, and Leslie came out of the hole beneath it, each of them kneeling or standing with their hands up. Leslie said later she'd felt the "whizz" of the bullet that entered the bunker as it went by her head.

Clem and two younger guys were apprehended near the foot of the wash, chained together, and walked up to Barker's in front of a truck. We were kept for hours on the dirt in Barker's front yard while deputies repeatedly spread out to search, and re-gathered. They were electrified, jocular, scornfully baiting us. "Where's Jesus Christ?" one called. "We wanna crucify him!"

After nine hours, we were all loaded into trucks and Jeeps, transported to Inyo County Jail, and variously charged with Grand Theft Auto, Receiving Stolen Property, and an unregistered gun.

Charlie had missed the bust. So had Cappy and Country Sue. The girls arrived late at Barker's, with Charlie later to follow. Finding that we'd all been arrested, they rushed down the wash to a town with a pay phone, to catch him before he left. When he answered the phone, Cappy told him, "Wait. Don't come! Everybody's been busted!"

He said, "I'll be right there."

Charlie

Your world outside was complex and you wanted much — even more than you understood, for to have a child you must have water, air, and the earth's food. The problems of the world are thousands of years old, set in thoughts of Kings and Emperors gone. You said you wanted change, freedom from your own thoughts, no war, peace, harmony and newness. You showed a love of awareness that you were robbed of by the schools that taught you what to think. And you laid down your lives upon the machine that was warring upon itself and the earth.

You were all my father also. I know only what I was taught and shown. I went as far with you as your love would carry you and death would be the easy part.

You've seen me walk away from movie stars and millions of dollars — for what? For a new experience. If someone else wants you and you freely want whatever it is, go. I would take nothing except the world if it was given. I already did when no one was looking.

Death died, and a TV camera was there to catch the last drop of blood, to sell the last heartbeat of fear, and they made a movie out of it, and the money kept buying and selling your love as fear, and the world's birds of prey keep feeding from your breast.

— Charles Manson # B-33920, c. 1981,
California State Prison

I've no thought of defeat. Unaware, I never gave up, never surrendered. I can be broken and dead but to lose is impossible because you cannot destroy the universe.

Lynette Fromme spent thirty-four years in prison after pointing a 1911 model Colt .45 pistol at the President of the United States in order to get her imprisoned friends back in a courtroom. There was no bullet in the chamber of the gun.